The Jungle War

Mavericks, Marauders, and Madmen in the China-Burma-India Theater of World War II

Gerald Astor

WILEY

John Wiley & Sons, Inc.

Library of Congress Cataloging-in-Publication Data:

Astor, Gerald, date.
    Jungle war : mavericks, marauders, and madmen in the China-Burma-India theater of World War II / Gerald Astor.
        p.   cm.
    Includes bibliographical references and index.
    ISBN 0-471-27393-7 (alk. paper)
    1. World War, 1939–1945—Campaigns—China. 2. World War, 1939–1945—Campaigns—Burma. 3. World War, 1939–1945—Campaigns—India. 4. World War, 1939–1945—Jungle warfare. I. Title.

D767.6 .A85   2004
940.54′25—dc22

                                                                                2003022629

Printed in the United States of America

10 9 8 7 6 5 4 3 2 1

Advancing from Thailand, the Japanese Fifteenth Army, although outnumbered by the Allied forces, swept across Burma, capturing Akyab and Maungdaw on the Bay of Bengal and marching north beyond Myitkyina and Kamaing, leaving only Ledo, near the India border, still in Allied hands. (U.S. National Archives)

Contents

The bulk of the Chindits in Operation Thursday flew from Hailakandi and Lalaghat to Broadway and Chowringhee after Piccadilly was found unusable. One brigade traveled on foot from Ledo. Subsequently the long-range penetration established bases and strongholds at Aberdeen, White City, and Blackpool. (From *Fire in the Night*, © 1999 by John Bierman and Colin Smith. Used by permission of Random House, Inc.)

Acknowledgments

I am indebted to David Quaid, Ray Lyons, and Werner Katz from the Merrill's Marauders Association, Inc., for their help in locating material dealing with the Marauders. David Richardson, a photographer and correspondent for *Yank* magazine during World War II, gave me good counsel about sources and photographs. Dr. Simon Robbins, the Trustees, and others at the Imperial War Museum in London enabled me to find memoirs of those who fought in CBI. As I found with previous books, Dr. Richard Sommers at the U.S. Army Military History Library in Carlisle, Pennsylvania, directed me to valuable materials at that institution. Through Dr. Ronald E. Marcello of the Oral History Program of the University of North Texas in Denton, Texas, I obtained transcripts of oral histories from a number of CBI veterans. Mrs. Lynn Gamma at the U.S. Air Force Library, Maxwell Air Force Base, Alabama, supplied me, through the good offices of my local Greenburgh Library, with some relevant oral histories. Denny P. Pidhayny of the 58th Bomb Wing Association provided me with documents dealing with that organization's efforts.

I also want to formally thank my son Ted Astor for his work in copying photographs and maps that illustrate this book.

Permission to quote from The Papers of Color-Sergeant Tommy Atkins received from copyright holder, T. Atkins, collection held in Department of Documents, Imperial War Museum. Permission to quote from The Papers of Trooper N. P. Aylen received from copyright holder, Joyce Aylen, collection held in Department of Documents, Imperial War Museum. Permission to quote from The Papers of Captain John Durant received from copyright holder, Margaret Durant, collection held in Department of Documents, Imperial War Museum. Permission to quote from The Papers of Brigadier A. D. Firth received from copyright holder, Robyn Firth, collection held in Department of Documents, Imperial War Museum. Permission to quote from The Papers of Lieutenant Colonel H. N. F. Patterson received from copyright holder, Mark Cardew, collection held in Department of Documents, Imperial War Museum.

Permission to quote from The Papers of Major David C. Rissik received from copyright holder, David C. Rissik, collection held in Department of Documents, Imperial War Museum. Permission to quote from The Papers of Lieutenant Colonel I. C. G. Scott received from copyright holder, Alan Scott, collection held in Department of Documents, Imperial War Museum.

Permission to reprint map of Chindit Operations from *Fire in the Night* by John Bierman and Colin Smith, 1999, granted by Random House.

Introduction

In late 1943, Philip "Flip" Cochran, after sixty-one missions in North Africa, credited with four enemy planes destroyed, holding the Silver Star, the Distinguished Flying Cross with two oak leaf clusters, the Air Medal with three clusters, the Croix de Guerre with star and palm, and celebrated as the swashbuckling model for a famous comic strip character of the day, Colonel Flip Corkin, returned to the United States to sell war bonds.

Cochran was eager to employ his talent and experience in Europe, where the invasion of France neared. He was summoned by Lieutenant General Henry "Hap" Arnold, Army Air Corps chief and, in Cochran's words, "he was right next to God, the grandest thing that ever came along and the rankingest person I ever would get to see." Arnold announced that instead of the assignment to "the big show" in Europe, Cochran would be posted to the China-Burma-India (CBI) Theater.

Cochran balked. He ignored protocol to rant, "I believe I have more combat experience than any fighter pilot in your air force. I'm going to be brash enough to tell you that I think I know more about the practical side of fighter aviation than anybody in the air force. I've done it the hard way and here you are sending me to some doggone offshoot, side-alley fight over in some jungle in Burma that doesn't mean a damn thing. The big show is in England. I think I can contribute a helluva lot more with what I know and have been studying for seven years."

"Side-alley fight" indeed—that was the status, particularly in the United States, of CBI throughout World War II. It was the most distant theater for Americans and on the outskirts of the British Empire. Ethnic heritage connected Europe to the United States, and the conflict in the South Pacific got the nation's attention because of the attack on Hawaii and the history with the Philippine Islands. Out of sight and

1

mind, perhaps, but CBI became a site for savage, murderous, brutal, terrifying combat among men against a backdrop of nature at its most primeval—thickly encrusted jungle; steep hills and mountains; canyons; gorges; swift, wide streams; monsoon torrents; blistering sun; infernal pestilence; starvation; and dehydration. Overhead flew the latest in combat aircraft, technological marvels when compared to the first contraption that lifted off at Kitty Hawk, North Carolina, only forty years earlier. But on the ground, while tanks and trucks worked some areas, the combatants often relied on the prehistoric wagons drawn by bullocks or pack mules, or else manhandled the cumbersome gear of modern war up the mountains, through jungles, and over streams.

Although an estimated 2 million men eventually fought in Burma alone, it remained a sideshow of the battleground because neither the United States, nor Great Britain, nor even China, most immediately affected, for their own reasons wanted to heavily commit their resources. Yet all of them eventually anted up enough to generate some of World War II's fiercest fighting. It was a war fought on the cheap, except for those who actually waged it.

Many involved in CBI were proper military types, graduates of the service schools or from regular-service, prewar duty and imbued with the knowledge of how World War I was fought in the French trenches. However, like any good side show, CBI drew military freaks, mavericks who never willingly surrendered their egos to the demands of soldierly discipline. Some of the CBI cast were old-fashioned adventurers, others garden-variety mercenaries, and a few might be classified as visionaries. They brought self-esteem, panache, singular ways of expressing themselves to subordinates as well as superiors, and different ideas on how to fight a war in the CBI environment. While individual personality seems to have been more of a factor than in the other war theaters, the ranks were full of ordinary soldiers, most willing to perform their duties, some eager to fight, maybe even behave heroically, but most hoped just to survive.

It was a truly polyglot army that faced the Japanese. The British fielded all-white outfits, Scotch, Welsh, Irish, English, Canadian, Australian, and New Zealand veterans of the 1940 rout in France, soldiers who had trekked the desert of North Africa, as well as fresh fodder from the training camps. They belonged to tradition-rich outfits such as the 1st Lancashire Dragoons, the Buckinghams, and the Royal Fusiliers. The empire disgorged regiments from West Africa—Nigerians, Yorubas, Sierra Leonians, Gambians, etc., some of whom knew no English. Out of India came Punjabis, Gurkhas, and Sikhs. In Burma, the Japanese fielded units drawn from rebels against the British Empire, the Indian National Army, and the Burma National Army. The

Allies countered by recruiting guerrillas from the almost primitive non-Burmese peoples in the hills, training and arming in some cases even fourteen-year-old boys.

The Americans included some who had fought in the South Pacific; others shipped to CBI from garrisons in the Caribbean. Draftees fresh from the States filled the ranks, and although the segregated U.S. Army allowed no African Americans to wield weapons in CBI, a large contingent would labor in service and engineering duties. The most numerous forces in CBI, of course, belonged to the two opposing Asian nations, China and Japan. The former outnumbered the latter, but the Nipponese were better educated, better trained, and far better equipped.

Reluctant to fight a war in CBI as some were, the stakes were enormous: immense tracts of land, inestimable natural resources, huge markets, richly endowed trade routes, and control of half the world's population. Advance toward the west by the imperial forces, if it broke through into India, would also link Japan with its Axis partners Germany and Italy to control the Middle East and its oil. CBI could not be ignored.

1

The Venues
and Opening Shots

The triumvirate of countries that composed the disdained CBI had much in common. They were all dependent largely on an agrarian economy bolstered by the exploitation of raw materials useful to the industrialized nations. Two of them, India and Burma, were subjects of the British Empire. As World War II dawned, the indigenous people clamored for independence, and rebellion simmered. China, while independent, was racked by internal forces struggling for dominance. Furthermore, the Western countries, along with Japan, had obtained economic and political concessions beyond the control of whatever faction governed.

The military-industrial juggernaut of Imperial Japan coveted China as a great warehouse of substances vital to fuel the economy, as a great bazaar for its goods, and as a buffer against the Soviet Union, where memories of the 1904 war still rankled. The largest entity in CBI, China proper covered 4.27 million square miles (the continental United States at that time was 3 million) and was home to 400 million people (U.S. census figures in 1940 counted 133 million). So large a land naturally encompassed a broad spectrum of climates. The topography ranged from broad river valleys—natural boulevards for military forces—that dominated middle and southeastern China, to high mountains, which marked the colder west and northwest. Seaports such as Shanghai, Tsingtao, Canton, and Amoy served maritime interests. China bordered Burma to the south, India to the southwest, and Japan's fief of Manchuria to the northeast.

Southeast Asia beckoned to the Japanese with shipping hubs such as Hong Kong, Singapore, and Burma's Rangoon, along with vast stores of rubber, oil, ores, and farm products in the Dutch East Indies, the French possession of Indochina (today Vietnam, Cambodia, and Laos), and the British colonial outposts of Malaya and Burma, and independent Siam (now Thailand). For the Japanese, the problem in Southeast Asia would become that every expansion required more troops, pushing their flag ever farther. Conquest of Indochina and Siam meant a secured military presence in neighboring Burma. That step in turn would bring the Nipponese to the Indian border, inevitably leading to still another confrontation. The Western powers would meet the Japanese most squarely in Burma. U.S. and British ground units saw no service in China, and the combat that intruded into India overflowed from Burma.

Burma (now known as Myanmar), with about 263,000 square miles, was roughly the size of the state of Texas. The population was about 17 million, composed of 10 million Burmese, 4 million Karens, 2 million Shans, and more than 1 million residents of the hill country, who were from ethnic strains known as Nagas, Chins, and Kachins. A sizable minority of noncitizens—Indians and Chinese—worked or plied professions in the cities. While various branches of Christianity deployed missionaries, the prevailing religions were Buddhism and Islam. Since the second half of the nineteenth century, Burma had been part of the British Empire, and as World War II neared, a strong independence movement gathered steam.

The best-known cities were Mandalay, which lay in a relatively dry triangle in the interior, and the port of Rangoon. The residents of a typical *ga* or village lived off crops. The five-month monsoon season and the intense tropical sun grew an astonishingly lush flora that in turn nourished a zoological cornucopia of animal and insect life. The latter, unfortunately, also bore a textbook of infectious diseases.

Four rivers flowed mostly north to south, following the elongated shape of the country. During the monsoon season these and smaller streams, known as *chaungs* (often arid ditches during dry periods), turned into swift-moving, even white-water torrents. The mighty Irrawaddy, 1,300 miles long and as many as 3 miles wide at some points, originated in northern Burma near Fort Hertz and traveled through the central portions of the land all the way to Rangoon, on the Gulf of Martaban. The Chindwin, a tributary of the Irrawaddy, approached the border with India. In 1941 both of these waterways were navigable by shallow-draft vessels, and a few bridges enabled vehicles and trains to cross them. The Sittang, between the two, was shorter, and its tidal currents made it difficult for boats and to build bridges. The Salween, the longest of the four, originated in China but was considered unnavigable; the only way to cross it was by ferry.

Burma's abundant stretches of mountains (*bum* in Burmese) mirrored the courses of the rivers and steep hills that also tended to stretch in north-to-south axes. These geological formations tended to completely wall off Burma from its neighbors India, China, and Siam. Siam and Indochina lay to the east, India to the west, and China was north.

A western, coastal sliver of Burma, the Arakan, along the Bay of Bengal, was almost totally shut off from interior Burma by mountains and the Irrawaddy. It was best reachable by boats from India or Rangoon. Not until the Japanese showed up did anyone realize that a determined military could push through overland. For that matter, there were few decent roads throughout the entire country.

The territory of India spread over a landmass slightly smaller than the continental United States at that time. As in Burma, India's 300 million people also splintered into a number of ethnic divisions and religions. The Hindus, with their caste system, created an additional divisive factor. The struggle for independence, led by Mohandas K. Gandhi, roiled the political and civil scene far more than in Burma. The India brought into World War II by its colonial master was something less than a willing partner. In fact, as in Burma, there were those who openly sided with the Japanese and even fought against the British forces. For the most part, the legions of soldiers drawn from various parts of India (Pakistan would not separate from India until independence in 1947 and Bangladesh was even farther up the historical timeline) remained loyal and fought for the crown not only in CBI but also in various other theaters.

In World War II the most important area of India was the province of Assam, which bordered northwestern Burma. An area marked by hills and mountains, it culminated in the towering Himalayas, the fabled "Hump" over which flew aircraft bound for China. The hot, moist climate of Assam favored tea plantations and fauna ranging from elephants and tigers to wee moles, as well as pestiferous insects loaded with tropical illnesses.

The Generalissimo and the First Americans

In CBI, World War II began in China, a country also beset by internecine strife. The contest for control of China pitted the Nationalist forces under Generalissimo Chiang Kai-shek, a hardened survivor of years of brutal internal bloodshed, and the equally determined and blowtorch-tested Communists. Hanging around like jackals were a galaxy of freebooting Chinese generals who acted like warlords hoping to preserve their private fiefs.

Western sympathy for China and antipathy toward Japan, an ally of the United States and Britain during World War I, dated back to September 1931, when the Japanese staged an incident near Mukden, Manchuria, and subsequently assumed control over Manchuria. Fewer than six months later, a Japanese expeditionary force sought to capture Shanghai, but the resistance of Chinese troops and the displeasure of world opinion forced the Nipponese to abandon the project.

During the following years, while Chiang Kai-shek and his Kuomintang Party solidified their leadership and unified China in spite of opposition from the country's Communists, the Japanese nibbled away at their nearby neighbor. In 1937, with the militarist and expansionist elements of Japan in the ascendancy, that nation's armed forces began a full-scale but undeclared war against China. In response, the factions within China declared an internal truce and vowed to present a united front against the aggressor.

Chiang Kai-shek's soldiers—many, ironically, trained by Japan's World War II partners Germany and Italy—mounted some resistance, but they were overmatched. They committed basic errors in strategy and tactics, failed to appreciate the need for intelligence, had little understanding of how to deploy supporting weapons, and lacked enough vehicles or firepower. The contribution of their fledgling air force was negligible.

The invaders captured major cities, including the capital of Nanking, from where news of massacres and terrible atrocities inflamed world antagonism toward the conquerors. Savage behavior aside, Great Britain, France, and the Netherlands, who possessed colonies in the region, and the United States—like them, having vast economic interests in the Far East—naturally regarded the extension of Japan's reach with alarm.

There had long been a highly visible American presence in China. Aside from the commercial interests, a substantial number of U.S. citizens inhabited the International Settlement in Shanghai, and China was a regular port of call for the U.S. Navy. As the government of Chiang Kai-shek skirmished with the Communist movement led by Mao Tse-tung, bickered with warlords, and faced Japanese aggressiveness, the figure of the U.S. military attaché at the embassy grew in importance and political stature.

In 1934, Colonel Joseph Stilwell received an appointment to that post from President Franklin D. Roosevelt's secretary of state, Cordell Hull. As a precocious adolescent, Stilwell had graduated from Yonkers High School, in New York's Westchester County, at sixteen, but a year later, as a postgraduate student, he engineered a series of pranks—smearing Limburger cheese over desks, roughing up the prin-

Lieutenant General Joseph W. Stilwell, an old China hand, lived up to his nickname of "Vinegar Joe" with his caustic comments on the Chinese leadership, his British allies, and President Franklin D. Roosevelt. (U.S. National Archives)

cipal, and stealing ice cream tubs and cakes. Nevertheless, his father, a lawyer and physician, secured him an appointment to the U.S. Military Academy (USMA) at West Point, Class of 1904.

A good student, Stilwell, in his diary, railed against the hazing and regimentation of plebe (freshman) life, collecting demerits because of his disdain for regulations. Stilwell never donned the persona of a spit-and-polish disciplinarian. However, he demonstrated an aptitude for languages; performed creditably in other classes; and enthusiastically engaged in football, track, and basketball, a sport he allegedly introduced to the academy.

When he graduated in 1904, one year after Douglas MacArthur, Stilwell elected the infantry and traveled to the Philippines to help suppress the last vestiges of the "insurrection." In line with the USMA's policy of using graduates as academic instructors, Stilwell then taught English, French, and Spanish, plus tactics. He spent his leaves traveling in Europe and South America. In 1911, detailed to the 12th Infantry Regiment, he visited China for the first time.

Fate brought him to Shanghai, where he embarked on a seventeen-day odyssey as an eyewitness to the turmoil caused by the overthrow of the Manchu Dynasty. Soldiers, bandits, villagers, and refugees driven from their homes by the conflict fought using everything from rifles and muskets to hoes, pitchforks, and staves. Gangs sacked and plundered towns in scattered orgies of terror and killing. Stilwell traveled about, soaking up a firsthand view of incredibly crowded slums with narrow streets or alleys; coolie labor; sewage-stuffed canals; opium smokers and bejeweled but slatternly prostitutes; shrines and pagodas; pirate traffic on the inland waters; and, more ominously, rivers strewn with corpses. He also became infected with his lifelong aversion to the British. While he admired their drill sergeants, saying, "their commands, appearance, and results beat our average officer 500 percent," he characterized the English officers as "a mess. . . . Untidy, grouchy, sloppy, fooling around with canes, a bad example for the men." Their traditional swagger stick became a symbol to him of all that was wrong with the British military.

The United States, like other industrialized nations, had imposed its commercial desires upon China in the forms of business concessions, bank loans, extraterritorial rights in the courts, and settlements immune to local control. American diplomats, however, had gained the country some goodwill by using the compensation money owed for the ill-fated Boxer Rebellion of 1899–1900 to educate Chinese students in the States.

None of that meant anything to Stilwell when the United States entered World War I. In 1917 he had been assigned to an overseas infantry division. His knowledge of French soon elevated him to the staff of General John J. Pershing, commander of the U.S. Expeditionary Force, as an intelligence officer. A brief tour with the British 58th Division, during which he prowled trenches, dugouts, and observation posts, only confirmed his Anglophobia. "These English are beyond me—most of them so very pleasant and some of them so damn snotty . . . too goddamned indifferent and high and mighty to bother about an American officer." (This Stilwell observation, along with many others from his early career, comes from Barbara Tuchman's *Stilwell and the American Experience in China 1911–1945.*)

While he came under artillery fire and observed at close hand death and destruction, he never commanded any troops in the field. After the Armistice and a brief tour as an occupation soldier, Stilwell returned to the United States, soured by the spectacle of politicians and generals bickering over the peace terms. He arranged for an assignment to China as an adjunct to the military attaché.

With his wife, he took up residence in Peiping (later named Peking and still later Beijing), where he immersed himself in a study of the host nation's military forces, including the warlords. As an agent of the military attaché, he traveled widely in the Far East, touring Manchuria, Siberia, Korea, and even Japan. Certainly aware of the grim life of the poor of the cities and the peasants of the countryside, Stilwell became enamored of the finer aspects of Chinese culture and the people who manifested them.

He added the Japanese to another of his dislikes. In Siberia, invaded by the Nipponese after the Bolshevik Revolution, he found the Japanese dilatory in carrying out the mandate for them to evacuate. Stilwell snarled, "The arrogant little bastards were . . . all over town this A.M. in American cars, posting M.P.s and sticking out their guts. . . . They need a kick in the slats in the worst way. They have systematically bothered and annoyed Americans about passports . . . and seem to go out of their way to make people despise and hate them." While visiting Japan he angrily observed the residents treating foreigners as inferiors. He compared them with the Teutons, "pale imitations of the Germans without the latter's brains and ability. Patriotic, well organized, brave, artistic, swellheaded [sic], and stupid." Underestimation of Japanese intelligence and ability would cost Stilwell in the future, but in this regard he was hardly alone.

Stilwell, in 1923, brought his growing family home and attended first the infantry course at Fort Benning and then, in 1925 and 1926, attended the Command and General Staff School at Fort Leavenworth, Kansas. Among his classmates was a 1915 West Pointer, Dwight D. Eisenhower. By 1926, Stilwell, now a major, had returned to China as a battalion commander in the 15th Infantry Regiment, stationed in Tientsin. To his dismay, the regiment hewed to customs that were anathema to Stilwell. The rules prescribed that officers when in uniform and not under arms would carry the abhorred swagger stick or a riding crop.

During this tour by Stilwell, the conflict for power between Chiang Kai-shek and other claimants to leadership, including the Communists, raged throughout China, with outsiders caught in between. Nationalist troops attacked foreigners, beating, shooting, killing some, looting the homes and businesses of others. Dispatched on a mission to scout the strength of rival elements, Stilwell endured the indignities of capture by a rabble in arms, threats to murder him, and a daring escape from his tormentors. Personnel changes shifted Stilwell to the post of acting chief of staff for the commanding general of U.S. forces in China. His boss, General Joseph Castner, insisted on forced marches that entailed covering 35 miles in 10 hours. Stilwell, a firm believer in exercise—he was an enthusiastic handball and tennis player—never faltered, and later, as a much older man, his endurance would stand him in good stead.

As an analyst of the Chinese struggles, Stilwell, in 1928, described Chiang as a man who might unify the county, and if he did, it would be through "resources he can find within himself." He tempered his praise for the Nationalist leader's progress as victories over unresistant troops. When Stilwell sailed home in 1929, he had, unlike many of his contemporaries, developed a fine sense of the difference between Chinese attitudes and those of the West.

By happy circumstance for his future, when he had first reported to Tientsin, Major Stilwell's immediate superior with the 15th was the executive officer, Lieutenant Colonel George C. Marshall. Although the association lasted less than a year, they hit it off sufficiently for Marshall to inscribe his junior in his memory book as a worthy officer. On Stilwell's return to the States he checked in at the Fort Benning Infantry School, now commanded by Marshall. When Marshall ascended to the post of army chief of staff on September 1, 1939, the opening day of World War II, Stilwell had a friend in the highest place. Assigned to instruct in tactics at the Infantry School, Stilwell lectured on the enormous value set on "face." Ironically, he would frequently disregard his own strictures about preserving the dignity of the individual during his CBI campaigns with Chiang and his relationships with other powerful figures.

Promoted to full colonel, Stilwell renewed his Chinese adventures, coming to Peiping in 1935 as the military attaché. With his rank and position he enjoyed the company of the best-educated and most artful of Chinese culture while avoiding the sterile social circles. He did not shirk his duty to gather intelligence for the War Department in Washington. As in his past tours, he traveled widely. From what he observed of the Chinese army, in the face of the increasing belligerence of Japan, Stilwell deprecated Chiang's military preparations. "No evidence of planned defense against further Japanese encroachment. No troop increase or even thought of it. No drilling or maneuvering. He [Chiang] can have no intention of doing a thing or else he is utterly ignorant of what it means to get ready for a fight with a first-class power."

Enter Claire Chennault

Although the political situation prevented overt support, in 1936, sub-rosa efforts to bolster China's military strength began. At the Pan-American Air Show in Miami, General Mow Pang-tsu of the Chinese air force gaped at a trio of U.S. Army Air Corps pilots who performed a dazzling series of stunts. On a yacht owned by William Pawley, an entrepreneur selling American aircraft to China, Mow met with the three fliers, Sergeants John H. "Luke" Williamson and Billy McDonald, and Captain Claire Chennault. Mow tendered an offer for them to come to his country to teach their skills. The two noncoms, unable to obtain commissions because they had never attended college and therefore at a dead end in their careers, accepted. Chennault hesitated. With a wife and eight children, he worried about giving up the security of the air corps. But after Williamson and McDonald departed, Chennault's health deteriorated to the point where a flight surgeon restricted his cockpit duties. His future military prospects bleak, Chennault grabbed a second opportunity in China. A letter from the Chinese government asked if Chennault would conduct a three-month survey of their air force at a salary of $1,000 a month plus expenses, a car, driver, interpreter, and the right to fly any plane on hand.

Chennault was destined to work in tandem with Stilwell, but his background was almost totally different. Born in 1890, Chennault, a Louisiana native, attended LSU and then the state's teachers' college, where he flashed an independent spirit, a resistance to conformity, and a willingness to rely on his fists when necessary to get across his point.

Married at twenty-one, he lurched from job to job until the United States declared war on Germany in 1917. Chennault enlisted and after his three months at Officers' Candidate School pinned on a second lieutenant's gold bars. At the newly created Kelly Field in Texas, Chennault persuaded instructors there to teach him, unofficially, how to fly. He piled up 80 hours in the air before the war ended and then wangled entry to the aviation cadet program. He had barely graduated before the army began to trim its ranks, and in 1920 he became a farmer.

Chennault wrote to his father, "I have tasted of the air and I cannot get it out of my craw." Fortunately for him, within a few months the army, having established the air corps as a separate branch, recruited pilots with commissions as regulars rather than as reserves. He embarked on a course in fighter tactics taught by veterans of France. He quickly displayed an aptitude for the craft, although he soon began to devise his own maneuvers.

However, the air corps, to the dismay of Chennault, had begun to turn away from fighter aircraft in favor of bombers. Theorists such as the American general Billy Mitchell and his Italian counterpart Giulio Douhet vigorously promulgated the virtues of heavy bombers that would fly so high and so fast that no one could intercept them as they carried out raids that would devastate any enemy. While Mitchell

Claire Chennault, scorned
by the U.S. Army Air Corps,
signed on with the Chinese to
direct that nation's air force
and created the American
Volunteer Group or Flying
Tigers. (Photograph from
U.S. National Archives)

retired in disgrace for his intemperate propagandizing of his view-
point, the approach won the approval of both the Americans and the
British.

Chennault and some colleagues doggedly insisted that fighters
still had a role, that they could battle the bigger aircraft as well as one
another. He innovated and refined tactics, rejected the traditional one-
on-one dogfight, and abandoned the standard V formation in favor of
two- or four-ship formations in which the pilots worked together to
destroy the enemy.

Outspoken and combative, Chennault convinced few superiors
with his arguments and irritated enough of them to damage his reputation. He criticized 1932 maneuvers directed by Lieutenant Colonel
Henry "Hap" Arnold, already an ascendant star in the air corps. Chennault would later claim that an outburst criticizing another top officer
cost him an opportunity to attend the Command and General Staff
School, a prerequisite for advancement to the upper echelons.

A 1933 paper he authored, "The Role of Defensive Pursuit," converted none of his adversaries and languished in the dustbins of theory.

A prophet without honor in his home country, the retired officer with the permanent rank of captain sailed for China in 1937. He brought his hard-drinking, highly competitive, blunt-spoken persona to a country where face and delicate diplomacy often governed decisions. While Chennault knew how to exploit his dashing image of the aviator—silk scarf; crushed air corps cap; angular, leathery face; and muscular physique—it hardly seemed that the man who arrived in Shanghai at the end of May fitted the job.

The rough-hewn American met the head of the Chinese air force, Madame Chiang Kai-shek, at the French Concession in Nanking rather than the U.S. turf in the International Settlement there to avoid Japanese spies or a squabble over American neutrality. At birth named Mei Ling and one of three daughters from the powerful Soong family, one sister had been the wife of Dr. Sun Yat-sen, the political and revolutionary leader who founded the Republic of China in 1912. Mei Ling's brother T. V. Soong was a powerhouse figure in banking and geopolitical circles. When the slightly built forty-one-year-old madame in a light print dress entered the room, Chennault did not realize who she was until his escort, another former air corps pilot and businessman, Roy Holbrook, said, "Madame Chiang, may I present Colonel Chennault."

Chennault recalled, "It was the Generalissimo's wife, looking twenty years younger than I had expected and speaking English in a rich Southern drawl [as did he]. This was an encounter from which I never recovered. To this day I remain completely captivated." He wrote in his diary, "Granted interview by Her Excellency, Madame Chiang Kai-shek, who will hereafter be 'The Princess' to me."

His infatuation with her lay not just with her physical allure. At this interview she listened intently to his ideas on the role of an air force, according him a respect for his theories that the authorities in the United States never granted. She asked him to survey the existing Chinese air force's personnel and facilities and deliver a report in three months. Chennault discovered the Chinese pilots barely able to do more than get the country's hodgepodge of obsolete military aircraft off the ground and then back to earth.

In the midst of Chennault's research came a confrontation at the Marco Polo Bridge, about ten miles from Peiping. Having already advanced into China on the pretext of protecting the puppet state of Manchukuo, formerly Manchuria, Japanese troops in 1937 were deployed at the western end of the span. The Japanese claimed a missing soldier was inside a small Chinese village and demanded the right to cross the border and find him. When the local Kuomintang garrison commander rejected the request, Japanese artillery shelled the village. At dawn on July 8, infantry and tanks marched over the Marco Polo Bridge to attack the Chinese forces, signaling the start of the war that would eventually envelop CBI.

Chennault immediately offered to serve in whatever capacity Chiang Kai-shek preferred. Chennault could not resist an opportunity to put into practice his concepts for aerial warfare. In the company of General Mow, the Chinese air force's uniformed commander, Chennault met with the generalissimo and his wife. When Chiang asked Mow how many planes were combat-ready, he said ninety-one, although the official records listed some five hundred. "Chiang turned turkey red," wrote Chennault in his memoirs, "and I thought he was going to explode. He strode up and down the terrace, loosing long strings of sibilant Chinese that seemed to hiss, coil, and strike like a snake. Madame stopped translating. Color drained from Mow's face as he stood stiffly at attention, his eyes fixed straight ahead." Madame Chiang whispered to Chennault that her husband was talking about executing Mow. However, Chennault confirmed Mow's figures, and at the urging of madame began to expound on his findings, the wretched state of the air force, and his prescriptions to correct the situation. The blunt facts presented to Chiang converted him into a believer. He spared Mow, and Chennault assumed the task of molding an air force that could battle the Japanese.

Just about a month after the incident at the Marco Polo Bridge, shells from Japanese warships in the Whangpoo River began to crash down on Shanghai, killing and maiming hundreds if not thousands of civilians. The barrages were in support of Japanese troops advancing on the city. At the request of Madame Chiang, Chennault organized a bombing strike against the naval vessels in the Whangpoo.

The raids were an unmitigated disaster. The poorly schooled flight crews did not adjust their drops to a change from their training altitudes and airspeeds. The explosions missed the targets and killed perhaps thirty-five hundred civilians. Chennault, in a Hawk 75 monoplane, had flown from Nanking to observe the action. Amid the smoke from fires and the rain squalls he zoomed low to check out a large naval vessel. As he came over the ship he saw a Union Jack painted on the deck and the winking lights of gunfire from its turrets. He pulled away quickly, but not before the gunners punched some holes in his wing and fuselage.

While Chennault wrestled with building an air force, Stilwell, in Peiping, now occupied by the Japanese, met with the conquerors, and in his typically irascible fashion did little to conceal his animosity toward the "arrogant little bastards." He railed at the leaders of China as "oily politicians . . . treacherous quitters, selfish, conscienceless, unprincipled crooks." Asked by the War Department about the ability to resist, he answered, "Not until they lose their inherent distaste for offensive combat." He dismissed the commanders of the Chinese soldiers. "The educated Chinese is astounded to be told that the Chinese officer is no good," and gloomily estimated it would require two generations to create effective military leadership. On the other hand, he believed that a strong army could be established because of the basic potential of soldiers if properly trained under good leadership.

Stilwell's dire predictions proved accurate. The Japanese quickly attacked Nanking. There Claire Chennault underwent his baptism in the terrors of an air raid, forced to sprint for the shelter of a dugout. As Japanese soldiers secured the ground around the Whangpoo, the Imperial Navy moved in aircraft carriers, from which planes could strike at vital areas. Aware of the Chinese limitations in both pilots and aircraft, Chennault, in one of his first acts, developed an early-warning system. He created a network of spotters who would transmit by telephone their observations of approaching aircraft. Armed with that information, the Chinese interceptors could take off and climb to an altitude that would allow them to dive on the marauders. Aided by Billy McDonald and Luke Williamson, Chennault instituted a crash course in tactics for his fighter pilots, teaching them how to work as a team and even how to exploit the beams of antiaircraft searchlights that would blind a Japanese pilot if he looked down into them. When the first bombers arrived after dark over Nanking, the Chinese pilots shot down seven of thirteen, and the enemy abandoned night missions against that city.

Initially, the Chinese scored well. The Japanese sent their bombers off without fighter escort. In three raids on Nanking, the Japanese lost fifty-four planes and crews, nearly half of the attacking force. As Chennault's pupils demonstrated the fallacy of the enemy strategy, the Japanese started to accompany their raiders with the high-performance predecessors of the renowned Zero, launched from the flattops at Shanghai. The prospects for resisting against the imperial air arm declined rapidly.

Historians who have researched the period, and Chennault biographers, have speculated on how much combat flying he did. While Madame Chiang told him not to engage in combat, he wrote in a 1951 letter to the widow of armaments expert Rolfe Watson, "In addition to training Chinese gunners and armament mechanics, he [Watson] kept the guns of my personal plane in the finest condition. My guns never failed to fire when I needed them." Chennault's wife, Anna, whom he married after World War II, insisted that he shot down at least forty Japanese planes. Biographer Jack Samson argued,

"Given Chennault's nature—volatile, quick-tempered, and fearless—it is difficult to believe he didn't fire back when fired upon. And with his experience as an acrobatic stunt pilot in air corps fighters planes, it is equally hard to believe he did not engage in combat against the Japanese fighters."

Jimmy Thach, a navy pilot who devoured the materials on Japanese aircraft that Chennault had furnished the War Department and who developed effective tactics for his carrier-based colleagues, believed that only one who had actually engaged the Japanese in combat could have been so authoritative. On the other hand, American mechanic Sebbie Smith told author Duane Schultz in *The Maverick War,* "I don't think he ever shot down any planes." Smith noted that only once did he find a bullet hole in Chennault's plane, most unlikely for anyone who tangled with as many as forty enemy aircraft. Chennault never claimed such feats.

The Chinese government retreated to Hankow, 400 miles up the Yangtze River from Nanking, and Stilwell reached Hankow in December 1937. While he was in residence, Japanese bombers, in spite of conspicuous American flags on the decks, strafed, bombed, and sank the gunboat USS *Panay.* The Japanese subsequently apologized, but the incident further worsened relations between Tokyo and Washington. Photographs and newspaper stories of atrocities committed by the Japanese—the rape of Nanking, with hapless civilians used for bayonet practice, the historic picture of a sobbing Chinese baby sitting in the ruins of the Shanghai railroad station, tales of the misery visited upon city dwellers by the bombers—inflamed American opinion. Stilwell joined in a successful effort to persuade President Roosevelt to authorize a loan to China to develop military defense.

With Chinese-born pilots in very short supply, Chennault began attempts to recruit foreign pilots for military purposes. Actually, one source was already on hand. Early in 1937, the Soviet Union agreed to supply Chiang planes and instructors in return for raw materials. The Soviets stationed complete squadrons in China with their own ground crews and command staff as well as accomplished pilots. The latter, theoretically on hand only to teach, flew combat missions between 1937 and 1939.

The Soviet airmen collaborated with Chinese pilots, most notably in an engagement near Hankow. Chennault had arranged for the two groups to take off one afternoon, seemingly on their way to another area. Enemy spies noticed the departure, but the fighters sneaked back to Hankow from a different direction. On the following morning, Japanese bombers and fighters approached the city, expecting no opposition. But forty of the Soviet fighters and another twenty of the Chinese lurked in the skies. The latter struck first, forcing the fighters to engage them and to burn up fuel and ammunition. When the bombers headed for home with a weakened escort, the Red interceptors pounced on them, wiping out a dozen bombers. Chennault's strategy also destroyed all twenty-four of the Japanese fighters. Only two Soviet planes were lost, but eleven homegrown airmen were knocked down, hard losses for an already depleted outfit.

Discouraged and with nowhere to turn, Chennault considered returning home. But when he learned that the League of Nations had condemned the Japanese for the invasion and that the United States and Great Britain were talking of an embargo on vital goods to Japan, he decided to remain in China. Still desperate to build an air force, Chennault enlisted a motley group of individuals—French, German, Dutch, and even American—in the 14th Volunteer Bombardment Squadron or 14th International Volunteer Squadron, stationed in Hankow. Paid $1,000 a month in Chinese dollars, the salaries amounted to less than a third of that in American money. Most of the newcomers proved more eager than able, and they compounded their deficiencies with a predilection for bordellos and bars. Their formation flying was described by one observer as "ragged as hell" and "plain dangerous to fly with most of [them]."

Through the machinations of William Pawley, the 14th received a batch of thirty single-engine Vultee bombers. Carrying a three-man crew and a heavy bomb load, the slow-moving planes had a range of 2,000 miles. A day came in March 1938 when Chennault scheduled the squadron for an early-morning mission. To steal added sleep time or a few hours for carousing, the 14th gassed and armed the aircraft a day before the raid. At sunset, a flight of Japanese bombers arrived and unloaded on the neatly lined up Vultees. The entire complement went up in fire and smoke. Most likely one or more of the volunteers blabbed about the proposed operation in a whorehouse or saloon. A spy relayed the news to the enemy, who launched the sundown attack. "What was left of the Chinese bombing force," said Chennault, "vanished in five seconds of flame and dust. With it went the jobs of the International Squadron pilots."

Japanese forces continued to advance ever deeper into China. Late in 1938 they seized Canton and then Hankow. The government moved to Chungking, deep enough into the heart of China to avoid a thrust by land. The air force, more a paper instrument than a functioning military branch, opened for business in the ancient city of Kunming in southwestern China, fairly close to Indochina and Burma. Pawley, under the rubric of the Central Aircraft Manufacturing Company, an agent for Curtiss-Wright in China, set up facilities to assemble and repair planes at Loiwing, near the border with Burma.

At Kunming, Chennault started to build a flying school. Although he had almost no pilots and few airplanes, he also began construction of a number of all-weather airfields. The one plentiful item in China was hand labor: men, women, and children toted the standard wicker baskets loaded with broken stones to line the airstrips, creating long, hard runways. He expanded the network to warn of air raids. Agents radioed, telephoned, and telegraphed the movements of Japanese planes almost from the moment they took off. However, Chennault remained pitifully short of combat-worthy aircraft. Not only did his flight school graduates lack the ability to fight the well-seasoned enemy, but also the plane shortage denied opportunities to acquire the requisite skills.

While Chennault coped with the deficiencies in China, Stilwell's penchant for doing things his way generated enmity within the Military Intelligence Division of the War Department. He insisted on drafting his own itineraries for his inspections, visiting a Soviet air base, returning to Peiping under the Japanese, and trekking to the front as the invaders approached Hankow. In that city he had met with Madame Chiang, and as with Chennault, she charmed him, eliciting compliments "highly intelligent and sincere." He spent five days at a battalion command post, observing up close the fighting, where he concluded, "The Chinese soldier is excellent material, wasted and betrayed by stupid leadership."

During a trip by Stilwell to Kunming, the two Americans who would be most responsible for their country's efforts in the CBI campaign first met. On the cusp of 1939, Chennault and Stilwell had dinner and a long discussion about the situation. Mutual respect was expressed, but that would dissolve after each assumed genuine command responsibilities. Five months later, discouraged with his professional prospects and the future for China, Stilwell headed home, expecting to put in his retirement papers.

2

The Japanese
Enlarge Their War

While Stilwell and Chennault dealt with the highest echelons in China, other members of the U.S. military were on the scene as war swept over the beleaguered land. U.S. Marines garrisoned both the International Settlement and other outposts such as Tientsin. Among those on duty in Shanghai was a former farmhand from Alabama, Henry Stowers. "I graduated from high school in 1926," recalled Stowers, "and joined the Marine Corps to get away from the cotton patch. I had actually planned to spend four years in the marines. The Depression came along during the four years. I peeped out and saw food lines, soup lines. You couldn't get a job for fifty cents a day. I ducked back in and got the re-enlistment bonus of I believe, fifty dollars and I reenlisted for four more years.

"I was playing on the All-Marine football team at Quantico and in 1937, the Chinese-Japanese war broke out. They took the whole football team, canceled our schedule, took the whole brigade, and shipped us off to Shanghai at the International Settlement for guard duty. It was voluntary in the sense that 'you, you and you are going.'

"We were in pillboxes, sandbagged deals during the day mainly because the Chinese and the Japanese still had a lot of short rounds and it would drop unintentionally on us." The Japanese concentrated upon the Chinese part of Shanghai, avoiding any conflict with the representatives and interests of other nations in the city. "We observed the Japanese and Chinese airplanes fighting dogfights over us, the Japanese bombers dropping bombs right and left on the city and the surrounding area. We had no part. None of us fired a shot."

Stowers and fifty others were sent to Peiping to dismantle the equipment at the American embassy. The embassy had been moved to Chungking, and they left a lot of supplies and a radio station. The Marine guard, a machine gun company, had been shipped out to the Philippines. "Everybody out there knew that Japan and the United States were coming to a showdown. Servicemen are so busy, out in the woods, on maneuvers, training, and waiting on orders. They don't sit and read daily newspapers and [listen to] radio broadcasts. With the old-timers [after eleven years, Stowers was a gunnery master sergeant] who had a lot of combat in Nicaragua, Haiti, and Cuba, you smell these things coming. Suddenly there is this atmosphere; you know something is about to pop and you don't get it from a magazine or newspaper."

While Stowers had served in Shanghai, another contingent of marines headed for the city of Tientsin. In the ranks was a young Texan, O. R. Sparkman, fresh out of boot camp. "Marines usually spent two years overseas and we were being sent as replacements for some who were coming back. You could put your name on a bulletin board to volunteer for [shipboard duty, Shanghai, or elsewhere]. Some got off the ship at Shanghai. I just kept on. I wouldn't volunteer for anything. I wanted to see how long I could ride."

About seventy-five leathernecks from a machine gun company, including Sparkman, finally arrived at Tientsin. "It was divided. Italians, French, British, and Americans had sections of it after the Boxer Rebellion. We had old German barracks. It looked like the old castles you see in Germany. They were old brownstone buildings, and each end had a staircase running up the corners to the towers. About all we did is stand guard."

Other than sports such as handball, tennis, and an occasional volleyball contest with the friendly Italian soldiers, the Tientsin marines sought rudimentary recreation. With their own bar across from the barracks, a fifth of gin selling for sixty-five cents, and a bottle of Canadian Club for less than a dollar, Sparkman reported, "Most of them drank all the time." While he professed to liking the Chinese, many marines did not respect the local people. On the other hand, Chinese citizens reciprocated; the culture held little regard for common soldiers.

Japanese Advances and Western Reaction

As World War II marched deeper into 1940, the Chinese were hanging on only through the determination of Chiang not to yield and the facts of geography. China was so large, its terrain often so inhospitable to military advances, that the Japanese land forces settled into a stalemate. From the air, however, the Nipponese continued to attack, battering both Chungking and Kunming. Short of effective planes and pilots, Chennault could offer little opposition.

The conquests by Japan in China alerted the Western democracies to the vulnerability of their interests in the Far East, but that did not trigger a direct military reaction. The sudden end to "the phony war" and the fall of France to the German blitzkrieg in June 1940, however, heightened the threat. As the French armies collapsed, the Japanese cowed the government in Paris with an ultimatum that specified shutting down the railroad leading from Indochina's Hanoi to China and acceptance of a Nipponese base inside Indochina.

Emboldened by the defeat of the Allies by the Axis powers in the West, Japan demanded closure of the Burma Road, the sole land supply route from Burma to China. The British bowed to the implied threat against both the empire's Hong Kong on the frontier near Canton, and India, which teetered on the edge of a revolt. To the outrage of China, Great Britain shut down the Burma Road, a torturous track constructed by two hundred thousand laborers. In fact, only a trickle of materials traveled along the Burma Road, but the symbolism was ominous. The Japanese interpreted the capitulations as indications of Western weakness and began serious negotiations to join the Rome-Berlin Axis.

Not satisfied with simply ending rail traffic via Hanoi to China, the Japanese soon took over airdromes that put their planes ever closer to the western Chinese cities. Waves of air raids battered Chungking and Kunming, reducing Chennault's puny air force even more as the enemy brought in its latest-model fighters. Hopes for some succor arose after Chiang arranged for his air force chief to travel to the United States. T. V. Soong, often a political adversary of his sister and the generalissimo but foremost a patriot, had wangled an opportunity to buy some of the newer American aircraft and to recruit volunteers.

Claire Chennault, as head of Chiang Kai-shek's air force, hurried home to arrange for an increased, if unofficial, participation in the defense of China. In 1939, a model of the Japanese I-97 fighter, the first Zero, fell into Chinese hands. Chennault flight-tested and painstakingly dissected the machine. He brought to the War Department its complete specifications and all the intelligence he could muster on its capabilities.

Advocates of direct support for Chiang had suggested that B-17 Flying Fortresses manned by U.S. airmen target the invaders, but Secretary of War Henry L. Stimson and the army chief of staff, General George C. Marshall, deflected the proposal, pointing out that this would be an act of war. They knew that the country was ill prepared for a conflict. Instead, Washington, urged on by T. V. Soong and other strong supporters of China, sought a less overtly confrontational means to parry the Japanese thrusts. The British now supported the effort, perceiving Chennault's air power as a deterrent to moves against the crown colony of Singapore, on the tip of Malaya.

Birth of the American Volunteer Group (AVG)

The most palatable solution posited transfer to China of 100 P-40s, the basic U.S. fighter. Chennault and Soong actually asked for 350 fighters and 150 bombers, but that was far beyond what the army air corps could comfortably accommodate. In fact, the Curtiss-Wright P-40C Tomahawks that would be designated for Chennault originally had been consigned to Great Britain. However, the RAF, never terribly enthusiastic about the plane for its purposes, agreed to let China have the P-40C models and await a later version.

With General Mow, Chennault had gone to the Curtiss-Wright factory in Columbus, Ohio, for a demonstration of the Tomahawk. The army pilot for the exercise was John Alison, who had earned his wings at Kelly Field, Texas, in 1937 with classmate Phil Cochran. Said Alison, "Supposedly, the horsepower limit for the plane was 980 but I pushed it to 1,400. I just pulled it straight over the runway, and went up and did an Immelman [a half-loop maneuver used to gain altitude; the demo aircraft took off with a minimum of gas, no armor plate or bulletproof tanks, and no radio]. I did a 360 right over the ground before them, did a wingover, a slow roll. I pulled the airplane up in a wingover and landed out of the wingover. It was a two-minute flight."

According to Alison, the Chinese observers enthusiastically agreed they needed 100 of the Tomahawks. Recalled the test pilot, "'That is not,' Chennault said, 'what you need. You need 100 of these,' as he tapped me on the chest." The air corps was not about to hand over a major portion of its qualified pilots. Later, Alison would serve with both Chennault and Cochran.

At least equally important with the procurement of the Tomahawks, Chennault secured permission to covertly recruit among the American military. Emissaries, bearing letters of authorization from Hap Arnold and Secretary of the Navy Frank Knox, circulated through army, navy, and Marine bases offering contracts with Central Aircraft Manufacturing Company (CAMCO), which contracted to handle recruiting and housekeeping details for the AVG. The pay for pilots ranged from $600 to $750 a month, with the lowest echelon of ground personnel pegged at $250. The pilots also understood that they would receive a bonus of $500 for each enemy plane shot down.

The American Volunteer Group signed up roughly 240 individuals—mechanics, armament specialists, radio experts, medics, and meteorologists as well as pilots. The chief motivations were a lust for adventure and a desire for money. David Lee "Tex" Hill recalled, "I was a navy pilot on the *Ranger* and we heard about it through a shipmate of ours. We came down for a flight one day and he grabbed Ed Rector and myself by the arm and said, 'Come with me.' We went up to a room and he said, 'Here's a couple of guys who will go with you.'" The "you" was retired navy commander Rutledge Irvine, one of several recruiters with military connections.

"This guy," said Hill, "had a map and it showed Burma and the Burma Road. He said they were looking for pilots to patrol this area. That sounded real good to us, adventurous. He explained it real fast. 'You'll get $600 a month, all you'll be doing is patrolling the Burma Road.' This was about March of 1941. Everything was real vague."

Rector, Hill, and Allen "Bert" Christman signed contracts for the American Volunteer Group. Hill explained, "I'd always wanted to go to the Orient because I happened to have been born in Korea. My father was a missionary there and I'd always had a desire to go back. We signed these contracts. Bert Christman, Ed Rector, and myself all had key positions. Eddie was in operations. I was assistant gunnery officer and Christman was on the administrative end. It knocked a hole in the squadron because at that time, the navy had undergone a terrific expansion. The *Ranger* was one of the few operational carriers the navy had at that time. Our skipper flew to Washington to see if he could stop it [the departure of three of his men]. He came back and said, 'I don't know what's going on, fellows, but this is bigger than me.'"

A pair of flight instructors at Randolph, Robert T. Smith and Paul Greene, unhappy with their duties, read a *Time* magazine piece that mentioned the recruitment. The pair learned that one of the agents was C. B. "Red" Adair. They obtained his address and telegraphed him, boasting of their thousand hours of flight time. But when Adair met them and discovered all their flying had been in trainers and never in fighters, he declined to accept them. Undaunted, Smith and Greene plied Adair with whiskey until he consented.

Deeply in debt, harassed by alimony demands, under strict orders from the Marine Corps for him to meet his obligations, pilot Greg Boyington fled to the AVG, leaving behind a well-earned reputation for carousing. He kept his financial woes and his fondness for booze secret from Chennault's representative. That probably would not have mattered. The CAMCO agent was Richard Aldworth, former member of a World War I American volunteer flying unit, the Lafayette Escadrille, and a vice president of CAMCO. As Chennault would learn, Aldworth was more concerned with signing people up than with their qualifications or deficiencies. Boyington in his memoirs claimed Aldworth insisted the enemy flew antiquated planes—mostly transports—were rotten pilots, and all wore corrective lenses. Asked how Aldworth knew the pilots wore eyeglasses, the glib answer was that this was seen in the remains after the shoot-downs.

Charles Bond, an air corps reserve pilot bored with ferrying bombers to Canada, heard about the AVG through the grapevine and contacted Adair. "The lure of adventure in a foreign country on the other side of the world was exciting. More important, however, was the unique and ideal manner in which this opportunity served to satisfy my dreams; a chance to get back into fighters, a chance for combat experience, which might help me secure a regular commission, and a chance to earn fast money, which would put me in a position to buy my parents a home."

Robert J. "Sandy" Sandell, a highly skilled aerobatics pilot, abandoned the army air corps because "There was a lot of fighting going on in the world for causes I believed were right and just—and I wanted to be in on it. I had been trained to fight but it didn't look then as if the United States would ever get into the war."

Joe Rosbert, a native of Philadelphia, graduated in 1934 from a local Roman Catholic high school with a scholarship for Villanova. After four years of chemical engineering studies, Rosbert said in his autobiography, *Flying Tiger Joe's Adventure Story Cookbook* (it includes recipes from comrades in the AVG), "A group of us students was gathered in the meeting hall to see a movie shown by naval officers. . . . They came in their impressive green aviators' uniforms and the movie they put on had the stirring, romantic title: 'Pensacola, the Annapolis of the Air.'

"After seeing the student pilots flying those navy planes, not to mention the beautiful beaches of the Gulf Coast and the palm trees waving in the breeze I could hardly wait for the officer to finish his talk before going up to volunteer for training to become a naval aviator."

Rosbert was called up in 1939 and by April 1940 pinned on his wings of gold and joined the fleet as a pilot of PBY patrol planes. The glamour wore off rapidly. "Finishing a routine patrol up the coast of California, I felt bored and depressed piloting the slow, cumbersome

PBY back to North Island. It was June of 1941. . . . For some time I had been thinking that, with a good part of the world at war, there must be something I could be doing that was more important than trucking navy patrol planes up and down the Pacific Coast."

One day, Irvine appeared with his seductive pitch—a salary that doubled what the navy paid plus the bonus for every plane shot down, although Irvine cautioned, "You probably will never see one." Rosbert immediately enlisted.

Robert Neale started his flying career in 1938, after, he said, "I was going with a young lady and she bet me I couldn't pass a navy physical." He succeeded and started his training at Pensacola in 1938. A year later he graduated and began serving as a dive-bomber pilot on the carrier *Saratoga*. "Commander Irvine came to interview pilots about the idea of going out to China to protect the Burma Road. He didn't know much more about it than I did, it turned out. I was interested for the simple reason that I was USNR [he had a commission in the reserve]. In those days, after four years of fleet you were through. I had put in for a for a permanent commission in the navy. They were handing out a few of them. I was turned down. I didn't have the faintest idea of what I was getting into, the country, or the people, living conditions. It was an adventure, not motivated by patriotism or anything like that."

The Burma Scene

While the Chinese struggled to stave off further depredations by the Japanese and Chennault formed his AVG, the British had already been at war for nearly two years. Despite the June 1940 defeat of the Expeditionary Force in France, barely staving off the German aerial blitz against major cities in the British Isles, and crushing defeats in Crete and Greece, there were some successes. Under General Archibald Percival Wavell, a brilliant military scholar who wore a black patch over his left eye, lost at Ypres in World War I, the Middle East Command battled the Axis forces in Africa to a standstill. Prime Minister Winston Churchill, somewhat infatuated with his own strategic insights, however, clashed with Wavell. Churchill replaced him with General Claude Auchinleck and named Wavell in June 1941 to the post of commander in chief of the empire's forces in India.

Until 1937, Burma, as an attachment to India, fell under the protection of the British Empire's military forces in India. But the separation of Burma placed its defense within the country, and neither the colonial officials nor the local government attempted to create an armed force capable of putting up much of a fight. Two years later, when the war began in Europe, the local army for operational purposes came under control of the British Chiefs of Staff, but finance and administration remained responsibilities of the Burma government. Nobody of consequence paid much attention to the situation; Singapore seemed a much more urgent site, and the likelihood of a Japanese strike through Burma's jungles and mountains seemed remote. Furthermore, Wavell reputedly regarded the Japanese forces as a relatively weak threat.

Nevertheless, modest steps were taken to create a defense should the Japanese attempt to add Burma to their conquests. A part of what became known as the Burma Frontier Force (BFF) included old mounted infantry, composed of units such as the Skinners Horse and Poonah Horse, stationed at Pyawbwe. A second lieutenant, I. O. G. Scott, posted to Burma in September 1940, described a scene redolent of the empire in its halcyon days. "Peacetime soldiering in Burma," he said, "was a lot of fun. We lived well at Pyawbwe. The colonel [Lieutenant Colonel Hugh Childers, a cavalry officer assigned from the 35th Bengal Lancers] had a lovely bungalow and in fact all Pyawbwe belonged to him. Using his men as laborers, he excavated a lake—indeed, a series of lakes—which filled up with water during the monsoon and remained full throughout the long dry season. . . . It is a very dry part of the world and became a sort of oasis.

"The only form of entertainment we had was by ourselves. Each week, turn by turn, the officers would throw a drinks party in their bungalows. For these weekly parties, the colonel always came dressed in a dinner jacket and his wife, Gladys, in a long evening gown with gloves. In fact, Hughie and Gladys dressed for dinner every night, even when dining on their own."

While the social niceties continued, the authorities also called for strengthening the local military power. The task was not easy because, as Scott's experience showed, it required melding people of different ethnic and cultural backgrounds. He had spent his first nine months in Burma shaping recruits into soldiers, producing two companies of "so-called trained men." He noted, "The first of these, a splendid bunch of Punjabies I took as my own company and Ian Turner took the other one—Sikhs—for himself. Our two companies formed the nucleus of FF4 [a reconnaissance battalion] to be joined later by two companies from the Bhamo Battalion of the B FF—one from the Burma Military and the other Kachin [an indigenous Burma element]. FF4 also had a mortar platoon and a wireless section. The mortar platoon personnel were Sikhs and the wireless, Karens [another Burma clan] so we had quite a mixture."

In October, Scott and his outfit, mounted on bicycles, received orders to prepare defensive positions about midway between Mongpan and the Salween River. He quickly discovered that even though the rainy season had passed, the trail through the heavy jungle never dried out, forcing the men to push or carry their bicycles. "The whole countryside was clothed in dense jungle and it was fairly obvious to me that our efforts at cycle training had been a waste of time as cycles would be a hindrance on the twisting mountain path which we had covered. The area looked dank and dreary after so much rain. The jungle path crossed and recrossed water many, many times as the path generally followed alongside a stream. We waded this stream more than thirty times between Mongpan and Wantham, each time up to our knees in water. Believe me it is not easy to wade a fast-flowing stream in full marching order and carrying an army cycle and to do it sixty times [including the return trip] in a day."

By the middle of November, Scott and his troops had constructed an encampment, set up a defensive stronghold atop ground he labeled The Ridge, and begun to patrol to the banks of the Salween. Away from the formality of the garrison at Pyawbwe, Scott said he truly felt himself part of his company. "I spoke not a word of English and as a result my Urdu improved a great deal. I soon discovered that the Punjabi diet of parathas and curry was infinitely better than the British officer diet of bully beef, so I messed with the men. We met our first 'enemy,' malaria, which struck down man after man and we could do little to combat it as we had no doctor and only a limited supply of medicines." Unable to get a physician to even visit his unit, Scott sent a letter to pharmacists in Rangoon, and paying out of his own pocket, bought a supply of quinine and other essentials.

War at the Rim of Southeast Asia

The British military boffins regarded the empire east of Burma in far greater jeopardy. Malaya, Singapore, and Hong Kong, strategically valuable and vital to commerce, lay closer to Japan. As a consequence, extra military resources, particularly air power, were deployed there.

Geoffrey Fisken, a New Zealand farmer from Gisborne who had attended college in Auckland, as a twenty-four-year old enlisted in the Royal New Zealand Air Force shortly after the start of the war. He remembered, "They called for volunteers for the East. I thought it was the Middle East so I put my hand up and it was the Far East they had meant. I finished up in Singapore. I was on flying boats there. I didn't like them and transferred to a fighter squadron.

"They were getting Brewster Buffaloes. The Americans were throwing them out because they were obsolete. [Some U.S. Marines still manned Brewster Buffaloes in June 1942 during the Battle of Midway.] In the beginning of 1941, we formed two RAF squadrons. The Buffalo was really so slow, but maneuverabilitywise it was quite good. But the rate of climb was just terrible. We [Squadron 243] had about fifteen or sixteen and the other squadron [488] had about the same." The command shuffled the deck, sending off 488 to Burma and replacing it with another group of New Zealanders, still operating the Brewster Buffaloes.

AVG Growing Pains

While the British mobilized and deployed forces drawn from all corners of the empire and took the faltering first steps toward a defense of their CBI interests, the planes and the personnel for the AVG, in two separate shipments, slowly journeyed toward the war in China. Given the youthful composition and the adventurous bent, it is hardly surprising that the volunteers were less than models of discipline and deportment once they felt themselves freed of the usual military restraints. Aboard ship, the volunteers wove a pattern of drinking and brawling. Whenever their vessel paused in a major port such as Honolulu, Manila, Hong Kong, Singapore, or Java, a good many immediately sought out the bordellos.

Once in Rangoon, they maintained a reputation for alcoholic binges, brawling, and roughhousing in their quarters, holding rickshaw races in the streets, yanking tablecloths off restaurant tables, shooting holes in the ceilings with their pistols. They also frequented the local bagnios. Charles Bond, among others, freely admitted to heavy boozing, but Greg Boyington established himself as one of the principal culprits, charging through a plate glass window, smashing his fist through a bamboo wall, wrestling a cow, and challenging people to fights.

Faced with the riotous behavior of his troops, Chennault attempted to impose order and discipline. The AVG operated with no rank distinction other than for their "colonel" leader, which obviated the usual symbols of military courtesy, salutes, and the use of "sir" except when someone addressed Chennault. Since they were ostensibly civilians, there was no possibility for a court-martial. Chennault created a board of staff officers and squadron leaders who could levy fines for violations ranging from disturbing the peace after midnight to public drunkenness, tardiness for work sessions, or absence from duty without permission. The ultimate weapon was Chennault's right to terminate employment, with the equivalence of a dishonorable discharge.

The AVG head was hampered in his ability to crack down because of his own predilection for pleasures of the flesh. Chennault had a healthy appetite for women, and he, too, savored strong potables. Still, most of the men respected him. Paul Frillman, a Lutheran minister fluent in Chinese who had planned to be a missionary but volunteered to serve as a chaplain for AVG, said, "I don't suppose anyone could have called Chennault 'glamorous' to his face without being punched. But he was a vain man, and obviously relished making an impression. Like MacArthur, he had immense natural magnetism on which to base his public figure." Describing Chennault's costume of mosquito boots, officer shirt with Chinese insignia, and beat-up air force cap, all of which emphasized his gamecock look, Frillman wrote, "Watching him for only a few minutes, anyone would get the impression of informality and lack of military pomp plus a quick, sure air of decisive authority."

Tex Hill confirmed Frillman's appraisal. After he arrived in Rangoon in July 1941, he first encountered Chennault. "I think anyone meeting him for the first time would definitely get the impression that he was a very dynamic, strong person and would get confidence in him."

The layover in Rangoon lasted only a short time before the group and their P-40s traveled to Kyedaw Field, eight miles from Toungoo, to prepare for their mission. The Toungoo installation was available because the RAF thought the monsoon season from May through August unbearable for Westerners. Whatever culture shock the volunteers experienced in the raw districts of Rangoon, their new home introduced them to the barely mitigated ambience of tropical Asia. Heat, humidity, rain, wooden barracks with bamboo walls, and invasions by an encyclopedia of insect life depressed even the hardiest spirits. To the Americans, the food served by the local cooks was barely edible.

Chennault, busy with administrative matters and establishing a relationship with the RAF, which owned the airfield and with whom he would need to coordinate activities, reached Kyedaw on August 21, 1941, to find his people in a sultry summer of discontent. Five pilots and several ground crewmen tendered their resignations. Chennault, probably figuring they would be malcontents who would poison the atmosphere, quickly allowed them to quit.

He then announced a rigorous program, a minimum of sixty hours of flight training in the P-40s, and seventy-two hours of lectures that would begin at 6:00 A.M. His demeanor again won converts, with even Boyington saying, "seeing Chennault and listening to him talk was the only thing about this deal I had seen so far that did impress me."

Chennault's program had more to it than a desire to instill a sense of order and purpose. Although by and large they were accomplished pilots, some recruits were former bomber or transport pilots, and others, such as Tex Hill and Ed Rector, were accustomed to navy dive bombers. Very few had ever been inside the cockpit of a P-40, and it was not the easiest of planes to fly. Those who previously flew big multiengine aircraft required considerable adjustment from the long, slow-speed takeoffs and landings. They had to become comfortable with the quick movements of a high-powered single-engine fighter.

Many of the recruits, such as Hill, developed an ability to handle the P-40, but to Chennault's chagrin others had great difficulty. Training crashes killed several fliers. On a single day, November 3, no fewer than eight of Chennault's fighter fleet required extensive repairs—smashed landing gears, bent props, or damaged wingtips—because of pilot error. He blamed Aldworth's casual acceptance of anyone who volunteered, and in November 1941 sent angry letters to Aldworth and to CAMCO decrying misrepresentation to pilots.

In the one to CAMCO he said, "Typical of these problems is the case of Pilot Officer E. [Edwin] S. Conant, who reported . . . with nine other navy pilots on October 29. Conant has the rating of a four-engine flying boat pilot. He informs me that for more than a year before your representatives accepted him for service with the AVG, he had never flown a land plane of any sort. He has no pursuit experience. I need hardly point out that a pilot so trained is hardly qualified for combat in Curtiss P-40s. I may add that the result of Pilot Conant's employment is precisely what might have been expected; he has crashed up three planes in the first week of flying.

"In telling the AVG story to pilots who may think of volunteering, nothing should be omitted. Far from merely defending the Burma Road against unaccompanied Japanese bombers [as Irvine and Aldworth had specified], the AVG will be called upon to combat Japanese pursuits; to fly at night; and to undertake offensive missions."

He concluded, "I prefer to have the employment quotas partly unfilled than to receive pilots hired on the principle of 'Come one, come all.'" To emphasize the seriousness of his complaint, Chennault dispatched a copy to T. V. Soong.

Still, with his limited resources, untrained pilots, slow accumulation of flyable P-40s, shortage of spare parts, and problems with machine guns, Chennault conducted a crash course in aerial combat against the Japanese. In the cooler hours of the early morning he led the fliers in simulated dogfights. He held daily classes in which he expounded on his knowledge of the various enemy planes, the formations and tactics employed by the Japanese, and the assets and weaknesses of the P-40. With a blackboard and chalk he diagramed teamwork in combat.

He passed out Japanese flight manuals to his people and told them, "Japanese pilots fly by the book, and these are the books they use. Study them and you will always be one step ahead of the enemy. . . . Bombers will hold their formations until they are all shot down. Fighters always try the same tricks over and over again. God help the American pilot who tries to fight them according to their plans. The object of our tactics is to break up their formations and make them fight according to our style." Because the P-40 could not climb as fast as the Japanese fighter nor maneuver as swiftly, the basic technique was to have an altitude advantage at the start. From there, the Tomahawk, with superior diving speed, could plunge down upon the foe. The network of early-warning stations was designed to give enough warning for the P-40s to reach the heights before the enemy arrived.

Several members of the AVG came across an illustration of a P-40 in North Africa, one of the handful being used by the British. The nose art featured shark teeth. The pilots asked their commander if they might decorate their aircraft in similar fashion. Chennault acquiesced, figuring the ornamentation might boost morale. The final version displayed an eye above an array of shark teeth over a mouth formed by the air scoop. Although this depicted a generic representation of a shark, somehow it became identified as a tiger shark. The label of "Flying Tigers" would come later.

As 1941 drew toward its end, relationships between the United States and Japan approached the breaking point. Many months earlier, the military and diplomatic staffs had begun to evacuate dependents. The commander of the Asiatic Fleet, in one of the more prudent gestures, ordered his fleet to sea rather than hang around ports in the Philippines. At Toungoo, Chennault, believing the AVG was now ready for combat, organized his forces into three squadrons. The 1st Squadron was headed by Texan Robert J. Sandell and nicknamed the "Adam and Eves," with nose art showing the biblical characters running around a large apple. The 2d Squadron was commanded by Jack

Newkirk, a native of an affluent suburb of New York City. The outfit lacked a moniker, but Bert Christman, a cartoonist by avocation,
painted a caricature of each pilot on the planes. Arvid "Oley" Olson,
from Los Angeles, led the 3d Squadron, whose aircraft were deco-
rated with a nude red angel in various poses. Chennault planned to
station all three units in Kunming, from where they could begin to
battle the Japanese.

3

First Strikes

P robably the first realization that the Japanese had decided to war on the Western democracies came with sightings shortly after noon on December 6, 1941 (in U.S. local time, almost thirty-six hours before the first attack on Pearl Harbor, which in the Far East calendar was December 8). Royal Australian Air Force Lockheed Hudson patrol planes on reconnaissance over the Gulf of Siam observed some thirty Japanese transports accompanied by destroyers. Agents in Indochina had earlier notified British intelligence of the convoys departing from Camranh Bay and Saigon, and the logical interpretation of the information was an invasion of Khota Bharu, Malaya, and areas of northwestern Thailand that would seal off Malaya and Singapore. The latter lay twelve hundred miles from Rangoon, Burma's chief contact with the outside world. Technically, Malaya was outside of what would be known as CBI, but in terms of the course of battle, the peninsula provided a gateway into Burma.

Having foreseen the possibility of a thrust into Malaya, the British had devised Matador, a plan to thwart any such aggression. However, it hinged on crossing the border into Thailand, and that country's government had warned that it would oppose whichever country first breached its sovereignty. A few days before the sighting of the Japanese convoy, Air Chief Marshal Sir Robert Brooke-Popham had queried London for guidance on the circumstances under which he could initiate Matador. He still had received no reply when the Japanese armada was discovered, and all Brooke-Popham could do was put his forces on high alert.

A thick cloud cover and rain soon hid the movement of the ships until the following day at 9:00 A.M (still thirteen hours or so before Pearl Harbor), when a vague report from a PBY on patrol reported

35

Japanese ships in the Gulf of Siam. Apparently the airplane was shot down before the crew could transmit further data. Other reports trickled in from reconnaissance missions, but although they added to the evidence of Japanese intentions, Brooke-Popham had now received a paralyzing response. It ordered, "For God's sake, do not allow British forces to occupy one inch of Thai territory unless Japan has struck the first blow at Thailand."

Shortly after midnight, when informed of Japanese ships only a mile offshore at Khota Bharu, Malaya, the commander of the 8th Indian Brigade directed his field guns to open fire. Enemy warships responded in kind. The time was an hour and twenty-five minutes before the first carrier-based Japanese aircraft appeared over the Hawaiian Islands.

Some thirty minutes later, the first Japanese soldier to step ashore on Allied soil, a member of a two-hundred-man force, struggled up the beach at Khota Bharu. The invaders found themselves pinned down by a thick tangle of barbed wire, a minefield, and deadly fire from pillboxes. The troops burrowed into the sand, gouged a path forward with their steel helmets, crawled over bodies, and tossed grenades at the fortifications.

In the early morning darkness, British bombers, along with shore batteries, attacked the vessels offshore, sinking two transports and heavily damaging a third. Major General Hiroshi Takumi, in command of the operation, said, "There was the utmost confusion all along the beach. Many officers and men were killed or wounded, many jumped into the water before their crafts had beached and swam ashore. The enemy positions were about a hundred yards from the water, and we could see that their posts were wired in; their guns . . . pointing directly at us."

Sir Shenton Thomas, the governor of Singapore, when informed of the Japanese strike at Khota Bharu by the military commander, displayed the then typical dubious appreciation for the ability of the adversary: "I suppose you'll shove the little men off?" After arranging for the detention of some twelve hundred Japanese men in the colony and seizure of any Japanese ships in the harbor, he advised his wife that she could return to her bed. Khota Bharu was four hundred miles away, and he believed by dawn that the invasion force would soon be repulsed.

The Far East military commander, Brooke-Popham, exhibited the same false notion of omnipotence. Seven months before, he had prepared a statement in the event of war, and now it was released: "We are ready. We have had plenty of warning and our preparations are made and tested. . . . Our defenses are strong and our weapons effi-

cient. . . . We see before us a Japan drained for years by the exhausting claims of her wanton onslaught on China."

While that fight raged on, radar detected incoming aircraft on a
course for Singapore itself. Half of the fifty-four planes bound for
Singapore aborted the mission because of foul weather, but the others
pressed on. As they neared the city, word was passed to Air Raid Precautions (ARP), the agency responsible for air raid sirens and a black-
out. Unfortunately, it was a Sunday night, and no one was on duty.
Indeed, it had been argued that there was never a need for manning
the ARP offices after dark because, claimed an RAF officer, Japanese
pilots could not see well enough to fly night missions.

When the raiders arrived over Singapore they found it well lit,
streets, harbor, and even the military headquarters all brightly illumi-
nated. Down plunged the bombs, and not until twenty minutes after
the final explosion did the lights go out and the sirens sound. The
principal military target was the airfield at Seletar; the Japanese all but
ignored Kallang, the base that was home to Geoffrey Fisken's 243d
Squadron. In fact, Fisken could not recall a single bomb falling on his
field. Initially, at least one squadron, the 453d at Sembawang, roused
its pilots and ordered them to confront the attackers. But once the
searchlights lit up the sky and antiaircraft shells, rifles, machine guns,
and even gunners from a flotilla that included the battleships *Prince of
Wales* and *Repulse* sprayed the heavens indiscriminately, Air Command canceled operations of the 453d for fear of deadly friendly fire.

Australian pilot Greg Board of the 453d remembered looking forward to an encounter with the enemy after intelligence reassured the
fliers that the Japanese used "all fabric-covered biplanes which wouldn't
stand a chance against the Buffalos." Fisken knew better, not only
from what he had seen in his reconnaissance flights but also from his
knowledge of what the defenders manned. "Some of the squadrons
were fitted out with old Swordfish [a single-engine biplane used as a
torpedo bomber] and some with Vildebeests. You could walk faster
than they could fly. They were mainly used for drogue towing [target
sleeves]."

While both Board and Fisken escaped any injury, the first raid on
Singapore killed 61 people and injured another 133. Fisken believed
that he and his fellow airmen often survived subsequent encounters
because of the confusion aroused by the insignia on their wings. He
explained that while the Japanese showed a rising sun of red and yellow, the British used a roundel of red, white, and blue with a large
yellow ring on the outside. "A lot of time Japs came at us and looked
and shook their wings and went away."

At Khota Bharu, despite the fierce resistance of the 8th Indian Brigade (composed of Indian troops with British officers), the Japanese secured a beachhead. As the Japanese began to overrun the lines defending Khota Bharu, Brooke-Popham, who had finally received permission to cross the border into Siam to prevent an onslaught that could cut off Singapore, dithered. Unfortunately, by the time he dispatched his forces, the enemy had waded ashore at the two vital points. Thai troops valiantly blocked the way, but they were up against overwhelming numbers and superior weapons.

The situation for the British crown colonies rapidly deteriorated. Within a week of the opening salvos the Japanese swallowed Kowloon and enveloped Hong Kong. Singapore faced a similar fate as Fisken and his comrades waged a losing battle in the air. "We found out," said Fisken, "there was no use trying to dogfight a Zero. At one stage I threw my wheels down and put my feet on the dashboard and hung on, to get around tight enough. I did get a shot at one, but they were too good and they had too many planes. Even if you did get a reasonably good shot at one, there was somebody else peppering you on your tail."

His squadron attempted to attack the ground forces at Khota Bharu but gave that up for aerial combat. "Once or twice we did have an advantage in height. We could have the speed to dive down on them. Then we would get two runs in by swinging straight through them and up on over. Then we would get out when their fighters came in and chased us. You could get in and get out fast as you can, because there were always so many of them.

"The only good day I think I had was when we had about three thousand feet of height on some bombers. Our cone of fire for all our machines was ninety-six square feet for all guns. It didn't matter whether you had twelve guns or four; they all covered ninety-six square feet. I reckon the Japs' guns were similar. I knew very well you could fly through it, because I got a hundred bullet holes in a Buffalo one day, and not one went in a vital part or in me. All we did was put on a bit of canvas and paint and patch it and then we flew it again.

"On this day I got two kills and a probable. The first two were beautiful—they went straight up in flames. Because I had changed my cone of fire from ninety-six square feet to twenty-five square feet [a much more concentrated burst], I had a lot more firepower. I knew I could shoot. I've had a gun in my hands since I was born. When we were allowed incendiary bullets, I jumped mine up so among every ten shots I had at least five incendiary and three armor-piercing and then tracers. I knew very well if I hit them, I was going to knock them down."

But the sheer numbers of the aggressors easily overwhelmed the best efforts of the defenders. Fisken and the handful of survivors of his unit shifted from the Kallang airfield to an Australian squadron operating from Semberwang.

The War in China Spreads

In China, at the start of December, the Western military presence had dwindled to almost token status. In Peiping, 141 U.S. embassy guards remained, with another 49 at Tientsin and 22 at Chinwangtao, a seaport 140 miles northeast of Tientsin. Many of these marines were scheduled to depart in the second week of December. In Shanghai, the U.S. 4th Marine Regiment had been shipped to the Philippines, and only a few remained to handle the final details for closing down shop. The U.S. gunboat *Wake* and the Royal Navy's *Peterel* lay at anchor in the Whangpoo, near Shanghai's International Settlement. Most of the crew from the *Wake* sailed to the Philippines on other gunboats, and a skeleton crew manned the vessel.

The Japanese moved first in Shanghai. After midnight of December 8 the U.S. sailors could not help but notice the flashes of signals between a nearby Japanese gunboat and the cruiser *Idzumo*, half a mile away. At 3:00 A.M., half an hour after the bombing of Pearl Harbor, a launch brought two officers and a dozen Japanese marines to the *Wake*. The acting skipper, Lieutenant Commander Columbus Smith, had no choice but to strike his colors. Although the ship had been rigged with explosives to scuttle her, there was no opportunity to set off the charges.

On the *Peterel*, Commander Stephen Polkinghorn still had a full crew, and when he received a message from the British consulate in Shanghai about the attack on Pearl Harbor, he directed preparations to scuttle his ship. A Japanese officer, backed by as many as fifty marines in a picket boat, boarded the *Peterel* and demanded surrender. Polkinghorn stalled, trying to give his men time to start the self-destruction. When the Japanese officer protested, Polkinghorn ordered him off the ship.

The Japanese in the picket boat backed off, and almost immediately, both the enemy gunboat and the *Idzumo* opened up with their three-, six-, and eight-inch guns. The *Peterel* answered with its puny three-incher, but the Japanese shells ripped into her. Flaming pieces of the vessel rose into the air before dropping back into the water. Polkinghorn issued the abandon-ship call. As a small cutter bore off the British sailors, Japanese marines fired at them with machine guns mounted on the captured *Wake,* instantly renamed *Tatara.* Wounded tars splashed ashore to become prisoners, like the remnants of the *Wake*'s crew.

Master Gunnery Sergeant Henry Stowers, in Peiping to assist in the dismantling of the embassy facilities and equipment, said, "It was before daylight and as a master gunnery sergeant we had separate quarters from the other men. I went to breakfast probably an hour before daylight and [because] we had only three or four officers, the senior noncommissioned officers took turns as officer of the day. On this particular morning our first sergeant, Dutch Miller, an old-time, twenty-year Marine, came charging in as we were eating in the staff NCO mess. Dutch was acting officer of the day. . . . He said the Japs were everywhere, all around, on the wall and everywhere [there were] machine guns. He said he was going down and run them off. We knew Dutch well enough to know that he'd try to do it.

"Somebody woke up Colonel Ashurst and he ordered Dutch to come down. There was a big ramp up about forty feet high and Dutch was up there demanding that they get out of there. Everywhere we turned we'd see machine guns pointed down to us, all around the embassy compound. Colonel Ashurst had secret orders not to offer any resistance. Actually, we couldn't. We were in the heart of the North China Expeditionary Force of the Japanese army, something like five hundred thousand. There were less than a hundred of us.

"Really, it was no surprise. We were working on sort of a deadline to get out of there. We were old professionals and we said, 'Oh, shit!' Eventually a contingent of six or eight officers, one high-ranking officer, came down. We could see them talking to Colonel Ashurst. He agreed to surrender to the Japs with not a shot fired.

"Next to some close relative dying, it was the saddest thing I ever went through. We had to line up and stack our arms, and that was about seventy to eighty men. Nobody had a machine gun, only rifles and pistols. We had to stack arms, back up four or five paces, and then the bugler blew taps and they brought the American flag down. The Japanese bugler blew their reveille or some bugle call and they raised the Japanese flag. Even though you were at attention, I [cast] my eyes down and every Marine there was crying. We all were."

In contrast to situations elsewhere, the Japanese did not mistreat their captives. "They were really very nice to us," said Stowers. "Colonel Ashurst had established social contact with the higher-ranking officers while he had been there. He knew the colonels and the generals and they had cocktail parties and so forth. We had our own food, our own cooks. The only thing different in our routine was that Japanese guards were all around."

One of the other U.S. Marines stationed at the embassy in Peiping that first week of December, O. R. Sparkman, remembered being on guard duty when the corporal of the guard told him that a Chinese roomboy said that a Japanese soldier had slapped him around while he was on his way to the compound. "We thought they just harassed him," remarked Sparkman, "but a wireless came in that said the Japs hit Pearl Harbor and we were at war. They did send word that at one o'clock they'd come in and take the compound over. That gave us quite a few hours to go over to the legation and burn all the papers. We hauled them out and burned everything we could."

Even if the Americans had wanted to put up a fight, they had no equipment. "We had three loose boxes of ammunition. We shipped all the rest to Chinwangtao [the port], and we were supposed to board the USS *Harrington*. It was a Monday and we were supposed to leave on Wednesday. It was a little hard to give up like that. I guess if they'd said fight, we'd have fought. But there wasn't much use in it. At one o'clock we were all standing out there at attention and they pulled down the flag. It was pretty hard to take."

Stowers said, "We had a lot of youngsters and possibly some of them thought we were embassy personnel, but all us old-timers, officers and noncommissioned officers, we were marines and knew we were prisoners of war."

In Chungking, Colonel Edward MacMorland, chief of staff for General Magruder, head of the American Military Mission to China (AMMISCA), kept a diary in which he spoke of a round of "return" dinners planned for their Chinese hosts, to begin on December 19. "Hope to have the Generalissimo for the first one," MacMorland noted on December 5. A day later he remarked, "Reports that diplomatic relations with Japan may be severed." On December 8, said MacMorland, "Awakened by General Magruder at 6:30 A.M. with the announcement that war has been precipitated by Japan with a surprise air attack on Manila. Details coming in over the radio. Our marines at Peiping are captured. The gunboat *Wake* has surrendered. Report of ships sunk east of Hawaii. One report that battleship *Oklahoma* is sunk. Japs also landing at peninsula north of Singapore. Reported that island Wake is captured and Guam under attack. Apparently many of CNAC [China National Aviation Corporation] planes destroyed in bombing of Kai Tai Airport, Hong Kong."

The China Connections

The AVG's origins were sub rosa, but more publicly, the Lend-Lease Act, passed in March 1941, included aid to China as well as a much more favored customer, Great Britain. The shopping list from China, however, went far beyond either the desirable or the possible. The requested items—from rifles, cannons, machine guns, tanks, trucks, etc., and, of course, airplanes—went far beyond what the United States had on its shelves. Furthermore, many, if not most, required technological skills outside the ken of the raw, untrained, uneducated, often illiterate Chinese soldiers. The roads and particularly bridges could not handle even the lighter tanks.

To organize and supervise the transfer and use of whatever Lend-Lease materials might make their way to China, Washington created AMMISCA under General John Magruder, both predecessor and successor to Stilwell in the post of military attaché.

The fragmented news that reached Chungking and those involved in AMMISCA mixed fact with fiction. The first Japanese planes to hit Manila arrived over Clark Field about eight hours after the strike on Pearl Harbor. The marines at Wake would hold out for almost two weeks before surrendering. But these were details. The bombing of Hong Kong and the landings in Malaya indicated the scope of the Japanese actions. MacMorland reported in his diary, "Conference at 9 P.M. with Generalissimo, the War and Foreign Ministers, British Ambassador, British Military Attache, Gen. Magruder. A thrilling meeting at which the part of China in the war was discussed. The Generalissimo says he is all out in help to the U.S. After all, he has the only land army that can be put into immediate contact in large numbers."

A day later, the extent of damage to the U.S. fleet remained unknown in Chungking. The AMMISCA chief of staff mentioned loss only of the *Oklahoma* and a destroyer, albeit recording three thousand casualties. The diarist noted that Radio Tokyo "is making extravagant claims, including one that 70% of the Pacific fleet is already sunk. Report from San Francisco of Jap planes near there [untrue]. Our people seem to be really stirred up at last. War has been officially declared with only one dissenting vote [pacifist congresswoman Jeanette Rankin] in Congress. All sorts of war measures being taken, including rounding up of Japs. Central and South American countries are also declaring war. Conference this afternoon with Gen. Ho Ying-chin [minister of defense], Gen. Dennys [Major General L. E. Dennys, British military attaché], Gen. Magruder, British and Chinese staff officers mainly over aid to Hong Kong against Kowloon Peninsula and Canton [occupied by the Japanese]."

Chiang actually volunteered to insert two Chinese armies, totaling perhaps eighty thousand troops, in Burma. Considering the battering his forces had absorbed in defense of their own country, the offer seems dubious, and Dennys suggested that perhaps a division or a regiment might be more reasonable. MacMorland seems to have been badly misinformed on the capacity of the Chinese army, but the British military attaché was more knowing.

On December 10, a succinct "bad news" led off with the information that both the *Prince of Wales* and the *"Republic"* [*Repulse*] had been sunk by bombs off Malaya. MacMorland wrote of the frantic flight from Hong Kong. "The CNAC has been busy every night, moving among others Madame Kung [wife of financier H. H. Kung, a rival of the Soong family], [who] left the flesh pots of Hong Kong with 900 pounds of baggage to hurry to Chungking. The laugh is now on the rich Chinese who have skulked in Hong Kong when their country needed them."

On December 16, MacMorland noted that a message from President Franklin D. Roosevelt was important enough to require an immediate meeting with the generalissimo, General Ho Yin-chin, other members of the Chinese staff, and the British military attaché concerning the defense of Burma: "Events are moving fast . . . war ferociously pressed by the Japs, their main effort in Malaya, attack on Philippines secondary. We have been pressing the Chinese to pin down the troops in China, but so far nothing much done. They need more time for preparations." Although the AMMISCA staff, which was on the scene, was supposed to provide guidance to the military staffs and the Roosevelt administration, MacMorland's ignorance of the parlous state of Chiang Kai-shek's forces is startling.

The AVG Enters the Lists

The American Volunteer Group still had not participated in combat lists on December 7. In fact, although the imminent signs of war abounded, the P-40s at Toungoo, like those at the Hawaiian and Philippine airfields, were lined up wingtip to wingtip, easy morsels for bombing raiders. The base, only 110 miles from a Japanese airfield in Thailand, was unprotected by antiaircraft guns and lacked an early-warning net like that created by Chennault in China. The news about Pearl Harbor and movements against the British in Malaya naturally sounded the highest alert, and measures were taken to disperse the planes.

According to Duane Schultz, the Japanese attack triggered highly emotional responses among the AVG pilots. Joe Rosbert was sitting around after breakfast when the editor of the AVG group newspaper suddenly handed out mimeographed sheets briefly reporting an attack on Pearl Harbor. "I could see the excitement overcome everybody. Some remarked that it was impossible that Pearl Harbor could be hit. It must be Manila or some other place close to Japan."

Another flier wrote in his diary, "We are stunned . . . we realized that we are right in the middle of one hell of a big war! . . . I wonder when we'll get a chance at them. We are very tense and prepared to do our best, but we have no replacements."

The first mission undertaken by the Chennault's minions sent a photo plane piloted by Erik Shilling, escorted by Ed Rector and Bert Christman in P-40s, over Thailand. The cameras recorded dozens and dozens of Japanese aircraft packed onto several fields, while ships in the Bangkok Harbor disgorged troops and matériel. Under strict orders not to shoot unless attacked, the trio returned to base. When Chennault saw the pictures he cabled an urgent plea to Washington for bombers to destroy the lush targets before the enemy could organize its forces, but none was available.

Not until December 20 did the AVG actually engage the enemy. Chennault's patchwork warning net in China reported a late-morning flight headed in the direction of Kunming, home for two squadrons. When the red ball signal rose to flutter atop a mast, the pilots, pulling on their flight suits, trotted to their planes.

The strategy devised by Chennault called for Jack Newkirk to lead four of his Panda Bears directly at the oncoming bombers. With Newkirk flew Bert Christman, Ed Rector, and Gil Bright. Another half dozen P-40s under Jim Howard from the squadron would fly high cover over Kunming, ready to attack should the raiders near the city and airfield.

From the radio in the Kunming operations shack crackled Newkirk's voice: "Shark Fin Blue [code name for the AVG and color-coded to identify the flight] calling base. Bandits sighted sixty miles east. Attacking." Silence followed, and Chennault now ordered a covey of P-40s from the reserves in the squadron, led by Bob Sandell, Bob Neale, and Bob Little, to look for the enemy. The commander reasoned that the location listed by Newkirk indicated that the enemy planes, because of thick cloud cover, were lost, and if attacked might flee to the Hanoi base. More time passed, and it became obvious that if the Japanese had continued toward Kunming, they would have already been overhead.

The six planes led by Jim Howard landed, having seen nothing of the enemy. Behind them by a few minutes, Newkirk and two others were soon on the ground. The leader explained, "We caught them, all right. We made one pass. My guns jammed and the radio went dead. So we came home. We lost Ed Rector somewhere along the way." He turned up later.

About half an hour later, the fourteen fighters dispatched by Chennault, when he believed the Japanese in retreat, appeared. As they came over the field, one P-40 did a slow roll, signifying victory. Once on the ground, according to Bob Hotz, who interviewed him for his book *With General Chennault,* Neale described the action: "We were flying along above solid overcast when we spotted the 10 Jap bombers. They were lost in the soup and trying to get back to Hanoi. They were going like the devil just above the overcast . . . they couldn't have been more than 3,000 feet above the ground. Evidently, they jettisoned their bombs to get more speed. When they spotted us, they put their noses down and ran hell-bent for election. We chased them for about 10 minutes before we caught them. Sandell sailed in first with the assault echelon, and I followed with my reserve flight. Bob Little stayed above, with the support echelon to cover our attack.

"We went in rat-race formation, everybody chasing the tail of the plane ahead [in the excitement of their first combat, the pilots had forgotten all of Chennault's tactics of working in two-plane tandems]. We opened fire, and the bombers seemed to fall into pieces. I saw pieces of engine cowling fall off into space. Glass from the gun turrets flew off in all directions. Engines smoked and caught fire. Tails just crumpled and fell off. . . . The air was so full of P-40s dashing all over the place that I worried more about colliding with a P-40 than about the Japs."

As their gas ran low, the Americans broke off the engagement, while the remaining enemy planes, four of them trailing smoke, scurried for their base. Reports from Chinese intelligence claimed that only one of the ten enemy planes managed to get home safely.

In terms of effect on the overall war, the action meant nothing; it was less than a pinprick inflicted on the Nipponese air force. But starved for good news, the Chinese newspapers lavished praise on the tiny air force that had so decisively defeated the Japanese. The stories christened the AVG "Fei Wing"—Flying Tigers. Until the overthrow of the Manchu dynasty, the dragon symbolized China, but after 1911, the tiger had become the national emblem.

Under Arvid Olson, Chennault's 3d Squadron, Hell's Angels, operating from Mingaladon Airfield at Rangoon, spotted their first enemy bombers a day after the successful defense near Kunming. However, when the Americans, along with RAF Brewster Buffalos, rose to meet the Japanese, the attackers hurriedly dumped their bombs on the nearest target and fled to their Bangkok base. On that same day, a lone Japanese photo plane flew over Rangoon at twenty-five thousand feet, well above the range for a P-40, and took pictures of the airfield and harbor.

One of Chennault's dicta said that the appearance of a reconnaissance aircraft indicated a raid in a day or so. On December 23, his prediction proved accurate. In morning heat of 115 degrees, as pilots lounged around in their shorts, the RAF reported fifty-four bombers en route from Thailand, with fighters joining them along the way. After a helter-skelter dash to man their fighters, the AVG scrambled fifteen planes and, with eighteen Buffalos from the RAF, climbed to eighteen thousand feet. Split into two flights, one led by George McMillan and the other by Parker Dupouy, both former army pilots, the defenders sighted the enemy raiders at sixteen thousand feet, with their Nakajima I-97 shepherds somewhat above them.

McMillan signaled with a waggle of his wings, and he dove toward the twin-engine Mitsubishi bomber formation, with the others of his flight close behind. The mottled green lead bomber exploded from the guns triggered by Charlie Older. McMillan blew up two others, while R. T. Smith ignited the wing tanks of a fourth victim and then a fifth. But now the I-97s had plunged into the fray, maneuvering for a tail approach. Somehow they missed Smith, who added another pair of the raiders, sending one down in flames and exploding the second. Older scored twice more against the bombers.

Dupouy's section greeted the second wave of bombers. As Neil Martin roared down on the formation, turret gunners from as many as twenty-seven aircraft concentrated their fire on him. Martin struggled for control, but his P-40 careened into a spin and smashed into the water off Rangoon. He was the first of the Flying Tigers to die in combat. Ken Jernstedt scored with tracers into one bomber's wings, and Americans Bob Brouk and Ralph Gunvordahl poured bullets into the vitals of two more of the enemy.

Japanese fighters sliced through their group of bombers to tail Henry Gilbert's Tomahawk. Their bullets slashed into the cockpit and started a fire that ended with Gilbert's plunge into the bay below. Several other Nakajimas mortally wounded the P-40 flown by Gilbert's wingman, Paul Greene. As his ship started a death spin, Greene bailed out. While he dangled in his parachute, enemy gunners attempted to machine-gun him. But Greene artfully yanked on his straps, and the oscillations enabled helped him to avoid the bullets before he finally hung motionless, pretending to be dead. Abandoned by the would-be assassins, Greene came to earth in a rice paddy, unhurt.

Bob "Duke" Hedman, by reputation a strict by-the-book pilot, had been the last man to get off the ground. He chose to dive through the escort fighters to hit the bombers, but on his way, he blasted a Type 96 before coming up behind one of the Mitsubishis and hosing it with a devastating ten-second burst. Although bullets had shattered his canopy, Hedman continued to pursue the foe. He successfully dueled with and destroyed two more fighters, even while his P-40 absorbed heavy punishment. Undeterred, he pursued some retreating enemy catching up with the remnants and put away one more bomber for an official score of 4 1/2 victories. Smith was credited with 5, making him the first Flying Tiger ace.

Charles Older recalled that he and a friend, Ed Overand, were off duty that day and planned on a shopping trip. "Just after breakfast we heard the airplanes winding up down on the field. We heard the Hurricanes go out first, then the 40s, so we figured something was up." The pair grabbed a couple of bicycles parked by the mess hall and pedaled to the field.

"All the airplanes were off except two P-40s sitting there unattended. I said to Ed, 'Why don't we hop in and go flying.' He said, 'Fine, but where are we going?' I said, 'I don't know. Let's get up.'" Aloft they found a flight of four others from the AVG and joined up as the trailing element.

"All of a sudden," remembered Older, "the leader started shaking his wings, which is an attention signal. I spotted coming in from the east at about three thousand to four thousand feet above us, a huge formation of bombers. I would estimate there were sixty of them, two-engine [planes]. A huge conglomeration of airplanes, more than I'd ever seen together. Up behind them another two thousand feet and back a couple of miles was a squirrel cage of Jap fighters. For some reason, they always seemed to be undisciplined. The bombers were in a crisp, precise formation. But the fighters were always in some kind of big mess back there.

"We didn't have a chance to get up on top of the bombers in the time we had before they hit Mingaladon. The only thing we could do was pour on as much power as we could, climb up underneath them, and make passes from underneath. We tried to get as much altitude as possible but couldn't even get even with them. We'd get to about five hundred feet of them, then dive down, pick up some speed, and come up underneath them in an almost vertical position, fire, and then roll out underneath them again. One reason we wanted to stay as vertical as possible was to get underneath their bottom guns, which could only fire down something like forty-five degrees. That way we could avoid a good deal of the crossfire from these bottom guns.

"I started making runs on the leader because I could keep well under the formation, whereas if I were making runs on the back man I'd be at a lesser angle with respect to the front bombers and they'd have a better shot at me. I can remember on the first or second pass, seeing the bomb bay doors open up. I looked down and I could see that Mingaladon was about ten miles away and they were starting their final bomb run. I remember also seeing a tremendous amount of tracers going by. Instead of red, like ours, they were silver. They looked like silver streaks of confetti going by. I also picked up a few holes in the airplane, in the wings.

"On about the third pass I was making on this leader, the whole bottom of it just blew out. I must have hit either the bombs or the gas tanks. I could see all this debris coming down and the airplane rolled out and went almost straight in. Immediately the number two man on the right side slid right over, took the lead. There was no hesitation. None of the other bombers varied an inch. They just kept the formation going, straight on into the target."

Older knocked down one more bomber before he ran low on fuel and ammunition. He put down on a runway pocked with holes. In spite of the fierce opposition, some of the twin-engine bombers had reached their target and blasted Mingaladon Airfield, blowing up barracks, the operations offices, and the radio shack and cratering the landing strip. The Japanese fighters vented their fury on the base and Rangoon itself, strafing city streets with deadly effect to civilians who had ignored warning sirens.

The RAF counted thirty-two wrecked Japanese planes in the jungles and rice paddies surrounding Rangoon. With three Buffaloes downed early in the battle, short on fuel and ammunition, the Brewster pilots had quit the fight well before the Americans. They claimed only seven victims, indicating that the AVG had accounted for twenty-five. Three P-40s had been destroyed in combat; two pilots, Martin and Gilbert, were dead. Olson reported to Chennault the loss of three more planes, two damaged in the air and one that crashed while landing on the pockmarked runway. Along with his congratulations, condolences for the dead, and reminders to disperse aircraft against future raids, Chennault instructed Olson to report the names of all pilots engaged "for bonus." The AVG intended to meet the terms of the contracts with its volunteers.

While Chennault husbanded his slim resources, confusion dogged efforts by the Allies to convene a council of war at Chungking. On December 17, to coordinate the campaigns against the Japanese, U.S.

Army Air Corps major general George Brett, originally assigned to investigate the possible use of heavy bombers in China, had become the American delegate to the meeting. At the moment he was in Burma, and in the interests of secrecy, Magruder felt unable to advise him of the urgency of his presence in Chungking. As a result, Brett, aware of the critical location of Burma, was busy in Rangoon. Far from attending the scheduled session in the Chinese capital, Brett asked Magruder to join him in Rangoon. MacMorland noted, "We suspect he [Brett] wants Gen. Magruder to give the Chinese Lend-Lease materials [accumulating in Rangoon] to the British, which very definitely cannot be done without the consent of the Chinese." Indeed, Wavell and his staff had cast covetous eyes on the supplies earmarked for shipment to China, having concluded that the empire soldiers would make far better use of them than the corrupt Chinese generals and their poorly trained legions.

In a historic first of a number of wartime meetings, on December 22, President Roosevelt and Prime Minister Churchill conferred with their senior service officers in Washington. The problems of China were among the many topics. But the arrangements for the American-British-Dutch-Australian Command (ABDA), to be headed by Wavell, left China out of the loop. Chiang would hardly have permitted his soldiers to serve under a foreign command.

Anxious to keep the generalissimo from feeling underappreciated, and aware of Sino-British friction, Roosevelt urged that Wavell make an extra effort to placate the Chinese leader. The Americans in particular wrestled with the proper posture to take in China—whether to send only a mission that would simply service as best as possible the needs of that country, or to consider China an active theater of the war, with heavy U.S. participation.

Hong Kong surrendered on Christmas Day, and the Japanese continued their advance toward Singapore. Over Rangoon, the Flying Tigers, together with British pilots, contested a Christmas morning mission by three waves of raiders, sixty bombers and thirty fighters in all. Again the Americans and their ally punished the enemy severely, as nearly a third of the attackers never made it home. The AVG claimed thirteen fighters and four bombers. Two P-40s went down, but Burmese natives brought both pilots back to Mingaladon. The Brewster Buffaloes again showed their vulnerability, with more than half of their seventeen ships shot down and six pilots killed. While the successes gratified Chennault and company, his tiny force could ill afford the high rate of attrition.

4

War Comes to Burma

The suspicion of Colonel Edward MacMorland, chief of staff for the American mission handling Lend-Lease to China, that the British intended to expropriate the war goods consigned to Chiang but still in Rangoon, was right on the mark. Sir Archibald Wavell, named commander of the newly formed ABDA combine, initially, in an egregious miscalculation, thought that the multipronged Japanese advances had stretched the Nipponese too thin for any concerted attack through Burma. He anticipated reinforcements of two British Empire divisions and a pair of East African brigades. He correctly foresaw that import of a massive number of Chinese soldiers into Burma and then feeding and maintaining them went beyond logistical capabilities. Coupled with Wavell's conviction that the Chinese troops had neither adequate training nor adequate discipline, he balked at any large infusion of them. In addition, the Burmese people had long resented the presence of civilian Chinese in their midst, and an ongoing northern Sino-Burmese border conflict generated hostile feelings on both sides. The notion of seventy thousand alien soldiers under their own independent Chinese command was no more acceptable to Wavell than the prospect of these troops serving under a foreign nation to the generalissimo.

The AMMISCA chief, Major General John Magruder, theorized that Wavell's reluctance to enlist Chinese soldiers meant that Mac-Morland was right. The British general intended to grab the Lend-Lease goods for his own purposes. A diplomatic and military dance centered on their disposition. The swift decline in the fortunes of Hong Kong, Malaya, and Singapore had forced Wavell, even as he declined to make use of the Chinese army, to take a harder look at the Burma defense situation. There was a desperate shortage of every-

50

thing, from trucks to bullets. Magruder argued that unless Chiang consented, the British could not take possession of the supplies, and Washington ordered Magruder to persuade the Chinese to acquiesce to a transfer. Of particular import was a treasure trove of weapons and ammunition on the SS *Tulsa*. Everything on the Rangoon docks and the cargo of the *Tulsa* and other ships was impounded until the ultimate destination of the matériel could be determined. Under a compromise, it was agreed that a committee would examine the stocks in warehouses and on the docks. Amounts that could be handled via the limited transport along the Burma Road would go to China, while the British took possession of the vast surplus that remained.

The impound sat poorly in Chungking, and when British soldiers seized 150 trucks from the Chinese offices in Rangoon, the agreement on sharing nearly foundered. On Christmas Day, at a meeting among the interested parties, the Chinese representative stunned his listeners with an announcement that the generalissimo had concluded that it was no longer possible to cooperate with the British in a war against Japan. Only after intervention at the highest level was Chiang pacified sufficiently to agree to aid in the defense of Burma, but the relationship of China and Great Britain would be tenuous. The bickering over the spoils continued.

Nor were Prime Minister Churchill and President Franklin Roosevelt on the same page. To begin with, the administration of Roosevelt, from the top down, believed that victory over the Japanese would not preserve the British Empire. In the president's eyes, Burma, Malaya, Indochina, and even India would inevitably secure their independence after the war. Instead of focusing on retrieving these countries for its ally, U.S. strategy aimed at support for China, for reasons of sentiment and the very hard truth that, properly aided, the country might tie down huge numbers of Japanese soldiers while providing a base for aircraft to carry the war to Tokyo. Burma was important not because it belonged to Great Britain but because it offered the best route to feed war matériel to China.

At the same time, the United States was in no position to resolve matters among the squabbling parties or to influence actions in the theater because of indecision over who on the scene should have command over American interests. The first choice to head the American military presence was Lieutenant General Hugh A. Drum, a veteran of World War I, when he served as chief of staff under General John J. Pershing. Drum, who, among other deficiencies, could not speak Chinese, alienated army chief of staff George Marshall and Secretary of War Henry L. Stimson with demands that his post include an abundance of American ground troops. The whole idea was to use the manpower of China backed by American guidance, Lend-Lease, and a substantial air effort.

Stilwell was then at work in the War Department, creating plans for an attack by the Allies in North Africa under the code name Gymnast. In his diary for the period he complained about "the Limeys," grousing about Roosevelt—"the Limeys have his ear, while we have the hind tit." With Drum rejected, Marshall and Stimson turned to Stilwell. When Chiang agreed that the American would be appointed his chief of staff, a post from which he could exercise command, newly breveted Lieutenant General Joseph Stilwell prepared to leave for China.

AVG Squabbles and Struggles

The early victories aside, Chennault continued to operate on a very narrow margin. He was enraged when Washington informed him that it intended to send Brigadier General Clay Bissell, as a member of Stilwell's staff, to command the Tenth Air Force in China and be Chennault's superior. During Chennault's stint at the air corps' tactical school he had vociferously disagreed with Bissell, a World War I ace and instructor. Bissell taught the conventional one-on-one dogfight technique and further ired Chennault with his insistence that fighters could not defeat heavily armed bombers.

In mid-January no fewer than eleven pilots quit; the AVG commander handed them dishonorable discharges for leaving while their country was at war. From Kunming, Chennault sent his 1st and 2d Squadrons—Adam and Eves under Robert Sandell and Panda Bears led by Jack Newkirk—to relieve Arvid Olson's 3d Squadron, Hell's Angels, at Mingaladon Airfield near Rangoon. Bob Neale, as second in command to Sandell, said, "I arrived in Rangoon after a rather harrowing flight. The maps were Chinese maps and I couldn't read them too well, and they were very small scale. I kept flying with these eight planes behind me. I didn't know any more about it than anyone else. My combat experience was the same as anybody else, my leadership ability was probably rock bottom.

"I called one fellow up on the radio and said, 'That was the Mekong River we just went over, wasn't it?' He said, 'No, that was the Salween. If you stay on this course for another fifteen minutes, you're going to run into Mandalay. We'd already had a few fellows get lost.'"

The Panda Bears actually arrived on station several weeks before the Adam and Eves. Frustrated by a lack of action, Newkirk scheduled a four-plane mission against Japan's Tak Airfield in Thailand. The squadron commander flew with Bert Christman as his wingman; Jim Howard, with Tex Hill on his wing, made up the second element. Christman developed engine trouble and was forced to return.

Hill recalled, "We went over at an altitude of ten thousand feet and dropped down on this airdrome. We could see planes parked there. When we made this run on the field, the first thing I know when we pulled up—hell, there were more of us in the circle. This Jap was on Jim Howard's tail, just sitting back there. I don't think Jim even knew we had been attacked from above until we got back. I shot this Jap off his tail. I was so excited, hell, I wasn't even looking through the gunsight. I was just looking through the windshield. We had tracer bullets, you might say it was just like putting a hose on a man. I just flew right up on the guy's tail and brought around on him. I could see [him] set on fire and [go] down.

"In the meantime, this fellow had made a pass at me from overhead that I didn't see. Why I didn't get it, I don't know because when I got back I had thirty-three holes in my plane. I began learning fast from that time on. I think my neck size increased about an inch—keeping your neck on a swivel, looking around.

"As we pulled up, there was a Jap coming toward Newkirk. He just turned into him head-on, just as Newkirk pulled off his first strafing pass. He just disintegrated. He was coming almost head-on into him." At this early stage the enemy seemed not to have realized the advantages of a P-40 against such a head-on attack. Armor protected the nose and cockpit of the Tomahawk, and its .50-caliber machine guns put out a much deadlier stream of fire than the smaller 7.9-mm rounds of the Japanese fighters.

For Neale, his first shoot-down occurred over the Gulf of Martaban. "They [the Japanese] would make a lot of fighter sweeps and they'd be stacked up all the way from ten thousand to fifteen thousand feet. There'd be twenty-five or thirty planes. These were all 996s and 997s. The 996 had a fixed landing gear, and the 997 had a retractable landing gear. They were very maneuverable. The gas tanks were nonsealing; their oil cooling system was a series of copper tubing in front of their radio. If you ripped into one of those tubes, they'd eventually go down.

"You'd make a pass through them and pick out a target. You couldn't try to turn. You went right through and came back for another pass. We never did any dogfighting or anything like that. We might make a few evasive maneuvers. My first plane was a 996 or 997. He went into the Gulf of Martaban. Charlie Vaughn saw the oil slick down there. I was confirmed by Charlie on that one. Actually, there'd

A P-40 with the distinctive nose art of the Flying Tigers carried an auxiliary fuel tank under the fuselage. (Photograph from U.S. Air Corps)

be more planes found than we ever claimed. A lot of time you'd hit one of these little 996s or 997s on a head-on run with a .30-caliber in the nose, and if it went through one of these oil lines—the series of tubing—he'd eventually go down somewhere. Reports would come straggling in from the natives, saying another Japanese plane."

Stilwell's Preliminary Fights

Early in February, Joe Stilwell made his last official rounds before heading for the Far East. He had drawn some comfort from Marshall's scolding of the military regime in India. Stilwell wrote in his diary, "Saw George. He burned up Wavell on British friction with Chinese." A few days later Stilwell noted, "Archie now claims he never refused help. Said he'd take the two [Chinese divisions]. . . . Somebody is a liar. Archie missed Peanut [Stilwell now referred to the generalissimo by this demeaning nickname] at Lashio and now they are both sore, each thinking the other ducked out on him."

A Republican, like most of the military, and contemptuous of a civilian's ideas on war, Stilwell actively disliked the president. When he paid his respects, he wrote, "F.D.R. Very pleasant and very unimpressive. As if I were a constituent in to see him. Rambled on about his idea of the war." He quoted Roosevelt, "a 28,000-mile front in my conception." Stilwell remarked, "Just a lot of wind."

The "fuss" over Chennault and Bissell boiled up on the eve of the departure of Stilwell, who said, "It seems that George Marshall promised Chiang Kai-shek that Chennault would be the ranking air commander." Dr. Laughlin Currie, Roosevelt's personal assistant and an adviser on China, had interceded for Chennault with the head of the air corps, Hap Arnold, "urging that a man other than Bissell go. Arnold hit the ceiling. I spoke for Bissell, and insisted that he rank Chennault. Arnold so ordered. Currie pulled in his horns. I told him my opinion of Chennault had dropped a lot since hearing that. It was arranged for Currie to send Chennault another wire telling him to get in the game and play ball or else. They are acting like a couple of kids, and they'll both have to behave."

The message from Currie, via T. V. Soong, stroked Chennault, relating that Arnold held the opinion "you are A-1" and "has fullest praise for the AVG" but said the air corps chief wanted a member of his own staff "to head [the] larger show. . . . Bissell has now changed to your views on tactics and Stilwell adds you will have free hand regarding tactics." As much a maverick as Stilwell was, he was not inclined to humor any prima donnas under his command, and few in the army air corps in Washington would champion Chennault. The issue, however, was far from resolved.

The Ground War in Burma Begins

In the CBI, the Japanese now vigorously pressed their case. The British forces in Malaya fell back toward Singapore, whose vaunted defenses all aimed against a seaborne invasion rather than one from inland jungles. Just as surprising, to the ABDA command, enemy troops from Siam crossed the border through mountains labeled impassable and streamed toward Burma's eastern city of Moulmein. Realizing his vulnerability, Wavell reversed himself and requested that the Chinese bring two divisions into Burma to protect the country's Shan states next to Indochina. Under the new strategy, the British Empire's own forces could then shift to the west for defense of Rangoon. It had dawned on London that unless the Burma-to-China route could be maintained, there was a grave danger the latter country would be unable to contribute much to the war. Then the jewel in the crown, India, might be threatened.

A tiny group from the Burma Frontier Force led by Lieutenant I. O. G. Scott, who had described peacetime soldiering in Burma as "a lot of fun" shortly after the Japanese committed themselves to war, had been ordered to cross the Salween River and patrol the area. A north-to-south waterway, the Salween flowed through eastern Burma, close by the border with Siam.

After Scott left his base camp with a handful of men, including one who spoke the Shan language, and reconnoitered an area known as Mong Hang, he returned to gather up his small company for a forward move. They were to be attached to the Jecol commando unit, and to bear their heavy supplies they had a troop of eighty elephants.

"It was my first encounter with elephants and I approached them with considerable caution at first but I very soon got used to them and began to realize that they are very gentle, very intelligent, and truly wonderful beasts," said Scott. "On New Year's Day we set off with our little army of about 120 men for Mong Hang. Firstly, we had to ferry our kit over the river and swim the elephants over. The Salween is about half a mile wide at that point and is fairly fast-flowing so I could see that it could be a problem! The 'head' elephant—an imposing tusker—was first coaxed to the riverbank by his *oozi* (mahout). He tested the water with his left toe, just as if he was worried lest the water should be too cold for an early morning dip. Finding it to his liking, he then moved slowly down the sloping bank into the river. He paused, turned his noble head around, and I swear he gave me a wink before setting off, trunk in the air, to swim over. The others followed without hesitation and very soon all eighty were on the way. One or two were swept downstream for almost a mile, but they made their way up the far bank and all assembled on the other side.

"Unfortunately, I had to leave behind about thirty men under my *subedar* [equivalent of a ranking sergeant], who were too weak from malaria to move with us. My company had dwindled to two platoons without hearing a shot fired in anger. In fact, I had more elephants than men." Scott dispatched a patrol under one of his *subedars* that actually penetrated well inside Siam. The noncom returned, "rather disappointed" in not encountering opposition.

The expedition did not sight any Japanese, but once back in Burma learned from the civil police that a large force of armed Thais [from Siam] had raided Namaklwe, the village closest to the border. Scott assigned some of his people to lie in ambush in case the marauders appeared again. A band of men armed with rifles and a machine gun appeared, and the Burma Frontier Force unit gunned them down, killing as many as ten and wounding others without absorbing a single casualty. "It seemed," said Scott, "we were at war with Siam, though the rest of the army might not have been at that time." For nearly a month Scott and others in the frontier force skirmished with Thais who slipped into Burma before the frontier force was relieved by Chinese soldiers.

The Empire Shrinks

Tentative as these incidents were, the full-scale war enveloped Singapore when on January 13, in a tropical downpour, Japanese bombers dumped ordnance on the city. The Japanese offensive drove the final elements of thirty thousand mainland defenders on a four-hundred-mile retreat that ended with them crossing a causeway to Singapore Island. When the last of these, the Scottish Argyll Regiment, preceded by the Sutherland Highlanders, with bagpipes skirling, reached Singapore, dynamite charges blasted all connections to the mainland. For another sixteen days, the hopelessly outgunned eighty-five-thousand-man garrison in Singapore strove to fend off relentless attacks.

New Zealand native Geoffrey Fisken recalled that his squadron was reduced to four planes attached to an Australian unit at Semberwang. "Our officers had left us. They had been sent back to England. A major, an Argyle or Sutherland Highlander, came in and said, 'Well, it's time you got out, boys. Set fire to your planes and get down to the wharf.' The petrol tanks were smashed open with a pickax and a Very pistol [flare gun] was fired at them and they went up POOF! We [drove] to the wharf because we all had cars left by civilians. We got on a ship with these Australian fellows who were coming out, got to Java and then Australia." On February 15, Lieutenant General Arthur E. Percival surrendered Singapore.

The fall of Singapore presaged the demise of an even more vital component of the CBI defense, Rangoon. Without that port, supplies and reinforcements to Burma and China would be restricted to the minimal traffic possible along a few narrow railroads, roads, and trails originating in India, or the tiny amounts brought by aircraft. From their airstrips in Siam, the Japanese sent wave after wave of planes against strategic targets, including Rangoon. Unlike China, where sites such as Chungking and Kunming lay far behind the front, only a comparatively few miles separated the raiders from the RAF bases and the AVG at Mingaladon. The proximity prevented the defenders from creating an early-warning net that paid such big benefits in China.

A Sittang River Debacle

The air attacks meshed with a determined push by a minimum of sixty thousand Japanese ground troops toward Rangoon and southern and central Burma. The British forces were partially betrayed by wretched intelligence. As late as January 21, Wavell reported to Churchill, "Large-scale effort directed against Burma seems improbable at this moment." That estimate delayed vital action. Finally realizing the threat, for the defense of the city and southern Burma, Wavell deployed the 17th Indian Infantry Division, composed of three infantry brigades—the 16th, 46th, and 48th—buttressed by sappers and the 21st Mountain Regiment of Artillery. The division had clashed with the enemy along the Salween River and then the Bilin River. Driven back, the empire soldiers headed for the bridge over the swift-flowing, thousand-yard-wide Sittang River on the northern flank. It was imperative for the defenders to make their way west, over the Sittang, and then block the invaders from using the bridge that spanned the river near where it emptied into the Gulf of Martaban. Passage over the Sittang would allow the Japanese to sweep southwest and envelop Rangoon. British sappers, harassed by sniper bullets, had wired the 1,650-foot-long steel crossing with explosives.

While the Japanese 33d Division raced through the jungle toward the bridge, the 17th Division, harassed by repeated low-level air attacks, carried out an exhausting forced march toward the objective. Mokpalin, a fishing village on the eastern banks of the Sittang River, lay near the bridge. On February 22, brigade headquarters and some of the Gurkha Rifles dashed across the bridge, but then a truck crashed on the span, slowing passage. Most of the 4th Battalion of the Gurkhas had already withdrawn to the temporary safety on the western side, leaving two sections as a rear guard behind sandbag positions on the bridge. Behind them, a small band of officers wielded submachine guns to cover them. Before the wreckage of the truck could be cleared, Japanese in strength came on the scene. They promptly established a roadblock between the 17th Division troops across the Sittang and those just streaming into Mokpalin.

At about 4:30 A.M. the 17th Division commander, Major General J. G. Smyth, conferred with his staff; Brigadier Noel Hugh-Jones, CO of the 48th Brigade, charged with holding off the Japanese; and other unit leaders. Hugh-Jones gloomily reported that he could no longer guarantee control of the crossing against the oncoming Nipponese. In fact, unless the order for demolition came before daylight, the enemy's automatic weapons would prevent the engineers from setting off the charges.

The destruction of the Sittang Bridge would delay the Japanese advance, but it also would trap two brigades of British forces, including the 3d Gurkhas on the eastern bank, with no easy escape from the overwhelming enemy numbers and firepower. In his memoirs, Smyth said he pondered his decision for several minutes and then he recalled, "Hard though it is, there is very little doubt as to what is the correct course; I give the order that the bridge shall be blown immediately."

As dawn emerged from its jungle-shrouded bower, a series of huge explosions shattered the air, followed by the whistling noises of flying chunks of steel. A quick but circumspect inspection showed parts of the bridge gone but bits of the span remained, offering perhaps some use for those intent on reaching the other side. Although not totally successful, the destruction at the Sittang crossing delayed the Japanese crossing of the Sittang.

Unaware of the dilemma that had faced Major General Smyth, the soldiers still on the eastern side fought their way toward the bridge that they believed might enable them to escape. Twin hills, covered with jungle, dominated the final approaches to the Sittang Bridge. Atop the westernmost knoll stood a pagoda, while the outcropping to the east featured a large stone Buddha. To the embattled defenders, they quickly became Pagoda and Buddha Hill. Having cleared Mokpalin of the Japanese, two companies of Gurkhas, with no artillery support, charged Buddha Hill. The enemy inflicted heavy casualties, forcing the Gurkhas to fall back to a third hill, on which the 48th Gurkha Brigade established an observation post.

The 3d Gurkhas dispatched a patrol in force, one led by the battalion commander. It ran afoul of a substantial body of Japanese who, according to one source, faked a surrender and then mowed down the British, including their battalion leader. Only a few men managed to flee.

A replacement regimental commander cobbled together a defense behind a sunken road, deploying soldiers from headquarters companies and some reserves. As darkness fell, the enemy launched furious attacks on OP Hill, but the British lines held while the Japanese fell back after taking heavy casualties. The struggle, however, further reduced the strength and supplies, particularly the ammunition of the Gurkha outfit.

As a new day approached, the temporary quiet was ruptured by the flashes in the dark followed by the sounds of explosions. The crestfallen men realized that the blasts meant closure of their escape route. They could only hope to infiltrate to the waterside, find anything that would float them across or else chance swimming the stream. Brigadier

J. K. Jones soon issued orders for those on the hill to hold their position, reinforced by a company from the Duke of Wellington Regiment until the following morning to cover a night river crossing for first the wounded, and then the other survivors of the ill-fated advance beyond the Sittang. Men in need of medical care were quietly removed to the banks of the river, well south of the bridge.

The remnants of various units released their mules and armed themselves as heavily as possible with the intention of blasting their way through any enemy positions to reach a point where they might ford the Sittang. They sifted through the jungle to the river about half a mile from the shattered bridge without encountering any foe. Beside the water they found the wounded from a number of units. Unfortunately, those who had retreated before them and made it over the Sittang had stove in most of the usually available small boats to thwart Japanese crossings. Quite a few soldiers drowned when they attempted to drift across the river in flimsy, hastily constructed rafts. Others succumbed to rifle fire as they tried to swim across. The Japanese small arms and mortars threatened to annihilate everyone; the situation was all but hopeless. Taking advantage of the night, the besieged found a sampan and a few craft that were still serviceable, and ferried many of the wounded to safety. Several thousand men, however, were either killed in the action, wounded, murdered when they surrendered, or else became prisoners for a three-year ordeal.

Fiasco at Rangoon

A. D. Firth, in command of a signals platoon with the Duke of Wellington Regiment, based at Peshawar on February 2, traveled seven days by train to the port of Madras. From there a small ship carried Firth and the other soldiers to Rangoon, a week-long trip. "The first broadcast of the fall of Singapore was just coming through on the radio," said Firth, "which filled us with a wild surmise. From the docks we drove straight to a hutted camp at Mingaladon and saw nothing of the city. We immediately started to unpack and distribute equipment. No animals, but plenty of jeeps from Lend-Lease stocks [undoubtedly most of which came from the disputed items]. The Flying Tigers were using the main road as a landing strip."

The Wellingtons crossed the Sittang River by train, heading east, and joined the 46th Brigade at Khaikto to form a rearguard perimeter. "Around us there was incessant small-arms automatic fire, probably nothing at all. I was sent, in my new jeep, to brigade headquarters to report our arrival. There was a steady stream of transport passing through westwards toward the Sittang River bridge. It was nearly dark. I asked this officer in front of a truck if I was now near the front line. His tired answer was, 'My dear chap, this convoy *is* the front line.'

"Having been in Khaikto less than twenty-four hours, we were ordered to move that afternoon to a rubber plantation just west of the town." During this hike, Firth and his companions suddenly found themselves being strafed by the RAF. "My baptism of fire in World War II was from the front end of a Wellington [a British bomber] about two hundred feet above me and coming straight at me with guns blazing." According to Firth, the unit suffered "many casualties."

The outfit resumed its trek. "It was a fearsome march to Mokpalin village the next day, no food, no water, and a heavy load of weapons and ammo, hot sun and dust, and quite a lot of pellets flying around." The signals platoon was temporarily diverted to assault a small hill, only to find that the enemy had deserted the site. When they reached their destination at Mokpalin there was still no water, food, or blankets, while sporadic small-arms fire punctuated the night.

Firth scrounged a Royal Artillery water tank and filled it from a stream. He organized his noncoms to collect firewood and boil the water. "We got the ingredients, tea, sugar, and milk, and the whole platoon started that fateful day with a full mess tin of hot, sweet tea. The adjutant told me to line the Mokpalin railway embankment, connecting up with the King's Own Yorkshire Light Infantry on our right [south] flank. This we did. About this time the village was thoroughly mortared and burned fiercely. I stayed where I had been ordered, until midafternoon.

"About 4:00 P.M., with a lance corporal called Burns, I walked down to the river, about six hundred yards away, carrying a private soldier with his knee smashed by a mortar. We loaded him on a banana trunk raft, where he lay comfortably enough and secure. Burns and I stripped off, except for my .45 Webley [pistol] round my neck, and swam gently across in warm sunshine for eight hundred yards, pushing the raft along. At this point there was no one else in sight. On the other side, we discovered a bullock car and a group [from another regiment] and we managed to catch them up. It was carrying their second in command. Our wounded man was made room for.

"Corporal Burns and I walked, still only in our pants and vests, in the direction of a general hubbub which turned out to be the Waw Railways Station, by which time it was getting dark. I was hauled into a carriage in which was the commanding officer of the Jats [an Indian unit] shivering with fever and wrapped in a blanket with one or two of his [subordinates]. These included a *jemedar* [native lieutenant], who the CO said was the chap who found the body of our murdered CO in a village downstream and extracted due vengeance! The train took us to Pegu, where I found the remnants of the battalion had arrived and were re-forming."

The battered Duke of Wellington Regiment troops remained at Pegu, about sixty miles northeast of Rangoon, for several days before vehicles brought some clothing, weapons, and other equipment. With the arrival of the 7th Armored Brigade, hastily shipped from North Africa and the campaign to take Tobruk back from Rommel's Afrika Korps, Firth's unit moved back to block the main road from Rangoon to Mandalay.

The Flying Tigers had continued to bedevil the Japanese. During January and February the Americans scored heavily even though badly outnumbered. When twenty-three fighters suddenly approached Mingaladon, intent on wiping out the Rangoon air defenses, only Tex Hill and Frank Lawlor got off the ground early. They engaged the entire aggregation, and Lawlor shot down four while Hill brought down a pair. As three more P-40s and a handful of RAF planes joined the fray, several more intruders were destroyed. Jack Newkirk led ten Tomahawks against some sixty enemy aircraft. He knocked out two and damaged another before forced to land his bullet-riddled P-40. He climbed into a patched-up Tomahawk to rejoin the battle, taking down two more planes for a total of four for the day. On February 25 the eleven P-40s still operational and eight RAF Hurricanes, the entire Allied air arm at Mingaladon, confronted forty enemy fighters and a dozen bombers. The Flying Tigers, in their most successful day of the war, accounted for nineteen of the Japanese with eight more probables, and the British added half a dozen kills.

After the shout of "Scramble!" Joe Rosbert, the erstwhile PBY pilot who had been given a partial credit during the interception of enemy bombers near Kunming in December, recalled, "We all jammed the doorway like stampeding cattle. While I catapulted onto the wing of my plane, I saw out of the corner of my eye, Boyington scrambling into his in just his khaki shorts.

"It seemed like hours to get to altitude, but it was probably only about ten minutes. Bob Little waggled his wings and pointed south. I could tell from his devilish grin that we were in for something. Turning quickly, I saw two formations of twenty-seven bombers each headed for the airdrome. I had a bomber picked out as my target and was getting my finger set on the gun button when we found ourselves in the midst of a group of fighters flying crazily in a bunch like bees.

In a flash, one appeared in my sight, at close range; the two ugly red suns on the wings stood out. I managed one quick burst and almost immediately flew through the smoke and pieces that came from the plane. As I dove down and away, I saw him catch fire and spin earthward.

"I took a heading towards Moulmein. Ahead and below I spotted a foolhardy Nip pointed towards home. I closed on him with all guns blazing. Although white smoke appeared behind his engine, he made a sharp turn and went out of sight below me. Looking back, there were two of his mates trying to train their sights on me. I pushed the stick forward so hard I almost catapulted through the canopy. As I hurtled downward, I crouched down expecting at any moment the thud of bullets on the armor plate behind. Finally I looked back on both sides. Not only had I lost my pursuers but there was nothing in sight." Back on the ground Rosbert counted one fighter down and another probable. One AVG flier, Ed Leibolt, bailed out, but he was never seen again.

Others also scored against the Japanese, but aside from wrecked aircraft, the Flying Tigers also were losing pilots, albeit slowly. Three Nakashima 97s caught Bert Christman and delivered a concentrated attack. As his engine stopped, Christman started to bail out, but a stream of machine-gun bullets struck him in the chest. He tumbled from twelve thousand feet, his chute never opened, and his body landed in jungle scrub. Ed Rector shot down the man who killed Christman, but that was little solace. A Japanese fighter knocked down forty-three-year-old Louis Hoffman, whose body was found in the smashed plane. Tommy Cole died during a strafing mission in Siam. Robert Sandell, credited with $5\frac{1}{2}$ victories, took off to test a plane with a new tail assembly. During his maneuvers over Mingaladon, the restored tail ripped away, and Sandell died in the crash.

The 7th Armored Brigade, attached to the 17th Indian Infantry Division that relieved the Duke of Wellingtons, had combat experience, but in the hot, dusty sands of Libya. Yanked out of North Africa when the British Eighth Army wrested Tobruk from the Axis troops, the 7th reached Rangoon during the third week of February. L. E. Tutt, a member of the Brigade's 414th Battery, described the chaos at the Rangoon docks:

"Our arrival was largely unsung. The smell of disaster was everywhere. There were no dock gangs to take our hawsers and to help us berth. There were no stevedores to help us unload, no crane operators, no one. We understood now why some of the ships we had passed going the other way and packed with civilians had saluted us on their sirens and the passengers' cheers. We must have seemed to be sailing right into the arms of the Japanese.

"Over the city there was a dense pall of smoke, the sound of demolitions and rifle fire. Our infantry friends had disembarked before us and were taking up positions to cover us while we unloaded the precious armor and artillery. There was order and counterorder as to whether we should unload or turn tail and withdraw. We were not heartened when a boat, already there when our convoy arrived, suddenly slipped her moorings and made for the open sea, churning the harbor water into a froth with the speed of her departure. The civilian population had all departed, Europeans by boat and the Asians in anything that would carry them northwards to India. With them had gone all the technicians and skilled dock workers needed to unload us.

"If we stayed, we would have to unload for ourselves, even if the Japanese turned up halfway through the proceedings. We also heard that our troops were failing to measure up to the enemy, that we had lost over half a division at the Sittang River. To us the answer seemed simple, leave with all possible speed. Someone decreed otherwise; we were soon carrying our kit down the gangplank and cursing the humid heat."

Riding a truck to a bivouac on a plantation, Tutt saw numerous bodies in the Rangoon streets—looters shot down by troops, and victims of the bombing and strafing attacks. When he returned to the city to assist in unloading the battery's gear, he noticed kites (vultures) gorging themselves on the corpses. "[They] rose with slow, laborious wing flaps as we passed. They were so sated that they could hardly get off the ground, and as they moved off, the dogs came in."

After three days of this duty, Tutt and his companions prepared to move off. "One [ship] jumped the gun and left before it was empty. It still had one of our guns and most of our ammunition on board. It took some pretty pointed signals from those in authority to get it to turn around so that we could finish the job. We were given tacit permission to help ourselves from the warehouses to anything that might be useful to us in the field. There was everything from big American cars to paper clips. After a few goes at charging along the quaysides on looted Harley Davidsons, we concentrated on supplies of food and tinned milk."

Rangoon sank into anarchy. According to Tutt, "The Burmans started to settle old scores with the wealthy Indians and Chinese who had grown rich in their country." Before evacuating all of their forces, the military authorities systematically destroyed anything that the Japanese might find useful. Fires consumed 972 trucks in various stages of assembly, 5,000 tires, fuel dumps, blankets, and other items that could not be transported. From the Lend-Lease stores in warehouses, the last defenders of Burma seized 300 Bren guns with 3.2 million rounds, 1,000 submachine guns, 260 jeeps, 683 trucks, and 100 field telephones.

Convinced his people could no longer operate from Mingaladon, Chennault ordered an evacuation. Neale said, "I spent all my time trying to figure out how to get the bunch out of there. I was assured by the British that I'd have planes to fly my ground crew out, and we were getting these trucks assembled—trucks assigned to the AVG, full of tires and supplies. Most of them never got there, they were stuck in the black mud on the way up there. My transportation officer was shipping us about one truck in about four and selling the rest. I didn't find out about that for quite a while." When the British air marshal mentioned to Neale that the radio detection system had left, the American arranged for the AVG contingent to fly out the following morning. Convoys of trucks carried personnel; a variety of items, much of which was nonmilitary; and a number of good-looking young women to Kunming while pilots flew the few still-functioning planes to the Chinese redoubt.

While Tutt and his battery had headed north, a skeletal rear guard defended Rangoon. Wavell conferred with his Burma commander, Lieutenant General Sir Thomas Hutton, and the governor, Sir Reginald Dorman-Smith. In a dispatch from that day, Wavell announced, "I arrived at Magwe [250 miles north of Rangoon] on the morning of 1 March and held a conference with the governor, General Hutton, and Air Vice Marshal Stevenson. There seemed to me no reason why Rangoon should not continue to be held at least long enough to enable the reinforcements on the way, 63d Indian Infantry Brigade and a field regiment, to be landed. There was no evidence of any great enemy strength west of the Sittang, 7th Armored Brigade still intact, and Chinese troops were moving down towards Toungoo."

In light of the savage beating administered to the 17th Division, Wavell's assertion that there was no indication of Japanese in great strength west of the Sittang is hard to comprehend. Governor Dorman-Smith was not reassured. He had ordered a complete evacuation of all civilians, and from Magwe he simply continued his own journey to Maymyo, still farther north.

Depressed by the swiftly deteriorating situation and Curtin's refusal to dispatch his Australian division to the rescue, Churchill had decided that a change of command might make a difference. He summoned General Harold Alexander, whose rearguard defense played a key role in the successful evacuation in June 1940 of the British Expeditionary Force from France. Alexander replaced Hutton, who had glumly forecast the loss of Rangoon.

Alexander arrived in Calcutta on March 4 and straight off headed for a firsthand view of the Burma front and in particular Rangoon, reaching the city the following day. Misled, perhaps by Wavell's convictions, Alexander plotted to hold Rangoon, but within a day he realized that Wavell had it wrong and Hutton was right.

On March 7 the remaining soldiers blew up the docks, the oil installations, the refinery, and other structures. The following day, the Japanese entered Rangoon, cutting off the one port through which war matériel might be funneled to China.

5

Further Additions
to the Cast

D elayed by problems with the transport aircraft, Stilwell, on February 14, finally left the United States. Not until February 25 did he reach New Delhi and begin to confer with the commanders responsible for CBI. When he met the commander in chief of the Indian army, General Sir Alan Hartley, and his spouse, he described them to his wife as "very kind." A day later in his diary he burlesqued Hartley's diction. Wavell flew in to Calcutta to greet the new Chinese chief of staff, bringing with him Major General Lewis Brereton, already anointed commander of the Tenth Air Force in the CBI theater. The airman hardly endeared himself to Stilwell, who told his diary, "Brereton slapping his fanny with his riding crop and darting around importantly. A shock to Brereton to learn he had anyone over him. Expected to be the Big Boy [U.S. theater commander]."

From Calcutta Stilwell traveled to Lashio, near the Burmese border with China. Chiang Kai-shek, on hand to wish the latest infusion of Chinese soldiers good luck as they headed out to assist in the defense of Burma, was "cordial." A session with the generalissimo went well. "Apparently he told the Fifth and Sixth [Chinese] Armies [in Burma] to take orders only from me as soon as I arrived. He seems willing to fight and is fed up with the British retreat and lethargy. Also extremely suspicious of their motives and intentions."

When the official translator had difficulty dealing with the interchanges, Madame Chiang took over his duties. "Madame made some caustic remarks about the British, and their broken promises. She kept me after the conference to talk about Chennault. Worried for fear he would be pushed aside. No objections when I said the AVG was to be inducted [into the U.S. Army]."

Stilwell commented on the Chinese leader's hostility toward the British. "The British are s.o.b.s and he [Chiang] won't take their orders. . . . How they hate the Limeys." The feeling was mutual. "Major General Dennys, the British military attaché in China, gave us a tirade on the 'bastardly Chinese.' . . . Dennys came in breathing fire and destruction. The goddamn Chinese won't rush in and save the British Empire. He's going to tell Chiang Kai-shek what to do and Chiang Kai-shek can jolly well better do it." Dennys never got the opportunity to deliver his alleged ultimatum; on his way to Chungking, he died in a plane crash.

As Stilwell entered the fray, the Allied line of defense stretched east to west about a hundred miles north of Rangoon, with British forces at either end and the Chinese troops in the center. The strategy called for an orderly pullback and then a counterattack against the advancing Japanese armies. In reserve were tens of thousands of Chiang's soldiers concentrated along the northern borders of Burma and Thailand. During a discussion with the generalissimo on the use of troops that he could now command, Stilwell accepted as "a lot of good sense" Chiang's notions on how he should present himself to the soldiers. "Look at it coldly," he told his diary, "and the Chinese are doing a big thing from their point of view in handing over this force to a *lao mao-tzu* [old hat] they don't know very well." On tactics, however, he dismissed his nominal commander. While Stilwell plotted to attack, the generalissimo wanted to wait, preferring a defensive posture rather than risk an offensive one.

Defeats in Burma

Within Burma, the people, alienated from the British, showed little inclination to fight the Japanese. The hastily mobilized, ill-trained, and ill-equipped Burma Rifles, composed largely of indigenous men, fell apart rapidly with wholesale desertions in the face of the stalwart Japanese units. Stilwell scorned the mobilization of British defensive forces: "seventy thousand on the [British] rations [list] in Burma and twelve thousand at the front! The difference is scattered around over the country in Frontier Guard detachments and the Burma Auxiliary Forces. Every 'home guard' puts on shorts, a Sam Browne belt, and climbs on the ration wagon. But nobody goes up front. There it's just a couple of brigades of Indian troops, one brigade of tanks, and about five battalions of British troops."

Those who were at the front were nearly swallowed by the Japanese juggernaut. No longer able to hold Rangoon, portions of the 17th Indian Division not engaged at the Sittang River bridge battle had traveled north. Some units wheeled west, toward the town of Prome, while others marched east, toward Pegu, behind the Sittang River. Well before Prome, at Taukkyan, however, the retreating troops bumped up against a formidable roadblock anchored by a well-armed enemy in the dense woods on both sides of the highway. The Japanese appeared to have trapped Alexander and his headquarters staff.

Cut off from Rangoon, unable to go forward, Alexander ordered an attack on the roadblock, but even against tanks and the lead Gloucestershire Regiment, the Japanese refused to budge. Fortunately, the main body of enemy soldiers apparently had not reached positions where they could pour devastating fire on the stalled column. Still, the Japanese were on the cusp of a major coup, the capture of thousands of soldiers, including the commander of all British forces in Burma.

The 414th Battery, with L. E. Tutt, had been part of a column that shifted to the east and Pegu. Alexander summoned them and additional armor and artillery for a full, brigade-scale attack the next day, March 8. "Some of the tanks went off in advance to spearhead the attack on the roadblock," said Tutt. "We followed at a more sober pace but were in time to take up positions to support the attack. The initial bombardment was from the guns of the 12th Mountain Battery. Troops and tanks moved forward on a grand scale. The tanks and some of the Sikhs probed forward and found that the Japanese had gone." Tutt and his artillery outfit protected the withdrawal to a new line of defense while Alexander hustled off to meet Stilwell.

The Japanese had thrown away a marvelous opportunity to cripple the resistance in Burma and leave India almost naked to an invasion. Historians have struggled to find the reasons behind the Japanese strategy. The best explanation is that the Nipponese high command had plotted a surprise encirclement of Rangoon. The Japanese position along the road to Prome was intended to prevent reinforcements coming from the north to aid in a defense of Rangoon. Once the main body of their soldiers swept across the Prome highway near Rangoon, the roadblock against southward-moving British forces was no longer necessary and removed. Either the Japanese did not realize that they could have gained a far greater prize than Rangoon, or else, as other campaigns indicated, once committed to a strategy, the Nipponese lacked the flexibility to alter their operations. This error aside, the situation in Burma for the British forces worsened. Some two hundred thousand Indians living in Burma, fearing both the wrath of their hosts and the oncoming Japanese, clogged the few roads out. Cholera, hunger, thirst, and exhaustion dropped thousands along the way, adding a humanitarian problem to the military one.

From his position, Stilwell alternated between fits of despair and towering rages at the incompetence, deception, and pusillanimous behavior he detected. When Stilwell left Chungking on March 11, Chiang assured him, "This morning I have issued orders to place the Fifth and Sixth Armies under your command." The heads of the armies, Generals Tu Yu-ming and Kan Li-chu, respectively, and the general staff representative, Lin Wei, were all therefore bound to obey Stilwell.

The American general never developed a smooth relationship with General Sir Harold Alexander, commander of the British army in Burma. Of their first meeting, Stilwell remarked in his diary, "Very cautious. Long, sharp nose. Rather brusque and *yang chi* [standoffish]. . . . Astonished to find ME—mere me, a goddamn American—in command of Chinese troops. 'Extrawdinery!' Looked me over as if I had just crawled out from under a rock." After a later session, however, he pronounced Alexander "pleasanter." Their dealings remained contentious, the Briton nonplussed that he commanded the war in Burma, yet a key element, the Chinese, were responsible only to Stilwell. Even the urbane, unflappable Alexander would find the hurly-burly of Burma a test of his disposition. Chiang would never agree to control of his troops by the British and had even argued that Stilwell should have overall command in Burma, but that was absolutely unacceptable to the British. At that, although Chiang had promised Stilwell a free hand, he frequently countermanded Stilwell's orders to Chinese generals.

Much of Stilwell's appraisal of the performance by the British grew out of the intelligence supplied him by Major Frank Merrill, a former army enlistee who then graduated from West Point in 1929, after having taken the examination for the academy no fewer than six times. Trained as a cavalry officer, Merrill had studied Japanese and left the Philippines after Pearl Harbor to become the American liaison with the British in Burma. Merrill delivered a summary of the ally's operations as "no plan, no reconnaissance, no security, no intelligence, no prisoners," while observing that the enemy possessed excellent communication and showed aggressiveness and high mobility. Merrill became a favored member of Stilwell's staff.

After more conferences with the generalissimo on the use of the Chinese forces in Burma and the overall strategy to preserve the avenues into China, Stilwell touched down in Maymo, about three hundred miles inside Burma. Maymo lay quite close to Mandalay, which, to Stilwell's chagrin, Chiang persisted in denoting as the key to defense.

Brigadier General Frank Merrill entered West Point from the enlisted ranks of the army before becoming a staff officer under Lieutenant General Joseph W. Stilwell. He was a member of the party that Vinegar Joe led out of the Burma wilderness during the 1942 retreat. (Photograph from U.S. National Archives)

With the front hundreds of miles farther south, Stilwell thought that "a cockeyed strategic conception."

In Maymo, the American commander also met Dr. Gordon Seagrave, an American Baptist missionary who had established a hospital and medical treatment in the Shan states. He offered the services of his trained staff of physicians and Burmese nurses to the Chinese Fifth Army. Seagrave wanted to come under U.S. command rather than British and was aware that Stilwell was in charge of the Chinese soldiers. Stilwell quickly accepted Seagrave's proposal, knowing very well how little in the way of health care was available to Chiang's troops.

Stilwell scorned the depth of the British presence in Burma, but for those on the scene the situation was desperate. I. O. G. Scott, who as a captain with his company of Punjabis in the Burma Frontier Force had been introduced to the elephant as a vehicle for war, now relied on a more common beast of burden, the mule. The campaign, after a warm flush of early victory, had become a nightmare. Working along the Salween River near the Siam border, Scott and his colleagues had easily vanquished Thai soldiers advancing under orders of the Japanese. However, as the latter steadily advanced in the southern part of the country, the frontier force troops were shifted during two days some six hundred miles by foot and by truck with no rations.

Scott settled uneasily into a defensive position from which, through binoculars, he spied the enemy in a village only half a mile off. But when an attack by the British forces failed, the frontier force soldiers embarked on a series of dispiriting retreats. Scott said, "The men, already tired after their exertions in the Shan states and the long journey by road, packed like cattle in trucks, had to march every night and dig in and patrol by day. We had 250 mules with Chinese muleteers, so the column even closed up was more than a mile long. I doubt if we ever traveled at much more than 1½ miles per hour, and at every hourly halt, many men dropped to the ground and fell asleep."

Disaster struck the long column as it trekked toward an assembly west of Toungoo. As the weary men approached Obogon village by the edge of a jungle known as Pegu Yumas, mortar shells exploded in their midst, followed by sustained fire from machine guns and rifles. The mules stampeded, and the ropes that tied them in bunches tripped the stumbling soldiers.

For a brief period, the troops regrouped in a thicket. There Scott awaited word from division headquarters. "Bahadur Khan [one of his subordinates] reported that a large force of Japs was converging on the copse. I had a look through binoculars and to my horror he was right. There were Japs galore coming across the paddy fields about twelve hundred to fifteen hundred yards away. I would have been stupid to remain in the copse with nearly two hundred mules and all the men bunched together. I ordered a rapid withdrawal into the Pegu Yumas. Just as we had got all the mules and most of the men into the jungle, the Japs opened fire with a mortar and dropped the first bomb right on target. It was by now almost dark and it was no easy task to progress up the steep and narrow jungle path but we continued until 2230 hours, by which time I felt we had broken contact with the enemy. We made painfully slow progress as it was largely bamboo, ghastly stuff to cut through. I estimated that we had covered about five miles, which I felt was far enough to go in the dark. I called a halt. There was no water so we could not cook food or even brew up tea."

It was March 20, and Scott, as the senior officer with some two hundred men—a mixture of Punjabis, Sikhs, Karens, Chinese, and a Bengali doctor—pondered his alternatives. He had no maps. When division headquarters finally responded to his radio inquiry it advised him of the location of the front and to withdraw as rapidly as possible west of Toungoo. Scott realized that his group was more than twenty-five miles behind the advance of the enemy. The only escape route lay through the forbidding jungle-covered hills.

"I gave orders for all kit which could not be carried to be destroyed. It was very sad to destroy our 3-inch mortars, and the Sikh mortar platoon personnel almost wept. All available rations had been cooked, so there was nothing in the way of food to destroy. We kept one wireless set to carry with us. We set the mules free near the water. We set off on our long walk, but had to stop as it was quite impossible to make any progress in the dark."

When daylight came, the men continued their torturous hike, the first goal a river named the Pyu Chaung. "We struggled on all day, cutting our way all the time, and evening came with no sign of the Pyu Chaung and worse still, no water. We were all almost exhausted. We had been going for twenty-four hours without water except for that which was in our water bottles and most of those were empty before noon as it was very hot and hard work. Talib Hussain had to be carried, as he was very ill with malaria and I must mention the devotion of Havildar Amir Hussain and Naik Adelat Khan, who took turns carrying him. We went up and down over ridge after ridge and all the time we were cutting at the thorny jungle to create a path. To make matters worse, the wireless set which we had carried had been dropped and was not working. I was no more than semiconscious, suffering from a severe bout of malaria. I suppose we traveled at about half a mile per hour at the best, and the night of 21 to 22 March was passed with all very thirsty and too exhausted to go to the bottom of the ridge, where water might be found. I doubt if anyone got any sleep that night but there was a very heavy dew, which was most refreshing.

"At about 0900 hours we came to the top of a cliff. I knew very well that the Pyu Chaung had to be at the bottom so we started to clamber down. I slithered and tumbled down clutching to thorny branches for support and by 1000 hours reached the bottom. There was a gushing mountain stream and I believe it was the most welcome drink I have ever had. Soon we were all down. Talib Hussain was lowered down by ropes."

After they reached the Pyu Chaung, the men crossed the deep, fast-flowing river by making a human chain. At a tiny village the inhabitants produced rice, salt, chillies, and eight chickens for a restorative banquet. Continuing the journey, Scott could hear gunfire in the distance, and on the fifth day believed the direction of the sounds indicated that the Burma division was not far off. Further maneuvering

through countryside to avoid contact with the Japanese at last brought
them to a road where a patrol sent out by Scott reported trucks that
bore Chinese soldiers were rolling south, while refugees headed north.
He intercepted some empty trucks and persuaded those in charge to
haul his men to safety. Many others in the frontier force were not as
fortunate; several hundred, including officer friends of Scott, were
killed or captured.

The defenders in Burma reeled from a severe pummeling administered by Japanese bombers to the air base at Magwe, a town on the
Irrawaddy River about seventy-five miles north of the front. The
raiders roared in, undetected by any warning system. They burned
dozens of Blenheim bombers, strafed ground personnel, and burned
hangars. Neither the RAF nor the AVG fighters got off the ground in
sufficient numbers to do much damage. The destruction forced the
RAF to pull out all of its aircraft and personnel from Magwe and set
up shop inside India.

The Flying Tigers moved to Loiwing, just over the border, in
China. A few days later, the group lost two of its leading aces, Jack
Newkirk and Mac McGarry. Newkirk, leading a strafing mission, dove
on what appeared to be an armored car. Flames sprouted from Newkirk's P-40, which crashed and burned. McGarry, returning from a
similar mission, bailed out over Siam after his engine spewed thick,
black smoke. Thai police captured him and he spent three years in
one of their jails before rescue.

New Faces

Unable to add large numbers of fighting men to ward off the impending collapse before the rampaging Japanese in Burma, the British top
command in desperation had reached out for leaders—shamans in
another culture—who might magically weld the limited forces into a
winning combination. Among these was William Slim. Volunteering as
a private soldier in 1914, supposedly because he could not raise the
money to buy an officer's kit, Slim received a commission almost
immediately. Wounded in the Middle East and invalided out of service, he wangled his way back to active duty to fight in Flanders and
later won a Military Cross.

Early in World War II, Slim had been in Baghdad, commanding
the 10th Indian Division, which had squelched a rebellion and bloodied the noses of the recalcitrant colonial French in Syria. Slim's orders
named him to take charge of the I Burmcorps (an official designation)
composed of the battered 17th Indian Division and the 1st Burma

Lieutenant General William Slim, who would eventually command all of the British forces in Burma as well as some units defending India, was one of the very few Allied officers whom Lieutenant General Joseph Stilwell respected. Slim orchestrated the major offensives in 1944–1945 that drove the Japanese from their conquests in India and Burma. (Photograph from Imperial War Museum)

Division. Tough-minded with a wry wit and less concerned with class, he figured to be more acceptable to Stilwell.

For his part, Slim, aware of Stilwell's reputation for a short fuse and "distrust of most of the world," in his autobiography *Defeat into Victory,* described the American as "tough, mentally and physically; he could be as obstinate as a whole team of mules; he could be and frequently was, downright rude to people whom, often for no very good reason, he did not like. But when he said he would do a thing he did it. True, you had to get him to *say* that he would quite clearly and definitely—and that was not always easy—but once he had, you knew he would keep to his word. He had a habit, which I found very disarming, of arguing most tenaciously against some proposal and then suddenly looking at you over the top of his glasses with the shadow of a grin, and saying, 'Now tell me what you want me to do and I'll do it.'

"He was two people, one when he had an audience, and quite a different person when talking to you alone. I think it amused him to keep up in public the 'Vinegar Joe, Tough Guy' attitude, especially in front of his staff. Americans, whether they liked him or not—and he had more enemies among Americans than among British—were all scared of him. He had courage to an extent few people have, and determination, which as he usually concentrated it along narrow lines, had a dynamic force. He was not a great soldier in the highest sense, but he was a real leader in the field; no one else I know could have made his Chinese do what they did. He was, undoubtedly, the most colorful character in Southeast Asia—and I liked him."

Wavell also brought in an extreme outsider, Major Orde Wingate. Wavell, from his experience in the Middle East and East Africa, foresaw Burma as highly suitable for some sort of guerrilla or behind-the-enemy-lines operations. Toward that end, he sought an individual with expertise in that form of combat. He would later write, "When I was struggling to hold the Japanese advance in Burma, I . . . summoned Wingate to organize enterprises against the Japanese communications. He arrived too late to undertake anything in Burma [in the spring of 1942] but in time for his quick brain to grasp the essentials of warfare against the Japanese in jungle country." Wingate would occupy center stage later.

The Burma Defenses Collapse

Alexander had planned for his troops to draw up a defense centering on Prome, 150 miles above Rangoon, on the mighty Irrawaddy River. The Chinese Fifth Army would anchor itself at Toungoo, covering Alexander's eastern flank. Unfortunately, the Chinese would not follow the script, either unable or unwilling to advance swiftly enough to establish themselves at Toungoo and protect Prome.

On March 23 the Japanese renewed their advance on Toungoo. Stilwell frantically tried to bring in Chinese reinforcements by rail from Pyinmana. After fits and starts, three regiments reached a position to counterattack. Almost immediately he told his diary, "Now they [the Chinese] are down again. They have 49 tanks [more armor]. They have 105s etc. [bigger guns]." Still, the 22d Division stayed put. The American blamed its commander, General Tu.

Stilwell appealed to the generalissimo, and argued with Chinese generals until he thought he had an agreement for an attack that would be coordinated with one by the British. "Limeys will attack in force with all tanks. Good old Slim. Maybe he's all right after all. Order of the day is that 'Chinese are attacking under extreme difficulties and it's up to the British to follow the example.' Gave this to Tu in plain language and called on him for a real effort. Full of excuses as usual."

For the hard-pressed I Burmcorps, the battle against the Japanese took on an even uglier cast, if anything in war can. A detachment of marines, commandos, and Burma military, assured by villagers of the absence of any Japanese, was surprised by an ambush. Some were killed on the spot, others escaped, but about a dozen of the wounded had to be left behind. The victorious Japanese soldiers tied them to trees to demonstrate to the villagers their prowess with bayonets.

With the defenses faltering, L. E. Tutt, as a member of the 414th Battery of Royal Horse Artillery, was among those engaged in a counterattack. "Slim's first orders," he recalled, "were that bits and pieces of the 17th Division should move south through Prome and attack the Japanese. He was a man who had never refused a fight, although he had a pretty strong suspicion that this was one he could only lose. He needed four things to give him a chance of beating the fresh and numerically far superior Japanese. A preponderance of artillery. They now had twelve times as many guns as had we. Air superiority. We didn't have a single plane. Superiority in tanks. They had four armored regiments against our two battered ones. Eager to fight, well-equipped infantry. Ours was tired to the point of exhaustion, had lost most of their equipment, and were sick with dysentery and malaria.

"When the attack started on March 29, we were immediately in trouble. Our gun positions were heavily shelled, our infantry was repulsed, and we lost some 350 men and 10 tanks. We withdrew a little way up the road, only to hear that the Japanese had infiltrated behind us and that our retreat back to Prome was blocked. This was very grave news, indeed. We had used a lot of ammunition in the abortive sortie and there was no possibility of further supplies reaching us. We also had a very large number of soft-skinned infantry vehicles with us and they looked like being lost if it came to an 'every man for himself' sort of do.

"Immediate orders were given to our battery commander to take Don Troop, a squadron of the 7th Hussars, and two companies of Glosters to uncork the trap. They reached and neutralized some minor blocks in the failing light and then reached the main one in a village that no 414th Battery member will ever forget the name of, Shwedaung. After one or two attempts in the dark to break through it and the loss of some tanks, it became clear that this one was held in force and it was going to take the combined efforts of the whole of our troops to open up a way of escape."

At daybreak, the artillery units of the 17th Division, from a range of only eight hundred yards, resumed their shelling of the roadblock, firing everything they had while infantrymen and the tanks of the 7th Hussars lumbered toward the enemy. The effort dented the line but did not break the block. In desperation, the commanders ordered the men to simply speed through the gauntlet.

"We were almost out of ammunition as were the tanks," said Tutt. "The battery formed up behind the tanks of the Hussars and the rest of the convoy of trucks followed behind. The tanks led off, blasting in every direction with everything that they had. We followed and immediately most of the enemy fire was directed at the soft-skinned vehicles. We copped everything, bullets, mortar bombs, and grenades. For the first time we saw the Japanese using their version of Molotov cocktails to set any tanks which stopped on fire. One of our twenty-five-pounders received a direct hit and was literally blown off the road. The headlong rush slowed and stopped. We were under very heavy machine-gun fire from a house at the very edge of the road. Lieutenant Simcox took over one of the subsections and they unhooked the gun. He fired over open sights and with about our last ammunition blew the house and the machine gunners to smithereens."

The men sought refuge in the monsoon ditches alongside the road. The gridlock invited the attention of Japanese bombers. "This was better than it might have been," said Tutt. "We were so close to the foes on both sides of us that we were a very difficult target to hit. Many of the bombs and bullets from the planes set on fire the wooden houses in which the enemy were situated; they were burnt to a crisp." A desperate final attempt to break out succeeded. The embattled troops smashed through the encirclement and held on long enough to rejoin the larger body of soldiers from the division. The engagement left 350 killed or missing.

Alexander decided on a new line of resistance based at Yenangyaung, an oil field center 110 miles up the Irrawaddy. The Chinese army was only too happy to draw its defenses around Pyinmana. Stilwell raged, "Through stupidity, fear, and the defensive attitude we have lost a grand chance to slap the Japs back at Toungoo. The basic reason is Chiang Kai-shek's meddling. . . . Had he not gone behind my back to Tu and Lin Wei, they might have obeyed my orders. He can't keep his hands off: sixteen hundred miles from the front, he writes endless instructions to do this and that, based on fragmentary information and a cockeyed conception of tactics . . . he wobbles this way and that, changing his mind at every change in the action."

At a meeting with Chiang, Stilwell claimed he "threw the raw meat on the floor. Pulled no punches and said I'd have to be relieved. Proposed independent army under my command as an alternative. Told him I could not use the Tenth Air Force behind such commanders . . . the commanders failed to obey and I had insufficient authority to force them to obey."

Actually, Stilwell carefully couched his words to allow the generalissimo to save face. Stilwell noted he had also said "with a straight face that his subordinates are not carrying out his orders, when in all probability they are doing just what he tells them. In justice . . . it is expecting a great deal to have them turn over a couple of armies to a goddamn foreigner that they don't know and in whom they can't have much confidence."

As would happen so often, a ballet of excuses, apologies, and flattery followed, culminating in a new announcement by Chiang to his generals and Alexander that Stilwell had full power to direct the Chinese soldiers. On paper, however, the official proclamation subtly suggested Stilwell was an adviser rather than a commander.

Whether the disposition of forces outlined by Stilwell would have made a difference is problematical. The Japanese had brought in fresh troops and additional artillery and armor. With the RAF based in India and the AVG extremely short of flyable planes, there was little opposition to be mustered against attacks from the air, which Slim described as "frequent and heavy." The commander of I Burmcorps set his headquarters at Taungdwingyi, along the line from Magwe in the west to Loikaw, near the Siam border. "I spent a good deal of my time on the lateral road from Magwe to Taungdwingyi," said Slim, "and I do not think I have ever disliked a road more. It was for most of its course, unshielded from the air, and throughout the hours of daylight, the Japanese kept a constant patrol of two or three fighters over it. A jeep was the safest vehicle; from it you had a clear view of the sky, and it was easy to spring in one bound from your seat to the ditch. One often did! Once when I was visiting his area, [Major General A. C.] Curtis, who commanded the 13th Brigade, went ahead in a closed car with the colonel of the Inniskillings beside him. A Japanese fighter swooped and riddled the back of the car. The colonel was killed instantly, and when we came up we found Curtis was bleeding from three wounds, all luckily superficial."

Slim prepared for the inevitable thrust of the Japanese centered upon the new line, the oil fields at Yenangyaung. "Japanese reinforcements, we knew, had been pouring in through Rangoon. Their old formations would have been made up in strength again and there would almost certainly be new ones added. The blow, when it came, would be heavy."

6

"We Got a Hell of a Beating"

On April 10, the Japanese renewed their offensive. The tactics presaged the experience of Americans in Vietnam a quarter of a century later. William Slim remarked that the enemy approach was "covered by numerous small parties of hostile Burmans and Japanese disguised as peaceful villagers. These tactics were difficult to counter, as the countryside was covered by numbers of genuine refugees trying to escape the battle area. It was always a toss-up for our men whether the group of Burmese men, women, and children, wandering past their positions with their creaking bullock carts, were what they seemed or Japanese with concealed machine guns."

Slim, acting on a promise of a Chinese division to buttress his own 17th India defense at Taungdwingyi, had deployed his 1st Burma Division some thirty-five miles to the west. But the Chinese unit never arrived, and when the Japanese ruptured the line of the 1st Burma, Slim realized that unless he shifted his 17th India to plug the gap, the enemy would sweep north along a broad avenue. While the British general moved his troops, sappers at the Yenangyaung oil fields prepared to detonate explosives to destroy the installation rather than allow it to become a prize for the enemy.

Stilwell left his headquarters for visits with his Chinese soldiers in the area around Pyinmana. When he inspected the 200th Division, he informed his diary, "fine-looking lot of soldiers. . . . On to 96th [Division] Officers lined up in dark at Pyinmana. Yu is commanding general, schoolteacher type. Indecisive, looks weak. On to 22d Division. Liao talked and talked. A lot of crap at high speed. He impresses me

80

as being empty. The usual bunk about losses; 14 days in line and 1,300 casualties. All the villages burning. Stink of corpses and burnt wood."

Alexander, now commander of the Allied effort in Burma, toured with Slim. "I took [him] with me when I visited both divisional headquarters," said the I Burmcorps chief. "We saw something of the start of the battle. We were machine-gunned from the air at Scott's headquarters, which, although well hidden in a big clump of forest, were betrayed, I think, by tracks into the trees or perhaps by Burmese agents. General Alexander, as usual, was quite unperturbed and refused to take shelter in a trench, as I did very briskly, preferring to stand upright behind a tree. I was very annoyed with him for this, not only because it was a foolhardy thing to do, but because we had been trying to stop the men doing it. . . . This was not the only time I found the Army Commander's courage above my own standard."

I. C. Scott, from the Burma Frontier Force (BFF) and who first came under fire along the Siam border, had been forced into a fast retreat north of Toungoo. Given command of several companies from the BFF, north of Myingyan and positioned at the juncture of the Mur and Irrawaddy rivers, Scott recalled, "We were quite close to corps headquarters at the time and in fact we were the only troops between them and the Japs as far as we knew. I had been given written orders from corps to patrol the Irrawaddy daily for a distance of about twenty-five miles on each side of the Mur River confluence, to cross the river daily, to destroy all boats which could possibly be used by the Japs, etc. The orders were so vague and so ridiculous, I decided to go to corps headquarters to seek clarification. I was again feeling like death with malaria and dysentery and I was quite ready to have a fight with the first staff officer I met.

"Corps headquarters was established in a rather ramshackle-looking [building]. On arrival I went in through a door into semidarkness and started to feel my way up a narrow staircase. I was more or less blind, having come in from the bright sunlight. I sensed rather than saw someone coming down the stairs, we met, and a voice said, 'And who are you?'

"'I am [commanding officer, BFF 4],' I replied, 'and I am looking for the half-wit who gave me these bloody stupid orders, which I want to discuss.'

"There was silence. The figure in the bush hat turned and started to go upstairs, saying, 'Follow me.' I followed and he entered a well-lit room where, to my horror, I saw that he was wearing the insignia of a general—he was in fact General Slim, the corps commander.

"He said to his G-1, 'This young man is looking for the half-wit who gave him some bloody stupid orders—must be you, old boy.'

"He gave me a pat on the back and said, 'Give him hell!' and resumed his descent of the stairs. I duly had my orders modified and returned to my command, having met the great man himself, which gave me great satisfaction."

But the pleasure of the incident gave way to another serious attack of malaria. A doctor in a medical unit found his temperature hovering between 104 and 105 degrees. Dosed with quinine, Scott fell asleep in an ambulance, and when he awoke, he was on the road to Shwegyin. When the vehicle stopped, Scott, feeling much improved, discharged himself and returned to his command, now near Shwebo. "I found myself, goodness knows how, attached to the headquarters of General Alexander. I had the honor to meet the great man himself, so within a couple of weeks I had met two of Britain's greatest soldiers."

Alexander and Slim tried to preserve the line at Yenangyaung with its oil depot. According to Slim, his mixed forces fought gallantly at what he called the Battle of the Oil Fields. "A brutal battle it was," wrote Slim. "The temperature that day was 114 degrees; the battlefield was the arid, hideous blackened shale of the oil field, littered with wrecked derricks, flames roaring from the tanks, and shattered machinery and burning buildings everywhere. Over it all hung that huge pall of smoke. And there was no water."

When his command tried to renew its drive the following morning the Chinese 38th Division, led by General Li Jen-sun, perhaps the most capable of the top Chinese officers, did not jump off until nearly four hours later than scheduled. Slim found the delay maddening but acknowledged that he was not yet aware "that time means little to the average Chinaman." In addition, he realized his ally lacked communications equipment, means to evacuate the wounded, and ways to replenish ammunition; in addition, the junior officers performed poorly.

Slim's 1st Burma Division had all but been destroyed by the intense fighting. It had been surrounded, and its effort to break out could not be coordinated with that offensive by the Chinese. Tanks from the outfit cleared a track leading to the stream known as the Pin Chaung, but ambulances and trucks could not navigate the sandy trail. While the wounded were piled on tanks, General Bruce Scott ordered other vehicles abandoned and for the men to fight their way to the Chaung on foot. In small groups, many managed to reach the objective. According to Slim, the parched mules went mad at the sight of the water, and the men flung themselves face down into it.

"The British, Indian, and Burmese soldiers who staggered up the bank were a terrible sight, but every man I saw was still carrying his rifle."

Once the Chinese 38th went into action, Slim was gratified by their splendid performance. They responded to the tank and artillery support the British provided, and he praised the actions taken by Li. The 38th broke through to rescue some two hundred from the Burma Division taken prisoner earlier. However, that did not save dozens of wounded left behind in ambulances by the battered 1st Burma. When an officer volunteered to sneak back under cover of darkness, he discovered all dead, their throats cut or with bayonet wounds to their bodies.

While Stilwell complained that the chief obstacle to effective use of the Chinese troops lay with their commanders and the generalissimo, Stilwell appeared not to take into account the enormous logistical difficulties in feeding, housing, and transporting soldiers who arrived with nothing more than what they could carry on their backs. Brigadier John Bowerman, an English officer, was responsible for administrative arrangements in the Shan states for the incoming units of the Chinese Sixth Army in the eastern sector across the Salween River. There they were expected to head off incursions from Siam. The infiltrators were usually Thais, such as I. O. G. Scott had combated. Additionally, the Sixth Army would block a flanking drive on the British and Chinese forces manning the Magwe to Pyinmana line in the center of Burma.

Initially, Bowerman reported some success with encampments created and local purchases of rice. During March the Chinese carried out successful patrols that, Bowerman said, "inflicted considerable losses on the Siamese in a number of encounters." But as more and more Chinese arrived, difficulties mounted. The fresh unit, the 55th Division, noted Bowerman, "was made up of newly formed and not too well disciplined units. The divisional commander, too, was not helpful and created trouble on a number of occasions." Orders from the Allied command for deployments were countermanded or ignored by the 55th's generals.

As the Japanese pushed forward and the Allied forces fell back, the Sixth Army's units failed to take up positions that would back up the I Burmcorps and the elements of the Chinese Fifth Army. Analyzed Bowerman, "The army [Sixth] was very widely dispersed and had no central reserve anywhere; thus a threat in any sector could only be met by troops actually there and as the [motor transport] situation was bad it was impossible to move any adequate body of troops over the long distances and rather indifferent roads."

The AVG Carries On, Barely

With the RAF driven from Burma to India, the Flying Tigers offered
support for the British and Chinese soldiers in Burma as well as
defending major targets within China. The base for troop operations
in Burma was Loiwing, just inside the border of China. From long
range, enemy aircraft sought to demolish the Loiwing installation.
Their bullets and bombs seriously damaged the shops and hangars.
On April 8, however, the Americans, patrolling at a higher altitude,
pounced on a flight of Zeros below. When the dogfights ended, ten of
the Japanese had been destroyed. But two days later, the Nipponese
obtained some revenge, catching the Loiwing contingent by surprise.
They demolished several planes, including both of the newest P-40
Kittyhawks, which came with improved speed, greater range, bomb
racks, and better radios.

That dented morale among the AVG people, but more troublesome were the missions against enemy ground forces. Strafing brought
the Americans down to earth, where their slower, less maneuverable
P-40s not only put them at a disadvantage against the Zero but also
exposed them to deadly antiaircraft fire. The Flying Tigers were further discomfited by the demands from Stilwell and Bissell, Vinegar
Joe's air chief, to perform low-level reconnaissance and at the same
time improve the morale of beleaguered troops by their presence. As
an old-line infantry officer, Stilwell had only a rudimentary understanding of what an airplane could do. Such assignments induced
considerable grumbling from the pilots. When they had volunteered,
they had expected to protect Chinese cities against aerial attack and
engage in high-altitude combat.

It was another sort of operation that almost broke up the AVG.
The RAF proposed a strike on the Japanese Cheng-mai base by its
Blenheim bombers accompanied by P-40s. The Americans arrived at
the rendezvous point, but the Blenheims never showed. That generated grumbling from the fighter pilots. Chennault was annoyed when
on April 15, as Stilwell had advised him, he was called to active duty
as a U.S. colonel. Nine days later he received a brigadier general's silver star, but the promotion of his old opponent Clayton Bissell to the
same rank preceded Chennault's by a day, making Bissell senior.

The British rescheduled the attack on Cheng-mai for April 18 (the
day of the carrier-based Doolittle raid on Tokyo). The American escorts
for the slow-moving Blenheims would have to sit for a protracted time
over the target, itself a hive of Japanese fighters. Fed up with so-called
morale sorties and facing another high-risk mission, a group of AVG
pilots demanded a meeting with Chennault. They expressed their anger

and frustration over what they considered near-suicidal flights using aircraft that were neither airworthy nor equal to that of the enemy. A number of them said they would not fly the mission.

Charlie Older, now operations officer for the 3d Squadron, was one of those strenuously objecting to the missions. "It seemed to us that most of these missions were being planned by some staff officer that knew nothing about the problems involved. There was little or no intelligence about the targets or how we would accomplish this. Everybody knew the Japs were loaded at Cheng-mai. They had probably a couple of hundred fighters there. And it was a long flight. It seemed as if the thing was almost being taken out of Chennault's hands by someone else. The general started asking me how I felt about these things." After reciting his lack of confidence in those allegedly behind such adventures as the Cheng-mai attack, Older explained, "There wasn't anybody afraid to fly. That's what we had been doing and that's what we were there for. We didn't mind risking our lives but we didn't want to throw them away. Then he tried to explain to me how some of these things were beyond his control, that these were joint strike plans, and so on."

When confronted by the dissidents, Chennault became irate. He warned that since he was now an officer in the U.S. Army Air Corps, they had no choice when it came to orders. That was an overstatement. While Chennault himself was now subject to military discipline, his fliers were technically still civilian volunteers and not covered by the Articles of War. He castigated them as cowards: "If you want to show the white feather, you can all quit."

That stunned the pilots. When one objected that he and his colleagues had shown their courage in the air, chancing their lives in combat against superior numbers and better airplanes, Chennault backed off slightly, claiming that the "white feather" meant insubordination rather than a lack of nerve.

At a second meeting, a petition of resignation carried the signatures of all but four to six of the thirty-four fliers at Loiwing. Chennault refused to back down, announcing that those who quit would be considered deserters and he would forward their names to Washington.

Tex Hill recalled, "Whatever the missions were, the old man [Chennault] had said that these things were necessary and, in his opinion, were justified. The first thing I knew, Oley [Arvid Olson] had called his people together. His squadron was at Loiwing and my squadron was there, too. [After] Newkirk was killed I was squadron leader of the 2d Squadron. They refused to fly this mission that was set up. It was a low-level mission, a combination of escorting these Blenheims and then going down and doing some strafing."

Hill said he believed that at the pilots' meeting, Olson had passed around a piece of paper for the fliers to sign. "It was a stand-up-and-be-counted deal. These people went on record. They wanted to show the old man that these missions should not be run. The people in my squadron, about eight of us, didn't sign that paper—Ed Rector was one, Catfish [Robert J.] Raines was another. It put the old man in a hell of a spot, because they either had to go or else. Mutiny. That's what it amounted to.

"I told the boys the reason I didn't sign. 'Hell, we're not a bunch of mercenaries over here. Hell, since we've arrived here our country's involved in war and this is part of our war. It's not just like a cold-blooded job or something like that and whatever has to be done, we've got to do it. We've got a man who's our leader who says this is the way it should be done; we've got to do it. We've got to advise him of all the facts and our thinking on the thing, but if he makes up his mind and says it's still necessary, we've got to do it.

"Ed Rector and myself and several of the boys there were prepared to run the mission. I know Bob Neale, who had the 1st Squadron, was at Kunming, and they were itching to get into something. They sent a wire from Kunming; 'If these guys don't want to go, bring us down there. We'll go.'"

Thanks in part to Hill's remarks and the cancellation of the latest Cheng-mai raid for logistical reasons, the revolt petered out. Several men, including the fractious Boyington, did go through with their resignations, and Chennault issued them dishonorable discharges from the AVG. The departure of Boyington, an outstanding flier and a leader in aerial victories, who never shirked his duty and accepted the dull duty of breaking in repaired planes, was welcomed by many, according to Duane Schultz. Boyington's consumption of alcohol, even for the hard-drinking Flying Tigers, drew censure. He was accused of having broken into the locker with the group's whiskey supply. Bob Neale even doubted Boyington's veracity on planes shot down.

His leadership no longer questioned, Chennault secured a promise from the generalissimo that he would not use the P-40s for low-level reconnaissance-morale missions in conjunction with the Chinese army. And within a few days, the relentless Japanese advance forced evacuation of the Tigers from Loiwing to Kunming, making the issue moot.

The Allies Desert Burma

When the war had begun, the British deployed some troops into the Arakan, the long strip of westernmost Burma that ran alongside the

Bay of Bengal. Several battalions occupied the island seaport of Akyab to prevent a seaborne invasion or land thrust. From Akyab, bombers could strike Calcutta and other Indian targets. As the situation worsened and after air raids on the seaport and a Japanese advance into the Arakan, on May 4, the entire garrison departed for India, leaving the enemy to occupy strategically valuable Akyab.

While some had begun to concede Burma to the Japanese, Slim still believed he might mount a counterattack that would preserve the British presence there. He approached Stilwell, proposing additional Chinese units to reinforce his forces. "I found him, as he always was," said Slim, "ready to support an offensive move and prepared to go a long way to help me. He promised me the 200th Chinese Division from [the] Fifth Army . . . and I had some hopes, too, of his sending another from Mandalay to follow up, though I could not get this firm." A dismayed Slim learned that his superior, Alexander, would not countenance transfer of the 17th Indian Division to aid the plan because of fear that the move would jeopardize the flank.

The 200th arrived on the scene as promised, and Slim was refining his plans when he suddenly learned that the division had hurriedly begun to pack up and return to its starting point. The situation to the east had deteriorated rapidly. Slim had believed that the topography of the Shan states provided excellent natural defensive positions for the Sixth Army. But small columns of Japanese motorized infantry, tanks, and armored cars deftly outflanked the defenses. When Stilwell conferred with General Kan he found him "terrified." Colonels Frederick McCabe and Harry Aldrich, from Stilwell's staff, pleaded with Kan to counterattack or at least patrol aggressively, but he declined. In a few days with his command splintered, Kan and three hundred survivors of the Sixth Army fled toward the Chinese border. Stilwell immediately recalled the 200th, hoping it might halt the swift passage of the Japanese troops toward northern Burma.

Indeed, Stilwell personally involved himself in the actions of the division aiming to halt the enemy at Taunggyi. His April 22 diary note read, "At Meiktila [a town west of the objective] found Tu [Fifth Army commander] by the lake. . . . Tu sour at being chased to the front. Lo [Stilwell's executive officer, but appointed by Chiang] made a speech (spoke of my 'determination' in these operations). Bustle during the night, getting 2d Regiment started. Tu wanted to wait till tomorrow."

On the next day, Stilwell growled, "On to pass 18 miles west of Taunggyi. Tai sitting on his ass. Japs in Taunggyi. Hesitating tactics. Contact with Japs about 10 miles west of Taunggyi. Surround Taunggyi tonight. Attack at daylight. Went up front in scout car. Brisk exchange of fire. Too thick to see much. The boys were still at mile 7, which was kind of slow going. A good deal of ducking and starting back going on. Fairly steady, on the whole. Brought back two [casualties]—leg wounds. 200th must take Taunggyi or be caught fore and aft."

According to Slim's memoirs, Stilwell himself led the division to recapture the town. "He was again greatly handicapped by the Chinese reluctance to obey his orders, and it was only by offering the stimulus of a considerable cash reward that vigor in the attack on the town could be assured." Stilwell's diary, as edited by Theodore White, makes no mention of any payment, but Barbara Tuchman's somewhat hagiographical biography of Stilwell reported, "At Lo's suggestion, he offered a reward of 50,000 rupees if Taunggyi were taken by 5 o'clock." She also said he personally took command of a Chinese company under intense fire and ordered it to stand fast until reinforcements arrived. Stilwell himself did not provide any reference to this feat, but he was later awarded a Distinguished Service Cross for this action.

The successes of the Chinese 38th and 200th Divisions, however, faded rapidly, and the Japanese resumed their advance. The invaders swept around the eastern end of the defenses, overwhelming the Chinese 55th Division on the way to the vital hub of Lashio. When the troops of the 55th melted into the hills, Stilwell urged a court-martial and possible execution of their commander, but the request was ignored. Earlier, Stilwell had voiced his approval of a Chinese general who had a captain and a lieutenant shot for retiring without orders.

Stilwell and the fragmented units of Chinese troops began to retreat. He seethed with anger as he watched trucks with gas, rice, and other valuables streaming north, concluding that Chinese commanders would enrich themselves selling the goods. Meetings with Alexander and his chief of staff confirmed, in Stilwell's words, "imminent danger of disintegration and collapse." Showing scant appreciation of their ordeal, he noted, "Alex has 36,000 men to take out! Where the hell have they all been?"

The withdrawal plan called for Slim and his I Burmcorps and the three Chinese divisions still considered cohesive units to escape via Mandalay, then across the Irrawaddy. The British forces would head due west to India, while the Chinese went north through Myitkyina. The choke point lay on the Ava bridge across the Irrawaddy at Mandalay. Once the defenders had crossed, the span would be demolished.

The retreat was on for the British forces, the Chinese armies, and the scattering of Americans seeking to avoid capture or worse. Bandits roamed freely, murdering and stealing at any opportunity. Renegade Chinese soldiers robbed, raped, and killed Burmese civilians. By April 29, with the disintegration of the Chinese armies and their command structures, Stilwell no longer was in a position to issue them orders. Initially, he expected his headquarters staff, composed of both Americans and Chinese, to travel north from Mandalay by railroad to Myitkyina, where planes could ferry the entire contingent to safety. But the rail line fell prey to groups plundering resources and small bands of soldiers exploiting it for their own uses. In fact, Stilwell's chief executive officer, General Lo Cho-ying, had commandeered at gunpoint a seventeen-car train that soon collided with another, blocking the tracks. "Unfortunately, he was not killed," growled Stilwell.

The Stilwell Exodus

Some of the group with Stilwell boarded the last plane out, but he elected to remain behind. With a motley military group of twenty-six Americans, thirteen Britons, and sixteen Chinese, plus Dr. Seagrave, with his staff and his Burmese nurses, as well as some civilians, including Indian cooks and mechanics, Stilwell now started his own Burma exodus. Opting for a circuitous route that would evade the Japanese, the group traveled miles in trucks, jeeps, and cars over rutted cart paths, often passing vehicles jammed with Chinese soldiers. For five days the caravan struggled with overheated motors, flat tires, and stalled cars that dammed the narrow roads. Flagging spirits perked up briefly as Seagrave organized a chorus of his Burmese nurses in "Onward Christian Soldiers."

On the morning of May 6, at a clearing in the northern Burmese jungle, fifteen newcomers—hungry, unkempt British commandos with Colonel Davidson-Huston—appeared. To Stilwell's perturbation, they had no rations, but he agreed that they could stay. Now Stilwell addressed a ragged, filthy, weary crowd of about a hundred. Dressed in a windbreaker, boots, leggings, and a well-worn World War I campaign hat, Stilwell announced that for the rest of the roughly two-hundred-mile trip to Imphal inside India, they would be obliged to walk. He admitted the trails were not well marked, but the obscurity also might prevent the foe from knowing their location. Because the monsoons were due in ten days and to stay ahead of the hordes of refugees seeking asylum, they would have to keep a pace of 105 steps per minute, no easy feat in the heat and dust, across streams and climbing the seven-thousand-foot-high Naga Hills between Burma and India.

He instructed them to discard anything they could not carry themselves and for all food to be pooled. Trucks and staff cars were to be abandoned that morning. The jeeps bearing essentials would be used as long as possible. He concluded, "We're all in this together now and if you will do what I tell you, I guess we'll make it."

Jack Belden, the *Time* and *Life* correspondent who had arrived to cover the war in Burma wearing a white linen suit, a pith helmet, and white buckskin shoes, recalled, "I'd been driving one of the jeeps and we'd been bumping and bucking along through terrible stuff and the cars and trucks had been breaking down one by one. When he told us to get rid of everything . . . I didn't have much, just my typewriter and a few odds and ends. . . . The girls, the little Burmese nurses, were throwing away all their belongings, their colorful skirts and silks, tossing all their garments up into the trees, laughing and having a good time. And you'd see a man take a bottle of whiskey from his knapsack, drink the last of it, and throw the empty bottle into the bushes. . . . An old Indian servant found two pairs of long winter underwear one of the American officers had discarded and put them both on! Things like this created a sense of romantic adventure about to begin and I found I was looking forward to it."

Major Felix Nowakowsky, Stilwell's finance officer, had been toting about $100,000 in rupees. "I was worried about carrying all that money. It was in a steel box, so I put it into my knapsack, but even so, it weighed about twenty-five pounds. I threw away everything else except my tommygun and a change of socks. I cut off my pants and made shorts out of them. Those and an army shirt and my army shoes were all I wore."

Jack Croft, a British officer cadet, had been with a party of retreating Britains who managed to ride a train to Indaw before he and a fellow cadet, Hughie Campbell, decided to head west on their own. "We had been walking for a couple of days when suddenly we began to hear a lot of noise in the jungle ahead of us, the sound of axes and saws and trees felled, and we could hear the grinding of motors. Then we heard a lot of shouted commands, which we began to realize were not Japanese, as we feared. We cautiously followed the noise, which led us into a clearing.

"Here what seemed to be hundreds of people were milling about, some parking lorries, others maneuvering jeeps. There were huge piles of equipment and stores on one side and some were being burned. We were standing there observing all this when we were suddenly confronted by a testy American officer who rudely remarked, 'My God, not more Limeys!' I took exception to this and said tartly though he might not like our company, neither were we too keen on his. But since we all seemed to be engaged in the same effort of escaping, wouldn't it be sensible for us to join together?

"We both cooled off after a bit and he conferred with the higher-ups, none of whom we knew at the time, and informed us that we had permission to join the group."

Martin Davies, a twenty-two-year-old British conscientious-objector driver for the Friends Ambulance Unit (FAU), had been working with the Seagraves operation. "Every day since daybreak we'd been battling our way through trees and an undergrowth and we had to stop every few minutes while it was cleared. Men with saws and axes were going ahead and we coming behind but obviously it was a losing battle and it was apparent that unless we hit a road, we were going to have to stop.

"Suddenly we broke out into the clearing. Beside it was a stream across which was strung a narrow bamboo bridge and on the other side of the stream there seemed to be no trail at all. We were told to park the vehicles and to collect ourselves in various small groups. The American soldiers were in one, the British in another. The ambulance drivers joined the Seagrave unit and the nurses. Some Chinese soldiers stood near and in a separate group were the servants and the Asian drivers and mechanics for the trucks.

"So we waited for the 'pep talk,' the hot story of what was going to happen next. I must confess that to us General Stilwell had a slightly comical appearance in that Boy Scout hat, and his American accent was a joke to us. We were slightly disrespectful about him among ourselves. We tended to discount the military on the whole, they were outside the orbit of our morality. We believed . . . the military concept cannot stand up to the man of reason.

"But thinking practically, we realized that we would be lucky to get out at all, and if we *had* to have a military solution to the situation, the sensible thing was to go along—Stilwell's way of doing things, even though we didn't feel confidence in him at the moment. We did realize that he was probably the only person within a thousand miles who *could* get us out of there."

The evacuees managed to drive their jeeps, carrying, among other items, radio equipment, across the fragile bamboo bridge, but the bulk of the party started a long hike. By a stroke of great good fortune two drivers happened by with twenty mules. They more than likely were contraband smugglers, but Stilwell pressed them into service along with some sixty bearers hired through the headman of a nearby village. The refugees traveled for about ten miles, but even the rugged jeeps could proceed no longer. Sergeant William D. Chambers, the radio operator, said, "When the general asked me that night what I thought about taking it [the radio] along, I had to tell him I thought it would hold us up. The receiver itself weighed about a hundred pounds and we'd have to take a fifty-five-gallon drum of gas to run the generator for the transmitter and we didn't have anything else to carry it in. He said, 'Tear it up.'"

Before destroying the set, Chambers arranged for Stilwell's senior aide, Lieutenant Colonel Frank Dorn, to send final messages. Chambers, using a cipher prepared by Dorn, then advised Chungking and New Delhi of their situation before signing off. While others poured sugar in the gas tanks of the jeeps or blew up engine blocks, Chambers swung an ax on his radio.

As they loaded up on May 7 for the first full day on foot, medical officer Captain Paul Grindley said, "Most of the American officers, including Stilwell, were carrying tommy guns or Springfield rifles, all the rest carrying their personal packs. I carried a tommy gun and a full pack, the total weighing about forty pounds. Before we left, Stilwell lined us up and told us that somebody had loaded two bedding rolls and all kinds of extra uniforms onto one of the mules and that anyone caught doing that again would be left to walk alone." The culprit received a private tongue-lashing from Stilwell.

The first day of the walk-out involved slogging through or beside the Chaunggyi River. For that May 7, Stilwell wrote, "Out at 6:30. A mess. Start ordered for 5:00. Easy pace down the river. Till 11:00. Holcombe out. Merrill out; heat exhaustion. Lee out. Slimey pooped. Nowakowski same. Christ, but we are a poor lot. Hard going in the river all the way. Cooler. All packs reduced to ten pounds." Stilwell originally permitted a five-minute break for each hour of the trek, but as more and more people lagged or fainted in the dry, torrid atmosphere, he stretched the rest period to ten minutes.

Grindley reported that Merrill, never in robust health, had suffered sunstroke. "After we cooled him off, we inflated one of the air mattresses and the FAU boys towed him along. Then Tommy Lee passed out and we put him on a mattress, too. After Holcombe was overcome, the porters made a bamboo raft to pull him on."

As one scorching day followed another, they camped at night, sought shelter in the midday heat, and resumed their steps while Stilwell frequently shouted out a cadence. The column heard and saw long-tailed monkeys as well as elephants and airplanes. They pulled voracious leeches off one another; nursed sore, blistered feet; and tended to infections and innumerable insect bites. Tempers shortened, goodwill evaporated, and Stilwell, to conserve food, put everyone on half rations. He ate last. When they reached the Uyu River, a branch of the Chindwin, the Americans built four rafts with roofs to shield against the sun. While many navigated downstream for hours looking for an appropriate place to halt for the night, another group stuck with the mule train traveling overland to a site where they could ford the river. "We swam some of the mules across," said Jack Croft, the British officer cadet. "Then we went back to bring the rest of them over only to find that the first darn mules were swimming back with us."

During the second day of floating on the Uyu, those on the rafts heard a plane. Captain Paul Jones said, "I stripped to my underpants in case we had to dive overboard to take cover. It came in at us very low; it had two motors. We couldn't identify it, it came right at us. We were a perfect target for machine-gunning. Then after making a couple more passes it started dropping food on the bank of the river and into the river itself, corned beef, cigarettes, biscuits, and dried milk. We all dived in after it and everybody got a big kick out of it. Even the Boss [Stilwell] in just his underwear carried a sack of the stuff out of the river."

Martin Davies from the FAU remembered, "I felt frustrated because we were told not to go out to pick up the food, that Stilwell was going to have the honor of getting the first sack. He waded right out into the river in his drawers and vest and in great triumph brought back the first sack. Having done that, he allowed his minions to go get the rest of it. After it was all brought in, we were allowed to take one tin each and I shared a tin of sausages with George or Tom and that was about the best meal I ever had. It was sort of a bonus. It was Stilwell celebrating. Obviously he had to conserve food, but he let us have some. He gave way to discipline that day."

The supplies dumped by the RAF cheered the Stilwell party enormously. Not only did they have more food and some medical items to treat their injuries and bouts of disease, but also the air drop signified awareness of their existence by headquarters in India.

The entire group united by the banks of the much bigger Chindwin River. The rains of the monsoon had yet to fall, and it was necessary to mush through a half a mile of sandbar before boarding long, narrow canoes, boats hollowed out of tree trunks. This transport was provided by local people with native paddlers fore and aft. In place of the Shan and Kachin porters, Naga tribesman assumed the duty of bearers. Everyone started to climb a steep path that wound through a teak forest up into the Naga Hills. But as they ascended, the temperature fell to a more comfortable level, and heavy rains began. They sensed themselves now out of harm's way, beyond the reach of the Japanese. Indeed, during the trek, a Briton named Tim Sharpe, secretary of the maharajah of Manipur, met them with ponies and additional bearers.

When they came upon a clear, cool stream after another grueling fourteen miles, Stilwell commented, "Soaked feet in brook. Rocky hillside in gorge. Tangkhuls [local tribe] squatting around their rice pots and fires. Lean-to shacks. What a picture, if we only had a movie camera. Thatched covered bridge. Chinese soldiers, Burmese girls, Americans and Limeys, all in the brook, washing and shaving and soaking feet. Rough sleeping."

Pelted by the rains of the monsoon, the journey continued, with receptions in villages that featured rice wine, cider, chicken, and even a local beef. Stilwell noted improvements in health, "Cripples getting fewer."

On May 20, two weeks after the group started its walk, Stilwell entered the Indian city of Imphal, true to his promise not to lose a single person during the odyssey out of Burma. He weighed twenty pounds less than when he started. Dorn, his aide, had shed a dozen more, and Holcombe was described as "emaciated, resembles Gandhi." After Stilwell flew to New Delhi, he defiantly announced that Burma would be retaken from the Japanese, even, as he admitted, "I claim we got a hell of a beating. We got run out of Burma and it is humiliating as hell."

End of the Rout

For thousands of other troops under British command, the way out required a swift démarche due west and over the Chindwin considerably below where Stilwell and company reached the other side. Alexander issued directions to Slim for an orderly withdrawal. Two brigades would fall back along the Chindwin to hold off the enemy farther south, and a strong detachment would occupy positions west of the river, in the Myitta Valley, to prevent an overland thrust in that area. The remainder of I Burmcorps, including Alexander and his staff, would follow a road from the temporary headquarters at Shwebo for some 110 miles to the town of Kalewa, on the Chindwin. There ferries could haul the remnants of I Burmcorps far enough for them to escape into India and be joined by the men who had been stationed in the Myitta Valley.

I. C. Scott, with his BFF unit attached to the 17th Indian Division, participated in the retreat via Shwegyin and Kalewa. In a dry, extremely soft riverbed, vehicles—trucks, cars, and even bullock carts—sank in the sand. Given a tank, a truck with a winch, and two tractors, Scott cleared the way, enabling the elements of the 17th to go through smoothly. He believed that his effort here is why he was later awarded a medal, the Chowringhee Star.

After a few days in Kalewa, Scott with his soldiers crossed the river and headed for India. "It was burning hot and the whole countryside had a parched look. There was little enough water for the army and the position was made much worse by the thousands of refugees, mainly poor Indians heading for their country. Everywhere they camped became foul ground and they camped everywhere. All one could see for miles and miles was a steady stream of refugees and with water in very short supply there were queues at each and every water point. Many dropped dead with exhaustion and their bodies were left to rot in the sun."

A. D. Firth, as an officer with the Duke of Wellington Regiment, driven out of Rangoon and across the Sittang only a few days after he arrived in Burma, had become part of the general retreat until the outfit reached Kalewa. After swimming their mules over the Chindwin, he and his comrades boarded two paddle steamers. Among the earliest to escape, the troops, along with a chunk of the 48th Brigade made up of Gurkhas, sailed upstream for two days to Sittaung, where they disembarked and sank the ships. From there, the group plodded toward the Indian frontier.

A major threat to the bulk of the British lay in the Japanese forces already attacking Monywya, a settlement also on the Chindwin about 125 miles south. Overwhelming a few soldiers and Royal Marines, the advance of the enemy surprised Slim in a bivouac area not far off. Hardly had some fleeing officers delivered the bad news than he heard the unmistakable *wump, wump, wump* of exploding Japanese mortars. It was obvious that the Japanese hoped to intercept anyone trying to cross the Chindwin. They were organizing an armada of launches to travel upstream and cut off Alexander and his portion of the Allied forces headed for Kalewa.

As the Japanese brought many more soldiers to Monywa, on May 2, Slim called on his available brigades to wrest the town back from the enemy. "One talks of brigades," said Slim, "but they were by now sadly depleted and the whole force did not amount in numbers to much more than one normal brigade group. The Japanese defense was stubborn as our troops fought their way into town. There was a particularly bitter struggle around the railway station, which changed hands three times. By 1500 hours we were well into the town thanks to a vigorous attack by the 1st Burma Brigade, fighting well after its reconstitution with two Indian battalions. Another Japanese attempt to push naval launches up the river was frustrated by our mortar fire."

Slim gave the word for a full evacuation, complicated by the throngs of refugees, including European women and children as well as his wounded. With only a few ambulances, the stricken troops were packed into trucks and a few civilian buses for a hideously rough ride. The most seriously injured did not survive. Slim sent the 1st Burma Brigade, including L. E. Tutt and the 414th Battery, cross-country on foot to a site beyond Kalewa for crossing the river. The torturous trip for others on foot or in the remaining vehicles brought them to Shwegyin, where five hundred to six hundred men, a truck or two, several guns, and a few jeeps were loaded aboard steamers. Unable to effect a direct crossing, the ships carried their passengers for six miles.

The site on the eastern shore was like a mini-Dunkirk, with thousands of soldiers crowded into a narrow, cliff-surrounded, basin-shaped area, awaiting their turn to board a vessel. The Japanese bombed and strafed, and although held off by a strong rear guard, lobbed mortars on the concentration of troops and equipment. By digging in, said Slim, the damage to humans was reduced, but the onslaught devastated vehicles and other equipment. However, the civilian Indian seamen on the ships panicked, and many deserted. The available vessels and lengthening turnaround time became further hindrances.

For four days the rescue effort slowly proceeded. On May 10 a large number of Japanese arrived by boat, some eight miles from Shwegyin. Outposted to maintain the perimeter of the basin, the 7th Gurkhas fought off two attacks by these Japanese. "Some time after the second attack," said Slim, "more probably during it, numbers of Japanese infiltrated between our rather widely spaced posts and got on the forward edge of the escarpment. . . . The Gurkhas, with my old friend the *subadar* major well to the fore, then put in a very spirited counterattack, right up the cliffs. There followed very confused fighting in which the Gurkhas and the Indians, who were still clinging in places to their positions, savagely clashed with large numbers of enemy in the precipitous jungle around the 'Basin's' edge. The situation was restored."

However, time was running out. A trickle of wounded were carried aboard the few boats still operating. When one of the final steamers had embarked its cargo of troops, Slim allowed some refugees to get aboard, where they clung to the rails or crouched in any crevice they could find. Slim scrounged three small vessels to slip under a cliff that shielded them from mortar fire and saw the last of the wounded loaded along with some of the administrative staff.

Slim ordered his artillerymen to use all of their ammunition in one final twenty-minute barrage against the enemy positions. While that fusillade checked fire from the enemy, the remaining able-bodied soldiers destroyed anything that could not be carried. The exploding tanks, guns, ammunition, and fuel erupted into night-shattering flames. The men then struck out on foot with mules bearing some necessities. Uniforms in rags, boots given out, their only defense small arms, they were in poor shape to resist further assaults by the Japanese, but the punishment meted out to the invaders had forced them to pause and reorganize. Hampered only by minor skirmishes with Burmese brigands, Slim and his cohort slogged to Kalewa. Other elements from the tattered remnants of I Burmcorps, some of which still had trucks, straggled to that town, where all crossed to the western banks of the Chindwin.

The BFF survivors with Scott had reached that side more than a week earlier. When they finally arrived in India, trucks took them to a camp. Scott said, "There was no organization whatsoever and it was complete chaos. Officers were ordered into one camp and their men into a separate camp, which was quite unacceptable as far as I was concerned. Rations were in short supply and there were no proper arrangements for the issue of rations. There was no sanitation. Latrines had not been dug. There were no tools for digging so we could not even dig latrines ourselves."

The rains came, bearing with them more malaria and dysentery. Finally tents and tarpaulins were distributed, enabling the troops to take cover. "The rain stopped the day before General Wavell dropped in to see us. He saw about two thousand men of the BFF all lined up and trying to look like soldiers. He did not, of course, see the one thousand lying sick or the two hundred or more wives and children of men of the BFF who were camped in terrible squalor in the area. I heard him say to Ted Cartmel [the camp commandant], 'There's a lot of weeding out necessary here!' No doubt he was right."

The journey of those with Slim was more painful. Beyond the reach of enemy guns, other miseries attended the broken army. The monsoon rains deluged them during a trek through a ninety-mile stretch of malaria-laden hills and jungles. Some assistance came from an India-based transport company that met them several days into the march. They carried off the wounded and sick, then alternately shuttled men a distance before returning to pick up those still walking.

Slim commented, "On the last day of that nine-hundred-mile retreat, I stood on a bank beside the road and watched the rear guard march into India. All of them, British and Gurkha, were gaunt and ragged as scarecrows. Yet, as they trudged behind their surviving officers in groups pitifully small, they still carried their arms and kept their ranks, they were still recognizable as fighting units. They might look like scarecrows, but they looked like soldiers, too."

7

CBI Doldrums

With Stilwell out of the picture and the British forces, including the command center, exiting Burma, the Chinese troops who had entered the country were now on their own, seeking escape routes. The 22d and 38th divisions and remnants of the 28th, 96th, and 200th straggled toward India. The redoubtable General Sun, having fought his unit so well in support of Slim, and then led them as an intact fighting force that maintained both discipline and morale into India, must have been sorely tried when the governor of that province of Assam, hearing that a "mere rabble" was on his turf, recommended that they be disarmed and confined. Only after Brigadier General William Gruber, Stilwell's representative in India, interceded with Wavell did the 38th receive an appropriate encampment in Assam.

To the east, other Chinese fared much worse. In the company of tens of thousands of refugees, they struggled to evade the Japanese pursuit. Food became scarce even though Kachin tribesmen generously provided from their own stores. American and RAF planes dropped tons of food along trails known to be used by the fleeing hordes and helped prevent mass starvation. In the anarchic flow, some of the Chinese soldiers resorted to looting and even murder of refugees and the hospitable Kachins. Advance Japanese units, hounds on the heels of fleeing prey, nipped at the departing troops with small arms and even artillery.

The Salween River Gorge

Aside from Chinese soldiers trying to stave off further advances, the only active units opposing the Japanese were the AVG fighters and

98

a handful of B-25 Mitchells. As they routed their opponents within Burma, the invaders swarmed northward through Bhamo and Myit-kyina toward the Chinese border. On May 5, brushing aside the fragments of the Sixth Army, a large Japanese column, coursing along the Burma Road, penetrated China and entered the Salween River gorge. On the map that placed them within 300 miles of Kunming, Chennault's home base.

The route through the gorge twisted over twenty-five narrow miles of hairpin turns down to the Hweitung bridge, suspended over the Salween. The Japanese soldiers bucked a river of humanity, civilians fleeing the war in Burma as well as shards of the routed Chinese forces. Japanese artillery opened fire over the Salween, blasting defensive positions and the first throngs who had crossed the Hweitung and begun to climb the hills beyond. Chinese sappers then blew up the bridge, trapping refugees, some of their fellow soldiers, and the enemy.

The destruction of the Hweitung bridge dammed the oncoming flow. Japanese soldiers still pressing forward could not retreat. These offensive forces hunkered down to await their own engineers, bringing up pontoons to construct a span over the Salween. Through the observations of his pilots, Chennault grasped a marvelous opportunity to wreak havoc on the stalled Japanese. However, the bombing and strafing envisioned would be unable to distinguish the civilians from the foe. He radioed Madame Chiang, "Last reports state Japs on west bank Salween River . . . and bridge destroyed. Japs meeting no opposition anywhere as soldiers, civilians, panic-stricken and fleeing east along road. Consider situation desperate and Japs may drive trucks into Kunming unless road and bridges are destroyed. . . . Request authority to attack targets in between Salween and Lungling City."

She answered quickly, "The generalissimo instructs you send all available AVG attack trucks, boats, etc., between Salween and Lungling City." Chiang also ordered General Peter Mow to join the assault, using whatever aircraft the Nationalist air force could muster.

The AVG brought added power to the mission. Not only did the new P-40Es have wing racks for small fragmentation bombs, but also armorers Roy Hoffman and Charles Baisden improvised belly racks that could carry 570-pounders manufactured by the Soviets and in ample supply at Kunming. The larger ordnance suited dive bombing, and former U.S. Navy pilots such as Tex Hill, Ed Rector, and others were experienced in the technique.

When the heavily laden P-40 Kittyhawks arrived on the scene on May 8, the Japanese were already starting to unload their pontoons along the banks of the Salween. Hill, Rector, Tom Jones, and Frank

Lawlor flew as dive bombers, while Arvid Olson and three others flew top cover. There was intense antiaircraft fire, but the 570-pound bombs crashed on the massed enemy armor and artillery awaiting an opportunity to move toward the pontoon bridge. The huge explosions tore out massive chunks of hillside that snowballed into landslides, sweeping away people and vehicles.

A dozen Soviet-made bombers and obsolescent Hawk IIIs, manned by Chinese pilots obedient to Mow's orders, doused those caught on the western slopes. No one could take cover as the Kittyhawks unloosed their thirty-five-pounders and followed up with blazing, .50-caliber machine guns. They worked the road over from the gorge all the way back to Burma. Soldiers and civilians crawled into ditches and shell holes, but many remained naked to the deadly hail. Fires unleashed by P-40s rearmed with incendiaries sprouted from damaged tanks and trucks.

The downpour of destruction lasted for four days as the AVG, with some aid from the Chinese air force, blasted and burned every town and hamlet west of the Salween to deny the Japanese caches of supplies. The attempted passage through the Salween River gorge was emphatically rebuffed. Postwar analyses suggested that the Japanese never intended to press on toward Kunming because that would have entailed a perilously long supply line and placed troops beyond air cover (no Japanese planes defended against the AVG at the gorge). The true objective was to close off access to India.

The Allies Regroup

The potential for an advance into China through the Salween River gorge had been thwarted, but Stilwell and Slim, chased out of Burma, were in no position to challenge the enemy in the field. Instead, they would spend most of the remainder of 1942 plotting campaigns to recover what had been so humiliatingly lost. At the close of May 1942 the Japanese not only had cut off China from any viable land approach, but also from their Burma bases the Nipponese could bomb Calcutta and most other major Indian cities.

Stilwell, almost instantly upon bedding down in India, had begun to script an offensive to wrest back the territory conquered by Japan and then drive the occupiers out of mainland Asia. He asked army chief of staff Marshall and Secretary of War Stimson to ship one or more American infantry divisions to CBI, explaining that with retrained, reequipped Chinese troops he could evict the Japanese from

Burma, push them out of Siam, and then drive the invaders back from their gains within China.

The last of these efforts would involve the bulk of the generalissimo's resident armies, which Stilwell candidly described as deficient in weaponry, communications hardware, and medical services. Additionally, the upper echelons of the Chinese military required vigorous pruning to remove corrupt and incompetent commanders. He advised that one solution lay in the selection of a field commander free of meddling from Chungking. While Stilwell did not nominate anyone, he was the obvious choice. His letter noted that he had recommended that the generalissimo execute several commanders.

Stilwell then left New Delhi for Chungking, where he delivered to both Chiangs his postmortem on the debacle in Burma along with proposals to reform and revamp the army. His letter to his wife said, "I made a report to the Big Boy. I told him the whole truth, and it was like kicking an old lady in the stomach. However, so far as I can find out, no one else dares to tell him the truth. . . . Very cordial welcome from both him and Madame."

He suggested that the Chinese Fifth Army, or what was left of it, remain under Stilwell's command in India, where he could supervise their training. The generalissimo did not commit himself. The American was unhappy because of the Chinese leader's belief that all that was needed were the stuff of war. "They have the same old complex— planes, tanks, guns, etc., will win the war. I got a bit hot and told him that the only way to do it was to thoroughly reorganize the ground forces. Madame jumped up and came over and sat by me and said the G-mo had to consider 'certain influences,' etc. I told her I of course understood all that. But with the U.S. on his side and backing him, the stupid little ass fails to grasp the big opportunity of his life." His host constantly confounded the American general by ignoring a basic problem: the Chinese peasant draftee, often illiterate and totally unschooled in even basic technology, could not simply be inserted into a tank or equipped with a complex piece of artillery.

Nor did those in charge in Washington satisfy Stilwell. Marshall advised the president that there existed neither the personnel nor the shipping to accommodate the request for one or two divisions and all the transport required. Instead, he promoted a plan devised by the War Department under the telling title Keeping China in the War. Logistical studies had convincingly argued that shipments to China by air over the Himalayas could never remotely meet the needs. The best long-term solution lay in a new Burma Road, a truck route that would require a truly prodigious construction program.

Even as Stilwell reluctantly faced telling the generalissimo that the help he asked for from the United States would amount to a mere fraction of that requisitioned, CBI assets were further drained. In North Africa, the Axis armies recovered from the wintertime British advances and rolled back its Eighth Army, capturing a key citadel, Tobruk, on June 21. Never in favor of Washington's fantasy of a 1942 invasion of the Continent, Churchill had persuaded Roosevelt that the best option open to the Allies lay in Operation Torch, a campaign in North Africa. To Stilwell's frustration, General Lewis Brereton, his Tenth Air Force commander, was notified to shift his heavy bombers, transports, and personnel to the Middle East for operations both against Europe and in support of Torch. Stilwell groaned under the burden of having to inform the generalissimo of another retreat from an earlier commitment. To add to the friction with its Allies, China was denied a place at the table with the Combined Chiefs of Staff, for, among other reasons, its lack of contributions to munitions supplies while demanding a share of them. Indeed, the amount of Lend-Lease designated for China shrank rapidly, starting with the entrance of the United States into a war against the European Axis powers, the genteel confiscation by the British for their forces in Burma, and then the absence of routes to feed matériel into China. The first airborne freight missions fell significantly short of what Chiang expected as matériel was detoured to the defenses inside Burma. There simply were not enough planes, pilots, or maintenance services to overcome the rigors of flights from India over the mountains to China.

The shaky relationship between Stilwell and Chiang began an almost irreversible slide into mutual distrust following the withdrawal of Brereton and the heavyweights of the Tenth Air Force. The generalissimo argued that since Stilwell served as his chief of staff with the Tenth Air Force commander reporting to him, in effect, Chiang had the right to assign the Tenth Air Force as part of his domain. However, the charter for Stilwell, issued by the War Department, named him commanding general of the U.S. Army forces in CBI, an independent operation whose units were not subject to any Chinese orders.

Washington attempted to placate Chungking, but Chiang listed "three minimum requirements" essential for the maintenance of the China Theater of War. He demanded that three American divisions be shipped to India to join with the Chinese in reopening the supply lines through Burma before the end of the year. Beginning in August, he expected five hundred planes for his air force and that the monthly transport of goods by air that month should reach five thousand tons.

Stilwell, while dubious about the timetable, supported the generalissimo. However, to clarify jurisdiction, Stilwell informed Chiang that the generalissimo was supreme only within his own country. He could not control organizations in India or Burma. Lend-Lease items became Chiang's only after title passed to the Chinese. "I am charged," said Stilwell, "with the supervision and control of Lend-Lease matériel and am to decide the place and time that title passes." Possession of the key to the storehouse of war matériel endowed Stilwell with considerable leverage.

Frustrated by Washington, Chiang focused his anger on its military representative and indicated he would like the prickly Stilwell recalled. General Marshall told Soong that it would not change matters if someone replaced Stilwell; the arrangements would remain as is. A flurry of diplomacy wrought a compromise. Stilwell had proposed a new Burma campaign, and that signaled to Chiang that his Western allies intended to forge a land supply link to China. The United States agreed to a target of five thousand tons a month over the Hump, although the amount would rarely be that high during the first months. In addition, while feeding munitions and other war gear into China, the United States, at Ramgarh, India, would train and equip the Chinese troops who retreated from Burma.

According to then colonel Haydon Boatner, Stilwell's chief of staff in India and an old China hand, the Chinese army remnants arriving at Ramgarh, in the Assam area, presented formidable problems. He notified Stilwell's infantry commander, Major General Franklin Sibert, "The condition of the army troops is pitiful. They are completely demoralized, disorganized . . . they are carrying out worthless equipment (switchboards with complete crusts of mud and rust . . .) although exhausted. They refused to throw any away at my urging for they claim they will be killed [by their officers] if they do so."

Boatner spoke of a substantial discrepancy between the number of soldiers on the rosters and those actually on hand. With the United States paying the men and issuing supplies, the Chinese commanders greatly inflated payrolls and needs. Boatner sounded a familiar note: "I cannot condemn too strongly the attitude and conduct of the Chinese. The local officers themselves have done nothing . . . pass every buck to the British or myself. Sun refused to allow his animals to pack food in the jungle and provided men . . . for depots only under the greatest of pressure. . . . Yang consistently refused to send any CEF [Chinese Expeditionary Force] headquarters personnel into the jungle."

End of the AVG

For Chennault's Flying Tigers, the war was in its final stages. He had been called to active service in April and then promoted to brigadier general. Dissolution of the AVG was set for July 4, 1942. Since the defeat of the Allies in Burma, several new airstrips in China had been built, and the first of the army air corps pilots, men fresh out of flight school, had begun to arrive. Flying Tigers taught them the tricks of aerial combat, but the first line of defense remained the veterans of the AVG. The army air corps hoped that the AVG pilots would accept induction and remain on hand. The recruiters refused to offer anything more than reserve commissions, and few of the pilots were interested. One who agreed to stay was Tex Hill, with 12¼ confirmed victories. He explained that Chennault had approached him and pleaded that he help activate new units. Ed Rector and three others also joined the air corps.

Chennault made an emotional plea for more men to stay beyond July 4. After almost a year in China and Burma and the ordeal of combat, they wanted to go home. Most were willing to go back to war, but not until they enjoyed a leave in the States. On June 30 Chennault proposed that the pilots extend their contracts two weeks to give him time to weld an organization strong enough to resist the enemy. His plea won over nineteen fliers and thirty-six from ground crews.

The extension agreement specified defensive missions against air attacks on cities, but the Flying Tigers volunteered for offensive actions as well. One pilot was killed and another shot down and captured during these raids. On July 4, the final official day of the AVG, a flight led by Bob Neale destroyed 6 enemy aircraft. Neale, who became the leader in planes shot down, finished with a score of 15½ destroyed in aerial combat. Chennault mourned the demise of the organization to correspondent Jack Belden: "The AVG is the world's finest trained bunch of fighting airmen. I regret their disbandment. Now I only look forward to meeting the enemy."

Shortly before the dissolution of the Flying Tigers, Clayton Bissell, as Stilwell's air officer, and perhaps expecting to add Chennault's forces to his domain, assigned Bruce Holloway to act as an observer for the final two weeks of the AVG's existence. Holloway, a University of Tennessee dropout, graduated from West Point and then earned his wings as a fighter pilot. He had volunteered for duty in China.

As a member of the new China Air Task Force he quickly recognized Chennault's tactical art and became a member of the 76th Fighter Squadron, one of four such units in the 23d Fighter Group. Eventually he would move up to become the 23d's commander. Over the course of a year Holloway had ample opportunity to appraise Chennault's personality and work ethic.

"He was a terrific field commander and tactician," said Holloway. "He did not get up there to the very top. He would have . . . if he had just had a little more tact and the ability to get along whether he agreed or not. He would go out of channels." Holloway identified two basic faults in Chennault's character. "He was the poorest loser that I have ever seen. We would play softball and he was the pitcher on my ball team. He was a pretty good pitcher except he would get tired after about the third or fourth inning. We would always be ahead then and we would always lose the game, couldn't get him out of there. He would sort of sulk off. Then we would go home and that night he would want to play badminton. Any one of us could beat him at badminton. Then he would want to play Ping-Pong. Any one of us could beat him at Ping-Pong, except Joe Alsop couldn't play anything.

"Then he [Chennault] would get lower and lower. If we had any whiskey, we would drink that. He would sometimes end up wanting to wrestle somebody and he would usually challenge Casey Vincent [his chief of staff], who was the biggest guy. Casey would stave him off usually until he went off to bed or we ate dinner. But once in a while he would grab Casey and would end up getting thrown over in the corner.

"He didn't know the meaning of the word *compromise*." Admitting to his own bias, Holloway continued, "He was, in my opinion, sorely tested in this regard, with the kind of people he had to put up with and work with, like Stilwell and Bissell, who sort of head the list of people that I have not much respect for. If they didn't get along with him, they were just categorically wrong and he was right."

The First Arakan Disaster

While Stilwell grappled with the Chinese problems and Chennault tried to build his Fourteenth Air Force, the British changed some horses. After the fiasco in the last-ditch defense, Alexander hardly paused on his way from Burma to India before he flew off to London to work on the plans for Torch. Slim received command of the XV Indian Corps, assigned to hold India's southern border and the Arakan, the long sliver of Burma stretched along the Bay of Bengal. Since the monsoon season precluded an immediate land-based advance into India toward Calcutta, Slim worried about seaborne strikes through the Hoogly River or a conflux of waterways known as the Sunderbans.

As the rainy season faded, the British command turned its attention to the Arakan itself, which featured a narrow coastal plain and the Mayu Range, a steep, two-thousand-foot-high, thickly jungled ridge. It ran from the border of India down almost to Akyab Island. The port and air base there, now in Japanese hands, provided a possible staging ground for control of the Bay of Bengal, advances against Calcutta, and the British staging site of Chittagong, with a subsequent reduction of supply routes to defend Imphal and northeastern India's province of Assam.

Because of a shortage of trained manpower, the British final plan for an offensive in the Arakan called for a straightforward overland advance rather than a more imaginative three-pronged approach that would have added seaborne strikes and a deep insertion behind enemy lines. In December 1942 the first Arakan campaign began. The 5th Indian Division advanced down the western half of the Arakan, while on the other side of the Mayu Range, the 7th Indian Division marched more or less parallel. At first the two columns, working their way south, met only minor opposition. Then unexpectedly stiff opposition from the enemy temporarily stalled the drives. While the British regrouped, the Japanese used the hiatus to reinforce their positions. Subsequently, not even a full-scale attack could dislodge the defenders.

According to Slim in his autobiography, "For the first time we had come up against the Japanese 'bunker'—from now on to be so familiar to us. This was a small strongpoint made usually of heavy logs covered with four or five feet of earth, and so camouflaged in the jungle that it could not be picked out at even fifty yards without prolonged searching." The bunkers contained as many as twenty men, equipped with machine guns. The structures resisted hits even from field guns and held up against medium bombs from the air. The Japanese aligned them to provide mutual support through covering fire.

To break the stalemate, the British brought up more troops and armor. One of the units was the 25th Dragoons, an organization parented by the Prince of Wales Own Regiment. Originally a horse cavalry outfit, the 25th, stationed in India, had been converted to tanks and armored cars. Trooper John McKnight of B Squadron served as a driver-mechanic. In its initial training, the 25th was armored in name only; McKnight's tank was a Chevrolet truck. "The regiment," said McKnight, "was earmarked for service in the Middle East and concentrated on desert warfare training. As the war situation worsened in Burma, the regiment's role was switched from desert to jungle training." They were eventually equipped with American M-3 and M-3A tanks, known as General Lees and General Grants, respectively. McKnight's particular tank was a General Lee. Along with a

75-millimeter cannon that poked out from the hull, the General Lee carried a 37-millimeter gun coaxially mounted on the turret with a .30-caliber machine gun. While the 75's ability to traverse was limited, the 37 could swing a full 360 degrees. Also part of the turret armament was a grenade launcher and a .50-caliber machine gun that could be deployed for antiaircraft use. Both of the larger guns fired either armor-piercing or high-explosive shells, and the 37 could spew cannister shot. Crewmen packed .38-caliber pistols, and a tommy gun was stowed aboard.

In India, extreme secrecy masked operations. McKnight's rank was changed from "trooper" to "craftsman," and his 25th Dragoons were listed as "Royal and Mechanical Engineers." Reinforcements assigned to the organization thought they had won soft noncombatant service but soon learned that they were scheduled to fight. All of the tanks were transported from the training site to a Calcutta installation, according to McKnight, "to make them waterproof up to a depth of three feet of water." When that had been accomplished, the 25th Dragoons loaded aboard U.S. Navy Landing Ships Tanks (LSTs) and under cover of darkness sailed across the Bay of Bengal for the Arakan coast.

As midnight neared, the drivers and tank commanders took their places in their General Lees. Signals from shore directed the LSTs where to head. "I was sitting in the driver's seat," said McKnight, "getting all excited when suddenly the ship came to an abrupt stop, as though it had run into a brick wall. It had in fact run aground on an unmapped sandbank and was stuck fast. Something had to be done quickly. The bow doors were opened and the ramp dropped. The water depth was tested, and it was six feet. The decision was made that to get the ship away safely, the tanks had to be unloaded."

Through the open bow, the LST crew jettisoned huge rolls of beach wire ordinarily used to improve traction on sand. With these on the bottom, the depth was given as four feet, although because of the contour of the coastal shelf, the tanks would pass through a six-foot-deep stretch before beginning to climb to the shallows. While the remainder of the crew crawled into the tank, McKnight wondered about waterproofing designed for three feet below the surface when he would travel through as much as six feet of the sea.

With his tank guided to a position behind the next one to disembark, the driver peered through his periscopes, which provided very little vision. After the tank ahead of him disappeared down the steep-angled ramp, McKnight received the order "Driver advance!" He could see little but his tank commander, who had his shoulders and head out the top turret, giving him directions to keep him in line with the ramp. "Letting the engine act as a brake to control the speed down the ramp, [when] I sensed that the tracks had touched the seabed, I pressed the pedal hard to the floor for maximum revs. We were on our way to the shore. We were now in deep water. periscopes were underwater. I couldn't see anything through them and had no sensation of movement. Water was leaking in everywhere above the three-foot mark, especially through the closed-down visor and periscope housings. Pretty soon I was soaked and shivering. The tank commander kept giving me steering instructions. He could see the marker lights on the beach. The engine was roaring away, sounding very healthy. I was confident we would make it unless we ran into a deep trench on the way."

Indeed, the armored behemoth crawled through shallower water and then onto the beach. A shore party guide met the tank and led it into a dense jungle atop the beach. McKnight, looking through his front visor, could see that he was following a track hacked out of the vegetation. After about half a mile he joined tanks that had debarked earlier. They were parked while the crews worked on camouflage.

After offloading, the armor traveled in the dark along a road between Chittagong, India, and Maungdaw, a Japanese stronghold in the Arakan. "All I could see ahead of me," recalled McKnight, "was the red-hot exhaust pipe of the tank ahead of me. I was assisted a lot by my 75-millimeter gunner, Ken Arnell, who was on the outside of the tank, lying along the barrel of his gun, yelling if I wandered off the straight and narrow. It was a nightmarish drive and it became even more so as we got close to the front line. As we approached a certain point, every artillery and ack-ack gun in the division opened up with nonstop salvos. The Japanese gunners retaliated by sending salvos in our direction. It was quite a traumatic introduction to active service. [When] the artillery gunners ceased fire, the Jap gunners stopped shooting, too. An eerie silence seemed to creep up all around us as we settled down for our first night in the line."

The terrain severely limited communications between the two Indian divisions. Royal engineers widened and improved the trails across the mountains for use by some motor transport. Farther south of the site of McKnight's baptism of fire, in an area occupied by the Japanese, an abandoned railway line tunneled through the mountains. Heavy artillery shelled both British divisions while shuttling in and out of the tunnels to avoid destruction from a retaliatory barrage. The tunnels connected a pair of towns—Maungdaw, the objective for those like McKnight to the west, and Buthidaung, on the eastern side of the Mayu.

To reach Maungdaw, the 5th Indian Division would first need to neutralize a stronghold built into a hill and code-named Tortoise. The bastion, dug deep underground and with interconnecting passageways, reduced the effectiveness of artillery and air strikes. Late in January, a renewed assault on Tortoise began. McKnight and his fellow tankers lay back a mile from the objective during a heavy artillery barrage that was followed by dive bombers that marked the target for a flight of American-made B-24 bombers dumping thousand-pound bombs. When the four-engine Liberators had finished their drop, the artillery picked up again until the tanks rumbled into close range and contributed their shot and shell to the siege.

"While all this tank activity was going on," said McKnight, "the infantry units had moved into their 'jumping off' positions. At a preset time, everybody ceased firing and the infantry charged up the slopes to finish the job, and were immediately repelled with many casualties. The Fortress Tortoise had withstood the onslaught and still dominated the approaches to Maungdaw.

"The battle continued for several days without success. A new plan of attack was devised by the tacticians of the 25th Dragoons. Hitherto when the tanks took over the shelling, the high-explosive shells were put on 'delayed action' so that they penetrated deep into the bunkers before exploding. The Japs learned to keep their heads down until the shelling stopped. Then they still had time to ascend and man the guns and decimate the poor infantrymen charging up the slopes. The new tactics used the Jap ploy to our advantage. At the moment our infantry started their advance, the tank gunners would change the ammunition from high-explosive, delayed-action, to solid-shot, armor-piercing. Solid shot does not explode, and as long as those shells kept arriving on target, the Japs, thinking delayed-action shells were still arriving, kept their heads down, allowing the advancing infantry to get established on Tortoise as soon as the tanks ceased fire.

"During the period we spent in this forward area, we were subject to shelling, mortar fire, dive bombing, and worst of all, night skirmishes with Jap patrols. Soon after dawn we would return to battle stations and resume our attacks on Tortoise until one morning we arrived to find that the Japs had had enough and withdrawn from their fortress during the night. The way was now clear to take Maungdaw and beyond."

On the other side of the Mayu ridge, the 7th Indian Division also had been stymied by hill fortifications similar to Tortoise. The command decided to transfer most of the 25th Dragoons to the 7th. That required navigating hairpin turns along a precipitous pass, named Ngakyedauk and quickly dubbed Okydoke, carved out of the ridge by the royal engineers. McKnight, guided both by his tank commander, who dismounted at times, and his gunner, lying atop the 75-millimeter gun barrel, negotiated the route.

The 25th hurriedly clanked seven miles south to the front lines and employed the same tactics used against Tortoise. After the infantry registered some gains, the tankers withdrew for the night, when they replenished their supplies, gobbled hot food, and then hunkered down for sleep. McKnight had just finished his stint manning a slit trench to defend against enemy infiltrators and crawled under his tank for sleep.

"I was awakened by someone shaking me and whispering, 'Get ready to move off in five minutes.' It was still dark when I crawled from below the tank. There was small-arms fire, grenade explosions going off all round the area. The tanks withdrew farther north and regrouped. The crews were informed that Japanese troops had advanced along the mountain ridges—which everybody had deemed impassable—and occupied all the high ground in the west, north, and east, cutting off all access to the Okydoke Pass in the process. They had also got in behind us. We were virtually surrounded. All units were ordered to withdraw [to the vicinity of the pass] and form a defensive box."

McKnight's crew received instructions to take up a position that protected the retreat of artillery units. In a lonely position on a trail flanked by thick jungle on either side, they nervously awaited the appearance of the enemy. "We were soon spotted by Jap artillery and they quickly tried to find our range by bracketing our tank with shells. The trick was knowing when to move before they got the proper range. We shuffled backwards and forwards quite a bit to confuse them. When things got too hot we made a beeline into the jungle trees. Even there, we weren't safe. They raked the trees with H.E. [high explosives], hoping to knock us out." Eventually, however, the tank was ordered to fall back and rejoin the rest of the troop.

Except for a few soldiers who had made their way west through Okydoke Pass before the Japanese seized control at that end, the surviving troops from the 7th Indian and the tankers settled into a defense centered on what was a supply area and called Administrative Box. The tactic dated back to the imperial days of Lord Kitchener in the nineteenth century, and the formation was a four-sided defense. In the Arakan, the box was adjacent to the eastern end of Okydoke Pass. The site featured Ammunition Hill, which stored the high-explosive shells and small-arms ammunition

The enemy surrounded Administrative Box and controlled all of the high ground. Japanese radio hailed the destruction of the 7th Division, and morale among the British troops sank. Broadcasts from India gave the embattled soldiers what McKnight called "a pep talk, telling us that we wouldn't be forgotten and we would be supplied with all our needs by air drops and most importantly 'to hold on and make history.'" Air force units backed up the promise. Over a siege of twenty-one days, usually at night to avoid enemy aircraft, the DC-3s skimmed the hills, often flying through a storm of small-arms and antiaircraft fire to unloose bundles of supplies. Some dangled at the end of parachutes, while others tumbled to the ground in free fall.

The beleaguered troops were lucky if they got four hours of sleep out of every twenty-four. At night the tankers deployed machine guns and tommy guns in slit trenches, then spent the day on maintenance of their vehicles and grabbed a meal. Attacks occurred day and night while dive bombers pelted the defenders or scourged them with strafing. On about the third day a salvo of shells penetrated Ammunition Hill, detonating its contents.

"We had been parked at our mini base," remembered McKnight, "and had to evacuate in a hurry as everything was exploding all around us. Small-arms ammo was going off like squibs [firecrackers] on Guy Fawkes night. There were huge chunks of shrapnel from the exploding artillery shells whizzing round our ears. We moved the tanks away from the cover of the hill and were now out in the open, making good targets for Jap gunners who were keeping their barrage going. I don't know how we survived that situation. There was nowhere to go to get away. It seems to me that Ammo Hill took about three days and nights to burn out and stop exploding, and when it did, the place looked like the end of the world. The smell of burning was always in your nostrils."

Still intact, McKnight's tank was summoned to assist a detachment of infantry defending a portion of the perimeter. One General Lee previously assigned left the scene after its commander, the 25th's adjutant, was killed by a machine-gun firestorm when he poked his head out the turret. A second tank committed to the task lost both periscopes to a shell blast and it, too, withdrew. McKnight drove his tank to the top of an incline, where a hail of small-arms and machine-gun bullets clattered against the hull. "Immediately, Mike McDonald (the turret gunner) went into action with the turret guns and the Jap guns fell silent. I was studying the area through periscope while this was happening. The Japs were taking cover in a *nullah* (ditch) about thirty to fifty yards ahead of our position. We were too close to them to get at them with the turret guns, even when fully depressed. To have moved back in order to be in range would have been worse. We would have gone back down the incline.

"Sergeant Clive Branson [the tank commander] told Mac to keep shooting at them to keep their heads down while he thought something up. I could see the Jap steel helmets scuttling back and forth between the bursts of Browning [machine gun] Mac was giving them. Sergeant Branson had worked out a solution to the problem of obliterating the Japs in the *nullah*. He radioed back to our H.Q. and arranged to get a 3-inch-mortar team to contact him by radio. After giving our map coordinates to their range finder, he got them to lob over a smoke shell that landed 'plus' from us. From that position, Branson was able to give them information to enable them eventually to land a smoke shell into the *nullah*. This caused panic among the Japs. They were rushing about trying to get out of the *nullah* but Mac kept their heads down with the Browning. Branson announced that he was asking for a 'flight' of H.E. mortar shells be sent over next. As we were so close to the target, we might get some damage ourselves and to brace ourselves.

"We were told to advance further for half a mile or so to make sure there were no more pockets of Japs who might threaten the ridge. We reported mines under the [caterpillar tread] and were told they must be 'duds' or they would have blown the track off when we first went over them. I started the engine and gingerly moved forward. Nothing blew up, so [I] drove like the clappers onto the trail. We went slowly, searching for Jap positions, and when we [took a left turn] I observed a Jap mortar team about a hundred yards ahead. I immediately fired my sponson gun into the target, as did the turret gunner. The target disintegrated. I had the feeling that as they didn't respond to our appearance, maybe someone had 'sorted them out' before we got there and they were already dead."

McKnight and his companions returned to their base, where they refueled and dined on a meal composed of American K rations and bully beef. They settled in for another night on the defense line. The area within the perimeter took on the look of a World War I no-man's-land. "Most of the vegetation had been destroyed," said McKnight, "and any structure that was erected was immediately destroyed by gunfire. Anything or anybody that moved became a target. The casualties mounted up. They couldn't be moved out of the area to a safe haven or cared for in anything that resembled a hospital or tented first aid station. They had to make it to a sheltered *nullah* adjacent to the entrance to Okydoke Pass. This was our Medical Dressing Station (MDS).

"During the night of February 7, a Japanese force of considerable strength overcame the defenders on the southern perimeter and found their way into the MDS. There they committed the most abominable, hideous, evil atrocities which almost defy description. The Japanese reputation up to this time was of the worst anyone could think of— low, evil, and degrading. But after that infamous night when they charged through the MDS, shooting and bayoneting the medical doctors and orderlies, bayoneting the helpless stretcher-bound wounded, killing the walking wounded, and destroying the medical equipment, their reputation took on a new low—bestial, inhuman, vermin to add to their already tarnished status.

"I, with the rest of my crew, were on duty on the northern defense line. We could hear the results of the 'brave Jap action' but were unable to give any help as we couldn't tell friend from foe in the darkness. As word spread through the Fourteenth Army about these atrocities, an intense hatred of the vile Japs was instilled into the hearts of all British and Indian troops and the hated Japs could never expect any mercy or compassion from the Fourteenth Army combat troops.

"That incident was the only time I'm aware of that the Japs broke through our defenses in strength. They tried often enough. At night we often could hear them in the distance, boosting up their morale, prior to an attack, by blowing bugles and repeatedly shouting *'banzai!'* Then we would be put on full alert. Anybody on a sleep period would be turned out to man the guns in the tank and weapons trench. Sometimes the Japs would come at us in a full frontal attack, but were never any match against the firepower massed against them. Sometimes they could try and get through with small patrols but they never succeeded in getting past the tanks. Or they used 'jitter tactics' by getting a small patrol close to our night positions and moaning and groaning, and calling out in English that they were wounded Indian soldiers needing assistance, or they would set off fireworks, hoping that you would react by firing your weapons. This would pinpoint your position for the benefit of waiting mortar crews, ready to send you a 'present.'"

The British command organized a joint attack by 5th Division at the western end of Okydoke and the 7th Division soldiers pinned down around the opposite terminus. The 25th Dragoon tanks led the 7th Division effort, entering the pass first. McKnight recalled good progress at the start, advancing through a teak forest with little opposition other than snipers. But as they started to climb the switchbacks of the mountains the Japanese resistance stiffened. "They were concentrated in force," said McKnight, "with well-placed bunkers and trenches. Having the advantage of height, they managed to stop our advance. The tanks went into action, destroying the Jap defenses and inflicting casualties. Our poor infantry were also taking many casualties from the murderous firepower, and the decision was made to abandon the attempt and withdraw to the relative safety of the Admin Box. The British casualties were collected and placed on the rear top decks of the tanks. We started to battle our way back. I felt for the wounded who were lashed onto the back of our tank. It must have been a rough and agonizing journey for them and dangerous, too, because of the hostile fire directed against the tanks.

"We managed to extricate ourselves without many more casualties until we got to the teak forest at the Admin Box end of the pass. A Jap force had got in behind us and felled a number of teak trees across the track, choosing spots where we would be confined to the track. This situation brought the withdrawal to a halt. Our whole force now [came] under concentrated machine-gun and mortar attack from well-concealed spots who had chosen the ideal spot to set up their ambush. The trees across the track had to be smashed up by tank gunners shooting H.E. shells to blast a path through the obstructions. Some of the tanks concentrated their firepower to silence the Japanese attackers whilst the destruction of the barriers was carried out. Some of the felled trees had to be towed or bulldozed to clear the way. Eventually we managed to fight our way back to the Box."

A subsequent series of efforts to break out resulted in some gains. When another outfit, the 26th Indian Division, began to make inroads into the Japanese positions from the south and east, a tank force that included McKnight set out to make contact. To reach the rendezvous point, the General Lees would run a gauntlet past a heavily defended antitank position that lay just beyond a sharp bend in the trail listed as Tottenham Corner.

"My tank," said McKnight, "was the last one in the column, thus becoming 'Tail End Charlie,' usually the most dangerous and vulnerable position. We had about one-quarter mile of track to travel to reach Tottenham Corner. This gave the drivers a chance to get a good lick of speed up before negotiating the corner. As I neared the corner, Sergeant Branson was in conversation with me over the intercom, reminding me of the perils that awaited us on rounding the bend. I was assuring him on my reply that I was doing my utmost to ensure that our tank would be going into the bend 'very fast' and would be at maximum speed at the far end. On rounding the bend and on the straight part of the track, we were met by a hail of small-arms fire and a very loud clang. Sergeant Branson came over the intercom asking, 'What was that?' I replied that it sounded like an antitank gun had hit us.

"A few seconds later, there was another loud clang. I noticed debris flying across my line of vision through my periscope. Immediately the 37-millimeter gun fired off one round. I thought Mike McDonald is quick off the mark. I was trying to figure out what the debris was when suddenly my earphones seemed to leap from my head, when Arthur Beers, the loader, yelled into his microphone as loud as he could, 'Branson is dead! He has been killed outright.' With my ears still ringing from that explosive message and concentrating very hard on driving the tank through a very hostile situation, I couldn't quite comprehend what I had just heard. Branson had been speaking to me a few seconds ago and now he was dead.

"The next message I got through my earphones, was 'For heaven's sake, Mac, don't you look round into the turret, or we might all be a goner.' All this time the column was moving along the track at a fair old lick and we had got past the danger area. Then our wireless operator, Ossie Stone, sent a coded radio message to the column leader, informing him what had happened. Ossie had codes for different situations. The one he sent for this was something like 'big nine is x cas,' [meaning] our tank commander has been killed. This message was received by the column leader with disbelief and quite a few signals had to pass back and forth before it was accepted.

"What happened inside the turret was Sergeant Branson was looking through his command periscope and it received a direct hit from a Jap antitank gun. Poor Sergeant Branson received the full force of this shot in his face and head and was killed outright. [He] fell across Mike McDonald as he dropped to the floor of the turret. While driving I was very conscious of the tragedy that had happened and the urge to look round was very strong. I resisted and concentrated hard on the track ahead. Unexpectedly, a hand holding a mug appeared in front of my face, and a voice in my earphones telling me to drink the contents. It was neat rum, which I gulped down greedily. My nervous system was a bit stretched at this time. All the crew had a tot at this moment to help to steady the tension."

Back at the Admin Box, with a new tank commander, McKnight and his associates in the 25th continued missions to harass the enemy at the perimeter, while from the other side, the 5th Division with the reserves of the 25th battered the Japanese. A battery of 5.5-inch howitzers enabled the rescuers to blast through the hills, and the foe retreated southward. There was no time for celebration; the foot soldiers and tankers once again plunged down the eastern side of the Mayu range. Employing the same tactics as those that subdued

Tortoise, the 7th Division advanced through the enemy stronghold of Buthidaung at the eastern end of the railway tunnel leading to Maungdaw.

The 2nd Durham Light Infantry, a battalion that had been among those pulled out of France in June 1940, had been shipped to India in 1942. In CBI the Durham Light Infantry was part of the 6th Brigade of the 2d British Division. After a plan to attack Akyab by sea was aborted, Captain David Rissik and the division's Special Service Company, of which he was second in command, joined an offensive aimed at Donbaik, a few miles short of Foul Point. Rissik remembered, "At five-thirty on the morning of March 18 we were woken by the opening rounds of the guns and mortars, interspersed with the stuttering of the medium machine guns. In the dim half light, the effect was not a little awe-inspiring: for into the mounting cannonade, dominated by the pounding of the field guns and the metallic thumping of the mortars, was interspersed the bursting of the answering Jap shells sending up splashes of dark flames as not a few fell around us. One hundred and twenty-four tons of shells were fired into the chaung area before the infantry were launched against it. During the lull which allowed the companies of the Royal Welch [battalion] to assault, the distant shouts of the troops could be heard as they raced into action.

"In due course that, too, died away and the silence was only broken by sporadic bursts of rifle and machine-gun fire and the pre-arranged concentrations of artillery coming down in accordance with their timed program. Shortly after seven o'clock, Alistair [a fellow officer] rang up the adjutant of the Royal Welch to find out how things were going. 'A bit sticky,' came the reply. At eight o'clock a call came through from brigade ordering us to move up. Everyone had been standing by for this and we were on the move almost at once."

British units—the Royal Scots, the Royal Welch Fusiliers, the Royal Berkshires, the Durham Light Infantry—altogether there were nine brigades engaged—banged against the Japanese in their redoubts. Slim mournfully recounted the inability to budge the enemy. "The final attack took place on the 18th of March. 6 Brigade made a desperate attempt to break through the strengthened Japanese defenses. Advancing again, straight in the open, over the dead of previous assaults, they got among and even on the tops of the bunkers but they could not break in. Like the Punjabis [driven off a month earlier], they were caught by the merciless Japanese counterbarrage and bloodily driven back. It was a magnificent effort, and it was the last. Donbaik remained impregnable and all hope of taking it was abandoned."

Worse yet, the Japanese attacked. They exerted great pressure on the British trying to hold the ground they had gained. Rissik stared at a mound of earth that lay between the opposing forces. "A solitary hillock amid the scene of desolation rose up like a vast dragon's tooth, draped about with the bodies of the fallen, left there to rot within a hundred yards or less of our own men. We could not bring them in; nor could the Japanese. Both sides waited with their fingers on the trigger for the first signs of movement from their opponents. Neither vulture nor jackal would venture near to do their grisly work for fear of the gunfire which continued with monotonous regularity. The air was filled with the revolting stench of death."

Several weeks of deadlock along the front elapsed. The British 6th Brigade, composed of the Durham Lights, the Royal Welch, the Royal Berks, and the Royal Scots, tenuously occupied positions in the vicinity of Donbaik but were compelled to withdraw on the morning of April 15. That same night, said Rissik, "The Japanese struck in an all-out bid to smash the brigade's ability to resist further and if possible to annihilate it altogether. They fell on the Royal Scots in the [Indin] rest camp and joined battle with unabated fury. A ding-dong struggle ensued throughout the night, dying down at intervals, only to be renewed with even greater vigor. The still, moonlit night reechoed with the rattle of small-arms fire, the grunt of bursting mortar bombs and grenades, and with the cries of attacker and attacked. The Japs streamed into the camp shouting in English, 'Royal Scots, don't shoot!' They were received by the full force of a stubborn and bitter resistance.

"Meanwhile, back down the road, brigade headquarters, isolated in a position it could never hold unaided, was set upon by another party of Japanese and overrun. Why it had elected to leave the protection of the Royal Scots defended ring is a mystery never solved. Had it remained it would assuredly have had to partake in the fierce struggle that continued there till dawn. But it would have at least remained an entity and it would, without doubt, have emerged still in control of the battle. Instead, it was surrounded on all sides, outnumbered and overwhelmed, and it consequently dissolved in confusion. The brigadier, Cavendish, was captured and with him his brigade major. [Cavendish was subsequently killed either by the Japanese or British artillery fire.]"

Troops from the Durham Light Infantry and the Royal Welch rushed to reinforce their comrades in the Indin rest camp. Stymied by the Royal Scots' desperate defense, the Japanese, when morning broke, had emerged from the fastness of the bunkers and the jungle and were clearly visible in the surrounding plain. "They were thus a perfect target for our guns," said Rissik, "which together with our mortars, were now directed upon their hiding places. The result was a glorious slaughter of Japanese who ran screaming from their cover only to be shot down in scores by light automatics, rifles, and mortars positioned around them like guns at a rat hunt."

Rissik, however, noted that it would not be correct to claim a victory. The reduction of the Japanese facing the 6th Brigade and others only allowed the British to make their way along the beach for an evacuation, signaling that the first attempt to retrieve the Arakan had failed. The British relinquished first their holdings at Buthidaung and then Maungdaw, retreating to roughly the positions from which they had begun the offensive. Battle casualties amounted to twenty-five hundred, with a higher toll taken by malaria and other diseases. A large amount of equipment was lost and, said Slim, "It was no use disguising the fact that many of the British and Indian units which had fought in Arakan were shaken and depressed."

What made the results most unpalatable was recognition that the heavily outnumbered Japanese—at a three-to-one disadvantage—had been able not only to defend themselves but also to score with counterattacks. Rissik, a junior officer, and Slim, at the top of the pyramid, both attributed the outcome to failures of imagination by the on-scene commanders and the persistent folly of feeding units into the maw piecemeal rather than deploying larger aggregations.

8

Enter the Chindits

Immediately after he had reached New Delhi, Stilwell had begun to plot a return to Burma, opening the route all the way from Rangoon into China. The plan, code-named Anakim, required the combined efforts of U.S., Chinese, and British forces, land, sea, and air. At this point in the war, Anakim proposed far more than it could provide. The Japanese were continuing to expand their holds in the Pacific and on mainland Asia, although they took a crippling body blow in the naval defeat at Midway, and the struggle for Guadalcanal raged on. The British, pinned down in North Africa and far more concerned about Europe, were not inclined to invest heavily in Anakim. The Chinese, cut off from their Lend-Lease except for the paltry air shipments, were in no position to ante up any forces of consequence. The United States, engaged now in North Africa and about to begin the torturous island-to-island campaigns of Douglas MacArthur and Chester Nimitz, lacked the resources for or, for that matter, a focus on Stilwell's area.

At Ramgarh, the program to build effective Chinese infantry divisions proceeded. Haydon Boatner issued instructions for the American liaison officers assigned to train the soldiers and officers. He directed advisers to hew to a delicately prescribed line. While charged with making the organizations battle-effective, they were reminded that they were "the connecting link between this headquarters and the Chinese unit concerned. You have no authority to issue orders direct to Chinese units." The restrictions would frustrate many advisers.

Chinese commanders in India lodged their own complaints. Stilwell queried, "Minister of War informs us that Generals Liao and Sun of New 22d and 38th Divisions report that uniforms issued their units are unsightly due to differences in colors, cut, and quality."

119

Boatner answered, "Uniforms and equipment being issued are best the Chinese army has had for years. In truly Chinese style they are complaining and their complaints approach blackmail now due to present orders for movement. . . . Everyone admits health and appearance of Chinese troops here is well."

When Stilwell queried about a report of the 22d Division not being paid since August Boatner replied, "On October 18, Lo [vice commander at Ramgarh] was notified in writing that 270,000 rupees [are] here and [are] ready to pay personnel of 22d and 38th Divisions for August and September. He refused payment, holding out for 450,000." Boatner then explained how he had doled out money, remarking that the 22d Division claimed allowances for motor and ordnance maintenance and hospital fees even though these services had been provided by others. He closed with the comment "Liao has reputation of being an unusually heavy squeezer."

Chennault Returns to the Battle

Claire Chennault's unit, activated on July 4, 1942, went by the name of the China Air Task Force (CATF). For the remainder of the year he commanded a force that flew P-40s and Mitchell B-25s, twin-engine medium bombers. John Alison, the fighter pilot who had demonstrated the P-40 for Chennault, working with Lend-Lease both in London and the Soviet Union, wangled a posting to China with the 75th Fighter Squadron. He reached Kunming about two weeks before the formation of the CATF.

Chennault sent Alison and the others from the squadron to an air base at Ling-ling. There they coped with a hot and humid summer and a frigid winter with no wool uniforms and such a shortage of sweaters and flight jackets that Alison made communal property of them: "When the mechanics got up before daylight to go down and warm up the airplanes, they had the privilege of wearing the sweaters and the jackets. When the sun came up it would get a little warmer and then they would give the flight jackets back." At the small mess, enlisted men and officers ate together. There was no running water, and everyone relied on outdoor plumbing facilities. There was no flight surgeon available, even when almost the entire contingent fell victim to food poisoning. They had no antiaircraft, only slit trenches in which to cower during air raids.

Alison flew his first missions escorting B-25s hitting Hangchow. Promoted to second in command of Tex Hill's 75th Fighter Squadron, Alison still had not tripped a machine gun at the enemy until one

John Alison, after becoming an ace with the Fourteenth
Air Force in China, became a co-commander of the 1st Air
Commando and flew a glider that brought Chindits into
Burma. (Photograph from U.S. Air Corps)

night. Previously, roused from sleep by an announcement of a night
raid, he had asked Hill, "'Has the AVG ever tried to get any bombers
at night?' He said, 'No, we never have.' I said, 'If they come tomorrow, I'm going to make the effort.'"

When the warning net apprised Ling-ling of incoming bombers,
Alison, with Major Albert "Ajax" Baumler, a veteran of the Loyalist
forces in the 1936–1937 Spanish Civil War, took off and began orbit-
ing the field. Alison, searching the night sky, suddenly spied six blue
spurts of flame, the exhausts from the twin-engine bombers. He
climbed to their altitude of fifteen thousand feet and maneuvered
behind them. Baumler remained out of the picture. Alison said, "As
I began to pull up on them, I called the radio on the ground and
said, 'Okay, watch the fireworks.' I counted my chickens before they

hatched. It was the first time I had ever fired a shot in anger. You have some mixed emotions. There must be fifteen people up there, and I am going to kill all fifteen of them. I remember saying, 'Lord, forgive me for what I am about to do.' I was going so fast I didn't know what I was doing. I went right in with them. Now I was trying to slow the airplane down. I was sideslipping so I wouldn't run into him. Before I could pull the trigger, they shot me down, just like that.

"I was right alongside the right wingman and he put the top turret on me. He [had] these two .30-caliber machine guns and he started right at the nose and went right to the tail of the airplane. Bullets went through the cockpit. I got burned in the left arm. He was shooting tracers. It didn't even break the skin, but I had an enormous blister on my left elbow. I knew the airplane was hit very bad. There was no time to be frightened; there was no time to do anything but react.

"Here the airplane was right ahead of me. I pulled the trigger. I am convinced I killed everybody on board, but surprisingly the airplane didn't catch fire. I think the reason is that I was firing right into the fuselage. I claimed him as a probable. We were fighting over a very broad river and I think the airplane probably fell into the river.

"I kicked right rudder, and I blew up the second wingman. Then I turned on the leader and I blew him up, but they dropped bombs and they hit the airfield, surprisingly. The two of them were falling in flames, the first one I didn't know what happened. I knew I was hurt bad so I started down from fifteen thousand feet. I was essentially right over the airport. I started down just as steep as I could with the throttle back to get the airplane into the airport.

"I had a five-inch hole right through the crankcase of the engine. It was just a little bullet hole where it went in and a five-inch hole on the other side where it came out. I had lost all the oil. The engine kept running. I got down to where I thought, 'Boy, I have got it made.' I had no safety belt in this airplane. They had a shoulder harness and [it] was made out of such stiff material that it absolutely restricted you in the cockpit. I couldn't turn. I just can't stand not to be free in the cockpit and looking in every direction, so I never wore the safety belt. I didn't wear any restraining gear figuring that nobody was ever going to shoot me down.

"I got down to about three thousand feet before the airplane really began to develop symptoms. The engine began to backfire; flames began to spurt out from under the hood. I guess I panicked a little bit because I dove the airplane from three thousand to make a 180-degree and come back. I was going so fast and when I headed back to the airfield, I had misjudged. It was dark and I was apprehensive. I dove the airplane right at the airfield; I was going to skid it in on the belly. The airfield wasn't five thousand feet long. The surface was clay, but I figured if I just got the thing on the ground and let it skid to a halt, I would be all right. But I was going so fast that this was impossible. I realized I wasn't going to be able to do that. I pulled up the nose and I opened the throttle, and the engine still ran. By this time, flames were now coming out of the cowling. The engine was still running, but I was headed right toward the river, and I must have had 120 knots even then. I was getting a little bit of power, just enough to drag me to the river.

"There was a railroad trestle I had to clear. There was no opportunity to maneuver the airplane. I was very fortunate that I missed the airport. All I had to do was go straight. I breathed a sigh of relief when I cleared that trestle and got over the top. I sat it down in the river. Knowing that I was going to put my face into the gunsight, I braced—I had the throttle cut and I had my left hand up on the cowling braced as best I could. I had my right hand on the stick. When the airplane hit the water, it was very rapid deceleration. I had the canopy open. We didn't wear helmets and goggles. My earphones had just been blown off my head and out of the airplane.

"I hit the water, and the canopy crashed shut. Bang! The airplane came to rest with the canopy out of the water, and I just rolled it back—it still worked—undid my parachute and stepped out on the wing, and the airplane sank. Water immediately put out the fire. I swam over to a log raft [from] a lumbering operation. I looked and there was a Chinese man running out across the logs. He reached down and got my hand and pulled me up. I had put my face into the gunsight, but fortunately it didn't knock me out. I had a bad cut on my forehead."

His rescuer helped Alison reach the shore, where a trio of Chinese soldiers trained their weapons on him. "I had my little flag out, and in my best Mandarin I was saying, 'I am an American fighter pilot.'" He was quickly accepted and taken to the home of an American missionary, who stitched up his wounds. Alison trudged back to the air base and surprised Hill and the others, who believed he had died crashing into the ground.

When the CATF was created, Colonel Merian C. Cooper, a veteran of the Polish-Russian War and World War I, had become the chief of staff. He noted that during the summer of 1942, when the majority of the AVG pilots refused to sign up and headed home, "We were really scraping the bottom of the bin for airplanes and pilots and ground crews. We fought with as little as five planes against fifty-three."

With his limited resources, Chennault nevertheless stung the enemy. Periodically, he dispatched his small fleet of B-25s with P-40 escorts against targets, particularly shipping in harbors. Cooper said, "We lost only one bomber plane; that was due to an accident which I considered unavoidable. We were forced to use Russian fuel, and five out of our twelve fighter escorts were forced down or had to return to their base. The rest of [the planes] functioned at very low power." Despite the handicap, Cooper said the Americans shot down eighteen enemy fighters "in addition to pasting hell out of Kowloon Peninsula and sinking two ships."

The CATF relied on surprise and deception to give its raiders an edge. Cooper cited attacks against Haiphong, the port occupied by the Japanese in northeastern Indochina (Vietnam). The predictable mission would send planes directly from Kunming. But instead, in one series of strikes, the raiders traveled from Kunming to Kweilin, a base north of Haiphong, paused to refuel, and immediately headed for the seaport. Said Cooper, "We knew they would get reports of planes coming over the direct Kunming–Haiphong line, and erroneously presume they were coming from the west. We immediately made a series of rapid raids—and then moved up to Hengyang and attacked the Japanese invasion route into Changshe [northeast of Kweilin]."

On another occasion, in preparation for hitting Canton, the pilots at Kweilin were kept ignorant of the plans. Cooper, with Chennault's blessing, suggested to half a dozen fliers that they visit the local Chinese restaurants and "talk pretty loud about the forthcoming raid on Hong Kong the next day. It takes about four hours for us to get accurate information from Canton to Kweilin [from agents], and we figured the Japs were as good as we were. We were pretty confident that we had prepared the Japs to believe we actually were going to attack Hong Kong. Believing [this], the Japs would figure when to get off the ground to intercept us. Instead of going [straight] in, we made a point to the north, then turned and drove straight in on Canton.

"It worked out exactly as the general had planned. There were approximately seventy Japanese aircraft fighters sent up, and we caught them all coming up. It was a field day. Johnny Alison was over the target forty-five minutes after we cleared out, carrying hundred-gallon belly tanks in order to remain out of the original fight, to report results. We had a minimum score of twenty-three or twenty-four victories and a maximum of twenty-seven. Our boys claimed about six more probables. In addition, he reported that both the vessels we hit in the river from fourteen thousand to sixteen thousand feet altitude—a ship of about six thousand tons and another of seven thousand tons—were on fire and sinking. He also reported that the docks off Canton were on fire. We then sent fighters down to strafe the airports. They cleaned up whatever was left at the airports."

Chennault was hardly satisfied with these achievements, mosquito bites to the elephantine Japanese presence in Burma, China, and Southeast Asia. While attempting to build effective ground forces, Stilwell also wrestled with the proposals of Chennault, who poured his ideas into the receptive ears of the Chiangs. Chennault argued that if he were given sufficient strength in bombers and fighters the Japanese could be defeated without recourse to a slow, more earthly approach, costly in manpower and war materials. Chennault's proposals appealed to the generalissimo because they would reduce China's investment of people and assets and allow him to husband his strength for an eventual confrontation with the Communists. Chennault also propagandized Washington through his staff member Captain Joseph Alsop, a reporter captured in Hong Kong and then repatriated. Still cloaked in the aura of an independent journalist, Alsop touted the gospel preached by Chennault.

U.S. Army chief of staff George Marshall, prodded by President Roosevelt, who saw an aerial campaign as a way to wage the CBI war on the cheap, dispatched his air corps chief, Lieutenant General Henry "Hap" Arnold, on a mission to determine the feasability of Chennault's notions. On his visit, Arnold, while a strong adherent of strategic bombing as the key to winning a war, recognized that in the Far East there was no way that could quickly become a reality. Neither Chennault nor Chiang appreciated the magnitude of the logistical obstacles. Few adequate airfields existed, and the heavy equipment required to construct them was scarce. While the number of combat aircraft could certainly be increased, the wherewithal for operating them simply could not be supplied, even with a massive increase in tonnage flown over the Hump.

Birth of the Special Forces

While Stilwell, Slim, and their forces had straggled to escape Burma during the spring of 1942, Wavell's recruit from the Middle East, Orde Wingate, had first set up shop in Delhi before moving to a camp some 250 miles southeast of that city. Born in India, son of a British army colonel and his wife, both religious fundamentalists, Wingate attended one of the "public" (private in American terms) schools of England, designed to churn out candidates for the military and colonial government posts. A voracious reader as a schoolboy and then at the Royal Military Academy at Woolwich, he displayed a studied disrespect for the rules and disregard, even contempt, for his associates.

Brigadier Orde Wingate created his legions of behind-the-lines fighters known as "Chindits" and preached his gospel of long-range penetration with the fervor of an Old Testament prophet. (Photograph from Imperial War Museum)

Assigned to the Middle East, Wingate commanded a company of some 275 native troops in the Sudan. He ruled the soldiers as if he were a fierce but benevolent potentate. He acted as counselor in the turbulent lives of the men, whose wives, concubines, and children lived in close proximity. He unhesitatingly applied a whip, a kick, or a punch when a soldier failed to follow his rules, or worse, showed insubordination. His contemporaries were distracted by his left-wing politics, his often scruffy appearance, and even more, by his strange habit of lounging about his quarters entirely naked.

In the British-controlled territory of Palestine in 1936, Arab residents of the area grew very unhappy with both the British rule and the increasing numbers of Jews immigrating. Nazi Germany's oppression of Jews had begun to produce refugees sneaking into the ancient Hebrew land. By terms of the 1917 Balfour Declaration, the governors of the land were supposed to use their best efforts to establish a homeland for the Jewish people.

When the Arabs revolted, concentrating much of their violence upon the Jews, but also targeting the colonial establishment, Wingate, unlike many of his countrymen, eschewed the usual anti-Semitism to actively side with the Zionists. He not only slipped representatives copies of intelligence reports but also started to participate and lead patrols of the Haganah, an armed Jewish defense force, against Arab attackers. Soon Wingate began organizing what were called special night squads for a kind of guerrilla warfare. The officer in command of the British in Palestine happened to be Archibald Wavell, who took notice of the unorthodox but effective actions of Wingate.

Wavell recalled, "I first met Wingate when I took over command in Palestine in 1937 and found him on my intelligence staff. I inquired about him and was told he was rather an oddity, clever but eccentric. He . . . knew Arabic well, but since coming to Palestine had developed pronounced Zionist tendencies and was now learning Yiddish or Hebrew. When I met him I realized that there was a remarkable personality behind those piercing eyes and rather abrupt manner. He was obviously no respecter of persons because of their rank."

The British intelligence service expected Wingate to lead a campaign of assassination and sabotage. But he thought in different terms: regular warfare conducted by units well behind the front lines. "Long-range penetration" (LRP) is how he labeled his operations in Libya and Ethiopia. His organization now went by the name of Gideon Forces, a tribute to one of Wingate's Old Testament heroes, and played an important role in driving Mussolini's army out of Ethiopia.

It was during the early days of World War II that Slim also became acquainted with Wingate. "I had first met [him] in East Africa, when we were both fighting the Italians, he with his Abyssinian partisans, whom in those days we impolitely called *shiftas* or brigands, and I with my more orthodox Indian Infantry Brigade. I had already in 1941 and 1942 had several lively discussions with him on the organization and practice of guerrilla warfare. With many of his ideas I was in agreement, but I had doubted if methods based on his Abyssinian experience would succeed equally well against a tougher enemy and in country not so actively friendly. Wingate was a strange, excitable, moody creature, but he had fire in him. He could ignite other men. When he so fiercely advocated some project of his own, you might catch his enthusiasm or you might see palpable flaws in his arguments; you might be angry at his arrogance or outraged at so obvious a belief in the end, his end, justifying any means; but you could not be indifferent. You could not fail to be stimulated either to thought, protest, or action by his somber vehemence and his unrelenting persistence."

Captain Norman Durant, who would command a machine-gun platoon in Burma for Wingate, said, "He was the worst-dressed officer I have ever seen. The most remarkable things about him were his eyes and his voice, both of which were sharp as steel and with both of which he seemed to stab anyone to whom he was talking. He was a man in whose presence anyone from Lt. General to Pte. felt uncomfortable and aware of his [own] faults and shortcomings. He spared no one in his criticisms and never used soft words to the victims, he had absolute mental and moral courage allied with a complete lack of pity, so that he said what he liked, to whom he liked, and where he liked."

During a long conference in which Wingate lectured his subordinates, Durant noted, "I never heard Wingate use the expressions 'it seems to me,' 'it is probably true,' 'in my opinion.' With him it was always, 'the Japs' reaction will be,' 'the result of this will be,' 'such and such cannot happen,' always with complete confidence in his predictions and reasoning. There was something awe-inspiring in his certainty and his dogmatism, yet something which inspired the fullest confidence, so that one went away saying, 'with him in command we cannot fail.' "

By the time he had come to CBI, Wingate's unique persona had obviously burst into full bloom. Around Wavell's headquarters he was sometimes referred to as Tarzan. Proper officers and old-line non-coms were put off by his dismissal of such niceties as shaving while on active service. To Wingate the grooming wasted ten minutes of a man's time. On occasion, he reverted to his unique style of uniform in tropical climes. Major George Bromhead, another acquaintance of Wingate dating back to the Palestine rebellion and assigned as major to the 77th Indian Brigade, recalled a day during jungle training: "An early monsoon was chumming on my office tent and the flies [entrance flaps] were sagging. Approaching through the mud came a pair of bare feet. As they came nearer, a pair of naked knees appeared, and then some more naked body and finally Wingate crunched under the tent flies wearing his Wolseley helmet and nothing else."

When official correspondence arrived, he told Bromhead to leave it in a pending tray, because most answered itself. "If it's really important, a reminder would follow." Mercurial and impulsive, Wingate bedeviled his staff with flights of ideas. While in England he had seen a collar stud that contained a magnetic compass. It was designed for espionage agents on the European continent, but he requisitioned three thousand of them for his people. When someone inquired who engaged in jungle warfare wore collar studs, Wingate answered he was aware of that but would have the devices converted in India to buttons on the trouser flies. Instead of a wristwatch, he depended on a portable alarm clock that he carried on his person.

Along with his singular behavior he continued to propound his theory of long-range penetration, which rather than in standard guerrilla form, employed small bands of men in hit-and-run raids or sabotage, relied on company- or even battalion-size forces to engage the enemy. Said Wingate, "In the back areas are [the enemy's] unprotected kidneys, his midriff, his throat, and other vulnerable points . . . the more vital and tender points of the enemy's anatomy. . . . [The] enemy would have to withdraw troops from the front in order to protect them."

Burma, however, was a far different topographical and tactical kettle of fish than the plains and deserts of the Middle East and East Africa, where the fight was against poorly motivated Italian soldiers. Wavell himself knew little about guerrilla activities and gave Wingate a vague charter to run all operations. During his first months in Burma and India, Wingate carefully studied the terrain, the resources, and the disposition of the enemy forces.

One of his chief deputies was royal engineers major Michael Calvert. A career soldier, Calvert, a former army welterweight boxing champion, fought in Norway during the spring of 1940 as part of an expeditionary force against the invading Nazi army. When the Allied troops were forced to flee, demolition expert Calvert blew up bridges and tunnels to block the pursuit. Posted to India, he had instructed at the Bush Warfare School at Maymo, Burma, where the purpose was not to teach jungle warfare but to organize guerrilla operations behind Japanese lines. He had already personally led parties deep in Burma, blasting railroad stock, bridges, and oil wells. When Calvert finally emerged from Burma, sick and half starved, he had to be hospitalized. Nevertheless, Wingate signed him up to report after his recovery. Behind Calvert's back, the troops referred to him as "Mad Mike."

Major Bernard Fergusson, from the Scottish Black Watch, a well-educated aristocrat who wrote poetry and contributed to *Punch* and other publications, had been blooded at Tobruk. Supposedly leaning toward a career as a missionary in the Far East after the war, he had preached in large churches, including St. Andrew's at Bangalore. Fergusson knew Wingate from his days in Palestine. While posted to Wavell's staff, Fergusson listened anew to Wingate and, as he wrote in his memoir *Beyond the Chindwin,* concluded, "Only in one direction did there seem any prospect of action in the near future. It lay in the person of a broad-shouldered, uncouth, almost simian officer who used to drift gloomily into the office for two or three days at a time, audibly dream dreams, and drift out again." Fergusson remained committed even after a major, departing from the training site, told him, "Wingate is crackers."

In August 1942, when Calvert returned to duty, Wingate, promoted to the rank of brigadier, commanded the 77th Indian Brigade. It was a misnomer aimed at hiding the nature of Wingate's charter. It contained no Indians. Instead, the complement included a battalion of young Gurkhas, enlisted from their homeland, Nepal; a battalion of the Burma Rifles that mixed Karen, Kachin, and Chin people; and some eight hundred Britons from the 13th Battalion, King's Regiment—Liverpudlians, Glaswegians, and Manchesterites—with an average age of thirty-three.

The 13th, originally ticketed for internal security in the British Isles during the 1940–1941 invasion scare, had been shipped east to handle civil disturbances in India. They were hardly ideal for Wingate's purposes, but manpower was so scarce that he took them on, hoping to transform a fair share of them into his kind of warriors. A scattering of Royal Air Force officers and noncoms also joined Wingate's forces. The script called for them to coordinate by radio the necessary air drops. Everyone would also learn to use mules that would bear heavy equipment, including the vital radios. About a hundred commando types from the cadre at the Bush Warfare School brought demolition skills and a reputation for brawling and drinking, vices that the puritanical Wingate deplored.

In official circles, the unit created by Wingate was known as Special Forces. The Burrifs—Burma Rifles—gave what the British soldiers called "Wingate's Circus" its more popular name. In Burmese culture, a mythical half-lion, half-dragon stone carving known as a *chinthe* guarded temples, and corruption of the word evolved into Chindits. It first saw print in an interview Wingate gave to a reporter shortly before the brigade went to war.

The organization underwent a brutal training period, with prolonged marches in sweltering heat and mock battles. They learned to leave established trails that could harbor ambushes and to hack their way through dense undergrowth. Philip Stibbé, a young lieutenant from the 13th King's, in a memoir, *Return via Rangoon,* reported "a constant stream of orders, pamphlets, information and invective showered down on us from Brigade HQ. . . . Saluting was to be cut down to a minimum. Everything was to be done at the double. Everyone must eat at least one raw onion per day. Only shorts should be worn when it was raining. Swearing must stop."

Wingate's ukases demanded that the Chindits ignore thorn bushes and plunge ahead, deterred only by thick stands of bamboo. He decried smoking and protested the issuance of cigarettes in rations, arguing that they induced coughing (noise that might alert the enemy in the jungle) and that the inability to supply them in the bush would affect those with an addictive habit. His biographers John Bierman and Colin Smith, in *Fire in the Night,* wrote that while he binged on whiskey, he preferred fresh buffalo milk, supplied by a quartet of the beasts milked by the veterinary officer. He showed little patience for anyone who claimed illness. He decreed that platoon commanders would first examine any individual who said he was ill. They, not physicians, tested temperatures and issued medicines such as aspirin.

Along with his extraordinary faith in the onion, Wingate fed the troops a diet based on cheese, dates, and a hard biscuit. These were ordinarily the three-day rations issued to paratroopers for their limited engagements, but Wingate expected his soldiers to live on these for extended periods. He inspired them to forage until they could subsist on the fauna about them—frogs, reptiles, and small birds. Inevitably, the regimen proved too much for many, the older, softer men unaccustomed to the food and highly vulnerable to malaria and dysentery. About two hundred of them—a quarter of their original strength—had to be replaced with younger or more fit men drafted from other units.

Those who survived the training ordeal developed a sense of self-esteem. According to *Fire in the Night,* Wingate converted the likes of Private Charles Aves, a draftee who as a civilian had been an enthusiast of those who chanted "Peace at any fucking price." Aves, in an audiotape on file at London's Imperial War Museum, said, "He realigned our perception of what was possible for ordinary people like ourselves. . . . We were just amazed. We were in awe of him. . . . Those of us who did not malinger and drop out we called Pukka Kings . . . those who did malinger and drop out we called Jossers [Liverpudlian slang for masturbators]."

The 77th Brigade's esprit benefited from the self-selection among officers, many university-educated, who added an intellectual quality to their eagerness to fight. Some gathered at night around the bivouac campfires to drink and debate books and politics. As 1943 neared, enlisted men caroused in their own fashion, swilling gin and beer, patronizing brothels, or engaging in more innocent pleasures, such as choir singing. Wingate had arranged for Australian-style "digger" hats as standard issue. With the left brim clipped up, "Wingate's Circus" flashed a distinctive panache.

As part of the strategy that began with the campaign in the Arakan, Wavell had plotted the insertion of Wingate and his troops into central Burma. The defeat in the Arakan, the delay because of logistical problems of a drive by Stilwell from China, and a proposed Indian army offensive from Imphal caused Wavell to waver on Wingate's operations. Absent the pressure from a three-pronged attack, the Japanese could concentrate on the Chindits, whose leader forcefully argued that having brought his people to their peak, it would be a mistake not to ascertain the value of long-range penetration.

Operation Longcloth, the title for the expedition created by the command in New Delhi, dispatched twenty-two hundred soldiers and nearly a thousand animals over the Chindwin. While the Japanese held the east bank and the British the west, neither side fielded enough troops to entirely man the long, sinuous river. The first objective for the Chindits was a north-to-south rail line used by the enemy to supply and reinforce their comrades in China. No one expected the 77th Brigade to seize control of the tracks; the cancellation of any incursion by Stilwell-led forces denied the capacity to actually occupy territory behind the Japanese front lines. However, demolition of the railway might force the Japanese to devote resources to protecting it and signal the ability of the British Empire to mount an offensive after enduring a series of beatings.

In mid-February the Chindits began crossing the Chindwin at two places, some thirty-five miles apart. They used inflatable dinghies, rafts hacked out of the bamboo, and vegetation and ropes. With coaxing, cursing, and whacks at appropriate moments, the mules, horses, and several elephants swam the river. Wingate had concocted an elaborate scheme to deceive the Japanese. The RAF dumped materials at a location on the east bank well away from the actual crossings. Major John Jeffries, a commando demolitions specialist disguised as a general, and his "staff" visited a riverbank village with a headman known to be pro-Japanese. Jeffries pretended to order vast amounts of food for the soldiers who would soon arrive. He spread out maps that purported to show the route of his forces, and he shouted bogus orders that named places the troops would attack. At the end of his charade, Jeffries and his companions marched off, and when out of sight changed their direction to meet elements of the brigade.

When the last of the contingent had splashed across the Chindwin on February 16, Wingate typically distributed a bombastic order of the day: "Today, we stand on the threshold of battle. The time for preparation is over, and we are moving on the enemy to prove ourselves and our methods. At this moment we stand besides the soldiers of the United Nations in the front-line trenches throughout the world. . . . Our aim is to make possible a government of the world in which all men can live at peace and with equal opportunity of service." In his role as an Old Testament warrior he wound up, "Finally knowing the vanity of man's effort and the confusion of his purpose, let us pray that God may accept our service and direct our endeavors."

To escape the eyes of the Japanese, initially the columns avoided trails, chopping their own paths through the undergrowth. Although the training stressed precautions against any evidence of their presence, the troops on this first combat experience deposited a trail of cigarette butts, paper, and cardboard. Wingate angrily scolded his officers for the discipline failings. The occasional brays from mules and whinnies of horses also discomfited the Chindits, but some animals could not be dissuaded from sounding off even if that brought a swift blow to the nose.

By the beginning of March, the Chindits had begun to surprise Japanese units with sudden assaults before melting back into the brush. The attacks mimicked standard guerrilla maneuvers, except they involved larger and more heavily armed troops. The six columns traveled forty to sixty miles beyond the Chindwin. To hide his real objective, Wingate sent several columns on pseudomissions, hitting sites well away from the railway. Meanwhile, Bernard Fergusson, with Five Column, approached a key site, the Bon Chaung railway gorge. Fergusson, who had been dropped a replacement monocle by the RAF after he lost his eyepiece, expected to demolish some of the gorge bridges and then blast the sides of the canyon to create an avalanche of rock covering the route. From another angle, One Column headed for a different sector of the railroad tracks, while considerably farther east, Three Column, led by Michael Calvert, the former Bush Warfare School instructor, marched on the railhead at Nankan.

Major George Bromhead, in command of Four Column, ran afoul of a Japanese ambush. When Bromhead learned that his radio had been destroyed and he could no longer relay the vital information for resupply of food and ammunition, he ordered a retreat. Half of his people headed for India, while others trekked almost a thousand miles to China. Two Column also stumbled into an ambush. Half of the men retreated to India, while the remainder managed to locate and join One Column.

Fergusson's Five Column and Calvert's Three Column struck on the same day. The latter, augmented by two platoons who strayed from Seven Column, blasted a pair of bridges around Nankan and blew up portions of track in seventy different places. In his memoir *Fighting Mad,* Calvert recalled, "We ran into some resistance but I had placed ambush and covering parties and booby traps all around us and the Japs had an unpleasant day. We did not lose a single man though many a Jap did not live to see another dawn. At one stage a group of the enemy really got the jitters and decided to chance their all in a charge. They came at us, yelling their heads off, but . . . they chose a spot which meant crossing open country with no cover. Every one of them died." A fortuitous mortar shot dropped plumb on a truckload of reinforcements. With the Japanese vanishing from the scene, Calvert and his associates set booby traps around the Nankan depot and then retired for the traditional tea break.

Fergusson encountered much stiffer opposition. He tumbled the bridge in the Bon Chaung gorge, and his dynamite charges blanketed the rail line with thousands of tons of rock. But Japanese troops had killed four and wounded another five. None of those injured could travel on their own for any distance. When the foe retreated and the demolitions had been completed, Fergusson was forced to leave the wounded with the headman of a village. He was well aware that once his troops departed, the local people would turn the British soldiers over to the returning Japanese. Only one of those left behind survived a nightmare of savage abuse during captivity. And although Calvert's Three Column had taken no casualties at Nankan, subsequent confrontations with the Japanese resulted in a similar situation for six of his men. They, too, were unable to hike back to India.

The grim fate of comrades abandoned to the less than tender mercies of the enemy depressed morale. But for the frustrated Wingate and the other Chindits, there was no means to extract wounded or desperately ill men.

Although the Chinese could not bolster his long-range penetration, Wingate decided to continue on, crossing the Irrawaddy rather than confine his legions to attacks against the more sparsely deployed Japanese in the northern hills, populated by Kachins hostile to the Nipponese.

Getting over the broad, fast-flowing Irrawaddy proved fairly easy at first as the Chindits persuaded many boatmen to ferry Fergusson's Five Column to the eastern banks without encountering opposition. But two days later, a firefight enveloped Three Column, led by Calvert. Fortuitously, however, their crossing had emptied their bivouac area, which was raided by Japanese planes. Wingate himself brought another thousand men with mules across the Irrawaddy almost a week later without any interference from the enemy.

The 77th Brigade had indeed engineered a long-range penetration in force, but at what was beginning to emerge as a high cost. Wingate's next objective, a bridge, lay more than a hundred miles off, over mountains. The Chindits were already in poor condition, not so much from action with the Japanese as from their long march and the shortage of rations. Bierman and Smith reported that when a message from Wingate advised that a long-awaited supply drop had been postponed, Fergusson responded with a quote from Psalm 22: "I can count all my bones; they stare and gloat over me." Wingate answered in kind with his own biblical reference, the Gospel of St. John: "Con-

sider that it is expedient that one man should die for the people."
Fergusson was, however, not ready to emulate Jesus Christ.

The deterioration of conditions led to near extreme measures.
Wingate had hoped to isolate Baw, a village targeted for a large air
drop. But a blunder by a young officer denied the Chindits the advantage of surprise when he brought a small number of soldiers into Baw
before the main body was in place. The drop zone became a contested area. Without a court-martial or any lawful military procedure,
Wingate summarily stripped the culprit of his rank. Worse punishment was meted out to two other members of the 77th. A British soldier and a Gurkha were discovered sleeping while assigned sentry
duty. Fergusson offered the offending Briton the choice of walking
back to the Chindwin on his own or the lash. He chose the latter, and
apparently accepted his punishment as just. The British officer in
command of the Gurkha, Lieutenant Dominic Neill, in a memoir at
the Imperial War Museum, said he arranged for that soldier's whip-
ping not to break the man's skin; otherwise he would have been
unable to carry his pack. "He was beaten so as to shame him . . . no
harm was done except to his morale and everything was forgotten.
He forgave us and we forgave him."

The Japanese, now fully aware of a substantial armed force within
their precincts, started to concentrate on the Chindits. An RAF strike
called in by Fergusson's column inflicted considerable damage on a
Japanese unit, and an ambush designed by Calvert wiped out as many
as a hundred of the enemy while losing only one of the Gurkhas. But
the Japanese continued to apply pressure; every battle weakened the
columns, now desperately in need of resupply. Rising temperatures
and an acute water shortage threatened further operations. When the
RAF radioed that it believed further drops too dangerous, Wingate
had no choice but to head back to India.

Fearful of strong Japanese retaliation, Wingate tried to conceal the
withdrawal and his routes. He resorted again to the Bible, directing
one group, "Remember Lot's wife. Return not whence thou came.
Seek thy salvation in the mountains lest ye be consumed." He created
another diversion, sending a message to Calvert to advance east, as if
the brigade intended to penetrate even farther.

Tricks aside, the bulk of the force hurried toward the first barrier,
the Irrawaddy. A drop by the RAF furnished supplies, but the Japanese were close on their traces. The mules and horses, so useful for
the penetration, now loomed as handicaps. All along, the small number that went lame or for some other reason could not work were
slaughtered. Facing a river crossing with the foe in deadly pursuit, the
Chindits could not afford the time-gobbling luxury of coaxing their
pack animals to swim. Wingate ordered all except those necessary to

haul radios and weapons killed. Releasing large numbers to roam free might tip off the Japanese of a hasty retreat and provide clues of their whereabouts.

Months of close association had bonded many soldiers and muleteers with the beasts. It had been difficult enough to dispose of them with a bullet in the head, but Wingate decreed that revolvers made too much noise. The murderers must slit the throats. Some units refused to carry out the orders and just let the animals go.

In any event, the Burrifs, acting as a rear guard, came under fire. Fergusson and his column, having set up an ambush, soon engaged in a frenetic night firefight. In his subsequent confidential report to Wingate, he reported that three cowardly British soldiers with the mules and bearing Bren guns ignored orders to bring them into play. The battle wounded and killed a number of Chindits, including Fergusson, hit in his hip by grenade fragments.

Meanwhile, Wingate had marched some seven hundred men at a punishing pace for two days, covering fifty miles of thick jungle before reaching the east bank of the Irrawaddy. Silver rupees bought cooperation from local villagers, who paddled canoes towing men in RAF life rafts. As the bridgehead party approached the west bank, pursuing Japanese lobbed mortars into the river and spattered the water with machine-gun and rifle bullets. Private Aves recalled, "One of the boats behind me was hit by a mortar and I suppose everybody was blown up or drowned."

The locals who manned the boats fled, leaving Wingate with few canoes to perform the ninety-minute round trip required. He quickly calculated that at best, ferrying his troops would require close to three days. With the Burma Rifles and Fergusson's column coming on, the Chindits would be bogged down at this site on the Irrawaddy too long, exposing them to the full brunt of the Japanese. Although at the moment the enemy guns had been silenced by the Chindit forces, the Japanese would certainly be rushing massive reinforcements to the choke point.

Wingate said, "Caught strung out on the banks we could easily be pinned down while [the enemy] brought up the superior forces at his disposal. Finally looking around, I saw most of the men asleep and exhausted. I therefore decided to abandon the crossing." The decision meant breaking the brigade into small pieces who would have to flee to safety on their own. Lest there be any confusion, Wingate shouted, "Disperse, disperse, get back to India!"

Lieutenant Dominic Neill, hearing him, said, "I thought the man had gone stark staring mad. . . . He had taken us so far but he wasn't going to take us back. Here we were a force of seven hundred strong [actually more] with a platoon already across the river and he wasn't prepared to cross." Neill accepted that getting over the Irrawaddy would mean casualties, but he believed there would be far fewer than if the Chindits broke up and scurried for India on their own.

While Neill questioned Wingate's wisdom, Bierman and Smith argued that the 77th's training prepared them for dispersal with an eventual reunion. Certainly, other specialized forces, such as paratroopers, expected that they would be in small, isolated packs behind enemy lines after they landed, and they were schooled to fight and maintain themselves until the opportunity came to join in larger groups. Having squelched the original Japanese attackers, the Chindits at the Irrawaddy brewed tea before beginning their separate odysseys. The columns commanded by Fergusson and Calvert also split their men into groups as small as forty.

Wingate personally led a party of more than forty from his brigade headquarters, and once finding an apparently secure bivouac area, remained on the east side of the river for about a week. A parachute drop floated down some supplies, including books, such as a new biography of playwright George Bernard Shaw, Mark Twain's *Innocents Abroad,* and Plato's *Dialogues.* The literature provided fodder for Wingate to lead intellectual discussions that ranged not only through the books but also on music, art, detective fiction, and even the Popeye comic strip character of Wimpy.

A two-day march evaded Japanese patrols and brought Wingate's batch to a site on the Irrawaddy where a single boatman, on six trips, carried the entire group to the west bank. From there they tramped another five days through jungle, forded waist-deep chaungs, and scratched at the relentless lice and mosquitoes. Daily dosages of atabrine warded off the severest symptoms of malaria, but diarrhea and dysentery took their toll, forcing them to leave behind five men. Fifteen-foot-high, razorlike elephant grass barred the last dash to the Chindwin, but Wingate, up front, led half a dozen of his people to the river. Using a life jacket, bamboo stalks for buoyancy, and swimming, the party made its way over the Chindwin and met a Gurkha unit five miles beyond. The remainder of the headquarters group followed the next night, preserved when the Gurkhas stifled a Japanese attack with mortars and machine guns.

Three other bands had struggled back before Wingate and others trickled in after them. Some lost significant numbers of their flock; about forty men refused to continue when they reached the Shweli River after they saw companions drown in the swift-moving stream. The Burma Rifles happened upon a pair of British soldiers tied to trees, shot, or mutilated with bayonets. Private Aves, hospitalized in

India for malaria, complained to Wingate about being abandoned. Aves said Wingate counseled, "We won't wash our dirty linen in public, will we."

The commander of the Chindits was deeply depressed by the experience of the first long-range penetration into Burma. Of the some 3,000 who infiltrated into the country, 2,182 returned to India, a staggering loss of 27 percent of the complement. Worst hit was the 13th Kings, the Liverpudlians, due perhaps to their relatively advanced age and bad luck. Almost half of their 721-man contingent did not return.

Nor could the Chindits afford to brag about their achievements against the enemy. "As a military operation," commented Slim, "the raid had been an expensive failure. It gave little tangible return for the losses it had suffered and the resources it had absorbed. The damage it did to Japanese communications was repaired in a few days, the casualties it inflicted were negligible, and it had no immediate effect on Japanese dispositions or plans." He pointed out that any shifts of Nipponese forces that occurred were due not to the Chindits but to the demands in the Arakan.

He mollified his critique, adding, "These are hard things to say of an effort that required stark courage and endurance as was demanded of and given by Wingate and his men. The operation was, in effect, the old cavalry raid of military history on the enemy's communications, which, to be effective, against a stout-hearted opponent, must be made in tactical coordination with a main attack elsewhere." That, as Slim noted, had been called off.

Reading the newspapers or listening to the broadcasts of the day, one would not have thought Longcloth a failure. Front pages in both British and American newspapers blared about the daring raid and the heavy blows against the Japanese. The press doted on the eccentricities of Wingate and his chief lieutenants. For the home front, the first long-range penetration scored a propaganda victory and lifted morale. Slim remarked that the adventures of the expedition distracted attention from the dismal results in the Arakan and as reported sounded as if the British "had beaten the Japanese at their own game."

Most significantly, Winston Churchill, who adored an unorthodox coup, gushed, "I consider Wingate should command the army against the Japanese in Burma. He is a man of genius and audacity and has rightly been discerned by all eyes as a figure quite above the ordinary level. . . . This man, his force, and achievements, stand out."

9

Detachment 101, the Burma Road, and the Hump

As the United States had inexorably marched toward full involvement in World War II, President Roosevelt, concerned with the paucity of intelligence resources available to Washington, in July 1941 appointed a millionaire Wall Street lawyer, William J. Donovan, as "coordinator of information" (COI). The charter for Donovan, a hero of World War I, where he earned both the nickname of "Wild Bill" and a Medal of Honor, extended well beyond just the gathering of information. The COI was actually a cover for an agency that not only engaged in espionage but also was charged with disseminating "black propaganda" and studying resistance movements. A year later, with the country immersed in the war, the COI became the Office of Strategic Services (OSS), which added missions of sabotage and guerrilla warfare.

As a Western democracy with ethnic roots deeply embedded in Europe, the United States could easily recruit agents and insert its own people into the target areas of the European and Mediterranean theaters. But in Asia, the OSS could count on far fewer connections with the indigenous people, and the pale-skinned, physically different Americans faced a much more difficult task in moving behind Japanese lines without notice by that country's troops or their numerous agents. As it did with all areas, the OSS compiled background books that spelled out economic, cultural, and political geographies. In Burma, for example, there were detailed descriptions of the Kachins, Shans, Nagas, Karens, and Burmese, educated guesses on which group would be most receptive to support of the Allies, and the best means to enlist

139

them in "irregular warfare"—sabotage, guerrilla raids, and collection of information.

To head a unit for duty in his bailiwick, Stilwell, having consulted with Donovan, nominated Carl Eifler, a hulking former Treasury agent, an army reserve captain with a promising background in the understanding of and relationships with Asians. Eifler in turn recruited John Coughlin and Vincent Curl, who had been serving with him in a Hawaii-based infantry unit. Coughlin roped in acquaintance William R. ("Ray") Peers, an army officer commissioned from the University of California at Los Angeles ROTC.

All recruits for the OSS, including those at the top echelons, were expected to have knowledge of military science and tactics, engineering, explosives, radio and other forms of communication, and photography; an aptitude for language was highly desirable. On April 14, 1942, Detachment 101 of what was still the Office of the Coordinator of Information became official, with a complement of twelve officers and nine NCOs. Eifler took most of the officers to Canada, where they underwent schooling by British commandos. They learned the arts of sudden assault and murder, how to blow up a freight train, and other tricks of guerrilla craft. In Maryland's Catoctin Mountains, Ray Peers and the remainder of the contingent practiced setting ambushes, and ran along narrow boards fifty feet off the ground to accustom themselves to the terrain of the mountainous jungles or traveling from housetop to housetop if necessary.

The advance party of Detachment 101, on the final leg of its journey to CBI, flew into New Delhi with Eifler and Curl lugging a suitcase packed with forty pounds of plastic explosives. No one in India seemed to know what to do with 101. In New Delhi, CBI headquarters, short on staff, tried to assign them to fill its needs rather than assist in deployment for the purposes for which they had trained Eifler and his comrades.

Stilwell's imprimatur was key to 101's future, and the OSS men had to wait for him to fly in from China. According to Richard Dunlop, who joined the detachment in 1944, the American CBI commander seemed to have had second thoughts about an OSS operation in his domain. In his book *Behind Japanese Lines,* Dunlop wrote that when Eifler reported to Stilwell, the general asked, "Well, Eifler, what are you doing here?"

"Sir, I was under the impression you sent for me."

"No, I didn't send for you and I don't want you."

In Dunlop's account, Eifler pleaded for thirty days, later extended to ninety days, to demonstrate what 101 could do. The general's parting statement after a second interview was, 'All I want to hear are booms from the Burma jungle.'"

In his book *Behind the Burma Road* (written with Dean Brelis), Ray Peers made no mention of a private audience between Eifler and Stilwell, but his encounter with the general indicated no reluctance to use the OSS. "He met with all of the officers and men of 101. He said he was anxious to have us get behind Japanese lines. Information was scarce and he believed anything we could reveal about the enemy would influence forthcoming operations. What he wanted was a group eager to knock to pieces the myth that a white man could not survive in the jungle."

A tea plantation in the lower elevations of the Naga Hills, on the Indian side of the Burma border, away from other military organizations with no need to know, became headquarters for 101 under the name Army Experimental Station. Technical specialists manufactured their own radios with long range and easy portability. The first team flew to Fort Hertz, also known as Putao, in northern Burma, the only remaining town in the country where the Allies could base an airfield. There the Americans, working with some of the local recruits, whom they had trained, probed the Japanese lines. They quickly realized that infiltration limited the number of operatives and meant slow, difficult work. The OSS leaders decided their best possibilities lay in parachute drops well behind the crust of the Japanese presence.

Peers noted one troublesome conclusion from this first attempt. The indigenous people put no faith in paper money; their favored mediums of exchange were either British silver coins or opium. "Our decision to use opium," wrote Peers, "was based on the fact that it would give our troops a certain amount of freedom, of buying power; we did not question it as just or unjust. The fact remained that opium, along with its multitude of sins, was also a palliative for the thousands of older people who suffered from a complex of maladies for which there were no cures. Even so, it should be noted that opium was not used to recruit guerrilla troops. . . . Opium was available to agents who used it for any number of reasons, ranging from obtaining information to their own escape."

While 101 now accepted the principal currencies required, the problem of flying people over the mountains and jungles to parachute well behind the enemy involved shortages of chutes and planes. Peers was part of a delegation that petitioned the Air Transport Command boss, Brigadier General Edward Alexander, for his aid. Peers described a scene in which Alexander voiced his regrets about his aircrews who crashed in the Burmese wilds and presumably perished from exposure, starvation, or capture by the enemy. Supposedly Alexander said, "I'd give anything to guarantee my people that they had a chance."

The OSS members responded, "That's why we are here."

"What can you do?"

"We can promise that if your crews crash in North Burma, we will go in and lead them out."

"That's the sort of thing they show in movies."

"No, sir. Those hills, those mountains, are Kachin country. They are on our side, and if we could get in and show them that we meant to stay, we should be able to get your men out." On that premise the ATC agreed to fly and drop men from 101 while it in turn "would act as an underground railroad for American and British aircrews."

Because of Japanese air strength in the targeted areas, the usual transportation was a C-87, a B-24 converted for cargo but still equipped with some .50-caliber machine guns. Instead of the usual backpack parachutes, the only ones initially available were seat chutes ordinarily worn by aircrews. With the aid of local artisans, the OSS people made woven bamboo containers to carry food, medicines, and other supplies.

The first real mission, said Peers, inserted two officers from the A Group about a hundred miles south of the critical hub, Myitkyina. From a base camp in that area they were to strike a rail line forty miles to the west. After the first pair arrived, another ten men joined them, leaping from the C-87 a scant six hundred feet above the ground. In superb physical condition, they actually marched a hundred miles over a circuitous trail through thick vegetation and up and down craggy ridges to reach their destination in just two days. Along the tracks they installed explosive devices timed to blow in as soon as an hour or as long as more than three weeks later. They also destroyed a large railway bridge near the town of Namhkwin.

A Japanese patrol surprised one pair engaged in demolition, and during the exchange of fire, one of the Anglo-Burmese lieutenants, trying to protect his companion by acting as a rear guard, was shot down. Enemy activity increased markedly, and only later did 101 learn that they were responding to the Chindit invasion occurring at the same time. For weeks, the A Group evaded the Japanese, collected information on their troop deployment, and subsisted on what they could forage along with the fruits of several airdrops. When they finally walked into Fort Hertz they had demonstrated the ability to produce the "booms from the Burma jungle" demanded by Stilwell. Although the first strike amounted to little more than harassment,

101 now was in a position to requisition proper parachutes, improve its techniques and equipment, and recruit new members from the indigenous population.

The New Burma Road

In a rare moment of prescience, Chiang Kai-shek, as early as January 1942, foresaw the conquest of most of Burma by Japan, thereby shutting down the supply route that began at the port of Rangoon and stretched the length of the country by rail and road to China. As a substitute, Chiang proposed a new road, from Ledo in India's Assam Province over the northern stretch of Burma and all the way to Chungking, China. The route followed a southeasterly path to Myitkyina and Bhamo and then intersected the old Burma Road, which led northeast into China and Kunming. The plan was predicated on evicting the Japanese from their positions at Myitkyina as well as Bhamo.

Much less realistically, the generalissimo claimed that such a highway over mountains, through jungles, and across rivers could be constructed in five months. The engineers from AMMISCA surveyed the route and announced that the project would require about thirty months. Although at that time Rangoon and southern and central Burma still remained in British hands, the War Department agreed on the urgent need for what would become known as the Ledo Road, scheduled to open in January 1945 with an initial capacity of thirty thousand tons a month, with a final goal of sixty-five thousand tons a month. As massive as that may sound, it could never bring sufficient matériel to support the proposed three hundred Chinese divisions or maintain China's four hundred million inhabitants. Instead it was expected to deliver enough trucks, tanks, artillery, and small arms to enable the Stilwell-led forces to capture a port on the coast for much greater imports and to secure bases from which the Japanese homeland could be bombed.

Overall supervision of the construction fell to Lieutenant General Raymond A. Wheeler, an engineer from the Services of Supply (SOS). The annual rainfall in portions of the terrain amounted to 150 inches, and during the monsoon season, more than 12 inches of rain might pour down in a single day. Wheeler's labor force would have to contend with mud, malaria, and leeches as well as an occasional Japanese sniper. The experts blueprinted as many as thirteen culverts per mile to defeat the inordinate runoff of rainwater. Not until the fall of 1942 did the engineers, Indian contract labor, and a battalion of

African American soldiers turn over the first shovelful of dirt. Eventually engaged in the project were eighty thousand workers, of whom fifty thousand were Americans and the remainder Indians or Chinese.

Richard L. Johnston, a native of Pennsylvania whose father was a steam-hoisting engineer, quit high school in 1932 to enter the Civilian Conservation Corps (CCC), a program of Franklin Roosevelt's New Deal that enlisted young men who built highways, improved the national parks system, and labored on the nation's infrastructure. As the country geared up for the war that began for it on December 7, 1941, Johnston found himself working seven days a week in sixteen-hour shifts. "I finally decided the war couldn't be any worse than this," he said. Although he held an occupational deferment, Johnston managed to enlist in the regular army in March 1942.

Unlike so many round pegs jammed into square holes, he received an assignment that took advantage of his skills, the Corps of Engineers. After basic training, he graduated from Officer Candidate School (OCS) and became an A Company platoon leader with the 382d Engineer Battalion composed of 1,242 enlisted men, all African Americans. "We had two black officers," said Johnston. "One was a warrant officer and the other a chaplain."

In June 1943 the 382d sailed to India with Johnston, now a captain, commanding a company. Sometime in September, at Ledo, the battalion was broken up, with Johnston's unit placed at "Mile One," where the road now lay about forty miles beyond Ledo. "I had 242 men and there were 5 white officers. First we cleared the area out, the jungle, and also got in a jam, for part of it was a tea garden [plantation]. It was right near the border up in the mountains. We cut down a whole lot of tea bushes and we caught hell for that."

Johnston's company worked at the "pushing point," the front of the project cutting through the jungle to lay the trace for the highway. "The Japs flew over and would bomb us pretty nearly every night. They called one 'Tojo' [the name of the Japanese minister of war] and the other 'Charlie' [the nickname bestowed generally on lone Japanese attackers]. They were individual planes, and you would hear them coming. They would bomb us, and we would shoot at them with our .50-caliber machine guns. We never got one of them as far as I know.

"There were Japanese snipers all along the road, so you would have to have what we called a guy riding 'shotgun' on the bulldozers with the operator. The rain was ungodly heavy. It would flow out of the culverts as fast as we'd put them in. Lots of times we would lose five or six miles because the road would be washed out by the rain.

Then we would have to rebuild it. I couldn't even give you an idea of how long it would take to build a mile.

"We worked all through the monsoon season. We ran gravel pits. There was no rock in that area. The mountains were pure mud. We ran gravel pits out of the river. We would take the gravel out with pans [large receptacles pulled behind tractors] and store it, to stockpile it. When the monsoons came, we would put it on the road. It was a dirt road or gravel road the whole way. There was no tarmac or asphalt."

The first trace or rough pathway stretched from Ledo to Shingbwiyang in the Hukawng River valley. It was a bit over a hundred miles. Beyond that point lay Japanese soldiers, and Wheeler's crews, working around the clock, covered three-quarters of a mile a day. Ahead of them by one day's march, a regiment of Chinese soldiers protected the road builders from the enemy. On February 28, the lead bulldozer crunched over the Burma border forty-three miles beyond Ledo.

Any sense of triumph was muted by the inability to advance supplies to the construction companies. Neither bearers traveling on foot nor elephants could haul the necessities, and when the monsoons hurtled from the skies in May, progress was all but halted forty-seven miles beyond Ledo. Torrents of rain created landslides that ripped away portions and washed heavy machinery over the sides. Malaria, scrub typhus, and ugly skin diseases fell upon the construction forces in full fury.

Hump Flights

The massive effort to build a road did not impress Chennault, and Chiang seemed to have lost his zest for the project. Instead, they beat the drums for huge, instant increases in the matériel hauled by air over the 700-mile Hump route from the Assam bases to China, and for more combat aircraft. In the summer of 1942, Stilwell had examined the efforts of the Air Transport Command (ATC) to sustain Chennault and provide the most urgently needed items for the Chinese. He declared the results inadequate. Stilwell noted that the China National Aviation Corporation (CNAC) pilots routinely flew in weather that grounded the AAF. There were also allegations of nonessential items, things for the benefit of China's rulers rather than the war effort.

With 45,000 tons of Lend-Lease supplies destined for China already stockpiled in India and another 7,000 tons consigned to CBI, the air ferry system obviously could not carry the mandated freight. The logistics faced by the Air Transport Command defied solution. The planes burned a gallon of fuel for every gallon they delivered to China. It took 18 tons of supplies to give Chennault the wherewithal to drop 1 ton of bombs. Stilwell argued for the deployment of 100 more cargo planes with their flight crews and ground personnel.

Although the ATC could not meet the initial goal of 5,000 tons monthly, the U.S. strategists had set a goal of 10,000 tons for the cargo airlift, stretching both planes and their crews. After an inspection trip Stilwell fretted, "The C-46 [the principal transport along with its relative the C-47] is full of bugs. Carburetor ices up. We have lost six over the Hump and the boys' morale is lower and lower." Losses on the perilous journey over the Hump during the three years of the ATC's operations amounted to 468 aircraft, an average of 13 a month. More than 1,000 airmen died flying the Hump, including those flown by the CNAC. An overall total of 600 planes went down, victims of the cloud-covered peaks, the weather, mechanical malfunctions, pilot error, and enemy fighters lurking just beyond the mountains to attack the unarmed, unescorted transports. Some airmen were rescued through the auspices of the OSS's Detachment 101, which recruited Kachins to help. In 1943, just as promised to the ATC's Alexander, they pulled out an astonishing 125 crewmen, but that was only a third of those lost during the year. Many died in crashes, expired in the jungles, or were seized by the Japanese.

When the AVG folded its wings, Joe Rosbert was one of a number of Flying Tigers who refused to remain with Chennault and his new command. Instead, Rosbert, along with sixteen others, had accepted an offer from the CNAC to fly the Hump between India and China, ferrying people and supplies. A private company, CNAC held a contract with the U.S. government to supply Chennault. "The program was very attractive," said Rosbert, "two weeks of flying from Dinjan in upper Assam to Kunming, then two weeks off in Calcutta. The pay was excellent, much more than we had earned as fighter pilots, and there was anticipation of a vacation in the States within a few months."

The drawbacks were mountains that poked fourteen thousand to eighteen thousand feet into the sky. Thick clouds often hid jagged peaks. Howling winds, rain, snow, and ice bedeviled pilots. Meteorologists covered conditions only at the two terminal cities. No navigational aids existed.

In the spring of 1943, after a vacation back home, Rosbert, with another pilot, Ridge Hammill, headed for Kunming with a load of medical supplies. For Hammill, previously employed ferrying aircraft to Africa, this was his first trip. The third member of the crew was a Chinese radio operator known simply as "Wong." Rosbert noted, "CNAC had decided to put parachutes on the flights for the crew. On the other hand, deicing boots for the wings had been removed. They gave the reason that the rubber rotted in the tropical sun of India. But I suspected the reason was to utilize the weight saved for additional cargo."

Only thirty minutes after takeoff, at sixteen thousand feet, snow and ice began to accumulate on the wings. Rosbert reassured his copilot that if they could make it halfway they would be able to complete the flight. But the ice built up to half a foot thick and they began to lose altitude. Rosbert decided to turn back. The C-53, a new version of the C-47, dipped down toward fourteen thousand feet.

"Ice had formed on the inside of the windshield. Using our hands to melt it, we could see nothing but snow. Then, suddenly, there was a swirl in the clouds, and directly ahead, a mountain." Rosbert tried a tight turn but heard "almost instantly a scraping sound under the fuselage. The nose tipped down and we crashed into the mountain of snow."

As he regained consciousness, a stunned Rosbert felt a sharp pain shooting from his right ankle through his leg. The aircraft was a wreck, debris scattered about. He stumbled to the rear and found Hammill alive, but bleeding from a gash on his face and complaining of pain in his ankle. However, Wong, the radioman, was dead.

After several days, fearful of avalanches, they left the shelter of the plane, hoping to make their way down to help. Plywood strips bound with parachute nylon acted as splints for their ankles while they used the aircraft's door as a sled for easier descent until it slipped away over a cliff. When they came to the edge of a fifty-foot drop, they tied the shrouds from the parachutes to a rock and let themselves down far enough for a final leap of ten feet into the cushioning depths of snow.

The pair staggered on, breaking their involuntary fast only with the remnants of a dead bird they found. Two weeks after they took off, they came upon a hut whose Himalayan inhabitants fed them a facsimile of cornmeal mush. Their hosts, said Rosbert, "looked like creatures out of the Stone Age: long black hair, G-string, abbreviated vestlike back cover with a pouch on one side and a long knife on the other."

In the company of the local people, the pair resumed the trek from what they learned were the Mishmi Hills. After a number of weeks, during which they were introduced to the opium pipe, a visiting headman named Ah Saw with a companion, Ma Lon, asked them to write a dedication on a piece of the map. Rosbert scrawled, "To Ah Shaw and Ma Lon from two pilots crashed on the mountain."

To their astonishment, Ah Shaw reappeared three days later with a sealed Indian telegraph envelope. Inside, the message read, "TO PILOTS AHSHAW AND MALON. SENDING RATIONS WITH MESSAGE STOP DOCTOR ARRIVING TWO DAYS LATER WITH AID STOP. MAJOR PHEIFFER AND CAPT LAX."

When the rescuers arrived, Rosbert discovered that his scribble on the map had been misinterpreted, leading the British scouting party to believe their names were Ahshaw and Malon. Final reunion with civilization required several more weeks walking through monsoon weather, over rickety bamboo bridges, and stripping away the ever present leeches, even though Rosbert's ankle was diagnosed by Dr. Lax as broken in several places. Altogether, it was forty-six days since they had left Dinjan. Rosbert was shipped to the States to recover from his injury.

Along with the miraculous survivals by aircrews who smashed into mountains or jungles, however, the Hump operations included a massive amount of smuggling, theft, black-market dealings, and the vice trade. At one point, the agents for the Army's Criminal Investigation Department were investigating more than three hundred alleged cases of criminal activities involving the transports traveling the Hump. Stilwell, who earlier alluded to "pilfering going on along the line," scribbled more specifics in his diary: "Officers pimping. Hauling whores in our planes. Sent for Chennault. He knew. More dope on gas-stealing ring." The corruption and black-market opportunities wrought conspiracy between Chinese and American freebooters. They stole and sold sulfa drugs, cigarettes, and PX items; smuggled gold; swapped foreign currency; and imported women from India and from China to staff bordellos.

Those aircraft that arrived in China carried back to India recruits whom Stilwell expected to train at the Ramgarh base. There was no shortage of Chinese, even when Stilwell insisted on a minimum of 400 fresh soldiers per day. Chungking not only complied but also boosted it to 650, the maximum that the facilities could handle. However, the newcomers to Ramgarh often went straight to medical facilities to treat them for malnutrition and disease. Stilwell in his diary reported one appalling incident where the Chinese general in charge ordered, "Put fifty in a plane naked. It's only three hours." He reasoned that since they would be issued new uniforms on their arrival it would be wasteful to send them clothed. The passengers on this trip traveled in their undershorts, and several died from exposure.

Despite the handicaps, Stilwell and a cohort of American officers and noncoms labored mightily to transform the raw material into soldiers fit for combat. There are films of the Ramgarh encampment that show rows of Chinese novices prone on the ground while Stilwell himself lay down next to them, patiently explaining the techniques of sighting and firing their rifles. As Barbara Tuchman noted, Stilwell not only wanted to instruct the troops, but also he hoped to set an example for the other American advisers.

Air War

The tiny U.S. Air Force in China struggled to mount a good fight. Chennault, as commander of the China Air Task Force, served not only under Stilwell but also was subordinate to Brigadier General Clayton L. Bissell, head of the Tenth Air Force, stationed in India. Because of the bad feelings from their time together during the 1930s, the former AVG leader chafed at the orders from Bissell.

The situation eased when Chennault received promotion to the rank of major general and command of the newly activated Fourteenth Air Force in China. Much to his gratification, that slid him out from underneath the control of Bissell. Bolstered by his new status, Chennault, backed by Chiang, renewed his requests for heavier infusions of fodder to the Fourteenth. Chennault chafed over the quality and quantity of what reached him in Kunming. Bruce Holloway recalled receiving a squadron of P-38 Lockheed Lightning fighters in August 1943. "That was a real Jonah. The guys never did anything right. Most of them were volunteers from an outfit in North Africa. They were pretty low-caliber pilots, most of them. We had great hopes for the P-38 because it had some altitude performance. But after they got to us, I had run three squadron commanders through trying to straighten them out, and they still weren't any good when I left in December 1943. They wouldn't make the rendezvous point or they would miss the target. They were always catching fire when they got hit. It was just a Jonah outfit."

Robert Breitweiser, who had become the operations officer for the Fourteenth, noted, "The problem was supply and matériel. We had very few planes and even the ones we had were second-line equipment and we couldn't keep them supplied with fuel. I laid on the biggest single raid of the war in East China. We had twenty B-24s, about twenty-four B-25s, and about thirty-five P-40s. That was it in a bombing raid on the Hankow railroad yards, and that adds up to less than a hundred airplanes. [In the European Theater of Operations the Eighth Air Force was mounting strikes of five hundred to seven hundred bombers, with hundreds of fighters as escorts.] That ran our fuel supplies down to where we had to sweat two airplane missions for a while until we could build it back up."

Anxious to reduce dependency on the small contingent of Americans, Chiang invested some of his slim capital in building the Chinese air force. John Alison, an eyewitness to the effort, said, "The Chinese didn't have any gasoline. We had come from America, where we could fly every day. The Chinese were lucky if they got four hours flying time a month. That's not enough to maintain proficiency, so they cracked up quite a few airplanes. Kids don't think, and we were kids [the American pilots]. They would talk about how the Chinese were cracking up airplanes. They said, 'The Chinese have no inherent flying ability.' I [would] lecture them. It's funny how people can look at other people's faults and shortcomings and ignore their own.

"The 74th Squadron [U.S.] was a training squadron we had at Kunming. We were getting these new pilots. In sixteen days, the 74th Squadron ground-looped seventeen airplanes at Kunming airdrome [six thousand feet above sea level], inflicting everything from minor to major damage on the P-40. I said, 'Fellows, you talk about the Chinese,' [which] would remind them that Americans right on Kunming airdrome, right in front of Chinese air force headquarters, cracked up seventeen airplanes in sixteen days. I said, 'Do you know what I bet the chief of the Chinese air force is doing? He looks out his window and sees these airplanes going ass over teakettle. I bet he is looking out and saying, 'Gee, it's a good thing the Americans are rich because they have no inherent flying ability.'"

Internal Affairs

The situation with the Ledo Road and the incessant demands from the generalissimo and Chennault for much greater resources occupied much of the discussion at Trident, a conference in Washington designed to plot the future now that the Axis powers had been forced out of North Africa, and what to do about Anakim. Chiang warned that unless China received three more fighter groups, the Japanese navy would steam up the navigable rivers all the way to Chungking. At Trident, Chennault argued that the Japanese no longer threatened central China as it had in the past, and that the Fourteenth Air Force, if given what he asked, could deliver punishing blows to the foe. He dismissed the Ledo Road and insisted that the necessities to win could be delivered by the ATC over the Hump. In his book *Way of a Fighter,* he said he told Roosevelt, "if we received 10,000 tons of supplies monthly my planes would sink and severely damage more than a million tons of shipping." Chennault wrote that the president banged his fist on the desk with glee, responding, "If you can sink a million tons, we'll break their backs."

Chennault's enthusiasm so infected Roosevelt that he invited him to contact his office directly, detouring around official circles. But the proposal neglected to consider the capacity of the Japanese to strike by land at the Chinese air bases and thereby limit their effectiveness. Stilwell took a low-key approach that focused on the need to continue the training program designed to field first the three divisions being schooled at Ramgarh and thirty more in Yunnan Province, to be followed by an equal number as agreed by the generalissimo. Without the Chinese forces, any plan to build a supply route sufficient for all was doomed.

Although Secretary of War Stimson and army chief of staff Marshall both sided with Stilwell, Roosevelt bought the scenario drafted by Chennault and Chiang. Joseph Alsop, the journalist turned captain on Chennault's staff, used his contacts with both Harry Hopkins, the president's chief civilian adviser, and Edward Stettinius, head of the Lend-Lease Administration, to promote the air war concept. Working behind the scenes to serve the desires of Chennault and Chiang, T. V. Soong skillfully lobbied influential figures. Marshall tried in vain to persuade Harry Hopkins, but while the civilian adviser ordinarily went along with the army chief of staff, he continued to favor the notions of Chennault. Marshall, never a fan of Chennault, while crediting him as "probably a tactical genius," like so many detractors regarded the former head of the AVG as ignorant of both strategy and logistics.

Throughout his period of CBI command, Stilwell entertained no doubts about the inability of air power to defeat the Japanese. He was certainly an advocate of the air transport system, constantly pushing for increases in cargo. He also asked for more combat aircraft, although he tended to think in terms of support for ground forces rather than strategic bombing. At the same time, Stilwell's growing contempt for the generalissimo sat poorly with the President.

Way of a Fighter, Chennault's autobiography, reported that Roosevelt asked Stilwell and Chennault for their personal opinions of the Chinese leader. Stilwell snarled, "He's a vacillating, tricky, undependable old scoundrel who never keeps his word." Chennault offered, "I think the generalissimo is one of the two or three greatest military and political leaders in the world today. He has never broken a commitment or promise made to me."

The upshot of Trident paid lip service to Anakim, promising efforts in northern Burma but not to the south and Rangoon. A message to Stilwell from Marshall concluded, "I think he [the President] felt that nothing for Anakim should delay Chennault's air operations." To meet the importuning of the Fourteenth Air Force, the Air Transport Command was reorganized, with a significant improvement in its deliveries. From only three thousand tons in May, the supplies flown over the Hump built up to as much as 13,000 tons a month only five months later.

Added Bomber Punch

Tony Tricoli, as a twenty-one-year-old from Jersey City, New Jersey, had enlisted in 1940 in the National Guard with his younger brother, "to protect him." After a one-year stint Tricoli was discharged, but three months later and ten days after the Pearl Harbor attack, he volunteered for the air corps. "I wanted to be a pilot but my eyesight wasn't good enough," said Tricoli. Instead he trained as a flight engineer and top turret gunner.

As a member of the 308th Bomb Group, he flew in an early version of the B-24—it had neither a ball turret in the belly nor a fully operational nose turret for machine guns, although there was a gun there that could be deployed. From India, Tricoli's crew often flew to Chungking, making several round-trip flights over the Hump to pick up gas and supplies from the Chabua base. Throughout his tour, Tricoli would travel to Chabua and back, sometimes detouring for a bomb drop on a Burma site.

On July 8, 1943, Tricoli flew his first combat mission, but engine trouble aborted his ship's participation. Two days later came a raid on Haiphong. "Mission wasn't too successful," he noted on a four-by-five-inch card. "Our bombardier dropped four in the drink and one close to a hangar on an airfield." The outfit struck Hon-Gay with thousand-pounders and a bundle of incendiaries. "Bombed at 8,000," he wrote, "strafed the town at 1,500. Some fun. Tit for tat, for those yellow dogs."

When the squadron landed at Kunming after a raid, Tricoli reported on a night in town. "Just like in pictures. Plenty of stench. Went to the club and had a steak. Rented a girl for 100 yen [about $1.25] an hour to sit at our table. I danced with the Chinese girl once. She wasn't bad but I wouldn't touch her. Neither did the other boys."

At Samah Bay, Tricoli saw his three-ship element attacked by a dozen Zeros from underneath, a highly vulnerable area in the absence of a ball turret. Because of the angle of the enemy approach, Tricoli never had an opportunity to trigger his weapon. When the 308th struck at Hong Kong on July 29, the eighteen B-24s enjoyed the company of thirteen P-40s and three P-38s. Heavy antiaircraft greeted them but no enemy fighters as they unloaded on the floating dry docks. Several days later Tricoli said, "Over the Hump again. Had to be on the alert this time. Japs have six of our P-40s. They landed at the Jap field in error. Afraid they may use them against us." In fact, he had already seen a B-24 captured by the enemy actually fly over the Chungking airdrome.

Although the first new versions of the B-24, equipped with ball turrets, had arrived, an August 21 assault on Hankow by fourteen Liberators showed the vulnerability of the big bombers. "We were attacked just over target by about 150 Zeros. We didn't have umbrella escort. We had a tough time. Our ship and one of the others were the only ones to drop their bombs. Lead ship *Rum Runner* was shot down. Our CO went down in it with the rest of the crew. A few were able to bail out but were gunned by the yellow rats. Tail gunner on *Thundermug* got it. Jerry and I helped take him out of the turret. Poor kid. Our ship got five Zeros. I got three and Lt. Robinson and Odie got one each. We also lost one of the 375th's ships. Our operations officer, Captain Adler, got it bad as pilot in *Hot Nuts* and Lieutenant Murphy got a bad shoulder as pilot in *Esculation*. The reason for this catastrophe was missing our fighter escorts."

Pick Picks Up the Pace

When the rainy season ended late in the summer of 1943, the ground began to dry, permitting resumption of the Ledo Road construction. The 849th and 1883d Engineer Aviation Battalions and the 382d Engineer Battalion arrived in September. A month later, Colonel Lewis A. Pick, a graduate of Virginia Polytechnic Institute, a World War I veteran, and an engineer who had cut his teeth on tough waterway projects such as the Missouri River flood control program in the United States, assumed responsibility for finishing the road.

Under Pick's direction the pace picked up, and by the end of November his bulldozers were chewing up real estate 82.35 miles from Ledo. Pick leapfrogged some of his earth movers beyond the spearhead, and they then worked their way back to the main drive. An advanced detachment set up shop at Shingbwiyang to await the first truck convoy. To supplement the supplies carried along the Ledo Road, the supply specialists now plotted a pair of pipelines running parallel to the road for a steady flow of aviation gas to the ATC and the Fourteenth Air Force and truck fuel for the China-based forces. The pipelines originated at tanker terminals in Bengal, and work on them began in November 1943.

Birth of the B-29 Project

While those concerned with logistics struggled to accommodate to their daunting responsibilities, the air force proposed a new operation burdened with multiple problems. The first Superfortresses, the Boeing B-29s, capable of a much extended range and greater bomb capacity, had begun to roll off the assembly lines. Washington planners saw the B-29s, staged first in India, as able to batter Japan from bases in China.

Austin W. Betts, a 1934 West Point graduate assigned to the Corps of Engineers, said that while he was at the army's Aviation Engineer Training Center in 1943, he was called to Washington for temporary duty with the engineer section directly under Hap Arnold. Betts said, "General Arnold was given the mission by President Roosevelt to see that Japan was bombed before election day [November 1944]. The direction given to the aviation engineers was to prepare a plan for engineer support that would build the appropriate airfields in the [CBI] theater with the provision that [they] not draw on any engineer support other than that already available to the air corps. I was not allowed to talk to G-4 or army Service Forces or anyone other than those immediately responsible to the air corps.

"The obvious purpose of the instructions given to me were to get a plan to General Arnold that he could then give to the president that would not have to go through the Combined Chiefs or the Joint Chiefs. When the plan that was finally evolved was presented at one of the summit meetings [Quadrant, Quebec, October 1943], it was a complete surprise to the other elements of the U.S. forces because General Arnold had given it to the president and the president said, 'We can do this.'"

Originally labeled Twilight, the script called for 280 B-29s, whose fuel, ordnance, and other necessities would be hauled by 412 transports. President Roosevelt asked Churchill to help build four air bases in India and told Chiang that five airfields would be required in his country. As the proposal entered the maw of the military planning machinery, some alterations occurred. Twilight became Matterhorn, but more important than the change in nomenclature, the feature of 412 cargo transports disappeared. The huge bombers were now expected to be self-supporting, ferrying themselves all of what they needed.

For Stilwell, the entire business was one more body blow. After Roosevelt informed Chiang of the B-29 scheme, Stilwell groaned to his diary, "FDR has undercut me again. Told Peanut all about Twilight, so I can't bargain on that." In the American's eyes, the prospect of bombers defeating the Japanese enabled the generalissimo to again avoid committing himself to reform of his army. Stilwell's petulance went so far he referred to the president as "Rubberlegs," an abysmal jibe at FDR's physical infirmities.

In a bluntly worded paper, Stilwell advised Washington of the continuing deficiencies of the Chinese military. He argued that instead of a paper plan for three hundred divisions, the Chinese should field a total of sixty well armed and well led. He called for the elimination of the many incompetent and corrupt officers. Most importantly, he stressed the desirability for the Chinese troops to participate as the "Y" force in an offensive to evict the Japanese from Burma, rather than to hold defensive positions inside China. A frustrated Stilwell found the generalissimo, while seeming to acquiesce, actually making no effort to implement the reform of his army. After accepting the proposed "Y" force plan, he balked when it came time to set things in motion. Instead, he reiterated theories on boosting the strength of Chennault's air units to strike at the foe.

10

Offensive Preparations

In August 1943, British prime minister Winston Churchill, U.S. president Franklin D. Roosevelt, and their Chiefs of Staff traveled to Quebec, Canada, for the Quadrant Conference. The surrender of Italy, now occupied by the Nazi armies, required new plans for the Allies. At this moment the floor was open for the first combined plans to defeat the Japanese. The consensus confirmed use of bases in China for B-29s to bomb Japan, hit enemy shipping and communications in the South Pacific, and eventually provide the staging areas for an invasion of the home islands.

The grand design expected the Chinese armies, trained and equipped under the guidance of Stilwell, to drive east toward the seas facing Japan. The critical need for supplies to these ground forces and the aerial offensive mandated massive increases via the route through Burma, as Stilwell constantly argued.

Present at Quadrant along with the civilian leaders and their top military advisers was Admiral Lord Louis Mountbatten, already chosen to assume command of a new entity, the Southeast Asia Command (SEAC) in the Far East. More singular was the attendance of Orde Wingate, whom Churchill brought along at the last moment. The prime minister, still enthralled by the exploits of the Chindits, which undoubtedly resonated with memories of his own behind-the-lines activities during the Boer War, wanted to use Wingate's operations as tangible proof of the British intentions to contribute in the campaigns against the Japanese.

Wingate fulfilled his sponsor's expectations with a presentation of his plans for a long-range penetration by more than twenty thousand soldiers. Before the rapt audience of Churchill, Roosevelt, and Mountbatten, Wingate eloquently described his plans for LRPs with a sizable number of men. The two heads of government vigorously questioned Wingate, going beyond even his own particular forte. Wingate responded at length with verve and knowledge. When they had exhausted their queries, Churchill said, "Brigadier Wingate, we owe you our thanks. You have expounded a large and complex subject with exemplary lucidity." Never nonplussed, Wingate rejoined, "Such is my invariable practice, sir."

Not only did Wingate secure the go-ahead for a second thrust by the Chindits, but also the Americans decided that they would create their own version of LRP. Listed originally as Galahad, the force, with an authorized strength of about three thousand, would train under Wingate and be under his overall command. However, Stilwell planned to deploy them in conjunction with the Chinese units, guided by American advisers in the northern Burma offensive.

As scheduled, Mountbatten, a hero of the Royal Navy who survived the sinking of his destroyer in 1940, and the man who led the British Combined Operations commandos in their first successful operations during the dark days of 1941, in October 1943 was nominated as supreme commander of SEAC. Stilwell became deputy supreme commander. SEAC covered Burma, Ceylon, Sumatra, and Malaya but not India. Operations in China belonged to the generalissimo, while Stilwell's domain included all three of the areas. While the disposition of authority paid homage to the individual national interests, it hardly offered a substantial foundation for an overall, well-coordinated strategy.

Mountbatten brought to his post the self-assurance of a man with a long, unchallenged, aristocratic background. William Slim described his new superior, whom Alastair Cooke once labeled "the most boring individual I ever met," as "youthful, buoyant, picturesque, with a reputation for gallantry known everywhere, he talked to the British soldier with irresistible frankness and charm."

The relationship of Mountbatten and Stilwell started on a promising note. Although impeccably tailored and groomed, Mountbatten rarely stood on ceremony and showed none of the traits the American associated with the leather-belted, swagger-stick Colonel Blimp types he so detested. Stilwell told his diary, "Louis is a good egg—full of enthusiasm and also of disgust with inertia and conservatism." Stilwell confided to General Alfred Wedemeyer, the U.S. officer selected as Mountbatten's American chief of staff, "I think he's fair and I think he wants to do something." But with his habitual distrust of the British, he added, "You watch him, Wedemeyer, keep your eye on him."

Congenial as Mountbatten appeared on the surface, he was not a man who could be bullied. According to Lord Louis, when he met Stilwell, the American said, "Gee, Admiral, I like working with you. You're the only Limey I ever met who wants to fight." Mountbatten mentioned General Sir Harold Alexander as a brave fighter. Stilwell answered, "General Alexander was a coward. He retreated all the way and never stood and fought." In a postwar letter Mountbatten wrote, "I pointed out that Stilwell had also retreated all the way and that nobody so far had called him a coward."

The same month Mountbatten took office, William Slim handed over his XV Corps to Lieutenant General Sir Philip Christison as Slim ascended to the role of commander in chief, Eastern Command, directly under Mountbatten. At their first meeting, Mountbatten indicated to Slim that the oft-talked-about offensive in northern Burma had been discarded in favor of a huge seaborne invasion in the south. Stilwell would have been greatly disturbed if he had been privy to that conversation. However, in November 1943, the Allied leaders agreed to launch a cross-Channel invasion of France in the spring of the following year. The possibility of building an armada aimed at Rangoon vanished.

Wingate Finds American Help

During Quadrant army air force chief Hap Arnold had listened to Wingate explain the physical difficulties embedding large numbers of troops far behind enemy lines and the agony of having to leave behind the wounded. At one session in Quebec the Chindit commander asked if some light planes capable of short takeoffs and landings could use airstrips hacked out of the jungle to evacuate the disabled. Arnold foresaw a major role for his airmen, not only in plucking the wounded from behind Japanese lines but also in taking the troops behind Japanese lines, carrying their supplies, and eventually flying them out.

To carry out the operations, he created top-secret "Project 9," which later became 1st Air Commando, USAAF. To develop and command the unit he summoned two veteran fighter pilots, Lieutenant Colonels Philip Cochran and John Alison.

Superficially, Phil Cochran personified the World War II fighter pilot, a combat daredevil, nonchalant about the niceties of rank, and zealous in pursuit of what he called "chicks." While thousands of colleagues matched his attitudes and performed similar feats, Cochran drew fame because he knew Milton Caniff, one of the leading comic

Lieutenant Colonel Phil Cochran, who led a fighter squadron in North Africa, inspired the comic strip character Flip Corkin and headed the 1st Air Commando, which carried the Chindits behind the Japanese lines, evacuated their wounded, and pressed the air war against the enemy. (Photograph from U.S. National Archives)

strip creators of the day. Caniff inserted Cochran as the character of Major Flip Corkin in his *Terry and the Pirates,* replete with the fifty-mission crushed cap and penchant for "chicks." But unlike most imitations of life, the adventures of the alter ego actually fell short of the achievements of the genuine article.

Cochran had brought a batch of replacement pilots to North Africa shortly after the 1942 invasion. They had arrived amid confusion that bordered on total chaos. Cochran seized an opportunity to create an operational outfit from the contingent he led, but discovered they lacked even basic knowledge of aerial combat. "Units told to supply some fighter pilots as replacements kept their better-trained people and assigned their youngest. We had one kid who was only three weeks out of flying school. Most of them had the required hours but instead of learning tactics all they had been told was 'take off, circle the field for a couple of hours and then come back in.'

"I was thirty-two, old for a fighter pilot, but I was fighter-steeped. We set up an advanced concentrated course with ground targets on the beach to teach them how to use their guns, which many had never fired, focused on what we had heard from the front, mostly on formations. After three weeks we started to become cohesive, act like a squadron. Having no [official] number or name, we called ourselves the Jokers. The boys developed an esprit de corps, began to think of themselves as better than anyone else. For some reason or other we had been issued red scarves. They weren't common, and they added to the sense of an identity."

According to Cochran, the situation resembled something out of World War I, with the opposing airplanes separated by only a few miles. It was a time when a German pilot might buzz them and drop a challenging message. "That would require an answer from us and we'd then beat hell out of something they hadn't protected, to say, 'All right, you arrogant bastards, we'll show you a little of what we're made of.' The first thing I did when I awoke in the morning was to listen for their planes patrolling overhead. Then we would call the [Lockheed] P-38s stationed farther behind the front, saying, 'All right, they are up there, come and get them. Sweep our area clear so we can take off because while they are up there, if we try to take off, they'll come down and whack us.' "

At first the air war had followed the World War I pattern, often involving dogfights among fighters, but the missions gradually evolved into support for the ground forces. Cochran recalled making four or five sorties daily, looking for opportunities, whether in the air or below. Operations became less free-wheeling and more formally orchestrated. Teletype machines replaced the uncertain telephone alerts. Radar picked up intruders well in advance. Intelligence improved. "There was less barnstorming, fewer guerrilla attacks," said Cochran.

Cochran urged an even greater ground offensive role for fighters. He scrounged some five-hundred-pound bombs and arranged for them to be attached to the wings in place of the auxiliary wing tanks. The entire stock of U.S. P-40s, P-39s, and P-38s began to carry bombs, while the Spitfires, unable to accommodate the extra weight, flew cover.

Credited with sixty-one missions, and four enemy planes destroyed, holding the Silver Star, the Distinguished Flying Cross with two oak leaf clusters, the Air Medal with three clusters, and the Croix de Guerre with star and palm, Cochran returned to the United States to sell war bonds.

The air force had produced a substantial improvement over the P-40 and the even less effective Bell P-39 with the Republic P-47 Thunderbolt. Cochran started to prepare P-47 pilots for war. Promoted to lieutenant colonel, Cochran rejected the "misconceptions" among his new pupils. He had already confronted Lieutenant General Henry "Hap" Arnold, the commanding officer of the entire air force, and bluntly harangued him about erroneous tactics being taught, when he was summoned to Arnold's office and informed that instead of the assignment to "the big show" in Europe, he would be posted to CBI. Cochran balked. He ignored protocol to rant,

"I believe I have more combat experience than any fighter pilot in your air force. I'm going to be brash enough to tell you that I think I know more about the practical side of fighter aviation than anybody in the air force. I've done it the hard way, and here you are sending me to some doggone offshoot, side-alley fight over in some jungle in Burma that doesn't mean a damn thing. The big show is in England. I think I can contribute a helluva lot more with what I know and have been studying for seven years."

According to Cochran, the air force chief growled, "I don't know what kind of an air force office I'm running here when guys come in and tell me they are not going to do something." The junior officer retreated. "I had to get it out. You would think less of me if I didn't tell you exactly how I feel." After a few more conciliatory exchanges, Cochran surrendered: "Okay, where and when?" Arnold laughed and responded, "That's better. I want to get that other monkey in here." The "simian" in question was John Alison, rotated back to the United States after his tour with the Fourteenth Air Force and an old friend of Cochran. They discarded the notion of cocommanders as unworkable and settled on a table of organization that made Cochran the top man and Alison his deputy.

Arnold spelled out the mission to the pair. "This man [Wingate] has really done some remarkable things. He has walked through the jungles. He has carried his supplies on mules. It takes him about six weeks to get his men through the jungle, across the rivers, and in behind the Japanese lines. The next time he goes in, I don't want him to walk. I want him to go by air. I want to make this an air operation completely independent of land transport. I want to demonstrate that you can use the air just like the navy uses the sea. You can land and maintain a force and support it in battle. I want you to go in there and take out General Wingate's wounded. We will make available the resources that you need."

Alison remembered, "Then, with a twinkle in his eye, he said, 'I not only want you to do that . . . but I want the USAAF to spearhead General Wingate's operations.' We gathered he wouldn't mind if we turned it into an air show."

When Cochran saw Arnold just before leaving for India and for final instructions, he said his superior held up a finger and fixed him with his blue eyes. "'You know what I want you to do, don't you?' I said, 'Yes, sir. . . . you want us to steal that show and make that as much an American effort as possible . . . and that's what we are going to do.' He said, 'Do it!' Man, that finger came up, and I'm telling you I don't think I would have ever gone home—I wanted to come home in a box before I faced that guy if I didn't get it done."

The Birth of Galahad

While Cochran and Alison moved to organize the 1st Air Commando, the U.S. Army proceeded with the plan to create a three-battalion ground force of about three thousand known as Galahad. Wingate and his people would train the Americans, all volunteers, and they would then fight under the aegis of the Chindits. The offensive deploying the Y Force of Chinese was scheduled to begin in December 1943. Wingate's own Special Forces would be committed in January 1944.

Stilwell knew nothing of this American venture until September 2, 1943, when he noted in his diary, "Victory again. Radio from George Marshall on U.S. (Combat) units for Stepchild. Only 3,000 but the entering wedge. Can we use them! And how!" Subsequently informed that while the soldiers would belong to Stilwell's overall command they would fight under the direction of Wingate, Stilwell spewed another diatribe: "After a long struggle we get a handful of U.S. troops and by God they tell us they are going to operate under WINGATE! We don't know how to handle them but that exhibitionist does! He has done nothing but make an abortive jaunt to Katha, cutting some railroad that our people had already cut, get caught east of the Irrawaddy and come out with a loss of 40 percent. Now he's the expert. That is enough to discourage Christ."

Wingate's forces were conscripted from available forces in India and elsewhere. In contrast, for Galahad, the War Department recruiters, primarily searching for infantrymen, approached troops with combat experience in the South Pacific, men serving in the Caribbean Defense Command (Jamaica, Puerto Rico, Panama, and Trinidad), and those with the army ground forces still in the United States.

James E. T. Hopkins had graduated from Johns Hopkins University Medical School in the spring of 1941 and was serving his first year as a surgical resident when the Japanese attacked Pearl Harbor. In his history of the organization, *Spearhead* (coauthored by John M. Jones), Hopkins said he volunteered for military duty in April 1942. Just about a month after he entered the army, Hopkins sailed from San Francisco to New Zealand along with the 37th Infantry Division. On Fiji Hopkins performed surgery on wounded from Guadalcanal. He said, "I developed a profound interest in the welfare of the infantry soldier. I was very disturbed by the number of casualties that had been and were being produced by the Guadalcanal conflict."

With combat on Guadalcanal over, Hopkins seized an opportunity to transfer to a combat outfit where he could be closer to the front-line soldier. He became a surgeon assigned to the 117th Combat Engineers and then the 148th Infantry Regiment of the 37th Division. As the combat for islands of the South Pacific intensified, Hopkins, with the 148th, arrived on the beaches of New Georgia. From a close-in view he saw the horrors of hand-to-hand combat, the dead from a massacre of wounded and their litter bearers, and perhaps worst of all, "inexcusable situations and problems . . . a tactical error that resulted in my battalion being trapped for four days. We came out with many dead and 127 wounded soldiers." Disenchanted, Hopkins said, "I concluded that future combat in the South Pacific under navy command would offer more of the same. I wanted a new start under a new command."

Immediately after the end of the New Georgia campaign, the appeal for volunteers made in the name of President Roosevelt attracted Hopkins and 131 others from the 37th Division. Medic Dan Hardinger, a conscientious objector, and six riflemen from the 1st Battalion accompanied Hopkins. The recruits from the 37th were part of a much larger contingent that included veterans of combat from the 25th, 43d, and American Divisions.

Second Lieutenant Victor "Abie" Weingartner said, "My whole battalion volunteered from New Georgia. We had been in combat for about thirty days and out of a battalion of eight hundred men and approximately thirty officers, we got four hundred replacements. Fifteen replacements were officers. We figured nothing could be worse than this, so everybody volunteered. Less than a hundred men and fifteen officers were let go. I was among the least valuable, I guess—because they picked me and sent me off."

Fred O. Lyons, a lieutenant, recalled, "I had been stationed in Trinidad for almost two years and had begun to feel that the war was passing me by, when one day in August 1943, Colonel McGee, my regimental commander, called me into his office. 'Do you want to volunteer for a dangerous and hazardous secret mission in an active theater?' A dangerous and hazardous secret mission! My heart gave a jump. But wasn't this what I'd been waiting for?

"'Sure as hell,' I replied. 'When do we start?' Colonel McGee asked the same question of all the officers and men in the regiment, and everyone gave the same answer, but in the end only eleven hundred were allowed to go. I felt lucky, for they took me."

John Jones, a Tennessee native and graduate of what was then the Tennessee Military Institute, a private high school, held an ROTC commission following graduation from Washington and Lee University. Called to active duty in January 1942, Jones had attended the Fort Benning infantry officer training course and become an instructor in the machine-gun section there. On hearing of the call for men to undertake hazardous overseas duty, Jones requested assignment and was accepted. He became one of some eighteen hundred soldiers from the Carribean command and the States to join Galahad.

Ray Lyons (no kin of Floyd) said that after the Germans seized Czechoslovakia's Sudetenland, he was convinced the United States would enter the war and enlisted in a National Guard unit in October 1939. "After 12/7/41, I and several other men volunteered for the paratroops. I broke my ankle and washed out of the paratroops and was reassigned to an engineer outfit in the 76th Division. Since I could not walk, I was made into a company clerk and later battalion clerk. I was very unhappy that my original outfit was overseas fighting a war and I was still doing the same training stuff. Every time an opportunity to volunteer for something came up I would volunteer." He, too, went on the roster for the secret new outfit.

"I should have known better," said Lieutenant Colonel Charles N. Hunter in his memoir *Galahad*, "but stupid-like I volunteered for a 'hazardous mission' in 1943 and as a result received orders to proceed as soon as possible from the Infantry School, Fort Benning—where I was chief of the Rifle and Weapons Platoon Group of the Weapons Section of the School—to Washington. I had no idea as to what I was getting into. My only clue was that I had been selected from all other volunteer lieutenant colonels because of my extensive tropical jungle experience." Hunter had spent considerable time in the Philippines.

Hunter was a 1929 West Point graduate, like Frank Merrill, a member of Stilwell's staff. Hunter became commander of the personnel bound for India and the still-secret operation. He recalled, "In Washington, I was completely briefed on current and projected operations, on the personalities I might come in contact with, and the fact that the War Department expected that Galahad would suffer approximately 85 percent casualties. They were *so* [his italics] right."

Under his supervision, the recruits from the Pan American Command and those enlisted from the ground forces in the States boarded a converted luxury liner, *Lurline*, for the voyage to India. On the way, the *Lurline* picked up the combat veterans on New Caledonia. The manifest for the recruits listed them as Shipment 1688, broken into three detachments that became known as Battalions A, B, and C. Throughout their service they would frequently be referred to by the alphabetic designations rather than the customary numerical ones.

It was not a luxury cruise nor even the usual passage for troops. Floyd Lyons said, "I found that we were to be given plenty of training for our mysterious mission. Day after day on the wide decks we jumped and crouched, slashed with bayonets, and parried with gun butts. We shot at bobbing Japanese cardboard faces, peered at cardboard mod-

els of Japanese tanks and airplanes. We had to learn a lot about fighting the Jap, and every minute counted. At New Caledonia we met
new members of our outfit, leather-faced veterans of Guadalcanal
and New Georgia. The veterans were assigned places in our units, to
give weight and experience to our novice ranks."

The Fourteenth Air Force Staggers On

The 308th Bomb Group pounded Burma frequently, taking off from
Chungking, dumping bombs on the targets, and then proceeding to
Chabua to pick up supplies, returning to the base via the Hump. On
one such venture, Tony Tricoli noted, "Had a full load, crossed at
twenty-three thousand. Hit a thunderhead and made a bad drop of
two thousand feet in sixty seconds. I thought it was the end. The gods
were with me."

The Japanese tried to retaliate with raids on the Chinese base,
sending as many as 35 twin-engine bombers against Tricoli and his
associates. The pace of the air war appeared to intensify. Tricoli noted
for September 16, "Five ships from 373d went over to Haiphong.
Three shot down over the target, another crash-landed at Kunming
(all dead). Only one really returned and many were shot up."

Tricoli was cheered by the receipt of the latest in B-24s, one with
a full nose turret. On November 27 he described a mission to Rangoon that included both the 308th and the 7th—56 B-24s escorted
by nine fighters, P-51s, and P-38s. "Formation was lousy," commented Tricoli. "I watched the 7th bomb Group go over the target
and seen the dogfights. A P-51 and a B-24 went down. It's not so
nice to see. We got over the target a few minutes later and were intercepted by about nine Zeros. I didn't get a shot at one. Yes, just one. It
was on the tail of a P-38 and I tried to help the fellow with no results.
The formation was in my way. The Zero got the 38. Our squadron
lost a ship and the crew was on their first mission. They rescued the
men when it went down in the bay."

On February 10, 1944, Tricoli proudly noted, "First bomber over
Shanghai this war. Caught them by surprise. Dropped mines. Flew
down Yangtze at mast level, flew over a dozen Jap transports. It was a
bombardier's dream. You could see the Japs smoking on deck." He
came closest to Japan with raids on Formosa (now Taiwan) and continued with the 308th until June. During his tour, Tricoli flew ninety-
seven missions, earning an Air Medal with a cluster and a Distinguished
Flying Cross. In the European Theater, bomber crews ordinarily rotated
home after twenty-five to thirty-five combat missions.

The Second Chindit Expedition Controversy

Wingate, cheered by the promises of Arnold to provide massive air-borne aid, after a leave, had arrived in September with only five months to raise, organize, equip, and train the six brigades he expected to insert behind the enemy positions in Burma under the heading of Operation Thursday. In Delhi, Wingate bumped up against a wall of obstruction by the general headquarters staff for India. The "curry colonels," as those in the field derided the noncombatants manning the bureaucratic heights, considered the policies announced at Quebec as political pap rather than strategies to be implemented.

While the Sextant Conference in Cairo confirmed the Allied plans for an offensive in northern Burma, the Teheran meeting, which included Soviet leader Josef Stalin, shifted emphasis. Stalin successfully lobbied his fellow Allies for a second front before the summer of 1944 to relieve the ordeal of his armies fighting the Germans. The schedule for an invasion of Europe drained away ships, planes, people, and supplies. Not only did that bode poorly for Wingate's demands, but it also dismayed the generalissimo, who once more perceived that his country no longer was a priority. That would translate into a reluctance if not outright refusal to follow any script that put Chinese assets in jeopardy.

CBI's smoldering internecine war on a political level and personal antipathies flared in the last half of 1943 to confuse military decisions. Mountbatten had supported Wingate at Quebec but was subject to the masters in London. They did not favor a massive British offensive across the Assam border to help open supply routes into China. They had less interest in forays into Burma for China's benefit than operations that promised to preserve the empire. Rangoon, Hong Kong, and Singapore were more attractive objectives.

In the chain of command, Wingate was nominally subordinate to Slim, head of the Fourteenth Army. Slim admired Wingate's determination and persistence but regarded alteration of the Chindits from small, lightly equipped units capable of guerrillalike operations into a force of twenty thousand as questionable. He was not happy that Wingate managed to appropriate one of the Fourteenth's top outfits, the 70th British Division. At one point during an argument over resources, Slim said that Wingate, while protesting he held personal loyalty to Slim, remarked there was a fealty above that. "I asked him to whom it was. He replied, 'To the prime minister of England and to the President of the United States.' He went on to say that they had laid on him the duty of reporting direct to them whenever any of his superiors, in his opinion, were thwarting his operations. With the greatest regret he felt that this was such an occasion, and he must, whatever the consequences to me, so report to the prime minister. I pushed a signal pad across my desk to him and told him to go and write his message. He did not take the pad but he left the room. Whether he ever sent the message I do not know, nor did I inquire."

Stilwell Spars with the British

The era of good feelings between Mountbatten and Stilwell passed quickly. Still in control of the U.S. Tenth Air Force based in India, Stilwell countermanded an order for operations against an apparent threat to the base at Fort Hertz. Although the Japanese advance petered out, Mountbatten was furious at the interference within his domain. Through appeals to higher authorities, he succeeded in bringing the Tenth into his tent. Its chief, Major General George Stratemeyer, accepted the arrangement in good grace.

For his part, Stilwell, by January 1944, castigated Mountbatten: "The Glamor Boy is just that. He doesn't wear well and I began to wonder if he knows his stuff. Enormous staff, endless walla-walla [talk] but damned little fighting." Later he sneered at the supreme commander as "a fatuous ass"; "childish Louis, publicity-crazy"; "a pisspot." He fulminated against the British, "The more I see of the Limeys, the worse I hate them"; "the bastardly hypocrites do their best to cut our throats on all occasions. The pig-fuckers." However, in the personal meetings with Mountbatten, Stilwell remained affable. The grease that prevented a rupture of the Anglo-American relations in CBI was supplied by General Albert Wedemeyer, the American chief of staff to SEAC. A skillful military diplomat but not a toady, Wedemeyer thought Mountbatten "intelligent, amenable, and apparently willing and anxious to get on with the job." The supreme commander in turn found Wedemeyer "100 percent loyal and straightforward."

Against stiff opposition from establishment circles and a weakening of Mountbatten's support, Wingate still managed to create his six brigades. The order of battle for Operation Thursday: the 3d West African Brigade (Thunder), 6th, 7th, and 12th Nigerian Battalions; the 14th Brigade (Javelin), 2d Battalion of the Black Watch, 1st Battalion, Bedfordshire and Hampshire Regiment, 2d Battalion York and Lancaster Regiment, and 7th Battalion, Leicestershire Regiment; 16th Brigade (Enterprise), 2d Battalion, Queens Regiment, 2d Battalion, Leicestershire Regiment, 51/69 Royal Artillery, 45th Reconnaissance Regiment; 77th Brigade (Emphasis), 3d Battalion, 6th Gurkha Rifles, 1st Battalion, Kings Regiment. 1st Battalion, Lancashire, 1st

Battalion, Lancashire Fusiliers, 1st Battalion, South Staffordshire Regiment, 3d Battalion, 9th Gurkha Rifles; 111th Brigade (Profound), 1st Battalion, Cameroonians, 2d Battalion, King's Own Royal Regiment, 3d Battalion, 4th Gurkha Rifles, 3d Battalion, Gurkha Rifles (added after May 16, 1944); Morris Force (named for Brigadier J. R. Morris), 4th Battalion, 9th Gurkha Rifles, 3d/4th Gurkha Rifles. The sixth brigade was to be the 5307th Composite Unit (Provisional) with the three battalions of Americans.

It was, on the face of it, the fullest expression of allies.

11

Long-Range Penetrations and Arakan Revisited

After the *Lurline* docked in Bombay, the three battalions of Shipment 1688 spent a short period at a site for transients before establishing its training base at Camp Deogarh, a tent city in a wilderness three hundred miles south of New Delhi. The contingent received a new name, the 5307th Composite Unit (Provisional). According to Charles Hunter, when the ship arrived in India, Colonel Francis Brink, from CBI headquarters, handed over a letter that placed Brink "in charge of training and everything else except actual command and discipline." The decision to give Brink responsibility for making the organization combat-ready miffed Hunter. He remarked that as a member of the general staff corps, Brink "was ineligible by law to exercise command of troops."

Nevertheless, Hunter described Brink as "aggressive, intelligent, and dedicated. . . . He was a rugged individual; I would have been happy to have been his second in command. Brink admired, was personally acquainted with, and was prepared to cooperate wholeheartedly with Orde Wingate, and the British in general. He had high hopes of becoming Galahad's combat commander, but Stilwell didn't like him."

While the Galahad contingent trained at Deogarh, Wingate suddenly put in an appearance. Sergeant Ray Lyons, the regimental clerk, remembered the day the British officer entered the tent. "I jumped to attention and said, 'Yes, sir! What can I do for you?' He told me he was Brigadier Wingate and he was there to visit Colonel Hunter. He looked like a crazy man. I must say that I instantly got the impression that his eyes were very wild-looking. When you looked at his eyes you got the impression that there was something wrong with this guy. He didn't seem to be a normal person."

Hunter said, "During his first visit Wingate addressed the assembled troops as is the British custom. He outlined his concept of long-range penetration tactics. Pride of authorship apparently led him to make statements that I questioned in my own mind, and I held the troops until he had left the area. I explained that his concept should not be considered too revolutionary and reminded the men that the United States had a long tradition of fighting deep in hostile Indian territory; that we should look at the coming operation in light of the history of our army in opening the West."

Hunter said Wingate advised the soldiers that if they would be deployed under Stilwell's command, they would not be withdrawn after three months, which was the limit he set for his Chindits. The Briton, said Hunter, "was apprehensive that [under Stilwell] we would be used to spearhead Chinese units. To this he was opposed. After he had departed, Merrill stated flatly that General Stilwell would not use Galahad to spearhead Chinese advances."

The 5307th engaged in joint maneuvers with Wingate's forces. The Gurkhas showed off their heavy curved-bladed knives, which seemed an improvement on the machetes that had been issued. The supply officer for Galahad managed to procure a generous number of the Gurkha cutlery. There was no animosity between the Allies. *Spearhead* remarked that in a war game, some British opponents allowed themselves to be taken prisoner, enabling them to share the more abundant American rations. "We admired them for their ability to train and live from day to day with less food, less pay, harder training, and a smaller chance of returning to their homes as soon as we had a right to expect."

Early in January, after Brink attended a conference with the British at Delhi, he learned that Stilwell had succeeded in having the 5307th removed from Wingate's operations to fight under his banner. Hunter accompanied Brink to the New Delhi airport, where Brink wanted to tell Wingate about this alteration in the order of battle. "We arrived at the airport just in time. Wingate's plane with Colonel 'Phil' Cochran as pilot was parked directly in front of the operations officer, ready and waiting for Wingate, who was inside. . . .

"Wingate greeted us affably, especially Brink, saying, 'Hello, Francis.' Brink informed Wingate that the decision had been made to relieve Galahad from his operational control. With this, Wingate's piercing black eyes clouded with anger, and he blurted out, 'Brink, you tell General Stilwell he can take his Americans and stick 'em up his ass.'"

Hunter confessed himself astounded to hear such a typically American GI expression uttered so vehemently by the Briton. Wingate had begun to stalk off, but he turned to Brink. "Francis, what I said was not intended to include you. You and I are old friends and I hope we always will be." He shook Brink's hand and climbed into his plane.

On January 4, 1944, Frank Merrill abruptly relieved a disappointed Brink. Hunter was also discomfited, having hoped for the top post if Brink was sacked. He noted that Merrill's basic branch of service was the cavalry, not infantry. Like Brink, Merrill knew Japanese, but although tall he was anything but physically robust and in Hunter's eyes "subservient" to superiors. On the positive side, Hunter said the new leader "exuded self-confidence and on joining the outfit managed to gain its respect and confidence."

Merrill, if anything, intensified the training, which was supervised by Hunter, the senior person with a genuine foot-soldier background. Blessed with a surplus of ammunition at Deogarh, the 5307th indulged in copious live fire exercises. Every man freely fired all of the weapons available, including the crew-served ones. One vital operation not practiced was supply by parachute. However, the end of the association with the Chindits cost the 5307th a detachment of North Burma Rifles. Their departure deprived the Americans of guides and interpreters. Also, Wingate's people collected many of the mules lent to the Americans, who then requisitioned and began to train their own.

The First Air Commando Meets the Chindits

As Galahad went its separate way, the 2d Chindit expedition brought together two wildly disparate characters: Wingate, the aristocratic, Bible-quoting, often vague philosopher, with Cochran, the plebeian, breezy, plain-speaking American pilot. When they met first in London following Quadrant, Cochran confessed himself bewildered by his new associate. To Cochran, the windy theorizing on the history of warfare interfered with a clear solution to the problems facing the 2d Chindit expedition. A second session, however, clarified Wingate's strategy of long-range penetration and crystallized the matter in Cochran's mind. The American perceived a close parallel in the behind-the-lines Chindit columns that coordinated strikes through radio contact, with the theory of fighter control that directed aircraft.

When Cochran returned to the States, he met with Alison, his associate commander. From firsthand knowledge of the mountainous terrain, the almost suffocating jungle vegetation, the swift-moving, often wide streams, and the absence of roads, Alison could say, "The obvious answer was to move the troops by air. We asked for gliders and transports and light planes. We knew there was not enough fighter aviation in that theater, nor bomber aviation to take care of the present commitments and also give our force the protection we wanted them to have."

Along with Arnold's strong backing, the 1st Air Commando capitalized on a letter from Marshall, which Alison quoted where it would help. "This is an independent unit which we have sent to Burma, and it is to be used to support General Wingate." With such sponsorship, adept scrounging, and sub rosa negotiating with Pentagon bureaucrats, the 1st Air Commando accumulated a squadron of P-51s; one of B-25s, along with about a hundred gliders and the pilots to man them; and a squadron of C-47 troop carriers capable of parachute drops of men and supplies as well as towing the gliders. The number of light, single-engine planes added up to roughly a hundred. Altogether, the 1st Air Commando enrolled about five hundred men, including aircrews and ground maintenance staff. Some of the sergeant pilots doubled as mechanics.

When the two leaders first observed the clumsy, C4A Waco gliders, Cochran remarked to Alison, "People that fly airplanes are fool enough, but anyone who gets into one of those things is a damn fool." Moments later, however, Cochran said, "Let's find out how to fly one of those contraptions ourselves." Having mastered that skill, Cochran experimented with a technique for tow planes to snatch gliders off the ground. Over time, he perfected the technique and soon the pilots assigned to the 1st Air Commando learned how to perform the maneuver.

Wingate still thought in terms of trekking to the interior, but at a meeting with Wingate and Mountbatten in India, Cochran boldly announced that the U.S. airmen would fly the brigade into Burma. Alison remarked that Cochran had nothing to back up his word other than his reputation. An operation of this nature had never been attempted, and the assembled strategists seriously doubted him. At a clearing in a central India jungle, Cochran and company put on a show. A pair of gliders, one with Cochran in the copilot seat next to the chief glider pilot, Bill Taylor, successfully landed. Troops from the Black Watch, Scottish infantrymen who had never seen the interior of a glider before but had dutifully loaded aboard, fanned out to create a defensive perimeter while waves of additional gliders swooped down to unload supplies, heavy equipment, and even mules.

Cochran saw someone running over the newly plowed field. "It was muddy and I saw him running and falling down in the furrows. Then I recognized him. It was the Man. He stumbled up in a wild hurry and gasped, 'Phil, you've done it!' 'I've done what, sir?' 'You brought these gliders in and landed the troops.' 'Yes, I said I would.' 'And you have!' This bit of talk gave him away. I knew then how much he had doubted, all along, that we could make good on the glider idea." Wingate thought that like many British, Americans tended to brag and overestimate their capabilities. In the demonstration, twenty-four gliders packed with troops had landed without incident.

Douglas DC-3s returned to snatch the gliders from the ground. Wingate, taken out by glider snatch, shouted to one of the officers, "Tell the RAF that I have not only seen it, I have done it!" Thoroughly convinced, he reported to Mountbatten, "Cochran's gliding was a complete success and can revolutionize the whole campaign."

On another occasion, Mountbatten remarked to Cochran that he had learned to fly sometime earlier and would like to try his hand. Recalled Cochran, "Taking off, the first thing he did was a ground loop. He had big feet and got them all over the pedals, and the plane went spinning around. I yelled, 'Get your feet off the brake!' He said, 'Which is the brake?' Airborne after the wing scraped the runway, Mountbatten flew for more than an hour while Cochran sweated the thought of a landing. It was hardly smooth, but the plane and its occupants survived. Later, Mountbatten sent a note apologizing for nearly crashing.

"General Wingate was an officer with vision," said Alison. "We had no sooner sold him on the idea of moving the troops by air than he immediately began to expand upon our operation and press us to do more. Instead of flying in a small percentage of his troops as first planned, General Wingate called on the Troop Carrier Command to carry almost his entire force after the troops of the Air Command Force had landed and built airdromes."

Using civilian labor and elephants, the outfit lengthened and widened bare airstrips in India at Hailakandi and Lalaghat to accommodate multiengine bombers and transports. The airmen pitched in alongside the workers, and no one paid much attention to their appearance until the new ATC commander, Major General William D. Old, inspected the base. He was appalled by the shirtless, bearded Americans, telling Cochran and Alison, according to the latter, "This is a rabble. This isn't a military organization. Off with the beards."

Cochran responded to an order for the men to shape up with a bulletin board announcement: "Look, Sports, the beards and attempts at beards are not appreciated by visitors. Since we can't explain to all strangers that the fuzz is a gag, we must avoid their reporting that we were unshaven (regulations say shave) by appearing like Saturday night in Jersey. Work comes before shaving. You can never be criticized for being unkempt if you are so damn busy you can't take time to doll up. But be clean while you can. Ain't it awful."

As soon as the bases in India were operational, the Americans began to fly missions. The first one consisted of two P-51s with Cochran and Colonel Arvid Olsen, an AVG alumnus, at the controls. Cochran reported, "We went over stooging around in Burma and shot up a few likely-looking targets and came back."

Cochran and his associates faced another unknown, the reaction of the beasts of burden to flight. He said, "How were these animals [the mules] going to ride? They [the Chindits] depended a great deal on them. They were their mobility in the jungle. Going along in the jungle, you'd be within a hundred yards of the enemy and the enemy wouldn't quite know exactly where you were. The soldiers were trained to strap all their military utensils, everything so they didn't clank. If the mule brayed or hee-hawed, he would give you away. The poor fellows had to be 'debrayed' [severance of their vocal chords]. We had these mute mules to put in gliders and aircraft and we didn't know how they were going to take to that sort of thing. We knew something of the nature of the mule and we were a little apprehensive. We had all manner of wild schemes of how we would do this. We searched the outfit to find any farm boy that had any experience or knew anything about mules. We found a couple of our guys who had mules on a farm. We had attacked the problem as though it were something you would have to sit down from square one and design something, as though it were one of these terrible, insurmountable things. This kid just cut that all out and said, 'Why don't we just try walking them in and see what they do.' Lo and behold, the mules took to it just like they take to everything else. It didn't concern them one bit. We asked the mule to go in the glider. He walked in and he stood there. We did take some precautions. We had a mule tender to go along and he had a ready revolver to clunk the guy between the eyes if he started tearing the glider apart. It wasn't necessary at all. The mules took off and enjoyed the ride, landed, and did nothing. As the guys in the glider said, 'They even banked on the turns.'"

Cochran and Alison obviously had been won over by the strength of Wingate's personality and his vision. Not everyone connected with the Chindit operations accepted the gospel or its messenger. His countryman Squadron Leader Terence Patrick O'Brien, a veteran of the futile effort to preserve Singapore and a pilot assigned as liaison between the Chindits and the RAF, said, "Wingate looked at you like the ancient mariner, 'long grey beard and glittering eye,' seeing you if at all not as a fellow human being with a life and mind of your own but as a tool for him to wield in some God-given fashion. Why risk your life for such an egocentric visionary? Or do him a favor?"

In his original manuscript from which he published an edited version, *Out of the Blue,* O'Brien continued, "There was no doubt about the passionate enthusiasm he roused in many of the officers. They spoke of him with a sort of religious fervor. After that famous meeting at the cinema in Jhansi when he addressed us in his flat, harsh voice, talking about the coming campaign, most of the officers came out with shining eyes, transformed into excited crusaders. They were so inspired by his personality that his actual words escaped scrutiny. A few, however, were not so completely bewitched, were uneasy about some of his military ideas and said so. These were matters beyond my competence, the most junior subaltern knew far more about ground fighting than I did, but I did know something about air war and I thought he was talking fearful nonsense on the subject of air support. He said we had no need of artillery, that the fighters and bombers of Cochran's force would act for us far more effectively than could any field guns, and far more massively. Certainly Cochran himself, speaking with enthusiasm, offered a willingness to try anything we might devise—'Just dream it up for us,' he said—but he made no such extravagant guarantees about his air support as Wingate did. Wingate was dogmatic as always: 'The planes are our artillery. They will bomb and destroy the targets you produce.'

". . . Anyone who has ever flown an airplane in action would have told him and them [the audience] this was nonsense. A major general in his position should have known that, because to think otherwise could at best lead to disappointment and at worst to a bloody shambles. . . . I had the practical experience in three theaters of war, in bombing and ground support, and had actually been lecturing on these matters just prior to joining Special Force. I knew he was wrong. The pilot drops his bomb towards a target, misses, and is finished; but when guns fire, the gunners adjust on the early results and then start hitting. To a pilot a miss is an end result, to a gunner it is the normal preamble to the bombardment proper."

O'Brien tried to argue the point with Gurkha officers in Wingate's legions, but he said they dismissed his caveats as typical service branch jealousy. They believed Cochran and company would deliver what the RAF would not or could not. The RAF squadron leader reiterated that

Cochran only promised to try anything asked of him. "But he was so enthusiastic and confident that people did not examine his actual words."

Operation Albacore

While the 5307th Composite Unit and the Chindits assisted by the 1st Air Commando prepared for their roles on the Burma stage, Stilwell had devised Operation Albacore, an offensive with the ultimate goal of capturing the key town and airfield at Myitkyina. The initial thrusts would liberate territory for the continuation of the road from Ledo. The Chinese 38th Division, trained and equipped at Ramgarh, India, and led by General Sun Li-jen, who had given a good account of himself in the 1942 Burma fiasco, would spearhead the drive into Burma's Hukawng valley. This offensive would later enlist other alumni of Ramgarh, the Chinese 22d Division and the 30th Division brought to India in bits and pieces. They would have American advisers working with them, and the 5307th Composite Unit and Kachin Rangers, recruited through Detachment 101, were expected to infiltrate the Japanese jungle positions to provide the appropriate intelligence for the Chinese attacks.

According to Barbara Tuchman, Stilwell, aware that his Chinese forces believed themselves militarily inferior to the enemy, attempted to ensure they had numerical superiority against any units that confronted them. The 38th Division advanced rather cautiously—too slowly for Stilwell's taste. He showed up with the regiments dug in along the Tarung River, just shy of the Hukawng valley. They had come under fire from Japanese soldiers, probing for openings to begin *their* own offensive into Assam.

On the scene, Stilwell rallied the troops with words, arranged for a barrage from big guns, and devised maneuvers to outflank the enemy. He could be seen hiking the trails from headquarters to smaller units and staying close enough to the front to worry others that he might fall victim to a shell or a sniper. In his diary, Stilwell commented that General Sun, after a "heart-to-heart talk, swears they are trying to do a good job for the *lao hsien sheng* [Old Man] and the troops are all bucked up to have me with them but commanders are uneasy for fear I get hit and they be held responsible. Insistent that I stay back and let them do it."

The fighting, including hand-to-hand combat amid foxholes and redoubts, raged for more than a week before the Japanese retreated.

At the end of December 1943, the 38th counted 315 dead and another 429 wounded, but the division could, for the first time, boast of having defeated the foe in Burma. However, when Stilwell urged the Chinese to exploit their gains, they stalled. "Sun not moving; preposterous demands for ammunition, air support, and artillery." The American spoke curtly to the 38th Division commander, pointing out that his organization had received more weapons, supplies, and medicines than any other Chinese unit. Before Stilwell would bring up tanks, larger mortars and U.S. infantry (the 5307th Composite), and flamethrowers (which were not yet in the theater), he wanted assurance that Sun would follow orders. Stilwell issued an ultimatum: "If I am double-crossed by the people I am trying to help I am through for good and I will recommend very radical measures." The hard talk was intended as much for the ears of the generalissimo, whom Stilwell suspected of holding the Chinese back, as for Sun.

Better results came from the other Chinese army unit. American adviser Major Desmond Fitzgerald had been assigned to the 65th Regiment in the 22d Division in the midst of the campaign. He reported, "Major (now Lieutenant Colonel) Jo Shih Kung, who commanded the 2d Battalion, quickly showed himself to be a first-class officer and leader. His vice commander was also an excellent soldier. Our battalion remained in reserve until the leading unit (the first battalion) encountered a strong enemy position at the mouth of the [Ahawk Hka River]. The strength of the enemy was estimated at four hundred to five hundred men. My battalion received the attack order from Colonel Fu Chun Liang, the regimental commander. The plan was for the 1st Battalion to engage the enemy on the north and northeast, while the 2d Battalion tried to cut the trail along the [river] south of the enemy's position. Colonel Fu's plan was in all aspects admirable.

"Our flanking movement proceeded slowly. The terrain was the most difficult I encountered anywhere in Burma—steep ravines and hills covered with closely matted jungle. It took the 2d Battalion three days to cut behind the enemy's position. The advance was conducted in an orderly manner and fire discipline was well maintained. The unit reached the assigned areas without being detected by the enemy. Animals could not use the trail that we had cut and the ammunition needed for the attack had to be hand-carried from the drop zone located north of the [starting point]. Nevertheless all our units were in position and preparations for the attack had been completed by January 22. I was not fortunate enough to witness the final phases of the operation at firsthand as orders for my recall to headquarters arrived. The outstanding success of the action and the aggressive conduct of the 2d Battalion were well known and were I believe a tremendous boost to the morale of the unit.

"For my part I admit that I guessed wrong. It seemed to me overoptimistic to expect the enemy to allow himself to be outflanked by a movement so necessarily slow and while it was in progress so vulnerable . . . this was not the last time I was wrong in estimating the capabilities of the Chinese soldiers and the tactical acumen of the Japs."

Colonel Smith, chief liaison officer to the 22d Division, had been with the outfit for a year and helped supervise the jungle warfare training that occurred after the division moved to the Ledo area. According to Smith, the officers and soldiers benefited from information from the 38th Division, already in contact with the Japanese. The 65th Regiment marched from Shingbwiyang, terminus of the Ledo Road construction, over thickly jungled mountainous trails.

"As the leading elements of the regiment reached a point some twelve miles north of Taro small screening forces of the Japs were encountered and the advance for several days was characterized by extreme caution on the part of the regimental commander who often used the excuse of lack of supplies and supporting artillery for the slowness of his advance. When the Jap was encountered, the Chinese fought well and the individual soldier was keen to meet the Jap in hand-to-hand combat. The heads of the first Japs killed were severed from their bodies and stuck on bamboo pikes and paraded about the bivouac area amid wild enthusiasm. When Colonel Foo [sic; his name was Fu] was reminded that such practice was hardly regular, he claimed they were not troops of his regiment.

"General Stilwell in command of these Chinese forces had issued orders to the regimental commander [Colonel Fu] to move his 1st Battalion from a new area in the vicinity of Shingbwiyang forward, as he desired the attack to move forward with greater speed, the prompt capture of the Taro Plain being necessary at this time to provide a base of operation for Wingate LRP columns, which were to pass through that locality at an early date. The advance of the regiment continued slowly, and General Stilwell's orders affecting the 1st Battalion were not complied with. As a result of this disobedience of orders, Colonel Foo . . . although in the field and in actual contact with the Jap was relieved. The relief of an American commander under similar circumstances would hardly cause a ripple. Not so with the Chinese army, where regiments are much more closely knit around their leader. The relief of the regimental commander caused much consternation in all the units of the division and particularly to Commander General Liao, who, in my opinion, was largely responsible for the failure of the 1st Battalion . . . more responsible than Colonel Foo."

Fitzgerald had mentioned the tight jungle of the area. Stilwell wrote to his wife, "Progress is slow; the jungle is everywhere and very nearly impenetrable. Yesterday, on a cut trail I took $3^1/_2$ hours to do 3 miles, tripping and cursing at every step. It takes a long time to even locate the Japs, and a lot more to dig them out. We are in tiger and elephant country although I haven't seen any yet . . . I've seen droppings and tracks. When an elephant leaves his card in the trail, it take a pole vaulter to climb over. I expect to see Tarzan any day now. The jungle is full of his long swinging vines. . . . The Chinese soldier is doing his stuff, as I knew he would if he had half a chance. It's only the higher-ups who are weak and they are still pretty terrible. The Americans are all doing a good job and they all enjoy the life."

The Road Builders

Behind the slowly advancing Chinese soldiers, the pickaxes, shovels, and earth movers ground away to extend the narrow road from Ledo. Colonel Richardson Selee oversaw the construction of the ten miles from Ningam Sakan to Yupbang Ga. As Christmas 1943 approached, Selee, in his diary, reported he coped with garbled communications from headquarters and new specifications, "changed suddenly from engineering 'by eye' with 'anything goes' to 32' roadway, easy curves, etc., etc. Companies B & E going back to widen and improve to meet the current specs. No parts, heavy casualties [injuries] and poor operating responsible for serious equipment problem. Since Dec. 1st can think of 4 or 5 pieces of heavy equip [sic] going over the bank. Cave-ins prevalent, yet withal, the work accomplished is miraculous. Dharjeelians employed by the thousands thru India Tea Assn. Ngas friendly with prices for knives and chickens going very high."

He noted an "effective service Xmas eve—extra beer ration . . . the band, orchestra and glee club outdid themselves. Christmas dinner of canned turkey, cranberry sauce, sweets, dressing, pie & cake & coffee-raisin bread & peas & chocolates. Usual work on 25th."

Two weeks later, he reported, "Got the nastiest letter ever today from PICK [sic]—said the production of the regt had gone down steadily since I took over: that I had failed to supervise and inspect at night in the good fashion that he does and accordingly I was a wash-out or 'words to that effect.' If he is right I am going to correct it—if he is wrong I am going to prove it too."

Selee's troubles continued, with frequent reports of heavy equipment that went off the precipitous road, daily pelting rains ("only 3.2 inches in few hours"), the theft of his jeep, inspections of the logging operations, shortages of gravel, tedious and difficult bridge building and culvert digging, soaring rates of malaria and venereal disease among his troops, and occasional deaths of drivers in accidents ("truck loaded with powder blew up, traffic guard tried to help drivers and was fatally burned.").

The Second Arakan Failure

To complicate matters for the Japanese, the British forces in the Arakan had begun to reassert themselves, creeping southward toward the objective of Akyab and the nearby airfields. On the surface that seemed to spell trouble for the campaign aimed at Assam, but if timed properly, it was reasoned that a counterstrike by the Japanese in the Arakan could well draw off forces that would have been available to defend the Imphal region.

Slim wrote and said intelligence accurately set the Japanese presence there at one division. Subsequently it was learned that an additional infantry division had entered the area. With his forces of almost three such organizations plus another in reserve, Slim believed he had the stuff with which to capture Akyab and the strategic jewels in its vicinity.

On the final day of November 1943, Lieutenant General Sir Philip Christison's XV Corps began its push, sending forward the 5th and 7th Divisions. Aided by patrols that pinpointed the locations of small enemy detachments, they advanced toward the tunnels through the Mayu range, which connected Maungdaw and Razabil, beyond which lay Buthidaung, all objectives during the first Arakan campaign. In the nearly one-year interval between the 1942 expedition and the latest one, the Japanese had busied themselves building stout fortifications at the entrances to the tunnels and into the steep, jungle-clad hills that overlooked the road to Maungdaw. The dugouts bit twenty to thirty feet below the surface, with mutually supporting machine-gun fire fields. Subterranean living quarters enabled the enemy to hide its presence.

Captain David Rissik, a veteran of the first venture into the Arakan, had been made an aide to General Christison. Rissik reported that along with the advance of the 5th and 7th Divisions on Maungdaw and Razabil, the strategy threw "a left hook" as the 81st Division moved down the Kaladan valley, east of the Mayu range. The

Japanese resistance stalled both the 5th and the 7th, and the British planned now to deploy tanks.

Said Rissik, "As a result of my experiences of the previous year, I had a somewhat prejudiced opinion of the fighting qualities of Indian troops. But here were two fresh Indian divisions properly trained and one of them with the laurels of victory in the desert still green upon its brow. The 5th Indian Division, who were to open the ball, were by no means the same division which had set forth for the Middle East some two years or so before. One brigade, a motor brigade, was left behind, presumably considered unsuitable for employment in the jungle. [In its place, the 5th] were given the 123d Brigade from the moribund 14th Division [chewed up during the earlier Arakan fighting], which refitted, rested, and reinforced from the better troops of the 14th Division . . . a useful addition to their strength and one which had some experience of jungle conditions. Nevertheless, the self-assurance with which the division descended upon the Arakan was not a little amusing. They could be told nothing: for had they not fought for two years in the desert with outstanding success? . . . So they learnt the peculiarities of warfare against the Japanese the hard way as did all new troops regardless of their experience under other conditions. The price as usual was paid in blood, though fortunately not much.

"In comparison, their neighbors, the 7th Division, gave the impression of having dash and ingenuity and of being only too ready to benefit from such experience as others had to offer them. Their commander, Gen. [Lieutenant General Sir Frank] Messervy, was ever concerned with new ideas as to how to keep the Japs guessing; and they seemed to make headway where the 5th Division, moving more cautiously, remained stationary. When the real test came, both formations acquitted themselves with utmost valor and the 5th Division hardly received the credit that it deserved."

The attack on the Razabil positions, January 26, kicked off with strong support from the air forces in India. Mitchells and Liberators from the U.S. Tenth Air Force, along with Vengeance dive bombers from the RAF, roared over the Arakan. Rissik reported, "At ten o'clock sharp the first waves of bombers appeared over the target area and dropped their bombs with [what] appeared to be good effect upon the Japanese positions [the fortress dubbed Tortoise]. They were followed by Vengeances whose accuracy, soon to become a bye-word, was all that could be desired. [Artillery smoke shells directed them toward the targets.] Then came another wave of Mitchells and here for the first and only time something went wrong. The pilot of one of the planes in the second flight must have misjudged the area in which his bombs were to fall and to our horror they were seen to burst well away to the west, where it was known that some tanks and troops of an India battalion were forming up. Fortunately, only slight damage was done. The *subedar* major of the battalion was killed and one tank received superficial damage. Otherwise the only effect was to frighten a number of RAF officers in the area observing the operation."

After the air strike, field artillery pounded the enemy and, said Slim, "pumped shells from their accumulated dumps into the smoking, burning, spouting hillsides. Then the guns suddenly paused. The Lee-Grant tanks [from the 25th Dragoons] roared forward; the infantry, bayonets fixed, yelling their Indian war cries, following on their tails. The dismal Jimmies who had prophesized, one that the tanks would never get to the line, two that they could never climb the hills and three, if they did the trees would so slow them up that the Japanese antitank guns would bump them off as sitting targets, were confounded. The tanks, lots of them—'the more you use, the fewer you lose'—crashed up the slopes and ground over the dug-in antitank guns. All was going well but as the infantry passed ahead of the armor for the final assault the guns of the tanks had to cease firing for fear of hitting our own men. In that momentary pause, the Japanese machine gunners and grenadiers remanned their slits and rat holes. Streams of bullets swept the approaches and a cascade of bombs bounced down among our infantry."

At headquarters, Rissik, unable to have seen the ebb and flow of the battle, learned that the attack had failed. "The infantry had not been sufficiently quick in following up the bombing and the Japanese positions were, in the majority of cases, dug down deep enough for the bombs to have had little effect upon them. The plain fact had to be faced that the Japanese were sufficiently strongly situated to prevent any further effective advance by the 5th Division without the planning and execution of more elaborate operations."

Slim admitted that this first assault did not rout the enemy burrowed deep into the hill. "It was the old problem of the First World War [of which he was a veteran], how to get the infantryman onto his enemy without a pause in the covering fire that kept his enemy's head down. It was solved in Arakan . . . by tanks firing first, surface-burst high explosive to clear the jungle, then delayed action high explosive to break up the faces of the bunkers this exposed, and lastly solid armor-piercing shot as the infantry closed in. With no explosion, the last few yards were safe, if you had first-class tank gunners and infantrymen with steady nerves who let the shot whistle past their heads and strike a few feet beyond or to one side of them. We had such tank gunners and such infantrymen—and they had confidence in one another, even when of different races." The prescription described by Slim enabled the British forces to nibble away chunks of Tortoise, but he noted, "in its very heart, desperate Japanese, with a courage that, fanatical or not, was magnificent, still held out."

Christison, as corps commander, reported Rissik, decided that "the main effort should be switched to the 7th Division front where the opposition had not proved to be as strong." The 7th Indian Division, on the other side of the Mayu range, punched into the enemy positions as the King's Own Scottish Borderers battalion captured a hillock that overlooked the main road between the tunnels and Buthidaung. Not even point-blank cannonades from a Japanese 155-millimeter gun could dislodge the troops, who included a relief unit of Gurkhas. To buttress the subsequent attack, a brigade from the 5th Division marched over the Ngakyedauk [Okydoke] Pass. The offensive succeeded in taking Buthidaung, and a new administrative box surrounded the supply depots, ammunition dumps, motor pools, and medical facilities.

Inside the box, the British scraped out a small airstrip capable of accommodating the standard single-engine, spotter, and liaison planes. The 1st Air Commando, said Alison, dispatched a squadron of their L-5s to assist the besieged troops. "They would carry a fresh man in and bring an injured man out. If a man were hit or wounded, very often in about an hour's time we could have him back in India in a general hospital. The doctors just thought this was the greatest thing that had happened to military medicine." The arrangement enabled the Americans to practice under battle conditions the service they had promised Wingate.

On a parallel track east of the 5th and 7th Indian Divisions, the 81st West African Division, commanded by Major General C. G. Woolner, traveled down the Kaladan Valley, through which the river of that name flowed north to south. West Africa covers a huge territory, and the members of the division represented several colonies: Nigeria, Sierra Leone, the Gold Coast, and Gambia. Formed into two brigades plus a divisional unit, they lacked a common language. The officers were predominantly white.

Peter Jeffreys, a white Briton and member of Woolner's staff, voiced misgivings about the operation. The march traversed an almost trackless expanse, with Woolner predicating his success upon cutting a path that would allow jeeps to supplement the manhandled or muleborne vital equipment. To sustain the troops, aircraft dropped their supplies.

Jeffreys recalled that the 4th Nigerian Regiment walked the sixty miles from the base at Chiringam, India, to Mowduk, just inside the

Burma border, "and reported the march a most fearful one. The rest
of 6 Brigade quickly followed them and a company pushed forward
unopposed into the Kaladan. I can remember well the feeling of wonderful elation I had on receiving the signal saying that . . . a company
of 4 NR was on the river near Daletme. One foot was inside the open
door before the Jap had slammed it."

Now came the most difficult part, constructing the jeep track.
The soldiers carved a path as they advanced. Said Jeffreys, "We were
not an expert force, I soon realized. I made mistakes. First amongst
them was the order that units should do the march from Chriinga to
Mowdok in four days. This gave an average of about fifteen miles a
day, but I had made no allowance for the hills! We later came to
reckon eight miles a day over mountainous jungle for a battalion with
full impedimenta to be a good marching performance.

"March discipline in many units was very poor; sanitary discipline
was low; water discipline did not exist . . . groups started discarding
loads; serious pilferage occurred at nearly all ration supply dumps
and baggage dumps. The Africans suffered a lot from the cold. We
could only carry one blanket on the man. We hoped to drop a second
from the air and then ferry it forward as we went. It was a pious hope.
Gathering supplies dropped was a considerable problem in thick jungle. Always a dropping zone [DZ] would have to be cleared of all
bamboo and scrub, 50 yards by 150 was the minimum size. Inaccurate dropping by the aircraft often resulted. If the jungle was thick
and hilly a parachute which dropped over the brow of a hill was unlikely to be found unless it had caught in a high tree. A varying proportion of parachutes failed to open or sometimes the load would slip
from its container and the result was usually ruined contents. An
accidental free drop of this nature was a great danger to personnel
below; during the operation several men were badly injured this way,
three of them fatally.

"The handling of the aircraft themselves must have been a most
hazardous task. Dropping at any height above 300 feet resulted in great
inaccuracy. In the very hilly country at the top of the Kaladan valley,
to fly as low as this was obviously an extremely difficult task." The
pilots, from the RAF, USAAF, and Royal Canadian Air Force, would
make four to six runs over the tiny, not-well-marked drop zones. Fortunately, in the Kaladan campaign, the RAF controlled the skies, and
the unarmed Dakotas, bearing supplies, went almost untroubled by
enemy aircraft. Probably no other area depended as much on air drops
as CBI, and the problems cited by Jeffreys were omnipresent. Although
Jeffreys figured his unit was probably sixty miles away, he heard the
sound of the thundering guns contesting for the Tortoise and Buthi-

daung. "All we knew was that the battle had been joined in a big way and while listening to that continuous but distant artillery roar, received instructions from Christison to push on ever faster for Kyaukta [seventy miles down stream from Daletme]."

When the division finally encountered the enemy, Woolner chose to advance on a broad front, hoping to find weak sectors that his forces could break through. That indeed occurred. From the 6th Brigade, elements of the 1st Sierra Leone Regiment crossed the Kaladan River to the eastern bank and then got over the Mi Chaung. The 1st Gambia engaged a strong enemy force at Kaladan village. That outfit, assisted by the 7th Gold Coast Regiment, struggled with the Japanese garrison while the remainder of the 6th Brigade and parts of the 5th forged ahead.

Said Jeffreys, "At this time, four of the six infantry battalions we had were all in combat with the enemy. The fighting was of a particularly unpleasant and tiring nature. The enemy positions encountered were invariably covering important defiles from which deployment was difficult; they were strongly and cunningly sited on precipitously steep ground and very carefully concealed. Holding their fire well, the Japs would let our leading troops come well forward, and then at close range inflict on us severe casualties. There would follow the slow, difficult deployment through the steep, thick, bamboo-clad country searching for the flanks of the enemy position in order to turn it. Inaccurate maps and the tangled, irregular ridges and spurs and reentrants made this a slow game and as soon as it succeeded the Japanese would trickle away through the thick jungle. A subunit sent behind to cut them off would find their job similar to trying to shoot rabbits in thick rhododendrons without any [pathways] cut in them. Our casualties were mounting rapidly, and if we were learning fast, we were also tiring quickly, too."

An African Soldier's Tale

Private Isaac Fadoyebo, a Yoruba from Nigeria, was a soldier in the 81st West African Division. His background and his experiences describe the enormous cultural chasm between many of the soldiers drawn from the British colonies and thrust into twentieth-century warfare. "I was born on the 5th December, 1925," said Fadoyebo, in an account of his life. "My mother and her parents had more than a feeling that she was being bewitched at home. Hence the thirty-kilometer journey [to a larger town with better health care] each time her pregnancy got to an advanced stage. The journey was usually made on foot and at night to avoid being seen by 'evildoers' who in their view were responsible for the deaths of five baby boys before the survival of my elder sister."

Fadoyebo grew up in a family marked by polygamy, and he reported his handsome father "featured prominently in brawls and litigations over women affairs." As the first son to survive, however, young Isaac was doted on by his father, a clerk in the timber industry, and granted the luxury of a grammar school education while his contemporaries worked on farms.

In 1941, Fadoyebo took the examination for teaching appointments. Only the five top scorers were accepted, and he finished sixth. He promptly enlisted, at age sixteen, in the army. He trained at the 44th General Hospital at Abeokuta, the capital for the state of Ogun, Nigeria. "The syllabus of the training course was not wide enough to cover real nursing work," noted Fadoyebo. "Nursing proper was being carried out by British nursing sisters and we were trained as sort of auxiliary medical persons [for use] with field ambulances on the war front."

The army also drilled Fadoyebo and his contemporaries in marching. They partook of a vigorous physical conditioning program "under the scorching sun" at the Enugu 1st Infantry Training Center. "At Abeokuta we were dealing with refined and educated military personnel: doctors, nursing sisters, qualified pathological laboratory technicians, and other highly skilled British officers and other ranks. In Enugu we met the opposite. We had to undergo military training supervised by indigenous noncommissioned officers who were rough in mind and in some cases callous to the extreme. We were not allowed to have access to the white commissioned officers. The highest rank we could deal with direct was warrant officer I, popularly known as regimental sergeant major. They would shout on us as if we were not human beings and generally developed hatred for those of us who had a bit of education. Not that the noncommissioned officers were naturally wicked; the feigned cruelty was designed for a purpose; namely to harden the body and mind."

At Enugu he was assigned to a company with a fair share of literate personnel, while other units were composed largely of illiterates. His E Company mates believed they were denied certain rights and privileges. "We later came to learn that the army was not the type of organization where an individual or a set of people could claim any right. Coming together for the purpose of forming a pressure group was a very serious offense. Anyone who tried it could be charged for 'mutiny,' a crime punishable with severe penalties."

The military required the Nigerian recruits to remove every bit of hair on their heads, and barbers regularly "scraped" their skulls bare. They wore khaki pants that ended between the knees and ankles, and woolen, long-sleeved jerseys. The authorities would brook no protests about the uniforms. "Imagine wearing a woolen pullover without underwear and staying in the sun marching for hours in a tropical country during the dry season; it could be unbearably warm." Absent dry cleaning facilities, the wool jerseys shrank with conventional washing. While Fadoyebo and others from his area spoke Yoruba, the dominant language was Hausa, and the British officers learned enough to be able to manage their troops.

After a four-week leave at home, where his father urged him to desert, Fadoyebo began a long trip by rail and by ship to India, assigned to the 29th Casualty Clearing Station, attached to the 6th West African Brigade, a component of the 81st West African Division. Most of the men with the 29th were from Sierra Leone, with the Nigerians to supplement them. In Calcutta, Fadoyebo witnessed an air raid. While he and his fellows had been trained to react to exposure to gas, they had received no instructions on how to behave when attacked from the air.

From Calcutta, the unit traveled by sea across the Bay of Bengal to Chittagong, the staging area for campaigns into the Arakan. Here the army issued green battle dress similar in style to that of the British soldier. Their commanding officer lectured them on their obligation to give only name and regimental number if captured. He told them, said Fadoyebo, "a Japanese soldier would normally prefer to die in the battlefield in the belief that his soul would go straight to 'Japanese heaven' . . . What a belief!" But indeed he would learn from experience that the enemy displayed "remarkable doggedness in carrying out their military duties. Their resourcefulness and powers of endurance in the battlefield were baffling."

The unit moved toward combat on foot and by canoe and bamboo raft. "Meals became irregular and scarce. We ate if and when food was available . . . conditions were such so we had to depend on parachutes for nearly all our needs. I was in the batch led by a young British sergeant who was in possession of a detailed map. We were in full marching order with all our belongings strapped round our body. The few things that could not go into the haversacks were packed into kit bags and each soldier, except the British noncommissioned officer, carried his on his own head. His kit bag had been picked up by one of the jeeps." To climb the steep hills, every man used a sharp-pointed stick he jammed into the ground before each step. Otherwise, said Fadoyebo, one risked falling backward and rolling to the foot of the hill.

Occasionally they encountered barefooted Burmese. "They peeped at us with excitement. The white-skinned soldiers were no doubt a familiar sight but we Africans attracted a lot of attention. I would not be surprised if some of them were seeing blacks for the first time."

Although the sergeant major carried a rifle, and the British officers and noncoms bore pistols, none of the blacks was armed. The advance party with Fadoyebo, floating down the Kaladan in canoes, paused for the night at the village of Nyron. "About 7:30 A.M." he remembered, "gunshots rang from the opposite bank unexpectedly and I and other members of my unit ran for cover. The Japanese troops were on the offensive. The slanting nature of the river bank rendered ineffective our efforts to dodge the enemy bullets. We could not do much to evade the gunshots. . . . The gunfire continued intermittently for more than one hour. A colleague of mine, Essien, and I took cover in the same place. Each time the Japanese stopped firing, I made abortive attempts to get away from the area. I did not know that I had been wounded and I just kept on trying to move away. . . . I felt I possessed of such a remarkable agility that I could run to safety in the event of an attack. Alas I was wrong in my estimation of my prowess. In addition to my not being able to crawl away I started to feel tired due perhaps to loss of blood.

"My right leg developed aches and pains. So was the left-hand side of my abdomen, immediately below my ribs. I made an attempt to peep at my right leg and the left-hand side of my body and I saw a lot of blood. I knew for sure that I had been hit by bullets on both parts of the body. I had a fractured femur very close to the knee and one bullet pierced my stomach. Luckily for me, that bullet did not go deep enough to injure my intestine or any of the food canal organs. It occurred to me that I was in serious trouble.

"While I was trying to examine my body, the movement might have attracted the attention of the Japanese soldiers across the river and as a result several shots rang out again, disturbing nearly all the grass around me. They all missed me miraculously. I heard the sounds of bullets flying past my head, uprooting the shrubs around the spot where I laid my head.

"I noticed that Essien, who was lying quite close to me, was in pain but I did not see any blood stain on his battle dress. I heard him saying, 'Take me, O God! Take me, O God!' After a short while I observed that he was struggling for breath, gasping. He could no longer repeat, 'Take me, O God, take me.' A few minutes later he stopped gasping and I presumed that he was no more." As the firing ceased, Fadoyebo crawled a few feet, stretched out his hand, and realized that his friend had died.

"At sunset, Captain Brown, a Scot, emerged from nowhere and came straight to me and said, 'Ebo, my boy, you are down.' He had always called me Ebo because he felt my name Fadoyebo was too long for him to memorize. I complained of thirst, pains, and tiredness. He went away and after a minute or two reappeared with a flask containing tea and served me. What a brave soldier. It was apparent that all those who were lucky to escape death or being seriously wounded had run away except Captain Brown. I regarded the tea he gave me as the 'Last Supper' because I thought I was going to die in the next few minutes. I was already down with severe gunshot wounds, no medical attention, and no hope of getting out of the predicament. . . .

"At that juncture, the invading Japanese soldiers charged in with bayonets fixed to the muzzle of their rifles and took Captain Brown away from me. I heard him telling them, 'I am Captain Brown, medical officer.' I did not and still do not [fifty years later] know what happened to him. I came to admire and respect the courage and gallantry he displayed. He was free to desert us like the others but instead he kept going round to minister to the wants of those who were in dire need of assistance. He was not wounded, not even a scratch on his body, and yet as a soldier and true to his profession, he stayed to succor comrades struck down by enemy bullets."

Another group of enemy soldiers appeared. One pointed a rifle at Fadoyebo and gestured for him to stand. He could not, and the Japanese, probably convinced he was not a threat, left him. He helped his fellow soldiers loot the bodies in the area. Among them were a number of Fadoyebo's acquaintances who lay close enough for him to identify. Finally the soldiers left and local villagers swarmed over the site to pick through the baggage that remained, bits of clothing and other items carried by the unit. When two individuals showed sympathy, the wounded Yoruba, using sign language, persuaded them to carry him a distance from the killing ground.

For nearly a week he lay in tall grass, fed by Good Samaritans, Muslims from India, who applied some herbs to his still open wounds. To his delight, the friendly Indians brought to him Sergeant David Kagbo of the 29th, who limped from a minor gunshot wound near his ankle. Subsequently, a British captain with two African soldiers, who had unsuccessfully tried to rescue the medical clearing unit, appeared. "The British captain, who had only a Sten gun and few rounds of ammunition . . . was a combatant in full battle order and complete camouflage. In addition to his green battle dress he had his face and hands painted green. What we black soldiers needed was just the green dress, as nature had already colored our body. The white boys had the exposed part of their body painted green to avoid being easily seen from a distance."

The captain had recruited a pair of coolies to bear an improvised stretcher for Fadoyebo, and a third refugee from the 29th, Tommy Sherman, suddenly joined them. The officer, armed only with his Sten gun with a few rounds of ammunition, started to lead the small party, hoping to smuggle them through the Japanese lines. Unfortunately, the jolting movement triggered such severe pain that Fadoyebo could not completely stifle his screams of agony. When a friendly Indian informed the captain of the presence of a large number of Japanese ahead, the British officer decided further travel with the groaning Fadoyebo risked the safety of everyone. He directed that the wounded man be taken back to where he had been picked up and Kagbo stay with him. Much later Fadoyebo learned the captain had successfully evaded the enemy but his acquaintance Tommy Sherman, who chose to try a different escape route, disappeared.

Although both of the soldiers were Christians, Kagbo had been raised as a Muslim. To gain further help, they tried to convey that they held the same religious tenets of their hosts. From them they received temporary succor, food, and water, but soon they were abandoned. The two men endured an attempted betrayal by a Burmese bandit who robbed Fadoyebo of his blood-soaked jacket and a pus-splattered blanket. He apparently notified Japanese soldiers of their presence, but fortunately for the pair, the enemy, whom they heard searching the area, could not find them. On the brink of starvation and dehydration, Kagbo and Fadoyebo tried to find help. The latter could only crawl a few yards before his agony became so intense that he said he preferred to stop and die on the spot. His companion left him but found villagers who carried the badly wounded man to a safer place. As a monsoon enveloped their location, they settled in to await healing through time and a better opportunity to seek their fellow soldiers.

The reinforced Japanese counterattacks in the Arakan stopped further advance by the British. Intelligence confirmed that the enemy intended to strike directly at India, making Assam a major front. Slim needed whatever resources he could mobilize for defense of the plain leading to Imphal. He buttoned up the Arakan, choosing to withdraw from the vulnerable area around Buthidaung but standing fast at Maungdaw, the tunnel sector, and the mouth of the Naf River. The achievements for the second Arakan offensive were not monumental, but they showed that under the right circumstances, the Japanese could be beaten.

12

Marauders and Thursday

U pon hearing of Axiom, a proposal from SEAC that called for a cessation of efforts to open the Ledo Road, Stilwell grew choleric. Axiom argued that the construction project would take far too long to complete and that it would be better to expand over-the-Hump operations. The scenario, under Mountbatten's imprimatur, renewed the idea of a seaborne attack via Malaya and Sumatra, with Hong Kong as a primary goal. In scope and logistics it required a vast investment of resources, well beyond the possible. Predictably, the refusal of the British to contribute to the land-based invasion of Burma furnished Generalissimo Chiang Kai-shek with an excuse to deny his American commander the troops necessary for Stilwell's strategy. It was apparent that only substantial monetary contributions from the United States would change Chiang's mind.

For once, Stilwell's position jibed neatly with that held by both President Roosevelt and his Joint Chiefs of Staff. They regarded Axiom as weakening the resolve of China to continue in the war and as a British attempt to ensure retention of its colonies. With D-Day in France fewer than six months off, there was no chance to commit to such a huge undertaking as Axiom.

Stilwell expected that the drive by the Chinese divisions in northern Burma, begun in late 1943, would receive a huge boost through the insertion of the 5307th Provisional (Composite). The original plan indicated that the men would operate for roughly three months before withdrawal. At that, the medical authorities told Merrill and Hunter that reliance mainly on K rations, periodically supplemented with C rations and ten-in-one meals, would not furnish sufficient calories. Although the lightweight Ks offered three thousand calories, the dry biscuit and cheese were not appetizing, particularly as a daily meal.

Often soldiers downed only portions of the K ration, thereby depriving themselves of vital ingredients. There was, however, the hope of supplementing the intake with the food that grew in the Burma bush, including even bamboo shoots and the water contained in the omnipresent stalks. Fodder for animals, however, was uncertain. Mules could dine on bamboo leaves, but horses would find little to their taste.

Water tanks would accompany the men at the start. Later they would need to rely on finding fresh, pure supplies in the jungle. No one realized that the standard-issue halazone tablets, while effective for most contaminants, would not destroy amoebic eggs, deadly carriers of dysentery. Nor was insect repellant available in adequate amounts.

On February 21, after cursing the nightly downpour, Stilwell said to his diary, "Went to Ningbyen and saw Merrill's gang. Tough-looking lot of babies. Told Merrill what his job would be." Stilwell's closing remarks to Merrill were, "Good luck! You know what I want. Go in there and get it for me." The absence of written orders, a marked departure from basic protocol but typical of Stilwell's way, would heap kindling on the fires of controversy later.

James Hopkins reported, "General Stilwell looked well beyond his sixty-one years. He had on a soiled field jacket, baggy khaki pants, leggings, and a cap. He lost a lot of respect when he failed to address the men in large or small groups."

A contrasting opinion came from Lieutenant Colonel George A. McGee Jr., commander of the B or 2d Battalion. In his account, excerpted for a study project by Lieutenant Colonel Henry L. Kinnison IV, he said, "The visit was carried out in an appropriate and effective manner; and it accomplished all that needed to be done, that is he saw the troops and sized them up and they saw him and appreciated his interest, and both were well satisfied. Although clearly not General Stilwell's style, this was no time for oratory and there was no need for exhortations and flattery. These were well-motivated soldiers, and any questions which may have been in their minds at this time, on the eve of being committed to combat, were not ones that General Stilwell could answer."

Merrill and his second in command, Charles Hunter, discussed whether to haul their troops as far as possible by trucks or simply to walk them into the depths of Burma. Hunter reported that he advised Merrill that the entire outfit should go by foot rather than ride from Ledo to Shingbwiyang. "I felt strongly that, from the standpoint of breaking in the animals and men, the long hike would solve several primary deficiencies . . . it would condition the men and animals, who most certainly would be getting soft after nearly three weeks spent in merely getting from Deogarh to Ledo [a slow, 1,000-mile train trip]."

Hunter noted that the 140-mile march would allow the pack saddles to be broken in, and the mule skinners would become better acquainted with their charges. The pack animals had only recently been received. There was a question of whether to sever the vocal cords of the mules to prevent brays that would announce Galahad's presence to the enemy. The deputy commander claimed he thought the mutilation unnecessary, but Kinnison's research suggests there was insufficient time to perform the procedure on the hundreds of animals.

Hunter also said he thought the long trek would "separate the men from the boys." While that might be true, any "boys" would then be many miles inside Japanese lines and perhaps a handicap to the "men" trying to fulfill the mission. In any event, against the advice of others, such as Wingate and Ray Peers, who argued that the arduous march would cut into the endurance necessary for a three-month tour, the decision to hike into the depths of Burma stood.

A Chinese officer from the 38th Division joined Merrill's command staff as liaison to the Chinese already in the Hukawng valley. That division, aided by the 1st Provisional Tank Group, an American-led armored force of ninety light and medium tanks under Colonel Rothwell Brown, had now progressed to the Tawang and Tanai Rivers. To the west, the 22d Chinese Division protected the 38th's left flank. Merrill held a staff conference to lay out the plan for Galahad. He explained that the first objective was to cut the road between Jambu Bum and Shingban and then hit the Japanese 18th Division command post. Merrill predicted that the first contact with a sizable Japanese force would occur on March 2d, within a week after they started. Walawbum was the first significant target, and the ultimate goal was Myitkyina, site of an airfield and the hub critical to further advance of the Ledo Road beyond Shingbwiyang.

At 10:00 P.M. on February 7th, Galahad hit the forty-foot-wide road from Ledo headed toward the interior of Burma. The nighttime departure was a security measure, but Tokyo Rose soon announced that two American divisions were now marching along the Ledo Road. Captain Fred Lyons said, "Lining both sides of the road as far as I could see ahead were the bobbing heads of men in green helmets, with green packs riding high on their backs. Mules ambled along, their packs lurching from side to side in rhythmic movement with the marching feet. Behind me stretched an endless line of faces, chalky white in the iridescent light from a Burma moon. As dawn approached, we pulled off the road and made our camp in the jungle till sundown. For 137 miles, we were disturbed only by the dust of 100 truck convoys roaring past with provisions for the Chinese army hacking at the Japs in North Burma."

Correspondents in CBI knew of the 5307th and, while censors and secrecy prevented them from revealing their mission, had seen them training. *Time* and *Life* reporter James Shepley, seeing them leave Ledo, hit on a catchy name: "Merrill's Marauders."

On February 24, the intelligence and reconnaissance platoons started out from the assembly area at Ningbyen on the banks of the Tanai River, which, as it wound south, became the Chindwin. Hopkins quoted from a soldier's letter turned in for censorship just before the start. "My pack is on my back, my gun is oiled and loaded, and as I walk into the shadow of death, I fear no son of a bitch." The trail meandered over flat terrain, often thickly overgrown, along broad but shallow streams that in the monsoon season would become raging torrents.

Fred Lyons observed, "The light that seeped through the tangled mass of vines, banyan trees, and verdure was hardly enough to make a tree visible two feet away." The men passed the word back when they encountered a root, while an occasional flock of baboons, hearing their approach, screeched and leaped through the trees. Galahad's warriors worried that the sounds might alert the Japanese. The dense vegetation proved ideal for ambushes, and the experienced Japanese soldiers exploited the lush conditions to dig in and conceal themselves.

Two days after leaving the assembly area and pointing toward the objective of Walawbum, the I & R platoon from the 3d Battalion Orange Combat Team, twenty miles southeast of Ningbyen and five miles ahead of the column, neared the hamlet of Nzang Ga. Corporal Werner Katz, a refugee from Germany and a combat veteran of the Spanish Civil War, the lead scout under Lieutenant Logan E. Weston, held up his hand to signal a halt. Katz told Weston that he heard noises ahead. With the Chinese troops in the vicinity, Weston warned against indiscriminate shooting. Both he and Katz had been in combat in the South Pacific.

"I was on a trail early in the morning," said Katz. "I suddenly came out of high elephant grass, I was thinking about America and New York when I saw an Oriental. He called me over but as I got closer I said, 'My God, that's a Japanese. Fortunately I got up my rifle and I hit him right between the eyes. He went down. On my left I saw a Nambu [machine gun]. One bullet hit my watch and the other grazed my nose. I fell into a small indentation in the ground." The

In the initial stages of the hike into Burma, three of Merrill's Marauders, uniforms intact and yet to face their grueling ordeal, waded across a shallow stream. (Photograph by David Richardson)

return fire of Katz, Weston, and another scout routed the enemy, leaving at least one dead and perhaps several other bodies hidden in the bush. Katz had the honor of being the first from the 5307th to engage the enemy and earn a Purple Heart.

Another column, the 2d Battalion, with Lieutenant William Grissom leading the I & R platoon, advanced toward the village of Lanem Ga. Private Robert W. Landis, a veteran of the 37th Division's New Georgia action, scouted ahead. A sudden burst of Japanese machine-gun fire fatally wounded Landis, the first of Galahad to be killed. Because of intense interlocking fire, the Americans were forced to retreat without recovering the body until the following day.

Merrill moved among the units, displaying an easy manner that ingratiated him with his soldiers. David Hurwitt, a radio specialist, recalled a moment when the commander appeared while they were taking a breather. "We didn't know where in the hell we were going. Benny [Silverman] turned to me and said, 'Hey, Sarge, where in the hell are we going?' I looked at him and said, 'Why in the hell are you asking me—why don't you ask the general?' I'll be damned if little Benny Silverman doesn't yell out, 'Hey, General! Where the f—— are we going?'"

To Hurwitt's amazement, Merrill walked over and sat down. "'Sergeant, where are you from?' [Hurwitt had lost his stripes because of an AWOL moment, but the imprint of the chevrons remained on his sleeve]. Hurwitt replied, "I have been to Guadalcanal and New Georgia. . . . He then questioned a couple of other guys and then he pulled out his map case and pulled out some maps. He then started telling us where we were going. And the more he related to us the whiter I got. He was telling us we were going to attack the Japanese headquarters. I kicked myself and said to myself, Why did I ask this dumb little bastard to ask the general and why didn't he keep his mouth shut?

"After the general got done with his briefing he stood up and said, 'Okay, fellers?' We had just about enough strength to nod . . . no general acts like this to a couple of enlisted men. I tell you that was a measure of our guy. He was the kind of man you could get to love, and I did."

As dawn peeked over the ridges and through the foliage on March 3d, all three battalions were about fifteen miles from Walawbum. The few confrontations with the Japanese had been of the sort experienced by Werner Katz, hit and run. On this day, as the 3d Battalion paused at the village of Lagang Ga, scouts warned that there were unseen Japanese in the area. Battalion surgeon Hopkins and one of his aid men, Dan Hardinger, suddenly saw seven men trotting along a trail that ran between the village and the river. "They were carrying a litter," said Hopkins. "They suddenly stopped, and a Japanese in front raised a Nambu light machine gun. All hell broke loose. Many men fired, and five of the enemy were instantly killed."

In *Spearhead*, Hopkins said that the battalion commander, Lieutenant Colonel Charles E. Beach, had been sitting in hip-high grass with his intelligence officer, Captain John B. George, when they spotted the advancing Japanese. George, at a distance of seventy yards, identified the shoulder patch and the machine gun as those of the enemy. George's first shot knocked down the lead man, and the others fell victim to fusillades from the Marauders. A short time later, a recon unit from the Khaki Combat Team of the 3d Battalion caught a batch of Japanese about to set up a machine gun. A firefight ended with three enemy dead. Beach's soldiers ran into several small clumps of Japanese and disposed of them in brief, deadly firefights.

The Marauders' march toward Walawbum continued. As night fell, Logan Weston, under orders from Beach, took his platoon across a small river and set up a defensive position in an uncomfortable swampy area. The following day, Weston's I & R unit began steps to occupy Walawbum. They climbed a knoll that overlooked the village. The platoon leader ordered his people to dig in. They were still at work when a machine gun cut down scout Private First Class Pete Leightner, out in front, as he draped camouflage branches over his foxhole.

"Before anyone could put a fix on the machine gunner," said Logan Weston in his autobiography, *The Fightin' Preacher,* "he disappeared into the dense jungle. Sergeant Paul Mathis, the platoon guide, and I crawled out and dragged Leightner back to the perimeter for safety. The men jumped into their slit trenches and braced themselves for a Japanese attack. They didn't have to wait very long. Through the brush, we could see the tan uniforms of the Japanese coming toward us, some with twigs sticking out of their helmets for camouflage. They were crouching, walking slowly toward our position. As soon as they were in range, we opened fire. The enemy soldiers hit the ground and fanned out, crawling closer and shooting ferociously. They chattered among themselves; some seemed to be giving orders. Then came the hollow snap of knee mortars being discharged from behind their front-line troops. Seconds later, the mortar shells exploded in the trees over our men. The mortars started coming in salvos, showering shrapnel throughout the entire area.

"'Watch for five Japanese coming around the right flank!' somebody yelled. Sergeant John Gately spotted the first one and killed him. Private Harold Hudson glimpsed the other four and started his tommy gun at the rear of the quartet, mowing them down. The main Japanese attack was coming in the center sector of my platoon's defense. A squad of enemy soldiers moved in closer, crawling, running a few steps, hitting the ground, creeping closer, and shooting."

The I & R platoon responded with a deluge of fire from rifles, tommy guns, and Browning automatic rifles. Weston instructed radio-man Benny Silverman to contact the main force of Marauders, now on the opposite bank of the river after driving off some of the enemy. Weston gave Silverman an estimate of the Japanese positions based on his grid map. Weston added, "Soon the crack of a mortar discharge answered from across the river. An eighty-one-millimeter mortar shell burst with a hollow boom behind the Japanese. I gave Silverman new elevation and azimuth figures. The next one burst a little closer but was still too far from the first one.

"'Anyone got a compass with mills on it instead of degrees?' I shouted over the noise. Near me, aid man Corporal Joe Gomez had just finished pouring sulfanilamide powder into Leightner's stomach wounds. He was working on the mortally wounded Sergeant Lionel Paquette, who had been hit in the head by a mortar tree blast. Unfortunately, he had previously lost his helmet and had not been able to replace it. Gomez opened a pouch at his belt and handed me his compass. 'We medics have got everything,' he grinned."

After the mortar crew lay down a smoke shell, a more precise reading could be established with the new compass. The mortars began to explode right on the target, and with Weston supplying the data, the eighty-ones walked across the enemy from flank to flank. "As fast as the mortar men could rip open shell cases," continued Weston, "they poured fire across the river. Still the Japanese kept coming. They edged into positions on all three sides of our platoon perimeter and were even trying to get between us and the river. Their machine-gun and rifle fire intensified. We tried to keep up with an artillery barrage that had developed, but our ammunition supply was getting pretty low. I estimated at least two hundred Japanese troops opposing us."

Suddenly the walkie-talkie manned by Silverman brought an order to withdraw and join the battalion on the other side of the river. According to Weston, his platoon had achieved the mission, distracting the enemy while the main body from the Orange Combat Team moved into position for a direct attack on Walawbum. The retreating platoon improvised litters to bear the wounded, fastening their fatigue jackets to bamboo poles, and waded across the stream.

Werner Katz remembered himself chest-deep in water, holding an end of a litter above the surface. "I looked back and saw a Nambu machine gun. I thought it was possible that this was the end, that I would die."

On the opposite bank, Private First Class Norman Janis, a full-blooded Sioux and typically known as "Chief," saw an enemy soldier squat down behind the weapon. "I got him in the head," said Janis, "and then another one took his place. I got him, too. There must have been seven of them and I got every one."

The Japanese rushed forward, attempting to maintain contact, but that brought them directly under fire from the well-entrenched Marauders directed by Beach. The Americans benefited from the work of Sergeant Henry H. Gosho, a Nisei (American-born of Japanese parents). "I couldn't believe my ears," said Gosho. "I heard an officer giving firing orders exactly like those I had been taught when I was educated in Japan and took ROTC. I told Weston and he rearranged our firepower to cover their firing orders."

Near the area occupied by the Marauders, the Khaki Combat Team from the 3d Battalion had marked out a crude airstrip. It was a near-spontaneous operation, for apparently neither Merrill nor Stilwell had addressed the issue that so vexed Wingate, what to do with the wounded. Some unknown hero arranged for the observation or spotter planes to remove casualties. The small aircraft, evacuating casualties, arrived and left in the midst of the battle. But Paquette succumbed before he could even be loaded into a plane, and Leightner died in the middle of his flight. Sergeant Clarence Bruno had died instantly from a shell fragment that pierced his heart, and several other men incurred wounds.

On March 5, with roadblocks established at several sites to stop reinforcement of those who garrisoned Walawbum, another Nisei, Sergeant Roy Matsumoto, climbed a tree and tapped into the telephone wires used by the Japanese. Matsumoto intercepted one call from a sergeant in charge of an ammunition dump. In the course of his conversation, the enemy noncom unwittingly gave the location of the site. The information was relayed to Allied aircraft, which soon attacked the dump. Data obtained by Matsumoto also enabled Merrill to deploy elements of McGee's 2d Battalion to set up effective blocks against the Japanese converging on Walawbum.

For the Orange Combat Team of the Marauders, on the banks of the Nambyu Hka River, March 6 began with unpleasant bangs: barrages from artillery and mortars. Fortunately for the Marauders, they had dug their foxholes deep and covered them with logs. As a precaution, the overhead trees, which could trigger deadly bursts of downward-ripping shrapnel, had been chopped down. Unfortunately, the animals could not be protected, and a number were felled before someone thought to remove them from the scene.

Sergeant Andrew Pung climbed thirty feet up a tree with a radio and directed mortar fire against the enemy. One shell burst amid a truckload of soldiers, flinging bodies to the ground. A Japanese gunner put a shell near Pung's perch, stunning him and causing the radio to slip from his grasp, but he descended without further injury. Throughout the daylight hours, the exchange of fire continued, with the Japanese using both artillery and mortars, while the more lightly armed Americans could counter only with their 81-millimeter mortars. The Marauders' machine guns stayed silent rather than reveal their positions.

Later in the afternoon, at least a company of Japanese soldiers attempted to cross the Nambyu under a blistering shower of shot and shell. The Americans heard shouts of "Banzai!" and yells for their surrender from the oncoming troops, chivvied by sword-waving officers. Despite the provocation, fire discipline prevailed until the foe was a scant forty yards away, at the water's edge. At this point murderous scythes of machine guns, tommys, BARs, rifles, and the ever-deadly mortars sliced through the Japanese ranks. Their bodies bobbed and sank in the river, but those on their feet kept trying to close on the Marauders.

Someone reported that along with the cries of "Banzai!" came an odd insult, "Eleanor [the First Lady] eats powdered eggs." Major Tony Petito responded with "Tojo eats shit," both in Japanese and English. Two American machine gunners, Corporals Earl Kinsinger and Joseph Diorio, veterans of Guadalcanal, each fired five thousand rounds from their heavy machine guns. Bullets perforated the water jacket that cooled Diorio's weapon, and he, with his assistant Clayton E. Halls, doused it with water from every canteen within reach. The machine gun became disabled just as the attack began to slacken.

It was estimated that as many as four hundred Japanese died in the futile effort to roust the Marauders. James Hopkins, the battalion surgeon, said he could not understand why his medical detachment had so little call for its services. In fact, to his amazement no one was killed, and of the three wounded, only one was hit seriously enough to require evacuation. Hopkins credited the results to a number of factors. The Americans occupied a bank ten feet above that from where the Japanese tried to ford the river. The defenders were extremely well dug in and exploited the advantages of the terrain. They made full use of the knowledge they gained in the South Pacific and, with abundant ammunition, created fire lanes that caught the enemy in a killing zone.

Under the prodding of Stilwell, the Chinese soldiers had resumed their offensive, and General Tanaka, harassed by the unexpectedly strong force of Marauders threatening to cut off his links to the Japanese lines south, chose to evacuate the area, leaving Walawbum to the Americans, who in turn would be relieved by the Chinese.

Captain Jefferson Davis Jr., a liaison officer with the Chinese 66th Regiment, a part of the 22d Division, who had survived hard fighting in the vicinity of Walawbum, expressed great frustration after a ten-day battle, aided by tanks against a strong force south of Walawbum. "We surrounded the Japs and finally drove them back. The Chinese commander of our brigade, Major Yu, refused to completely surround them, leaving an avenue of escape for the enemy in traditional Chinese fashion. Thus we lost the chance to completely destroy them." The policy was another aspect of the Chinese military philosophy that resisted change even after the most intense efforts by the American trainers and advisers.

Operation Thursday:
The Second Chindit Expedition

As the Marauders established themselves at Walawbum, Orde Wingate was about to commence Operation Thursday, striking with a force more than six times as large. Almost up to the final moment before the start of the adventure, it had been touch and go. Whitehall in London remained adamant against committing an early 1944 major offensive into Burma. Only pressure from the United States for action in Burma plus Wingate's personal, messianiclike fervor obliged Mountbatten to allow Thursday to proceed.

Wingate had developed his concept for long-range penetration beyond the scope of his original foray, Longcloth. He now added the notion of "the Stronghold." He would create bastions within the Japanese-controlled areas that would serve as bases that could receive aircraft of all types, store supplies, hold wounded until they could be extracted, and act as centers for locals resisting the enemy. He preached to his subordinates, "The motto of the Stronghold is 'No surrender.'" Most of his commanders were enthusiastic after listening to him.

An RAF liaison, Squadron Commander Terence P. O'Brien, accompanied Peter Wilmott, a friend, when he brought his platoon of Gurkhas to one of the airfields for training with gliders. O'Brien reported that while few Gurkhas had ever flown, they had seen many planes in the skies. However, none was familiar with gliders. The engineless machines mystified them. "Most of the men believed it was just a mockup, something designed for training only. Proper ones, of course, would have engines."

After Wilmott instructed his unit about the way a glider functioned, pointing out the circling birds above as examples, he expressed to O'Brien some doubt whether the men accepted his explanation. "He was right," said O'Brien. "They hadn't. When we were gathered about the [glider] the *havildar* [sergeant] said casually to Peter (in Gurkhali, of course), 'It has one engine? Or two?' He obviously believed it was a mockup."

O'Brien attempted to dispel the confusion. He showed the *havildar* the tow mechanism underneath the fuselage, and in his limited Gurkhali vocabulary described the entire flight process, using his hands to demonstrate. Wilmott chimed in that it landed just like an airplane. The Gurkha countered that an airplane used an engine, but Wilmott rebutted that airplanes did not need engines to land. At that precise moment, an arriving C-47 roared in, motors still pounding, and rolled down the strip to the airfield. The entire platoon looked at the two Britons, puzzled.

As a last resort, O'Brien ripped a piece of paper off a message pad and folded it into a paper airplane to demonstrate flight and landing without use of a motor. Said O'Brien, "I launched the little paper plane in front of them and in the dead still air, with no reason whatsoever for unruly behavior, the thing perversely turned over on its back and dived steeply into the ground with such force that the nose crumpled back at right angles." No words or hand gestures could now persuade the soldiers. But obedient to the discipline imbued in them, they would stoically load aboard gliders and find that the contraptions worked roughly as described.

With Thursday's first air drop scheduled for March 5, Bernard Fergusson's brigade had already entered Burma on foot, marching south on Stilwell's right flank. Two gliders, loaded with folding boats, outboard engines, and gasoline, were towed by air to the Chindwin River and softly set down on a sandbar. Not only were the necessities delivered to Fergusson, but also for reuse the pair of C-4As were plucked from the scene by a C-47.

In addition to their strikes at enemy installations, the 1st Air Commando performed general reconnaissance while searching for specific locations suitable for bringing in gliders, transports, and fighters. Prior to the start of Thursday, Wingate, in consultation with Cochran and Alison, picked three plots—Broadway, Piccadilly, and Chowringhee, named for famous streets in the United States, the United Kingdom, and India, respectively. Once these were designated, Wingate issued strict orders banning further overflights because he feared the Japanese would know his intentions.

His RAF liaison, O'Brien, scoffed at Wingate's restriction. Pointing out that there was no sign of Japanese radar or tracking systems in Burma that could have detected the areas of British interest, O'Brien noted, "A PRU [photographic reconnaissance unit] aircraft flying at thirty thousand feet across a country provides no useful information whatsoever about its target interest; the swathe of cover is far too wide to assess its purpose. The RAF had a [PRU] based near Calcutta which was actually making sorties almost daily over Burma at this time. They could have given continuous cover of the planned sites without any security risk, simply with oblique shots on the periphery of their normal track, but they were never asked. Wingate had decided that photographs were a risk, and that was the end of the matter.

"He [Wingate] was surrounded by more pilots willing to help than any army commander ever had before. And his own army staff were not idiots; they were highly skilled professionals . . . they must surely have known something about aerial reconnaissance and could have advised him—had they been allowed, or dared. Apparently they were not or did not. Hard to believe that some people could have been so meekly deferential, and one man so barbed against advice."

Although Cochran had obtained photographs of the sites arranged for topographical studies and mapped them (O'Brien was under the impression that the places had been selected more casually), he wanted a final look. On his own, said Alison, Cochran sent out a B-25 from the airfield at Hailakandi, with Lieutenant Charles Rushon, head of the unit's photographic section, to photograph Broadway and Piccadilly. Just fifteen minutes before the tow planes and gliders were to take off from the Lalaghat air base, a breathless Rushon arrived from Hailakandi with still-wet enlargements of the proposed landing sites.

Broadway and Chowringhee were clear, but teak logs sprawled over the Piccadilly site. "I was going to land at Piccadilly, where we would set up forward Air Commando [Force] headquarters," said Alison. Studying the photographs, the airmen and Wingate mistakenly believed that the Japanese had set up the obstacles, but a more likely explanation was that loggers had simply used the open area to deposit the trees.

Piccadilly was obviously unsuitable, and brigade commander Mike Calvert persuaded Wingate to put all of the gliders (eighty in the plan but fewer actually made the trip) into Broadway, rather than splitting them with Chowringhee. If the Japanese opposed his landing, he wanted his forces concentrated, rather than have half of them on the other side of the Irrawaddy.

On the night of March 5, 1944, at 6:10 P.M., the airborne part of the 2d Chindit expedition started out from India. The gliders were loaded with bulldozers, tractors, jeeps, mules, soldiers of General Wingate's forces to guard the landing area, and members of the Air Commando Force to direct the building of airdromes.

John Alison piloted a glider towed by the second airplane. Cochran, on Wingate's orders, stayed at headquarters with the Chindit chieftain. According to Alison, the insertion of Chindits into Burma by air was probably the most difficult glider tow ever tried. "There was a three-quarter moon shining, and although this was good light for night flying, the haze was bad over the mountains and over Burma, which made it difficult to see the planes from the gliders which they were towing. The DC-3 [C-47] had to climb eighty-five hundred feet to cross the mountains through turbulent air on a flight into enemy territory that lasted three hours and fifteen minutes. The gliders were overloaded with men and machinery; parachutes were not worn. Every pilot left our home base knowing that once he was committed to this flight the airplane that was towing him did not have enough gasoline to turn around and tug his glider all the way back home. Every pilot knew that no matter what the outcome of this venture, he was going to be deposited 200 miles [officially the distance was 165] behind enemy lines, and if everything did not go right, 200 miles is an awfully long way to walk through jungle country."

Back at Wingate's headquarters ground observers flashed word of red flares, the distress signal for downed gliders. Three tow ships returned to base with the discouraging news that the ropes to their birds had snapped, meaning a total of six gliders lost even before passing over the border into Burma. Alerted to the broken lines, the home base messaged the convoy of transports and gliders to fly "high tow," a maneuver that stationed the gliders above the tow ship and less likely to break off.

"From the photographs," said Alison, "we had estimated two logical places on the field where the Japanese might have machine guns. The first two gliders were down and their crews out immediately and on the dead run for these two points. Fortunately, the enemy machine guns were not there, and as my glider came over the field I saw the green flare, which meant that the first two gliders were not being fired upon and my landing could be accomplished without [harassment]. The pilot on the end of the other rope from the tow airplane cut, and I followed right behind him. He came into the field and had to purposely crash his glider to keep from running into the first one [there]. My landing was uneventful. I had the solution for successful glider landing at night; I used the close-your-eyes-and-pray method."

The pathfinder gliders, first to touch down, set out flare pots to facilitate succeeding waves of gliders. However, the field proved far less accessible than expected. For many years, the local people had logged teak and during the wet season, slid the huge logs across the ground down to a river. Over time the technique gouged deep ruts that elephant grass covered, making the trenches invisible to aerial photographs or reconnaissance. "They formed perfect glider traps," said Alison, "and there was no way to avoid them. The gliders arrived overhead in large numbers, and when a glider starts down there is no way to stop it. As each one hit the trenches the landing gears would come off and the gliders would go in a heap. We tried to arrange the lights to spread the gliders all over the field to avoid collisions, but this was impossible—they were coming in too fast to change directions, and glider after glider piled into each other while landing.

"It was dark, and standing on the field you would try to shout to the gliders as they whizzed by at eighty to ninety miles an hour to give the pilot some directions after he hit the ground. You would try to get the injured out of the wrecked gliders, but there just wasn't any way to stop it. You had to be on the alert at all times for gliders rushing down the field and be mighty quick to get out of the way. You don't hear a glider coming toward you—it doesn't make any noise; then all of a sudden it's on the ground and you hear the rumble of its wheels and you look out into the darkness and try to tell where it is going to go. There is not much use starting to run until you know that. It was a dramatic evening but we lived through it, got our equipment down, and got our men down without too many casualties."

Actually, thirty-one men were killed at Broadway, including Captain Patrick Casey, the engineering officer expected to direct the clearing of debris and construction of the airstrip. Another thirty individuals suffered serious injuries. Only thirty-one of the original sixty-eight gliders launched actually reached Broadway, and virtually every one was beyond salvage. A handful went down in enemy territory. But more than five hundred men, three mules, and thirty tons of equipment were on hand.

Realization of the hazards at Broadway forced those already there to send a radio message using the prearranged code to halt all flights, "Soya Link, Soya Link, Soya Link!" (The British hated an ersatz sausage manufactured from soybeans. "Pork Sausage," a tastier meat, was the signal for a smooth operation.) When Cochran heard the catastrophe signal he assumed the Japanese had attacked and said he urged Wingate to throw in "everything we've got. Get them down on the ground and win that battle in there and try to get our people out." Wingate refused and lectured the American about the folly of trying to snatch victory from obvious defeat.

"The entire second wave of gliders was stopped by radio and returned to base," said Alison. "In the first wave we had enough equipment to build an airfield, and it wasn't necessary to jeopardize other men's lives, as our patrols reported no Japanese nearby." The soldiers immediately constructed their fortified square, slit trenches, foxholes, and barbed wire with supplies in the middle of the box. Chindit headquarters then received a much more encouraging word, indicating the troops were not under siege.

"The next morning," said Alison, "the landing ground presented a desolate scene. There were parts of gliders strewn all over the field. There were [a number of] dead and many wounded. The British brigadier was a little discouraged. He was worried about the wounded, as they limited his ability to maneuver in case of an attack by the enemy. We immediately radioed for our light planes, and just before noon, L-1s and L-5s landed, picked up the wounded, and flew back into friendly territory unescorted.

"I talked to our engineer [Casey's deputy], Lieutenant Robert Brackett, and said, 'Can you make an airfield in this place?' He replied, 'Yes, sir, I think I can' and I said, 'Well, how long will it take?' He replied, 'If I have it done by this afternoon, will that be too late?' He wasn't just kidding—that night the first DC-3 landed at Broadway at seven-twenty, and altogether sixty-five sorties arrived that night, bringing in about a thousand men, fighting troops, mules, machine guns, and equipment."

Norman Durant, feeling he had wasted four years of his life in an antiaircraft unit and filled with loathing and abhorrence for his CO, had eagerly accepted the challenge to volunteer for service in Wingate's operations. Posted to the 77th Brigade of Mike Calvert, he had command of a machine-gun platoon in the South Staffordshire Regiment. He noted that his platoon happened to be composed of aging reservists. Durant was the only one under thirty, and the average was thirty-three. Somewhat frustrated by the unwillingness of his older enlisted men, Durant rid himself of a platoon sergeant and two others in favor of three younger privates who, while ignorant of machine guns, were intelligent enough to be taught.

On D plus 1, Durant, with eight men, four mules, and a complete Vickers machine gun and ammunition, boarded a Dakota for the trip to Broadway. "The inside of the planes were fitted with bamboo poles and the idea was to get the mules in pairs well forward and then box them in pens, lashing the bamboo so close they could not move, no matter how much they got thrown about. Eventually by cajoling them with handfuls of corn and by turning out the lights inside the plane so they couldn't see what they were getting into we managed to get three of the mules secured, but the fourth was as obstinate as only a mule can be. Every time he was walked towards the plane he would stop about ten yards short of the ramp and neither heaven nor hell could move him. We managed to put a bit of sacking over the animal's head and then led him very fast in intricate circles until he didn't know whether he was coming or going. When he was really dazed we pushed him up the ramp into the plane, lashing him in before he realized he had been tricked."

As he awaited departure for Burma, Durant said the only emotion he remembered was impatience. The RAF pilots gave a last word of advice: "Strap yourselves in; if a mule breaks loose, shoot it." Indeed, when the engines revved up, the mules became frantic, attempting to bash their way through the sides of the aircraft. It was not as smooth as Cochran claimed. As the plane rolled forward, one animal slipped to the floor and started to thrash about. Fortunately, the troops were able to get it upright again and soothe the others.

"We had to climb to ten thousand feet," said Durant, "to clear the hills and it became uncomfortably cold. I took my blanket out of my pack and wrapped it around me but I was never to be comfortable for the climbing gave me the most excruciating earache. I was extremely glad when the pilot told us to prepare for the landing. Through the window we saw an amazing sight. On the ground were the long-lit lights of a flare path, flanked by the lights of planes which had already landed. Every now and then a bright signal lamp flashed out instructions or a jeep's headlight lit up the crowds of hurrying men. We felt the bump as we landed and the screech as the braked wheels bit into the ground and then we slowed up and were moving off the strip.

"The doors were flung open, we tossed the loads out, cut the mules loose, and pushed them unceremoniously out into the night. I looked around and could hardly believe my eyes. Here we were, behind the Jap lines, within thirty minutes' flight of Jap airdromes and there were more lights than show in Calcutta. Every five minutes a huge transport would land or an empty one take off; over a loudspeaker instructions and orders were booming out. Two jeeps dashed about replacing burnt-out flares, torches flashed, and men shouted. The only jarring notes were the skeletons of the gliders which had crashed the night before."

A guide directed Durant's platoon to a bivouac in the woods, where the mules were unsaddled, sentries posted, and the other soldiers lay down in their blankets to grab a few hours of sleep. In the first light of the morning, the troops quickly breakfasted and then dug foxholes. Because of damage to some of the airplanes and the wrecked gliders, the full battalion had not arrived, and plans to move out were delayed until the following morning.

"During the day," said Durant, "a B-25 landed and we saw the grotesque figure of Wingate step out. Already he had a large beard—quite unnecessary in view of the fact that he was directing operations from Assam, where he had every facility for shaving and was wearing his famous Kitchener-type toupee, the only one of its kind worn in India. Everybody melted away and pretended to be engaged on some work of vital import, but he was in excellent humor, conferred with the brigadier, and then was whisked back to the north."

Terence Pat O'Brien, the RAF liaison officer, had been lounging around the airstrip, awaiting a scheduled landing at Chowringhee five days later. While still digesting the news of the adventure of the previous night at Broadway, he was suddenly informed that because of the loss of the Piccadilly site, his group would leave for Chowringhee that night as part of a nine-glider group. The flights would carry a tractor, some engineers who would use the machine to make the strip suitable for planes, a band of soldiers to provide security, and O'Brien's own RAF radio unit.

With his kit packed and handed a 100-rupee note "in case of a crash this side of the border," O'Brien climbed in the copilot's seat of a C-4A Waco glider. He had not been reassured after a captain from headquarters nonchalantly spoke of the smashups at Broadway and the broken bodies and then cheerily declared, "But you'll be all right. Good luck."

"You gaze in delight at a glider soaring away from a sunlit hill," said O'Brien, "free as a seagull floating the cliff edge, silent and smooth. . . . You think you could sail across the countryside with never a whisper from the buoyant air, so quiet you would hear the bark of a dog from the earth down below, so light you would keep bouncing gently on faint eddies of the air. But not in the Waco. The Waco was more like a noisy, wallowing barge than a glider.

"When the tow plane revved its engines, the settling dust boiled up furiously, the white tow line shivered taut, we started forward with a jerk that knocked me back in the copilot's seat, and there was a high-pitched shriek that momentarily pierced through all other sound. The pilot had the stick jammed forward, our nose was scraping along the harsh surface of the strip. I would not have been surprised had the floor begun to smoke from the friction. The dust cloud was so thick that we could not see the nylon tow any more. . . . He [the pilot] suddenly heaved back on the stick, the screeching stopped, and now we had the roaring sound of a Waco sliding and wallowing about in full flight. It was a composite sound, of a violent wind nearly double hurricane force beating against the frail structure, of a creaking and whining and cracking of that structure under stress, and of the roar of the laboring aircraft now visible in the clear moonlight 150 yards ahead of us."

When O'Brien peeked behind him he saw the Gurkhas packed in so tightly that only the outside push of men had forced the door shut. They were not strapped in, and if there was a crash, O'Brien believed that all 10 of them, together with the radio, batteries, fuel cans, and everything else, would be hurled at 150 miles per hour at himself and the pilot in front.

"The pilot tried to keep the tug aircraft steady just above us, but the Waco was so sluggish in response that from time to time the line would slacken before the elevator could correct. You waited then for the fearsome penalty. There was no escaping it. When the line taut-ened again, there would be a savage jolt accompanied by a thunder-ous clap as it slammed against the underpart of our fuselage. You felt sure the flimsy structure would be smashed apart. I kept wishing we had parachutes."

The moment came for the pilot to drop his tow line. "We were on our own," said O'Brien. "He pushed the stick hard forward and we finally came out of the diving turn heading straight for the long central line of the pear and at an alarming speed. Even then, with the aircraft gone, the Waco was still making a great racket as it rushed towards the ground, the noise making the speed seem even more fearful. He brought us in low over the trees, so low you could pick out branches, then the moment we had clear ground ahead, he straightened out his arms and dived the thing straight down at the ground. A terrifying approach.

"The landing speed was far higher than I had expected. . . . There was a distinct crashing sound when we hit the high grass and almost immediately a crackling thud against the ground, squashing us into our seats; then we zoomed up clear on rebound for a moment before he once more rammed the stick forward and slammed us into the grass again. This time he managed to keep us down."

The RAF flier lifted his feet and they slammed into the instrument panel as they jounced over the grass, stumps, logs, boulders, or other impedimenta. The craft flitted over a depression in the ground before slewing around in a bone-hammering stop. Miraculously, no one was hurt. Unfortunately, the glider bearing a tractor crashed, destroying the vital earth-moving machine. Alison, who had left Broadway to direct operations at Chowringhee, was distraught. He told O'Brien that the plan called for one hundred aircraft to land there the next night, but without the bulldozer, the field could not be prepared.

The RAF flier remarked, "This attitude illustrated the difference between his approach and ours. He knew what machinery could do and he rejected as worthlessly trivial the substitute we offered . . . to us the substitute of twelve men with kukries and four spades did seem to be a genuine alternative." A British sapper officer, "energetic, practical, and confident," organized the men to start work clearing the strip at 11:00 P.M. They could work safely out in the open until five in the morning. They plunged into the tedious labor of shoving the gliders out of the way, cutting the tall grass, smoothing out small ridges, and filling depressions. They cleared a sufficient stretch for a glider to arrive shortly after dark with the vital bulldozer. The party at Chowringhee had been concerned that the noise they made in their manual labor and the loud crackle from stepping on teak leaves would bring the Japanese down on them. "The bulldozer engine," said O'Brien, "ripped apart the cover of quiet under which we had been living for the previous twenty-four hours. We had been speaking to one another in lowered voices, never a shouted call, the cutting of wood banned." Still the enemy never showed. And the work went on apace, until Chowringhee was ready to accept the C-47s.

"On the third night in Burma," said O'Brien, "the Wingate magic worked. The airstrip by midnight was like a fairground at its extravagant peak, wheels of colored light circling about in the moonlit sky, cones of brilliant landing lights flashing across the trees and strip, red and green beams from the signal lamp at the edge of the strip, aircraft rumbling in, taxiing, and taking off, fiery red of roaring exhausts, clouds of dust whipped up to float across the stars, files of clanking men following blue guide lights, asthmatic calls of devocalized mules, a jeep scurrying about with headlights blazing, shouting men, clattering mule ramps, thumping doors, squealing brakes.

Alison noted, "[Chowringhee] was held for three nights, two thousand troops put down. Then we abandoned this strip. The day after, the Japanese found and bombed it. All of our people were gone. Fifteen hundred of them walked to the east to operate against the motor line of supply from Lashio to Bahmo to Myitkyina, the main Japanese line of supply for the 18th Division, facing General Stilwell." Another hundred men disappeared into the bush to recruit local people to fight against the Japanese. Less than one week after the first glider bounced to a halt at Broadway, more than nine thousand Chindits had flown in and then moved out to hit the Japanese. Eight days after the air commandos first arrived, the Japanese struck at Broadway with fighters. Fortunately, a flight of Spitfires happened to be on hand and they shot down half of the attackers and drove off the others. The first stage of long-range penetration had been achieved.

13

Chindits and Imphal

The majority of troops involved in the second long-range penetration traveled by air into the recesses of Burma. But the 16th Infantry Brigade, composed of the eight separate columns, with three thousand men and four hundred animals, commanded by Brigadier Bernard Fergusson, had started to set out on February 5 on a four-hundred-mile walk into the Burmese interior.

Color sergeant Henry "Tommy" Atkins at sixteen had worked as a houseboy for the Charterhouse public school in England before 1937, when he enlisted in the territorial army. He had served in Palestine, Crete, and Syria and seen desert combat at Tobruk before sailing to India with the 2d Battalion of the Queen's Royal Regiment, one of Fergusson's units.

Atkins marched with the 21 Column (the 16th Brigade numbered eight columns) of approximately four hundred men, some seventy mules, and a dozen ponies, all strung out in single file. Both humans and animals bore heavy burdens. Atkins said, "The going was atrocious. A working party of sappers were sent ahead to cut steps into the hills so that the mules could get a footing on the climb ahead. These steps were smashed in less than no time and had to be rebuilt again and again. Cutting parties working with the sappers would be widening the path so that as the mules passed along their loads would not be ripped off by the protruding undergrowth. When it did happen it was a safe bet that the mule would panic and the next thing the mule would be tumbling down the side of the hill. There was nothing for it then but for a party of men to 'off packs and equipment,' descend the hill, release the load and harness, cart it all back up, get the mule back, reharness, reload, and set off again, only for it to happen again.

211

"Descending could be equally frustrating and very hard on the knee joints. One descent was so steep the mules were offloaded, given a smack on the rump, and they almost literally slid down the hill for the next hundred yards or so on their haunches until they reached the bottom. In the meantime, a bamboo slide had been made and the mule loads and their harnesses were passed down this chute by the men lining either side. Of course at the bottom, the mules had to be rounded up, reharnessed, reloaded, and the climb started all over again. As darkness fell, we would just stay on the spot we had actually stopped, try to find a flat spot to lie down, and get some sleep. Only, there weren't any flat areas. It was very wet and still raining, almost impossible to light a fire to get a warm brew up. Was it any wonder we were behind schedule almost before we had started?"

Trooper N. P. Aylen, as a member of the 45th Reconnaissance Regiment, a unit within the Chindits' 16th Brigade, was also with the contingent that walked rather than flew into Burma. His adventure began on February 13th, three weeks before the first tow plane roared off toward Broadway. "My section, No. I, consisted of men drawn from various parts of the U.K.," said Aylen, "including a London bus conductor, a Newport metal worker, a Glasgow quarry worker (strong man of the section), a Taunton butcher and Taunton confectioner, and an accountant, myself. We also had three Karens (Burma Rifles) attached to the section.

"Each man carried rifle or other weapon, ammunition, two or more grenades, two or more Bren gun magazines, five days' rations, water bottle, ground sheet, blanket, spare clothing, washing kit, mess tin, and personal kit—total weight about sixty pounds. In addition, each man took his turn carrying the section Bren gun (twenty-four pounds). The first two or three miles along the road were easy going except that our necks were almost dislocated by the weight of our packs. But presently we left the road and took a track up a steep gradient. Before long the track was littered with 'extras' with which many of us had burdened ourselves, but which we now found impossible to carry."

Although they had engaged in a vigorous training regimen for four months, the march taxed them severely. The daily order to move out came at dawn, with a one-hour break for breakfast and then another pause from noon to three in the afternoon before resuming the hike until nightfall. Ten minutes of each hour were allotted for rest. The pace was quick enough that if a man fell out, he could not catch up until the ten-minute halt. They cooked meals of tea and bully stew, or soup and corned pork loaf from some of the American rations. The air forces became their source of supply.

"Drop day was always a special day. . . . The dropping included a number of luxuries—bread, tinned fruit, rum, etc., and these were usually consumed on the day of the supply drop as it did not pay to carry luxuries on the march." Shortly after the first of these, his recon troop went off on its own to reconnoiter the group ahead of the column. To carry out the mission, the troop cut its midday three-hour rest to one. The most dangerous terrain lay while crossing the numerous valleys between ridges and fording the countless streams, some of which were deep enough to reach the chest of smaller men.

Some three weeks after they began, as the airborne contingents had begun to emerge from gliders and transports at Broadway and Chowringhee, the column reached the banks of the Chindwin. Captain Rodney Tatchell, a thirty-five-year-old former architect and an engineer, now a commando platoon leader, said, "On the afternoon of February 28, we suddenly came within sight and sound of the river. It was an amazing spectacle and looked rather like a bank holiday at Brighton. The Leicesters, who had gone ahead of us, had nearly completed their crossing. Inflatable rafts, folding boats, and outboard engines had been flown in by gliders onto a convenient sandbank, and craft were busily crossing and recrossing the river, a good half mile wide with a respectable current. To get the animal over, the drill was for muleteers or grooms in the rafts to lean over the stern gunwale grasping the head ropes; the rafts were then towed across by the outboard-engined boats. It all went like clockwork and nobody swam except for pleasure." Wingate landed on the sandbar in a small plane and signaled his approval for the progress.

Tatchell noted, "Dakotas arrived, made a circuit and, without landing, snatched off the gliders into which all the gear they had brought in had been loaded. Now we really were in Jap-occupied Burma. Strict jungle discipline became the order of the day. This entailed jungle silence; voices kept low, no noisy chopping of firewood. All traces of bivouacs had to be obliterated. Various elements of the column [would] halt; each man would then left or right turn as the case might be and then on a whistle signal, march some little way off the track before re-forming and taking up their bivouac positions, thus making it less obvious that a large number of men had entered the jungle at the same point."

Similarly, Atkins and his fellows encountered no difficulty in getting over the Chindwin. "I was resting on the far bank of the river after crossing," he said, "waiting to disperse into the jungle. Two men came walking along the riverbank. One was attired only with a towel wrapped around his middle, wearing a battered bush hat, a fearsome-looking beard, and a monocle in his eye. This was, of course, our brigadier. The other man was dressed in a crumpled old suit of khaki drill, an old toupee worn well down on his head. He was, of course, General Wingate. I couldn't help thinking, blimey, that was our 'top brass' responsible for all our doings. I wondered what the more conventional-dressed brass hats of the European Theater of War would say if they could have seen them."

The objective for the 16th Brigade was one of Wingate's proposed strongholds, "Aberdeen," another three hundred miles beyond the Chindwin, near the Meza River and the village of Manhton. For Norman Durant with the 77th Brigade led by Mike Calvert, the mission was a block to be established on a series of hills overlooking a railroad and near the road hub of Mawlu. The site would be dubbed White City. Some historians have debated whether White City qualified as one of the strongholds planned by Wingate. In essence, with a hefty contingent of troops and an airstrip, the place certainly took on the major characteristics of a stronghold rather than a more simple block in place only as long as it shut off a route for reinforcements and supplies.

Attack on India

At the very moment that both the Marauders and the Chindits struck in Burma, the Japanese commenced their own offensive, one that had been planned well before the Allied forces began their operations. It was partially due to an unforseen consequence of Longcloth, Wingate's first expedition into Burma. Both the Japanese and the British had regarded the forbidding Naga hill country between Assam and Burma as a natural barrier to hostile forces. But the Chindits had demonstrated that it was possible for sizable forces to negotiate the terrain. In fact, the Japanese suspected the major purpose of Longcloth had been to determine the feasibility of a strike from Assam. To preempt that strategy and make inroads into both the Hump flights and the construction of the road from Ledo, the Japanese planned an offensive aimed at Imphal, the major hub for all of the action involving northern Burma.

The British were not unaware of what was coming. Aerial reconnaissance reported a buildup of enemy forces, with obvious signs of a mass crossing of the Chindwin in the making. It had been for fear of such an offensive that Mountbatten and his staff gave Wingate a go-ahead without enthusiasm. And in spite of the foreknowledge, the empire forces were poorly prepared to offer initial resistance to the oncoming Nipponese. Slim, as commander of the Fourteenth Army, sloughed off proposals from "senior visiting officers who urged me 'to fling two divisions across the Chindwin'" in anticipation of the enemy offensive. "I noticed that the farther back these generals came from, the keener they were on my 'flinging' divisions across the Chindwin."

Instead, Slim decided to concentrate his IV Corps in the Imphal plain for a direct confrontation with the Japanese Fifteenth Army. He withdrew the 5th Indian Division from the Arakan and added two brigades of paratroopers to reinforce the garrisons defending the area. The battleground chosen by Slim, the great eight-hundred-square-mile Imphal plain, which lay beyond the Naga and Chin hills, whose peaks poked five thousand to nine thousand feet toward the sky, supported an incredible abundance of flora and fauna. The battleground included rice paddies, peach and banana trees, and a cacophony of blossoms, tigers, poisonous snakes, deer, elephants, and game birds amid which bred fearsome diseases such as malaria and scrub typhus. Both sides would find the environment as mean an enemy as the gun-toting humans.

The scenario drafted by Lieutenant General Renyo Mutaguchi of the Fifteenth Army envisioned a three-week campaign to attain the objectives of Imphal and Kohima. Mutaguchi had earned a reputation of being courageous, aggressive, pigheaded, bad-tempered, and above all absolutely unconcerned about the human costs of his strategies and tactics. During the first week of March, while the Marauders seized Walawbum and Chindits entered Burma from the northwest, both heading south and east, Mutaguchi's Japanese Fifteenth Army drove west. The adversaries were ships in the night, passing one another without notice. The flights to Chowringhee passed within twenty miles of the Japanese on the move from Homalin.

Mutaguchi's troops forged ahead on the premises that they would supplement their initial supply of rations by cattle confiscated from villagers and then capture British supplies. They knew of a vast dump of war stocks near Tongzang. Beginning in the first week of March, columns of Japanese soldiers made their way over the Chindwin and climbed the steep ridges until they cut the highway between the major Allied staging site at Imphal, seventy miles from the Burma border, and the town of Kohima, fifty miles to the north. Another thirty-five miles or so northwest of Kohima lay Dimapur, a crucial rail hub whose line led near Ledo, jumping-off point for the new Burma Road.

According to historian Louis Allen, in his book *Burma: The Longest War, 1941–1945*, Japanese strategy followed the earlier successful pattern of envelopment of their enemy. But the British no longer met the challenge by retreating when surrounded and fighting their way through roadblocks. Instead, they now held their ground, even when encircled, forging the "boxes" that had served them so well. Between the rout of 1942 and March 1944, the British had laboriously built roads to link Kohima, Imphal, and southern India. These highways fed the resources necessary to strengthen defenses, but the north-to-south axis, so close to the front, made them highly vulnerable to a thrust by the enemy and indeed they were among the first objectives seized by Mutaguchi's offensive. However, the British forces no longer depended on these lifelines for supply once the shooting started. The Allied air arms kept the combat units in food and ammunition.

Sporadic sparring between the two sides had been ongoing since 1942 at the lower extremities of Assam, from Tiddim to Kalewa on the Chindwin. It was in this area that the Japanese first encountered the British. Under Slim's strategy, the 17th Indian Division was to back up, leaving one of its brigades to meet the enemy forty miles from Imphal while the remainder of the unit passed into his reserves. The first advances of the Japanese overran Kalemyo and Tongzang with its depots, eighty miles south of Imphal.

When the Japanese advanced on Tiddim, the intelligence garnered by the 17th Indian Division was inadequate. A three-pronged attack struck as much as a week ahead of the estimates by Slim and Lieutenant General Geoffrey Scoones, his IV Corps commander. The swift, undetected passage of the enemy cut off the avenue to the Imphal plain for a major portion of the 17th Indian Division. It appeared as though the Japanese had wrecked the strategy devised by Slim. However, a battalion from the Japanese 33d, occupying key choke points on the road, found the site hard to hold. Showers of artillery shells fell on them. The Japanese commander, Hiroo Saito, aware that he was now the besieged, ordered a night attack. Said Allen, "Advancing along the ridge to the hilltop, his men were met by heavy machine-gun fire from the flank. Bodies tumbled into the valley, the battalion broke up in disorder, and Saito and his orderly were cut off. They made their way south to regimental HQ, and the other survivors reached Luntak." The 17th Indian Division, battered more than expected, was still able to withdraw toward its preassigned location at Tangzang.

Major General D. T. "Punch" Cowan, the commander of the 17th, warned against a focus on the enemy forces with an order, "Forget those bloody Japs and keep your eyes on the ball." The object in question was the roadway, and a battalion of Gurkhas, wielding bayonets and their kukries, stormed one block to wipe out those manning the position. The Japanese realized that they could not afford to delay.

The 15th Division, commanded by Lieutenant General Masafumi Yamauchi, charged with the conquest of Imphal itself, was ordered to "advance through the hills like a ball of fire." Accordingly, the division, although severely depleted from earlier combat and the ravages of disease, leaped over the Chindwin using both boats and pontoon bridges. A long caravan of horses and bullocks toted dismantled mountain guns, while soldiers straggled forward bearing boxes of ammunition for the artillery.

The Japanese with the 33d Division even brought up a handful of tanks for an assault to break through at another point along the crucial avenues to Imphal and Kohima. They ran into an assortment of Gurkhas reinforced with General Lee tanks. Poor tactics by the Japanese enabled the defenders to blast the enemy armor, but the 33d doggedly continued its advance.

At this point Slim said in his autobiography, "Not only were enemy columns closing in on Kohima at much greater speed than I had expected, but they were obviously in much greater strength. . . . I had been confident that the most the enemy could bring and maintain through such country would be one regimental group, the equivalent of a British brigade group. In that, I had badly underestimated the Japanese capacity for large-scale, long-range infiltration, and for their readiness to accept odds in a gamble on supply. . . .

"We were not prepared for so heavy a thrust; Kohima with its rather scratch garrison and, what was worse, Dimapur, with no garrison at all, were in deadly peril. The loss of Kohima we could endure, but that of Dimapur, our only base and railhead, would have been crippling to an almost fatal degree. It would have pushed into the far distance our hopes of relieving Imphal, laid bare to the enemy the Brahmaputra valley, with its string of airfields, cut off Stilwell's Ledo Chinese, and stopped all supply to China."

Desperate situations demand desperate remedies. Slim had always envisioned the 5th Indian Division and some commando units stationed in the Arakan as a ready reserve he could transfer to the Imphal front. But he expected that the movement, if and when needed, could be on an orderly basis largely by trains. The urgency of the moment called for an immediate deployment by air. However, most of the transports were involved in the Hump flights to China, and the authority to divert the planes for Slim's purposes required approval by the U.S. Chiefs of Staff in Washington. A plea by Slim and his RAF deputy, Air Marshal Sir John Baldwin, to Mountbatten won his support. Mountbatten, privy to the intelligence that governed Slim's actions, had been well aware, as early as March 5, that a potentially decisive situation loomed. He had asked General Sir George Giffard, his commander in chief of the Eastern Army, to begin the shipment of reinforcements by road and by rail. Giffard, however, had done nothing.

The supreme commander cabled his superiors in London, "The dangers of Japanese success and the magnitude of the defeat we may inflict on them are both greater than in the case of the Arakan." Therefore, unless ordered to the contrary, Mountbatten said he would begin to use planes working the Hump to ferry troops from the Arakan to the Imphal front. The military in London agreed and quickly advised their Washington counterparts of the absolute necessity for the diversion of transports. Winston Churchill contributed a personal telegram to Franklin Roosevelt, noting, "The stakes are pretty high in this battle, and victory would have reaching consequences [as would have defeat]."

Everyone acquiesced, but Mountbatten had not waited for their approval. On his own responsibility he ordered that thirty Dakotas be made available. The airlift started on March 19. In addition, Slim recruited Wingate's 23d Brigade and later the 14th Brigade as additional reinforcements. The two units had been left in India by the Chindit leader as reserves who would rotate with those already behind the Japanese lines. Predictably, news that he had lost command over the two brigades ignited Wingate's fury and brought a threat of resignation. But with some twelve thousand of his people now engaging the Japanese deep inside Burma, Wingate calmed himself, recognizing he still had the resources for a signal achievement.

Stilwell learned on March 16 of the crisis building on the Imphal plain. "After lunch *bad news* [his italics] from Imphal. Limeys have the wind up. Flying in the 5th Division from Arakan and looking for more troops. This about ruins everything." On March 18, the day before his sixty-first birthday, his gloom deepened. "Japs crossed [border of India] on 16th . . . Imphal threatened. This ties a can to us and finishes up the glorious 1944 spring campaign." In fact, his operations by the Marauders and the Chinese troops continued.

Chindit Operations

As the siege of the Imphal plain deepened, the Chindits began their campaign. Lieutenant Hugh Patterson, from the Royal Engineers, boarded a transport with ten men from his commando platoon and four mules for an uneventful trip to Broadway. Dakotas brought the remainder of his unit the following night, and on March 8, as part of the 50 Column, they departed the landing strip. Their primary objective was demolition of a bridge and the railroad serving Myit-kyina. The destruction would hamper Japanese supply and presuma-bly aid the oncoming Chinese divisions and Marauders striking for Myitkyina.

"The column commander," said Patterson, "chose to cut across country through the virgin jungle, thus avoiding [trails] and the enemy. My platoon [composed of soldiers from the Royal Engineers and the Lancashire Fusiliers] was usually called upon to deal with the marshy bits. The men were all right but the mules, with their heavy loads and narrow hooves, were often up to their bellies. We got them over by making rough causeways out of bamboo and saplings. On the twelfth and thirteenth of March we crossed the Gangaw range, climb-ing to nearly four thousand feet, quite a job with seventy pounds of equipment on one's back. After cutting through very thick jungle, the head of the column reached the main road running parallel with the railway just south of Mawhaung. At this point they were ambushed by a small party of BTA (Burma Traitor Army) and a few Japs. By the time those had been disposed of it was about 1830 [6:30 P.M.] on the fifteenth of March. I then set off with my demolition party for the railway bridge over the Ledan Chaung. I took about twenty of my commandos, and was given a platoon and a machine-gun detachment as protection. Six mules carried the explosives. I wanted to reach the bridge before dark, so took a risk and walked straight down the main road until we were near the bridge."

The group arrived at the bridge at about 7:30 P.M., and Patterson saw some figures bolt in the direction of the village. He speculated that those fleeing were the BTA guards stationed at the span. Behind a protection perimeter, Patterson and the commandos spent some ninety minutes placing 350 pounds of explosives. Although he would have preferred to bag a train on the bridge, Patterson, realizing the enemy knew of his presence, blew the crossing.

"Sergeant Kemp and I lit a fuse to make sure. I remember him saying to me as we walked away, 'This is something I've wanted to do all my life, sir.' Next moment we were both blown flat on our faces by the blast of the explosion. Bits of metal and bridge hummed through the air and thudded down all around us but luckily no one was hurt. The bridge was a satisfactory mess—all spans and piers were de-stroyed and a big crater made in the north abutment. We finished off by laying a lot of traps and time bombs to discourage repair parties.

"It made a fine bang. I was told later that they heard it at Broad-way, forty miles to the east. Mike Calvert sent a signal, 'Both saw and heard your bang—keep it up.' On the night of the sixteenth, the com-mandos were turned loose on Mawhaung railway station. Here we burned out about ten coaches and wagons, blew up the overhead water tanks and pump house, and repair crane. Again the enemy failed to put in an appearance. We found out subsequently that there were not more than a dozen Japs [there] and they left in a hurry." When they left, the entire area had been strewn with booby traps and mines.

Five of the first gliders to touch down at Chowringhee carried the Blaine detachment, named for James Blaine, a sergeant major during Longcloth. Commissioned in the field, he had risen to the rank of a major, and for Thursday he led a sixty-man volunteer group known as Bladet. Lieutenant Arthur S. Binnie said, "The first glider with Blaine and myself in it overshot the strip and tore into the jungle, shedding its wings and splitting open throughout the length of the wreckage. [We were] alarmed but relatively unharmed. The one carrying the mules actually looped the loop very near the ground, pancake-landed, and the mules walked daintily out over the wreckage and started to graze.

"The unit bivouacked for the night in the nearby jungle, the bivouac including the American pilots who were to be flown out by light plane at first light. They were very unused to jungle and I don't think they slept much, seeing lions, tigers, and Japs everywhere. During the night, Blaine realized that he had been injured in the glider crash and was incapable of taking a long march in enemy territory. He was, therefore, to go back with the U.S. pilots and I, by chance, the senior lieutenant, took over command.

"This was, initially, quite a shock, as apart from CSM [Company Sergeant Major] Chivers and a couple of engineers, the remainder of the detachment were new to action. It had been anticipated that Blaine's experience would be essential to the success of the operation. I was fortunate in having CSM Chivers to lean on throughout the patrol as he had been with Blaine in the first expedition and was an excellent Wingate-type soldier."

When they rose at dawn, the unit set off for their objective, a bridge over the railway between Mandalay and Myitkyina. "We blew the bridge and a nearby pumping station," reported Binnie, "and cut the railway line in several places. During the patrol, the mule carrying the wireless set went over a cliff, falling two hundred feet, and we were incommunicado for most of the patrol. Eventually the radio was resuscitated enough to permit contact with India and we arranged one supply drop without which we would have probably perished. We were congratulated by Wingate." How much the Japanese were misled by their presence cannot be determined.

Norman Durant with his machine-gun platoon, as part of a company of the South Staffordshires, set off on a nine-day march toward a configuration of hills from which they could eventually establish one of Wingate's strongholds. After an uneventful week trudging through the bush and fording streams, Durant said, "We had our toughest time when we had to climb a forty-five-hundred-foot peak. . . . The day before we climbed it we had a supply drop so that we started the ascent with six days' rations, and by the time we reached the top our packs felt as though they contained a fortnight's. The paths were very steep and narrow and on one or two occasions fully loaded mules slipped over the side and had to be hauled up from where they had ended on ledges or wedged against trees.

"By the greatest stroke of luck the Japs had not anticipated our move and on the sixteenth we moved into the area we were to occupy for the next seven weeks, a group of about seven small hills to the north and east of which was thick wood and to the west the road and railway and then open paddy and to the south open paddy and in the distance Mawlu."

Durant, with his Vickers guns and a pair of rifle platoons, began the grueling task of burrowing into the earth with entrenching tools and machetes. "That night we got no sleep for we were too busy digging in. At dawn we stood to in the foxholes we had dug. I had hardly put on my equipment before a terrific yammering began on the hill opposite. I remarked to my sergeant that the 'locals' were making a lot of noise. To see what it was all about I strolled down to the forward section positions when to my amazement I saw six Japs, equally unconcerned, walking down the hill opposite toward the road. They weren't more than eighty yards from me, so snatching a Bren gun from one of the men by me, who was unsighted by the thick bushes, I fired off a magazine from the hip. I think that in my excitement I missed the lot but it certainly gave them the surprise of their lives. At that moment firing had broken out behind me and Noel Day came running forward to say that some Japs had infiltrated onto Hill A (which was lightly held after we moved out the night before) and had killed two of his men and wounded one.

"I moved a Vickers back and sprayed the area, flushing six Japs, who made off down the hill towards the railway, two never making it but the rest getting away. After this there was an hour's quiet and then one of my platoon reported several Japs moving towards us across the open paddy from the direction of Mawlu. I moved both Vickers up into the positions from which they could do the most damage and for the next two hours we were engaging groups of Japs as they [ran] from cover to cover. We killed quite a number of them, including an officer who stood up, and waving his sword, urged his men on. But there was a company of them and plenty of covered approaches so that they eventually reached the ground behind the hill in front of us."

Toward noon, fusillades of rifle and light machine-gun fire from what was called Pagoda Hill raked the ground occupied by Durant and his associates. From another hump, Hill D, gunners lobbed mortars and grenades. Durant said he kept moving his machine guns to avoid the attacks focused on them. Durant also heard occasional screams from the foe's positions, informing him that the Japanese were also taking punishment. "By now," he said, "a third of us were casualties, including the rifle CO. His second in command, who was hit in both feet, and one of the platoon commanders got a bullet through the buttocks. We were extremely glad to get a message over the wireless that the brigadier [Mad Mike Calvert] was on his way with two companies of Gurkhas and would counterattack any feature held by the Japs."

Calvert later remarked, "I was determined we must win our first engagement." When he climbed a ridge he saw the Japanese "milling about a pagoda on top of a little knoll." On a lower height he could see the Staffords like Durant enveloped in clouds of dust erupting from the shells exploding around their positions. Calvert realized that the exposed Chindits could not survive long.

Durant reported, "The next hour was absolute hell. The Japs stepped up their mortaring and grenading and it became quite obvious that at any moment they might rush the road and attack from Pagoda Hill. Consequently, the arrival of the brigadier at 1600 [4:00 P.M.] hours resembled the moment in an American film when the police, with sirens screaming, speed up in time to help the hero, whilst the audience applauds wildly. The first we knew of his arrival was when the firing on our left stopped and we saw the Gurkhas attack Hill D and then the brigadier himself came striding up our hill, rifle and bayonet in hand, took a quick look round, and then said to Major [John] Jeffries, 'How many men can you spare to attack Pagoda Hill?'

"'About twenty.' 'Right, we'll go straight up.'" Calvert recalled in his memoirs, "I then told everybody we were going to charge Pagoda Hill. There were reinforcements on our left flank (the Gurkhas) who were going to charge as well. So, standing up, I shouted out, 'Charge!' and ran down the hill with Bobbie [Thompson, his RAF liaison officer and [his] two orderlies. Half of the South Staffords joined in. Then looking back I found a lot had not. So told them to bloody well 'Charge! What the hell do you think you're doing?' So they charged, machine gunners, mortar teams, all officers—everybody who was on the hill."

According to Durant, "George Cairns, the mortar officer and I, hearing this, picked up some grenades, got out our revolvers, and prepared to go, too. We had been shot at all day and everyone felt like getting in the Japs and exacting a bit of retribution, besides which I was very keen to see just how many casualties my guns had inflicted on the enemy. Seeing me ready to go, Jenkins, my platoon sergeant, picked up a Sten and I knew it was no good ordering him not to come. The Japs on Pagoda Hill were now a bit concerned over the arrival of the Gurkhas and we were not fired on as we doubled down the forward slopes of our hill onto the road. As we got to the bottom the brigadier said to me, 'Take a party round to the left and clear the houses' and to Jeffries, 'Take the right side and the pagoda.'

"I went up the hill like a two-year-old and halfway up met a path which led round to the left of the hill about twelve feet below the pagoda, obviously finishing up by the houses. I shouted over my shoulder to my sergeant to follow up with the party and unencumbered by any equipment . . . rounded a corner and came into view of the houses. I'm not quite certain what I expected to see—the place deserted, or the Japs on the run—but what I actually saw was a Jap section climbing out of their trenches under the nearest house and coming straight for me, the leading two with bayonets fixed and rather unfriendly expressions, about twenty yards on my right. I fired my revolver twice and nothing happened." He learned later that the hammer had worked loose.

"It is strange how at a moment like that the mind can think of a hundred things during the space of a split second. I remember that even as I ran forward my brain was working faster than it has ever done before or since. I realized that my sergeant was a good thirty yards behind me, out of sight round the corner, and the men with him were probably a bit behind that. Time was too short for them to be of any help. I had a four-second grenade in my hand, but it was useless against the two leading Japs because in considerably less than four seconds they were going to be embarrassingly close. I also knew that if I stopped or turned round I was asking to be shot.

"That didn't leave me very much choice of action and I took the pin out of the grenade and still running forward, threw it over the heads of the first two amongst the Japs who were scrambling out from under the house, did a swerve to the left . . . took a flying leap over the side of the hill. As I swerved I felt as if I had been violently kicked on the knee, and although I never heard the shot, I realized that I had been hit. I was only about twelve feet down the hill with no cover at all and for a ghastly moment I imagined myself crippled and unable to move, having to lie there whilst the Japs following up got to work on me with their bayonets. I remember saying to myself as I anxiously looked up the hill, 'What the hell did I volunteer to come here for? This is the last time I'll do anything like this unasked.' But no one appeared and [although wounded] I moved back along the hill about thirty yards and climbed onto the path just below the pagoda.

"My sergeant later told me what happened after I'd jumped. He had come round the corner with two or three men and they had shot the leading two Japs. The grenade I had thrown had caused casualties and the remaining Japs were moving back to the west side of the hill. Seeing no sign of me, the sergeant thought I had been captured and was being bustled away. . . . He went quite berserk, grenading like a lunatic until the area of the huts was clear. He then moved back round the hill and was relieved to see me there."

But before the reunion with Jenkins, Durant witnessed "a horrible hand-to-hand struggle going on farther up the hill. George Cairns and a Jap were struggling and choking on the ground, and as I picked up a Jap rifle and climbed up toward them, I saw George break free and picking up a rifle bayonet stab the Jap again and again like a madman. It was only when I got near that I saw that he [Cairns] had already been bayoneted twice through the side and that his left arm was hanging on by a few strips of muscle. How he had found the strength to fight was a miracle." Others reported that Cairns's injuries came from a sword-wielding enemy officer.

When the Chindits appeared to flag, Calvert rallied them again. The furious assault led by him routed the remnants of the Japanese. Durant sat down while someone applied a field dressing on his leg. "The hill was a horrid sight, littered with Jap dead, and already the ones who had been killed there earlier in the day were black with flies. Stretcher bearers were removing our wounded and our mercifully very few dead. Noel Day had been killed, shot through the back of the head by a Jap feigning dead, but on trying to repeat the ruse he was spotted by Noel's platoon sergeant, who promptly kicked his head in. We found out then what we never afterwards forgot—it doesn't pay to leave wounded Japs breathing." At least sixty enemy corpses bestrewed the immediate ground claimed by the British forces.

Durant's friend George Cairns did not survive his terrible injuries, succumbing three days later. He was posthumously awarded the Victoria Cross. He was one of three officers among the twenty-three dead from the South Staffords in the Pagoda Hill battle. Bierman and Smith's biography of Wingate asserted that Calvert was the only brigadier in World War II armies to personally lead a bayonet charge.

After further medical treatment, Durant endured morphine-induced nightmares but awoke able to perform his duties. On the following day, the Japanese mounted another attack at the other end of the Chindit block. Several more officers were killed, and Calvert ordered a large force to eradicate the enemy still in a nearby woods. Jeffries, a commando who fought in Longcloth, personally led the attack. He, too, was killed in action, but the threat to the area was significantly lessened. Calvert brought up more of his forces to enlarge the perimeter, build an airstrip, and dig bunkers covered by railroad ties. The site became one of Wingate's planned strongholds as air drops from the RAF and Cochran's command showered supplies. Because of the many parachutes that festooned the surrounding bush, it became known as White City.

Broadway, White City, and the other airfields hacked out of the bush naturally drew the attention of the enemy. The residents and the aircraft constantly coped with Japanese raids by land and from the air. Alison said, "Not only did the strips enhance the capabilities of the Chindits to disrupt supply lines and mount large-scale guerrilla attacks upon the Imperial Army but also they enabled aircraft to fly offensive missions deep in Japanese-controlled territory."

Alison described the effectiveness of the tactical air support. "The Japanese were in Mawlu in some strength; they had mortars and machine guns and they were firing on our positions. General Wingate's forces moved in north of the town [White City] to a point overlooking [it]. The first mission we had we came over and the British smoked the ravine near the town through which a small stream ran. The Japanese were in this ravine. Our B-25s came over very low with frag [fragmentation] bombs and completely saturated the gully with frags, causing a terrible commotion. The firing stopped and the British were outspoken with their compliments from the ground. The radiotelephone work was very good that day.

"General Arnold had given us the privilege of picking our fighter pilots and we had some very good ones. The British, by radio, called their shots for them. First they would put down smoke, then give more directions by radio. 'Will you hit the buildings? There's a machine gun nest over there,' and the bomb would go right in. 'A hundred yards north of that point there are some Japanese—put your bombs in there.' The boys would drop right where they were calling them. The British were terribly impressed.

"We had 75-millimeter cannons in our B-25s and the action went something like this: 'Bombers from ground. Do you see that white house in the southern part of the town?'

"'Yes, we see it.'

"'Will you get that for us?' Then they would fly right up to the front door and let go.

"'Now, do you see the house with the red roof about a block up the street?'

"'Yes,' the bombers would say.

"'Will you get that for us?' And the bombers would fly up to the front door and let go with their 75-millimeters. The Japanese had to base their airplanes so far away that they were hamstrung." Their nearest airfields were too vulnerable for use.

For the most part, Cochran and Alison got along famously with Mountbatten and Wingate. However, on one occasion, Cochran lost his temper with the Chindit leader. Unknown to the American, Wingate had arranged for some RAF Spitfires to set down at one of the airfields during daylight hours. Although the RAF fliers had repulsed a Japanese fighter-bomber sweep against Broadway with heavy losses, Cochran explained, "The worst thing to do would be to land fighters on that field in the daytime and have the Japs see them. You're just waving a red flag at a bull. He did it and don't you know the Japs came in and got them and just about wiped them out. They got one guy who was just taking off. They got one on the ground. They had to come in and beat that place up and those airplanes were just like drawing flies. This incensed me probably more than anything ever had in my life. I felt Wingate had betrayed me. I said you do that any more and we're off you. You did a thing you shouldn't have and you double-crossed us. You undercut us. He looked me straight in the eye and said, 'I did, didn't I.'

"That just about cut me off. Naturally I was fuming and I imagine my language wasn't that good. I learned later that the office was not soundproof. I was told later that his whole staff and all the soldiers, everybody in the place, heard my tirade. I was accused of very bad manners by those who didn't know the seriousness of it. I can see I did sound like an arrogant Yank. We had a little bit of a different relationship after that, but still a solid one because we had it out.

"Wingate was man enough to take criticism. He brought in an aide and he used his peculiar archaic words to the man who had a poised pad and pencil, 'Take a screed to the prime minister of Great Britain.' Then he started out, 'to the prime minister, to Lord Louis Mountbatten, to General Slim, to General Marshall, to General Arnold,' and went all down the list. He read off a very concise signal of admission that he had done it, that he had been wrong, and he apologized. Whether that ever got to the prime minister, Lord Louis, or General Arnold, I don't know, but it sure was a good show. It satisfied me, and I stormed out a little bit placated. I got those Spitfires the hell off that landing strip. We had been planning to put our P-51s there but we were going to fly them in late in the evening so the Japs wouldn't see them. During the night [we would] load them with bombs and do close support in the early morning, fly on back to the bases, stay out in the daytime so they would not be seen."

Mountbatten and Slim both regarded the second Chindit expedition as lacking any genuine military objective. Without a coordinated offensive the operations behind the enemy lines would at best sting and harass the Japanese. But there were close to a quarter million Nipponese soldiers in Burma, and the only genuine threat to their holdings lay with Stilwell's Chinese-supported thrust from the north.

Wingate gave Fergusson orders to attack Indaw and its airfields with his 16th Brigade. The monocled brigadier pleaded for a respite. His troops, having only just completed their four-hundred-mile trek from Ledo to the Aberdeen stronghold, were, as John Knowles, one of the RAF liaison officers, described himself, "completely beat." Some units had split off on assignments; others were still en route. The brigade was not only exhausted but also seriously understrength. Fergusson was partially mollified by a pledge that the 14th Brigade would fly into Aberdeen and back up the 16th. But Slim told Wingate he needed the 14th elsewhere, to disrupt the supply and communications of the Japanese divisions attacking toward Imphal. No one informed Fergusson of the change.

Rodney Tatchell, with the 16th Brigade, said, "We passed through Aberdeen, which was then under construction and here we had to spend time preparing a landing area for gliders. We pressed on south, crossing [three chaungs]. Then we had a disaster. My column was just entering our night bivouac soon after crossing the Ledan Chaung on March 24. The mules were being unloaded when there was a sudden flurry of automatic firing and the noise of grenades exploding. It seemed that we had chosen to bivouac a few yards off a motorable track not shown on the map and not spotted by our recce platoon. Our arrival had coincided apparently with the appearance of two lorryloads of Japs. It is hard to say who were the most surprised, they or us. There was a lot of confused fighting during which a number of the enemy were accounted for; our only casualty was the colonel, who had his right hand shattered when his pistol was hit by a bullet. The worst of it was that many of our mules were killed or stampeded in fright, leaving their loads on the ground, including our precious wireless sets. A general dispersal was ordered; the various constituent elements of the column split up and had to make their own way to the rendezvous." That assembly was achieved, but the group's mule power was badly depleted and bereft of radios.

"The planned attack and capture of Indaw and its airfield turned out to be a near shambles," reported Tatchell. "By the time the 16th Brigade arrived within striking distance it was already worn out after its long approach march. So far as my column was concerned, we were, after the loss of so many of our mules and of vital equipment, virtually no longer an effective fighting force. The element of surprise we had hoped to achieve by our circling approach from south of Indaw had been compromised. Two columns of some other brigade had crossed our front and given out [to villagers] that they were to attack Indaw."

The defeat at Indaw was due to more than the loss of surprise. Both sides fielded weary soldiers. However, the enemy had an opportunity to at least partially dig in, and most importantly, brought its artillery into play. Although the RAF and air commandos did their best, as Terence Pat O'Brien said he foresaw, the absence of field pieces tipped the odds in favor of the Japanese, particularly since the reinforcements Fergusson expected had not been committed. Five days of furious fighting could not dislodge the enemy, and Fergusson ordered a retreat.

Wingate never knew what happened at Indaw. Following another meeting in Imphal, Wingate boarded one of Cochran's B-25s for a routine flight to the field at Hailakandi, where he expected to confer with the American. The B-25 had originally picked up Wingate at Broadway, and its pilot, Lieutenant Brian Hodges, was bothered by the performance of one of his engines. He asked Lieutenant Claude Rome, the British officer in command of the garrison, to urge Wingate to wait for another plane. Wingate dismissed the notion, and after he spoke to Hodges for a few moments, the B-25 was readied for the flight. Rome later commented that the Mitchell bomber "fairly staggered off the runway, using every inch of it."

They had, however, made a successful voyage to Imphal. There the plane sat for ninety minutes, but despite Hodges's concerns, the aircraft was neither inspected nor serviced. A few minutes after 8:00 P.M. on March 24, the B-25, with Wingate; his aide, Captain George Barrow; two British war correspondents; and the five-man American crew, lifted into the sky. About twenty minutes later, the plane nosedived into a three-thousand-foot-high hill, killing everyone.

Mountbatten, an early champion of Wingate but somewhat disillusioned by his frequent contretemps and near-monomania with his own ideas, in the flush of mourning wrote his own wife, Edwina,

"I cannot tell you how much I am going to miss Wingate. Not only had we become close personal friends but he was such a fire-eater, and it was such a help to me having a man with a burning desire to fight. He was a pain in the neck to the generals over him, but I loved his wild enthusiasm and it will be very difficult for me to try and inculcate it from above."

Slim, who deployed the word "genius" when speaking of Wingate, noted, "The immediate sense of loss that struck like a blow, even those who had differed most from him—and I was not one of these—was a measure of the impact he had made. He had stirred up everyone with whom he had come in contact. With him, contact had too often been collision, for few men could meet so startling a character without being either violently attracted or repelled. . . . The trouble was, I think, that Wingate regarded *himself* as a prophet and that always leads to a single-centeredness that verges on fanaticism, with all its faults. Yet, had he not done so, his leadership could not have been so dynamic, nor his personal magnetism so striking."

The reactions of those who served under him were mixed. His 16th Brigade leader, Bernard Fergusson, in spite of bitter memories of the Indaw experience, called him "a military genius of a grandeur and stature seen not more than once or twice in a century. No other officer I have heard of could have dreamed the dream, planned the plan, obtained, trained, inspired, and led the force. There are men who shine at planning or at training or at leading, here was a man who excelled at all three, and whose vision at the council table matched his genius in the field."

Rodney Tatchell displayed an ambivalence probably felt by many. "I think we all felt that the carpet had been pulled from under our feet; the bottom had fallen out of the campaign. Nevertheless I must record that the first reaction of the troops of my column [still vainly striking at Indaw], exhausted and somewhat demoralized as they were, was one of relief. Wingate was certainly a slave-driver; he himself had limitless powers of endurance and expected similar qualities in those who served under him. Perhaps his successor, it was felt, might prove to be more humane—or at least less superhuman."

Controversy over Wingate boiled after the end of the war. Fergusson pronounced himself "damned angry" because he said his requests for the promised 14th brought no help. In his memoirs, Slim indicated that the brigade was deployed at Indaw, but this was not true. The issue of the deployment of the 14th aroused debate years later, when a British official history of World War II dealing with the war against Japan criticized Wingate for his strategy and orders involving

Indaw. Part of the problem lay in his somewhat vague language on the deployment of the 14th.

The Chindits would campaign for two more months, but the circumstances of the war in Burma and the absence of Wingate would reduce their contribution to more of a bloody diversion than a real turning point.

14

The Northern Burma Campaign

Although the British command declined to throw the weight of its forces against the enemy in northern Burma, and wrestled with the battle for Imphal, I. C. G. Scott, formerly with the Burma Frontier Force in 1942's desperate retreat across the Irrawaddy, led a daring expedition. It was a token effort on behalf of the offensive begun by the Marauders. "In February 1944," said Scott, "I was sent down south to Durip Ga with our commando platoon, which was a party of about forty specially selected men, with orders to 'hot up' the Jap lines of communication from Myitkyina to Sumprabum [the northern bastion of the Japanese occupation]. This meant we would be operating up to sixty miles behind the Jap forward positions."

On the heels of the British and Chinese evacuation of Burma in 1942, many of the soldiers enlisted from the Kachin people in the Frontier Force and the Burma Rifles had returned to their homes, places such as Durip Ga, to protect their homes and families. They retained their weapons and soon formed small guerrilla bands that harassed the Japanese. British officers had infiltrated into Burma to organize these units, and by January 1943 they were known as the Kachin Levies. Now the Kachin people not only traded with the commandos but also assisted in laying the ambushes. Knowing the lay of the land well, they ferreted out the most promising positions shown on a map to set up ambushes.

Scott marveled at their skill. "Kachins just disappeared into the jungle. One moment they could be seen, then they were gone and in complete silence! Through the jungle he [sic] slid like a panther stalking his prey until he reached a point overlooking the road. There he stopped and listened. The Japs also traveled very silently on the road and he did not want to be found by them whilst doing his recce. Perhaps he would have been a furlong or so out in his point of arrival at the road but do not forget that he had no map or compass and relied entirely on his knowledge of the jungle to get him to the selected area which I had taken from the map." For rapid escape after the ambush, which was sure to bring counteraction from the foe, the Kachin scouts created a small path, one difficult for the enemy to spot.

After a day's march, Scott, with the headman from Durip Ga and several of the levies, made a final reconnoiter and located an ideal site for the guns, atop a steep bank overlooking a road a mere fifteen to twenty feet away. He set up nine separate places for groups of three or four men to cover the road, which curved sharply along a stream. The soldiers dug foxholes, cleared enough jungle for fields of fire, and were instructed on the escape routes. Ropes were stretched from each group to Scott's command post. A yank on the rope signaled the approach of the enemy. No one was to open fire until Scott himself started.

"The second night came," said Scott, "and I was just trying to settle down for a bit of sleep when the creepers started to twitch madly. I got up quickly and peered down the road, which was lit up by the light of a full tropical moon and was almost like daylight! Sure enough, there were dark shadows gliding up the road from Myit-kyina—the Japs had come into the arms of my ambush! Everyone was wide awake immediately and eager fingers were caressing the triggers of their weapons.

"We let the first party go by as I hoped for a more inviting target and sure enough a large party of Japs came round the corner, possibly fifteen to twenty men. Not a sound did they make as they moved along the road. The temptation to open fire was very strong when they came to the area just below me and I nearly bit the Sten gun I was holding, so great was my excitement. However, I heard the sound of bullock carts, the squeak of wheels, and the snort of the odd bullock and it was quite clear that this was a supply convoy destined for the garrison at Sumprabum. The carts began to appear round the corner away to my right and we could hear the drivers urging their animals on and to my horror they were speaking Gurkhali! It was clear to me that these drivers had been enlisted by the Japs to drive the convoy and I felt pretty awful about shooting at them but there were Japs marching on either side of the carts and some sitting up on top of the loads.

"I let them come round the corner until I had fifteen carts within the arms of my ambush and I had a lovely target of Japs and carts filling the long, straight bit of road to my right. It was a beautiful target and I tapped the Bren gunner on the shoulder, and as he opened fire, so did I, firing a full burst of Sten ammunition into the middle of the line of carts. Everyone was now firing like mad. I threw three grenades down the bank onto the road just below me and I heard several more going off to my left. The air was full of the strong smell of cordite and there was much shouting and bellowing of bullocks as carts plunged down the steep bank to the stream below, taking with them their loads of ammunition and rations. There was, in fact, complete chaos.

"However, the Japs recovered very quickly from the initial surprise, and they began to return our fire, some from down in the stream and others from the road behind stricken carts. For above five or six minutes this went on. Then light mortars or perhaps grenade dischargers opened up on us and then a heavy mortar started to fire from an area off to the right. Obviously this convoy was very well protected, as the Japs were in considerable strength. The first salvo of Jap bombs fell in the jungle behind us, but they started to get closer so I gave the order to break off the action and to withdraw. We quickly thinned out, leaving a few men to carry on firing to cover our withdrawal for a couple of minutes.

"Down the narrow escape path we stumbled as quickly as we could. There was no need for silence now and we gathered at the rendezvous in ones and twos, collected our gear, and I did a check. To my great relief we were all present and so off we went as fast as we could to the hidden village. Back at the village they heard the firing and they knew the show was on. A party of villagers set off immediately to act as stretcher bearers should there be casualties. Hot water was prepared at the village, ready for the wounded should it be necessary. Thank goodness we did not need it for that purpose when we arrived at the village, but we did need the tea made from it."

The presence of Scott's unit and the Kachin Levies saved a number of American airmen. He remembered an incident when the transport aircraft ran afoul of Japanese Zeros and one crashed in the dense bush. "The chances of survival when coming down in the jungle must be very slim indeed. One of the crew was killed by fire from the Zero. The captain and the second pilot were both wounded, the skipper in several places, but in spite of his wounds he managed to keep control of the plane and brought it down in really thick jungle almost in one piece. The wings were torn off but the fuselage continued to plow a furrow through the jungle until it came to a halt up against a teak tree. It was clear that the pilot had kept his hands on the controls until he came to a stop and he was thrown forward into the windscreen, which smashed his face very badly. His crew were uninjured in the crash as he had ordered them to the rear of the aircraft and they all owed their lives to this very brave man, a Captain Hirshberg.

"The copilot, although badly injured—he had been hit by at least a couple of bullets—but kept his head and set off in search of help. He told the others to remain beside the plane until he returned. Fortunately, the crash had been seen by the Levies who were not very far away and he was quickly picked up by a patrol. By then he had forgotten where the plane was and the Levies had quite a job finding it." The survivors were taken in a convoy to an airstrip and evacuated.

Galahad Advances

The ultimate beneficiaries of Scott's raids, Merrill's Marauders, had cheered the sight of advance units of the Chinese 38th Division, bringing with them pack artillery. The field pieces would compensate for the absence of anything more substantial than a mortar to duel with the Japanese guns. According to Charles Hunter, the transfer of Walawbum and the vicinity to the Chinese encountered some bumpy patches. Two patrols, one American and the other Chinese, fired on one another because of confusion over a recognition signal. Three of the Chinese were wounded, and only after Galahad's medics treated them and they were evacuated by airplane was the incident smoothed over. U.S. fighter planes also mistakenly strafed a column from the 38th.

"For the first time," said Hunter, "we were to experience the Chinese soldiers' careless habit of making off with everything not tied down or personally carried. We were told that, by theater policy, this was not stealing. It would have to be tolerated. The Chinese moved in and bedded down in our midst and proceeded to contaminate the area thoroughly, defecating not only in the river, but all over the bivouac area as well." The officer staff, however, was gratified by compliments from Stilwell on the Marauder performance in the first operation.

On March 6 Stilwell had welcomed a visit to his Taipha, Burma, outpost by Mountbatten. "Louis in at 2:45. Sixteen fighters escorted him. (We had four fighters working on the battle.) Went to headquarters and he made a dumb speech." A day later Stilwell noted, "Up at 5:30 and in to Maingkwan and south a mile or so to ambush location. Plenty of dead Japs, horses and junk. Louis much impressed. Doesn't like corpses." In a letter to his wife, Stilwell repeated his dig at Mountbatten. "Louis has been up but didn't like the smell of corpses. Now it has been proved that I was right about Chinese troops and the opposition is entirely tongue-tied. It's grand. Louis and I get along famously even if he does have curly eyelashes." Stilwell's diary made no mention of the supreme commander's extreme discomfort.

The friction between the Marauders and the Chinese was eliminated when Merrill withdrew his forces to a place devoid of Chinese while planning for his next operation. The deployment was complicated by a mild chaos in the command structure. Hunter noted that Stilwell seemed unaware of the precise movements of his forces, an inevitable product of the vague field orders he issued. Once again Chungking muddied the scene with a message from the generalissimo calling for a halt to the advance of the two Chinese divisions until the British resumed their push in the Arakan. Chiang apparently was unaware that far from able to mount an offense there, the ally was desperately defending its turf in Assam.

Both Stilwell and Mountbatten agreed on the value of a greater effort by the Chinese in Burma. The American radioed Marshall urging him to promote a second front by Chiang's troops in the form of the "Yoke Force" coming down the Salween River. The Briton appealed to Roosevelt and Churchill to intercede with the generalissimo. The Chinese leader refused, arguing he lacked the resources to open a major campaign, since he needed his armies to fend off the Communists, whom he claimed were on the verge of an offensive against the Nationalist government. The reply sat poorly with Roosevelt, whose advisers reported that only a single Japanese division blocked the Salween River route.

Stilwell plunged ahead with his own strategy. He directed the 5307th's 1st Battalion to march due south over the Jambu Bum, a range of mountains, followed by the Chinese 113th Infantry Regiment. Then the Americans would veer west, setting up a block on the main road below the village of Shaduzup. That would enable the Chinese to attack the town without worrying about Japanese reinforcements coming from the south. The two other Marauder battalions, working parallel to their colleagues, would drive even farther south to control the road from Kamaing to Shaduzup. As Wingate had predicted, Stilwell, once in command of Galahad, used the men as the spearhead for the Chinese soldiers. The strategy was alien to the British general's concept for long-range penetration, but on the other hand, the Chindits were not part of a general offensive that deployed several divisions and intended to hold territory.

The Japanese began to show increasing resistance. On March 14 alone, Red Combat Team of the 1st Battalion engaged them no fewer than eight times in the short space of 1½ miles. The foe, although inferior in numbers, used the terrain effectively, deploying both machine guns and knee mortars. The Marauders countered with their own mortars, and with the Japanese hunkered down, enveloped them from their flanks and rear, only to have survivors slip away to dig in farther down the trail. The two combat teams, working together, continued their advance, while a mobile medical detachment from the Seagraves Hospital Unit treated wounded and arranged evacuation. Air drops continued although the steep hills, abundant vegetation, and proximity of the foe hampered recoveries. Skirmishes occurred almost daily.

While their comrades advanced on Shaduzup, to the east, the 2d and 3d Battalions, under the command of Hunter, had pursued a seventy-mile track over rugged mountain terrain that first led south and then turned west as part of the strategy to shut down the Kamiang road. Their ultimate objective for the block was to be at Inkangahtawng. At the village of Naubum, which had a tiny airstrip, they met Captain Vincent Curl, who commanded the OSS 101 forces on the ground in northern Burma. He had organized a bunch of Kachins, ranging in age from thirteen to sixty, into the Me Proph Pum or Lightning Force. They wore green shirts and shorts and carried rifles, tommy guns, and other weapons. Their ambushes kept the Japanese out of the area while they gathered intelligence and rescued downed fliers. The Americans named them Kachin Rangers.

As the heavy-weapons company from White Combat Team made its way over a small stream not far from the objective of Inkangahtawng, small groups of Japanese patrols intercepted them. Brief exchanges of gunfire followed before the action broke off. Realizing that the foe was aware of their presence, the heavy-weapons company started to embed themselves in a perimeter close enough to a road for their mortars to hammer anyone approaching. Before the Marauders finished work on their foxholes, the enemy started to pound them. In his half-dug position, machine gunner Jack Thornton responded, but a tree burst from a knee mortar mortally wounded him. Throughout a rain-drenched night, the two sides exchanged lethal punches. The GIs from the 2d Battalion could hear truck motors, slamming tailgates, and the sounds of reinforcements arriving at the Japanese position.

At about 7:00 A.M., the Japanese began their attack, creeping through the eight-foot-high kunai grass on the left flank until they suddenly broke into the clear, a mere twenty yards from several points of the perimeter. The entire front erupted in bullets. Corporal James Phillips, on the extreme west flank and closest to the charging enemy, saw a Japanese lieutenant swinging his sword in one hand while clasping a pistol in the other. Phillips fired a burst from his tommy gun, but the officer continued forward. The corporal said he emptied his magazine at the lieutenant, who finally fell with his body almost cut in half. His head banged against the parapet of Phillips's foxhole. To the chagrin of Phillips, while he replenished his ammunition, another Marauder, risking enemy gunfire, scooped up the dead officer's sword, pistol, and pocketbook.

The situation for the 2d Battalion became untenable and McGee obtained orders from Merrill for a withdrawal back across the river under cover provided by the Khaki Combat Team. The troops set up a defense at Ngagahtawng on level terrain. Sergeant George Rose manned a machine gun facing a cleared field beyond which lay a stand of trees. Less than twenty feet from him was a shack, presumably once used for grain storage. Other than a single camouflaged soldier who suddenly appeared in the open field, the only evidence of the enemy were scattered shots during the night and the ominous "sounds of trucks coming and going, the banging of truck tailgates, the thud of feet landing on the ground, and Japanese chattering," remembered Rose. "It sounded like ten thousand of them. We knew we were in for it the next day.

"When daybreak came, the Japanese were still firing random shots at us but now made a charge. Suddenly someone yelled, 'Fire for effect! Fire for effect!' All at once there was a blinding explosion right in front of us: an 81-millimeter mortar shell hit the top of the Nips' shack. From the direction it came it had to be one of ours. Those of us manning the machine-gun were only a few yards from the shack. The ground around us shook like a giant earthquake, tossing us around in our foxholes and slit trenches. A thousand church bells were ringing in my ears. Before the smoke cleared away, Harry [Hahn, one of the machine-gun crew] jumped straight up, yelling that he couldn't hear anything. Grabbing him by the arm, I pulled him back into the foxhole. For a moment or two I was deaf, but not enough to keep me from hearing Ellis Yoder screaming for help. 'The gun won't fire and Avery is dead!' he shouted.

"I scrambled over to see what happened, only to view a terrifying sight. Darrel Avery was dead and his brains were scattered all over the place. A piece of shell had pierced his helmet. Ellis and I jumped into the emplacement and pulled him away from the gun. While examining the damaged machine gun I discovered the bolt was binding and the water jacket around the barrel was leaking. It had to be repaired as quickly as possible because at any moment the Japanese would come charging out of the woods and across the field after us. With the machine gun out of action we were dead meat.

"It was my custom to always carry an extra bolt in my pocket, and that day it paid off. The most difficult job of my life was to disassemble the gun and replace the damaged bolt as quickly as possible. In less than three minutes I had it back together and ready for action. The leak in the water jacket was beyond repair. With all the tape we had, even our Band-Aids, we could not stop the leaks."

The same 81-millimeter shell wounded the second machine gun crew, platoon leader Lieutenant Phil Piazza and his runner, Bob Mills. Robert Thompson and Albert Wankel hurried forward to replace the injured men on the number-two gun while the wounded were evacuated. "About forty minutes later," said Rose, "all hell broke loose. About forty Japs came out of the woods and they had to cross an open field of approximately 175 yards. Wave after wave came; they came as close as 20 feet from the machine gun." The unsuccessful charges piled up so many enemy dead that the Americans were forced to kick the corpses out of the way to maintain their fire lanes.

The pressure upon the beleaguered Marauders continued for hours. Not even fighter-bombers called in by the battalion commander, Lieutenant Colonel George McGee Jr., through Merrill's headquarters, could discourage the Japanese from their assault, during which it was estimated that they attempted sixteen times to overrun the perimeter. One of them actually penetrated far enough to stick his bayonet in Leonard Wray's foxhole. Wray grabbed the rifle barrel and jumped out of the hole. When the foe broke off wrestling for the weapon, a BAR from another foxhole cut him down.

The block created by the 2d Battalion was part of the strategy to shield the 1st Battalion and the Chinese forces coming south to envelop Shaduzup. But the latter were making very slow progress, and the 2d Battalion's position was becoming increasingly precarious. With ammunition running low and indications that even more reinforcements would soon be on the scene, McGee finally received orders from General Merrill to abandon the block and withdraw toward the village of Manpin. Behind them, machine gunners set up positions to deter the enemy from a precipitous rush. Warren Ventura was one of those posted to protect the rear of the retreating Americans. The Americans, behind a rearguard defense by the Khaki Combat Team of the 3d Battalion, pulled back and bivouacked at Sharaw, four miles from Manpin. The battalion counted two dead and twelve wounded, with enemy casualties estimated at more than two hundred.

In his memoirs, Hunter said he believed that Merrill erred by withdrawing the 2d Battalion too quickly. He argued that the retreat would leave the 1st Battalion challenging Shaduzup naked to an onslaught by the Japanese. Regardless of whether Merrill should have usurped Hunter's prerogatives, it was clear that the various units of Galahad were having considerable difficulty communicating. Rain, mud, heat, steep hills, and enemy fire all interfered with the functioning of the radio equipment, causing great difficulties in transmission of messages.

In Hunter's view, McGee's column lost some essential military discipline as it trudged toward a final destination of Nhpum Ga. At the tail end he could find no officer; no radio; and worst of all, no rear guard. In fact, as Ventura reported, there were blocks behind the column. But the pullback did have its problems. The men were struggling to follow a trail up a steep ridge, setting their own pace, some falling out, unable to take further steps without a rest. Shortly after Hunter plopped down in the village of Nhpum Ga he said, "Two hysterical and exhausted soldiers, staggering and half falling, appeared on the trail leading up to the village. The GI in the lead screamed that the 2d Battalion was being shot up and needed help. They were followed by others. Major Schudmak, Galahad surgeon, was close by. We grabbed the two leading men as they started to fall to quiet them down in an attempt to learn what was happening, only to have them mumble unintelligible sounds. I told Doc Schudmak to stick a couple of syrettes of morphine in them. This effectively stopped their panic inducting [sic] screams." Battalion surgeon James Hopkins also reported cases of men showing signs of great emotional stress.

For the final week of March, the entire Galahad force engaged the Japanese in an ordeal that featured an almost continuous series of running battles under the most grueling conditions of terrain, temperature, and pestilence, with dysentery and diarrhea common. A particularly nasty creature, the leech, bedeviled the soldiers. Medical officer Hopkins said, "Men and mules were equally susceptible. . . . They fell from vegetation onto their victims. Their attachment apparatus was very efficient and allowed them to attach to any part of man or beast. During daylight hours they would attach to a part of the body where they could not be seen. Their small bodies would quickly become swollen with blood. Frequently their presence would not be recognized until the Marauder inspected his body at rest periods or at night. At times the leeches would rupture, and the blood sucked from the men would soak through their clothing. The leeches were removed by touching them with a match or lighted cigarette. The area where the leech had been attached would tend to bleed for several minutes, since the leech had injected an anticlotting chemical into the area of attachment. Frequently the leech would ignore easily accessible skin areas and would attach in the ear canal, in a nasal passage, or on an eyelid, scrotum, or penis."

The number of casualties and the conditions nearly overwhelmed the Marauders. Major A. Lewis Kolodny, the 2d Battalion surgeon, and his medics were sorely tried, not only because of the many desperately wounded but also they themselves were within easy rifle shot of the front. Kolodny noted, "A Japanese sniper in a tree was taking potshots at us. Finally one of the bazooka men hit him, and his rifle, with three notches on it, fell to the ground." The tree bursts inflicted horrendous injuries. "There was one man who had the top of skull sheared off, exposing his brain. There was nothing we could do for him. I had a sergeant who had been a plaster man for an orthopedic surgeon and we put plaster casts over some of the leg wounds. Maggots would eat the dead tissue and after the men were evacuated and they removed the casts, the wounds were clean. But there were a couple of cases where we had to perform amputations, with bayonets."

A three-man patrol led by Lieutenant Brendan Lynch ventured beyond the perimeter and made the unfortunate decision to return through another area. Before they could be recognized, the embattled soldiers unloosed a volley of shots. One man died instantly, and Lynch went down with a bullet in his leg. He could not be immediately evacuated, and gangrene claimed his life.

While the predicament of the 2nd Battalion deepened, in the vicinity of Shaduzup, the 1st Battalion probed its objective. One day shy of two weeks from the start, scouts reached the banks of the Mogaung River and reported a considerable number of enemy in the area. Many were seen bathing and some using grenades to harvest fish. Further reconnaissance revealed a sizable encampment, with large amounts of food and clothing stashed nearby.

The patrol estimated that they faced at least a company of Japanese. Major Caifson Johnson, the commanding officer for the White Combat Team, having personally waded the river to determine the feasibility of a crossing, picked out a location and then drafted a plan for six platoons to ford the stream. "We could hear them jibber, jabbering," said Johnson, "and went in with fixed bayonets." As dawn broke and the first cooking fires blazed up in the enemy encampment, the Marauders fell upon the unsuspecting soldiers, catching many half dressed or in a latrine. Rifles, automatic weapons, grenades, and bayonets ripped into the stumbling, shocked victims. Those who survived broke and ran for cover. A Japanese truck carrying cooked potatoes and soldiers blundered into a machine gun's lane of fire, with devastating results to the riders. The attackers seized possession of the site, gobbled down the cooked rice and fish left behind, and even donned some unused underwear, which fitted only the smaller Americans.

Private First Class Ted Zakotnik recalled, "After the skirmish was over, we started feasting on their rations. A guy said, 'Look at this.' We were sitting eating out of their utensils, canteens and whatnot. 'I wonder what this red is on the potato." I said to him, 'Those are red skin potatoes.' It turned out it was blood from their dead bodies in the truck."

According to Zakotnik, Chinese troops arrived toward evening and began to relieve the Marauders, who retreated back across the river. They dug foxholes and the Japanese, having regrouped, shelled them with mortars and heavy artillery, both 150- and 75-millimeter pieces. "There was an overhead tree burst," he reminisced, "right over a fox-hole, and killed them both in the foxhole. I remembered screaming during the night. I went over to the foxhole [and] other soldiers said, 'Zak, there is no point in coming over here. They are beyond help. They're gone.' The medics came up. What we did was just throw the dirt back into the foxhole, over them, just as they were."

The battle that had unfolded at Shaduzup demonstrated the effectiveness of the strategy worked out by Stilwell and executed by the men of Galahad. The modest success was not without cost; a number of Marauders had been hit in the initial phase of the attack, including one who later died of his wounds. The barrage that began at midday and lasted through the night killed three and wounded an additional ten as the dug-in Americans repulsed frontal attacks into the murderous maw of mortar fire, machine guns, and grenades but could not retaliate with their own artillery. It was the same weakness that afflicted the Chindits. Their only comfort came from the Chinese pack artillery, which began blasting away at the enemy.

The I & R platoon, commanded by Logan Weston, and a rifle platoon, under Lieutenant Warren Smith, leapfrogged one another, throwing up blocks that deployed mortars and machine guns, while the 2d and 3d Battalions continued their travels away from Inkangahtawng, passing through Manpin and Warong toward Auche. Weston's fifty-three-man group fought off a company-size Japanese force at Poakum long enough to enable a successful withdrawal toward Warong. Weston and his unit were joined by the riflemen under Smith for another confrontation at Warong. A fierce firefight broke out as the two platoons delayed the enemy. Still, once they gave way, the Japanese occupied the village, from where they could observe the next point of call, Auche. As the 2d Battalion, behind the 3d, pulled out of Auche, the first artillery shells from the Japanese whistled into the area. One soldier and several animals were hit.

The two battalions negotiated a narrow, rugged trail along the crest of a ridge. Merrill designated Nhpum Ga as the place for the 2d Battalion to organize its defensive stance, while the 3d Battalion would march five miles farther north, to Hsamshingyang, to protect an airstrip for evacuations and drops as well as to prevent any Japanese from attacking from that direction.

Getting to Nhpum Ga required a maximum effort by the bone-weary 2d Battalion. Nhpum Ga sat atop a knoll reachable only by a slog through ankle-deep mud. The exhausted mules, unfed for several days, slipped and fell frequently. They could regain their feet only after the troops unloaded their burdens, which then had to be repacked to continue the journey. Intermittent artillery bursts accompanied them.

When they had staggered to Nhpum Ga, they found themselves almost instantly under siege. The seemingly tireless enemy began the first of its attacks even as the Americans frantically dug their holes and emplacements for their heavier automatic weapons and created a perimeter roughly two hundred by four hundred meters. The initial assault seemed aimed at testing for weak spots and was thrown back without the need to resort to the machine guns, thereby betraying their locations. Throughout the first night on the hill, March 28–29, the Japanese were content to hurl occasional mortar and artillery ordnance, a harassment designed to interfere with needed sleep.

Successive attacks chipped away at the real estate controlled by the 2d Battalion. A critical loss came with a savage attack that shut off the sole water hole. Japanese mortars and snipers made any approach to the site impossible. McGee posted every available man on the perimeter, putting his muleskinners, photographers, and headquarters personnel on the firing line. Coming from Hsamshingyang to break the encirclement, the 3d Battalion stalled behind a strong roadblock created by the enemy.

On March 28 Galahad reeled from an entirely unexpected blow. Hunter said, "I left Nhpum Ga just behind a platoon of [Charles E.] Beach's battalion [3d] and some MPs who were responsible for patrolling the Nhpum Ga–Hsamshingyang trail. I passed through them and continued on my way alone to Hsamshingyang. I found Merrill lying in the middle of a path in the bivouac area occupied by Galahad headquarters. He told me the doctors would not let him be moved. . . . Doc Schudmak, the Galahad surgeon, was there and motioning me out of Merrill's sight; we discussed the general's condition. Doc told me that Merrill had collapsed where he was now lying and shouldn't be moved or disturbed. In Doc Schudmak's opinion, Merrill was suffering from a heart attack and should be evacuated."

Because darkness had begun to fall and the last aircraft taken off, Merrill could not be removed that day. He was installed in a hastily improvised shelter and a message on his condition sent to Stilwell. He agreed to the evacuation of Merrill, but the Galahad commander insisted that any wounded leave before him. It is Hunter's memory that not until March 31 did Merrill depart. The orders from Stilwell passed the scepter to Hunter but not the rank.

As depressing to morale as the news of their chief's illness, the troops, particularly those at Nhpum Ga, labored under an ever-worsening situation. Fred Lyons remembered, "Nhpum Ga, the ridge . . . almost spelled doom for a third of Merrill's Marauders. There were a thousand of us and we were trapped. The sneaking, crawling Japs weren't so bad, for we eventually could spot them, but the mortar fire lobbing inside the wagon wheel [perimeter] was raising hob with our supplies and killing off animals and men. Without a stream, we soon were in need of water. We cleared the bamboo inside the perimeter and cut open the joints, getting as much as a cup of water from each joint. But the bamboo didn't last long with a thousand men. There was some water in elephant tracks, and I tried to skim off the scum and drink that. Although I put halazone in the chalky-tasting stuff, tried to doctor it with lemonade tablets, and even tried coffee and cream, it still tasted just like what it was, wet mud."

A series of radio messages from McGee to headquarters spelled out the desperate situation: "We have been hit on three sides. Platoon from Orange was cut off and are making their way back through the jungle. My rear is blocked. I cannot withdraw north. Something has to come up to take the pressure off. Casualty report today three dead, nine wounded. . . . Will need sixty and eighty-one ammo tomorrow badly." Over the following days the daily casualty reports hovered in the same range and McGee's requests for relief became increasingly urgent.

The radio pleas brought some succor, air drops of water-filled plastic casks. Said Lyons, "When I saw those dangling sausagelike bottles come floating down . . . I breathed a fervent prayer of thanks." When Lyons requested cigarettes, the depot at Ledo responded in abundance. "The packages had little tickets on them saying they had been donated by American Legion posts and civic clubs. It made us feel for a while that there was such a place as the United States. From the strain and lack of sleep, men's eyes became glazed and staring. They began to call the ridge Maggot Hill as the carcasses of horses inside the perimeter decayed and the stench of dead Japs outside it became more and more violent. Shells pounded in, and we kept pouring it out."

Lyons recalled, "Hearing of our plight, the cooks at the rear echelon in Ledo stayed up all night to fix us something special. Sick of K
rations, we lived on coffee and cigarettes for eight days. Then came,
floating down under great white folds of silk, box after box of fried
chicken. With the fighting under way only three hundred yards off, it
was a strange sight to see a bunch of battle-worn GIs elbowing one
another to be first for the leg or the breast. Just as the feast was being
passed out to the second line, Jap artillery fire began lobbing in and
the boys scattered."

The 3d Battalion at Hsamshingyang sought to support their comrades a few miles off. John A. Acker, a staff sergeant in charge of pack
animals for the Khaki Combat Team, recalled a visit by Major Edwin
J. Briggs, that unit's commander. "His intent was to check our positions, encourage morale, and see how we were doing generally. As we
talked about the condition of 2d Battalion, I mentioned the fact that
we, of the 98th Field Artillery [his original unit], had been discussing
our need for artillery. I told Major Briggs that if we had some guns
we could fix the Japs up. His question was, 'Could we fire the guns if
we had some?' We assured him that we could. There was nothing more
said about it until the next day Major Briggs asked me to assemble
men for two gun crews."

Acker recruited thirty men, mostly old artillery hands, to work the
guns, handle the ammunition, pack the gear, and serve as picket line
guards. On April 2 they gathered at the drop area as planes droned
toward them. By prearrangement, the pieces of the 75-millimeter pack
guns were marked by differently colored parachutes, six chutes for
each 75, and the reconstituted artillerymen began to claim the different items and haul them to a designated area. In fifteen minutes they
were assembled, tested, and pronounced ready to fire.

Broken down again, with six mules to carry the individual pieces,
a pack train bore the weapons, ammunition, and other supplies to a
site about a thousand yards from Nhpum Ga. According to Acker,
the location was ideal. Because of a hill in front of the Americans, the
enemy's flat-trajectory guns could not fire low enough to hit them. If
the Japanese raised their sights the shells would whiz overhead, to
explode harmlessly in a ravine behind the gun position.

The two pieces lofted their first shells on April 3, aiming in the
direction of Auche, from where the Japanese were believed based.
"We had no forward observer," said Acker, "and the best we could do
was fire off our map position. We were effective to the extent that we
could stop the Japs from firing at B [2d] Battalion. We were firing
blind with no one to report our effect." After two days word came
that the enemy had shifted its artillery to Kauri, closer to Nhpum Ga.

To strike the new area, the Americans reduced their powder load and raised the elevation, which hurled shells up over a hill to fall on the enemy positions.

On the night of April 5 Roy Matsumoto, along with several others who spoke Japanese, slipped close enough to the enemy positions to listen to conversations. Matsumoto heard enough to believe that an attack was coming at a sector of the perimeter held by troops commanded by Lieutenant Edward McLogan. The officer withdrew his men to the crest of a little ridge—"McLogan's Hill"—leaving behind booby traps in the foxholes they abandoned and concentrating their tommy guns and BARs atop the ridge.

At dawn, as Matsumoto had surmised, a reinforced Japanese platoon began an assault with the customary cries of "Banzai!" "Death to the Americans!" They swarmed over the positions the Marauders had left during the night and then hesitated. Matsumoto stood up and shouted in Japanese an order to advance. The soldiers then charged up the hill, with a sword-wielding officer at the front. When they came within fifteen yards of the perimeter, McLogan signaled his men to open fire. Dozens of Japanese went down under the murderous streams of bullets, and a second group followed them as Matsumoto reiterated his bogus command to charge. Some dived into the old foxholes, setting off the booby traps. After half an hour, fifty-four bodies were strewn over the hillside, with no Americans hit.

On a forced march from their previous position at Shaduzup, the 1st Battalion, short on rations, arrived on April 7 within striking distance of the Japanese menacing the 2d Battalion. According to Hunter, the prevalence of dysentery, diarrhea, and malaria limited the number of available soldiers to only 250. They were immediately deployed for a flank attack over the high ground to the west or right side of Nhpum Ga. Meanwhile, other units would feint to the extreme east or left, to draw off mortar fire.

Acker and the two gun crews, however, were working blind. On April 7, to their surprise, a captain from the 1st Battalion radioed, "I'm sitting here along the trail between Kauri and Nhpum Ga and I can see the Jap artillery guns. You are firing about four hundred yards behind them."

Said Acker, "Boy, what great news. I asked him to watch for me and tell me what effect we had with the next round. We adjusted fire and he reported we were two or three hundred feet short of the target, but right in line. On my next order to fire three rounds . . . he reported we were right on target. The Japs were squealing and running all around. He watched as we pulverized the area and reported we had destroyed their artillery. What a day! We never heard from that artillery again. This eased the pressure on the hill a lot. We realized that the seventh of April was Good Friday and what a good Friday!"

The combined efforts of the two other battalions drove the Japanese from their siege at Nhpum Ga. On Easter Sunday, Major Briggs and Hunter walked into the village, where McGee greeted them. The rescuers brought a long column of animals and men with improvised litters to remove the sick and wounded, close to 100. A constant flow of small planes arrived and carried out the casualties. Hunter reported 52 dead Americans and 163 wounded during the battle around Nhpum Ga. Another 77 had to be hospitalized because of illness. The body count for the Japanese in the immediate area was some 400, with others probably down beyond the immediate perimeter area. An estimated two battalions of infantry reinforced by an artillery company had been badly hammered.

As Stilwell had planned, the Chinese 113th Regiment successfully held the roadblock established by Galahad's 1st Battalion on the Kamaing road. That enabled their comrades from two other regiments to successfully attack Shaduzup and occupy the town.

The entire Marauder force now entered a rehabilitation and training program. Hunter declared, "Close-order drill was prescribed, and the sight of the jungle veterans attempting to regain some semblance of spit and polish caused me to walk around with a sly grin on my face most of the time. . . . One would think only a crackpot or a genius would prescribe close-order drill for a jungle outfit deep in North Burma. Actually, soldiers like to drill. It is good exercise, creates a feeling of comradeship, acquaints the men and officers with each other's good and bad points, and it requires little preparatory work." Whether the men actually appreciated the therapy given by Hunter remains unreported.

15

Imphal and Kohima Besieged, Chindits Beset, Marauders Perturbed

The campaigns by the Chindits and the Marauders would certainly be for naught if the Japanese thrust into India succeeded. Without the bases in Assam there would be no way to exploit a northern Burma supply route. For Slim, the situation continued to deteriorate, even with the airlift that brought the 5th Indian Division from the Arakan to Assam. The most critical sector became the front north of Imphal, the Japanese drive toward Kohima. Beyond that small town lay Dimapur, the foundation for what flowed into China and northern Burma.

The British forces, helped by a network of hills and from fortified positions, fought hard enough to halt the push directly toward Imphal. The Japanese, who had enlisted a unit from the Indian National Army, troops rebelling against colonial rule, could not break through.

To the north, however, the Japanese progress was significant. They attacked a pair of important villages, Ukhrul and Sangshak. Ukhrul fell quickly as the Nipponese turned their attention to Sangshak, eight miles south. The three thousand defenders, members of the 50th Indian Parachute Brigade, hunkered down in a tiny perimeter two hundred yards by eight hundred yards, a space that allowed concentrated firepower. It also made for a fat target: a shell could hardly explode in the area without shrapnel spraying the soldiers. When the embattled troopers dug into the ground they struck bedrock at only three feet, limiting their protection to shallow trenches.

The original strategy for the advancing Japanese battalion from the 31st Division, which easily swept through Ukhrul, specified a direct path toward Kohima. But the general from the 31st Division, accompanying the battalion, thought he saw an opportunity to eliminate opposition at Sangshak with a quick strike. He ordered a detour, and when the battalion commander urged a night attack without waiting for their artillery, the general consented.

The 50th Indian Parachute Brigade, however, packed both 150-millimeter guns and 3-inch mortars in their arsenal. When the Japanese flung themselves forward, they encountered a buzzsaw of shells, grenades, and bullets that chopped them to pieces. Transports dropped supplies, much of which ended up in Japanese hands, but fighters escorting the cargo planes ravaged the Nipponese who scurried after the rations, water, and ammunition.

The battle for Sangshak raged on, with a second Japanese battalion entering the bloody hillside turf. Corpses piled up, only to rot in the sun while hundreds of wounded defenders lay amid puddles in the trenches. The Japanese battalion that had made the first attack had lost more than four hundred killed and wounded and no longer functioned as a cohesive fighting force. On March 27, after the defenders had again repulsed an assault the previous day, the Japanese survivors of the two battalions that had hurled themselves at Sangshak moved into the village before dawn. All they found were corpses and discarded weapons and equipment. During the night, under cover of an artillery barrage, the 50th Indian Parachute Brigade had pulled out.

The victory at Sangshak delayed the Japanese advance by a week, allowing the British to install the 5th Indian Division from the Arakan into the Imphal plain and to bring added forces to Kohima. And among the trophies taken from the Japanese killed in the early charge was a dispatch case with papers and maps that spelled out the strategic approach of the Japanese. Lieutenant General Geoffrey Scoones, the British commander for the area, now knew the enemy's plan.

To the south, another wing of the Japanese offensive headed toward Imphal. The British showed themselves prepared to meet these adversaries. When a twelve-tank column clattered up the road toward the village of Tengnoupal, antitank guns blasted the lead armor, blocking the road. The guns pounded the column until the ones to the rear could only retreat. They were lucky that RAF aircraft did not catch them in a stationary, open position, where all of them would have been destroyed.

The defenders, however, had too much territory to cover, and while the terrain and absence of adequate roads or trails denied full use of armor, the Japanese infantry swarmed forward. The British reverted to the tactic of fortified boxes snuggled into the hills. At a number of sites, in fierce close encounters, men wielded bayonets, grenades, and rifles against an overlay of exploding artillery and mortar shells, all to deadly effect. Both sides absorbed substantial losses.

The strategy for the capture of Kohima, four thousand to five thousand feet above sea level, called for occupation of the village of Naga, a few miles north. The key to the defense and the main safeguard of the vast storehouse at Dimapur, fewer than fifty miles away, was a ridgeline formed by a series of hills that overlooked the road looping around Kohima on its way to Dimapur. The siege of the defenders on the ridge began April 6 and dragged on for two weeks. Mortars and shells rained down on the garrison, starting at sunset. After dark, waves of infantrymen began the torturous climb up the slopes against the outnumbered and outgunned defenders.

The Japanese were not to be denied. And although the British garrison was relieved after being encircled, and three hundred wounded evacuated, the Japanese held most of the seven-thousand-yard-long ridge covering the vital road. However, the Nipponese high command, in Slim's view wrongheadedly, would have achieved more if they had simply bypassed Kohima and marched straight on to Dimapur. Slowly the British built up their strength until Slim estimated his forces outnumbered the Japanese by at least two to one. A series of painfully costly attacks battered the now well-entrenched enemy ensconced on the ridge. More than three weeks of fighting would finally evict them.

The strategy aimed at Imphal roughly replicated that at Kohima: parallel columns seeking to outflank the objective and surround it. The campaign reached a high-water mark when the 15th Division of the Japanese crossed the mountains northeast of Imphal and cut the main road to Kohima in March. While that was as far as they could advance, they would not be forced to withdraw for some three months.

Decline of the Chindits

While the men of Galahad recuperated from their ordeal during the second phase of their campaign, the Chindits, to the south, attempted to carry out the premises of long-range penetration. Upon the death of Wingate, Slim chose as his successor the 111th Brigade leader, Brigadier Joe Lentaigne, an army officer since 1918. In his memoirs, Slim said he was guided by the need to install an individual known to the men, "one who had experienced their hardships and in whose skill and courage they could trust." Slim insisted that seniority had nothing to do with his selection of Lentaigne, but in passing over the likes of both Fergusson and Calvert, experienced leaders, he named a much more conventional soul, one not given to tantrums or opposition to a senior officer's decisions and who lacked the imprimatur of Churchill.

The biographers of Wingate called Lentaigne "a brave but essentially conventional Gurkha officer who had never been wholly convinced of Wingate's theories of long-range penetration." Military historian Shelford Bidwell, in *The Chindit War,* characterized Lentaigne similarly, and another source claimed the new leader was physically unfit for the campaigns, possibly because of his fondness for whiskey. Without the forceful personality of Wingate, the new Chindit commander did not demur as Slim spun off the 23d Brigade for the defense of Kohima. The ultimate insult, on May 17, would cede operational command of the Chindits to Stilwell, with all of his prejudices toward the British.

Lentaigne flew out of Burma on March 30 to confer with Slim and the other senior CBI officers in India. According to Louis Allen's history of the war in Burma, Lentaigne believed that both Broadway and White City were on the brink of conquest. Actually, Broadway had held firm with the aid of Cochran's fighters and the RAF plus the import of the small twenty-five-pound cannons brought in by transports. White City, however, was a much more threatened specimen.

Rodney Tatchell, with the 21st Column under Bernard Fergusson in the abortive attacks at Indaw, having digested the news of Wingate's death, was part of a retreat. "In view of our sadly depleted state, we were ordered, in Fergusson's words, to 'slip across the Katha/Naha railway; and on into the Kachin Hills, east of the main Myitkina railway, north of White City and so to Aberdeen. It was thirty to forty miles farther than the direct route but much safer with more cover and better water.'" Fergusson was adamant that his people needed rest and decent food before they could function, having engaged in a hard battle after a march of seven weeks with rations.

"As we covered the last few miles," said Tatchell, "we were passed by a column of [the] 3d West African Brigade, newly flown into Aberdeen and on their way eastwards. They looked a splendid lot, in marked contrast to our dirty and bedraggled condition." He told of the luxury of staying put for a spell, enough to eat and drink, the ability to sleep and wash. "Dakotas constantly came and went, bringing in reinforcements and supplies and flying out the sick and wounded. We were re-equipped with new clothing and excellent American blankets. Officers and NCOs also received the new .30-caliber carbine in place of the abominable Sten gun."

Lieutenant Colonel Philip H. Graves-Morris, who had captained a company during the 1941 fighting in Eritrea, led the 84th Column, which arrived at Aberdeen on the night of April 2. Working alongside his unit was the 65th Column. Their initial mission was destruction of the rail line running between Wuntho and Indaw. Graves-Morris learned of a company of enemy soldiers a few miles off, relatively an easy task for the column, but "orders were to proceed with all speed, undetected if possible, to deal with the objective."

After a ten-day march through thick jungle, up and down severe slopes, and across innumerable streams, the outfit bivouacked with the intention of blowing up a bridge south of the Bon Chaung railway station. Aerial photos, dropped earlier, showed three targets, two iron-girder side spans of about forty feet with a hundred-foot length in the center. After sighting a troop train rattling over the gorge, the plan was to destroy the crossing with a train on it. Charges were prepared and laid for the most northern of the crossings. Hopes for complete surprise vanished when two Japanese scouts came upon Chindits performing reconnaissance. The pair died quickly, but their comrades began cautiously exploring the area. When a Chindit sentry blasted them with his machine gun, the Japanese went into a defensive stance. Sappers blew one of the smaller girder bridges.

The railway station and the main conduit were well protected by bunkered troops. A full-scale assault demolished the depot by means of flamethrowers, small cannons, and mortars. Platoons drawn from both columns advanced on the Bon Chaung bridge itself, methodically eliminating its defenders but at some cost to themselves. Muleteers ferried forward loads of explosives. The demolition specialists sought to place the charges. A corporal took a fatal wound from a sniper, and when a fellow sapper rushed forward to remove him from his exposed position, the sniper mortally wounded him. Nevertheless, a successful detonation totally wiped out the Bon Chaung span.

Graves-Morris reported, "The next problem was evacuation of the wounded and the map showed there were suitable paddy fields on the banks of the Meza River which could be converted into a landing strip for light planes. This entailed a grueling climb up a steep gradient with a merciless sun beating down through the leafless plane trees and a choking dust. The casualties, on improvised stretchers, had to be manhandled by men already so weighted down by equipment that additional stretchers had to be made to carry their packs by even more men. It took nearly a full platoon to carry one casualty as the stretcher bearers needed frequent relief. Many of the men had now not drawn water for over twenty-four hours and only undrinkable blackish water appeared from the holes dug in a chaung at the mid-day halt."

When the sorely beset columns finally came to a river, Graves-Morris said, "The animals went mad at the sight of water—their thirst seemed insatiable, and they had to be dragged away for fear this sudden immoderate drinking would have ill effects." An airstrip was marked out and soon six cargo planes, with fighter escort, dropped precious supplies. "To the great joy of everyone, five light planes, piloted by 'Cochran's young ladies,' arrived and evacuated the eleven casualties."

When Graves-Morris referred to "Cochran's young ladies" he meant, of course, the single-engine rescue planes. Cochran said, "You would fly airplanes [the L-1s and L-5s] in and out of the strips. They would collect the wounded at the immediate site, come into the big bases of Chowringhee or Broadway, offload, and go back with a replacement and some ammunition and bring out another wounded. Then when the DC-3s came in at night with supplies or personnel or equipment, the wounded would go into the DC-3s and be taken to hospitals in the rear. Wingate's first request [at the Quebec Conference] was more than adequately supplied. The wounded not only didn't lie in the jungle anymore to die, they were the best cared for guys in the business. They would get out the same day and they'd be in hospitals.

"This was the very necessary and very proud work of those liaison guys. They were the beloved of the British soldier. I remember when I would go in, you had a load to take in and a load to take out. I remember bringing one kid whose leg was all shot up. I got him out and I've never seen such appreciation from that boy. There were many instances where the kids on stretchers, pretty well shot up, would kiss the hands of the pilot. We not only amazed them, but they were mighty proud to be associated with us, and a great camaraderie was set up between the forces. We admired each other."

Cochran's air force also flew tactical missions. During March and April, the 1st Air Commando destroyed some eighty enemy airplanes; blasted eight bridges; and demolished seven ammunition sites, fifty-five buildings, and numerous trains and locomotives. The air commandos brought a new dimension to ground support. Cochran and Alison, while gathering equipment and supplies in the United States, had seen experiments with rockets mounted on aircraft. The engineers at Wright Field in Ohio were still working on manufacturing a tube to carry the weapons underneath a wing. Cochran and Alison found a local machine shop, arranged to fabricate effective tubes, and shipped them to India. American P-51 pilots used them on strafing runs against enemy ground targets in Burma.

Cochran himself flew occasional missions, but ordinarily he allowed someone who regularly participated to command the operations. On one day, Cochran led a four-plane section of a sixteen-ship strike. "The fighters carried a couple of five-hundred-pound bombs and we were after a supply depot. We were flying over Mandalay and I announced, 'I've got the target spotted. I'm going to go down as close as I can. I may need help from other eyes.'" Cochran had forgotten that he was not in charge. "We made a tactical error. Instead of setting up cover, which was routine, I started to peel off." Diving to low altitude, Cochran and his associates examined the area beneath them for their target. "As I started back up, collecting my guys, we were jumped by a horde of Japanese fighters. They were all over us. They weren't kids; they knew what to do. We were in a tough position, we were low, and we were climbing. We didn't have our speed, none of our flights were intact to help each other. My judgment was don't try to snatch victory from defeat. I said down and out. We weren't going to do any good by staying there and fighting. We had valuable pilots and aircraft. This was not our true mission, which was to support Wingate, and here we were doing a strategic air war thing. We had P-51s, which could roll over, dive, and run away from these guys, but we had handed them all of the advantages. We were outnumbered and fighting them from a very bad position. All the odds against us. They had Zeros, which could outmaneuver us. I ordered break it off and get out of here. I kept saying get out of here.

"Since I had been over the target, the main part of the enemy was between me and home. I was going to have to run the gauntlet. I started on a course for home, wide open, giving it all I had. They kept coming at me. I went by the first; he wasn't in position to get me. But another got above me and he had speed and came down at me. Supposedly I had more speed than any Japanese airplane and could outrun anyone. I decided I wasn't going to stand and fight him. I kept going lower and lower and he kept on coming. I could tell I was gaining and he was close enough to fire at me but was not effective. I just had it to the fire wall, running like a scared rabbit. It wasn't terribly brave, I admit, not like in storybooks [or in *Terry and the Pirates*]. I'd made enough errors for the day. I hopped trees, getting low enough to keep out of his gun range.

"I overheard a conversation between two of our pilots. One of them said, 'I think Cochran was in that plane on fire which went down and I didn't see anybody get out of it.'" The rumor filtered through the radio back to headquarters. Journalists there picked up the news during debriefings. Someone filed a report to the wire services. Oblivious to the wildfire account of his demise, Cochran recalled,

"We came limping back and we were disgusted with ourselves. We berated each other. Pilots said we should have stayed and fought. I felt we had not followed proper procedure, retaining half of the force as aerial cover. I criticized them and myself for not having done that and their leader for not having trained them to do it. I criticized myself for taking over a mission of that size. They weren't used to following me and I was not their squadron commander. We went over our mistakes. We had been complacent, careless, not watchful, gotten beaten. I explained it was a bad place to fight and we lost three men that day. One of them killed that day was my number four man. That was the burning plane seen."

Meanwhile, word of the apparent loss of Cochran reached the offices of Major General George Stratemeyer: chief of the Far East Air Command. A teletype tersely wired the 1st Air Commando base: "To Cochran from Stratemeyer: Verify or refute Cochran's death today." The alleged deceased pilot replied, "Hell no! I am not dead!"

White City Falls

Norman Durant, who emerged from the Battle of Pagoda Hill with a minor leg wound, had traveled a short distance to what would become White City. "Then followed a period of excessive boredom," he said, "when there might not have been a Jap for miles. Sometimes air patrols encountered them but they seemed to be giving the block a wide berth, the general opinion being that they were waiting for reinforcements to have an all-out slap at us.

"It [White City] was now a complete Babel, for it contained: British troops, West Africans, Chinese, Burmans, a New Zealand RAF officer, Indians, and an American-born Jap who acted as interpreter (or interrogator) of prisoners. Life was very tedious but luckily there was a pleasant stream on the southern perimeter and every afternoon, I used to spend an hour or so there." The inhabitants of White City lived in deep, narrow trenches covered with logs and earth. Ordinary field rations sustained the soldiers except for an occasional drop of bread, margarine, and canned milk. Durant remarked on some West Africans' first encounter with American K rations, which they opened and then cooked everything, a mixture of cheese, crackers, lemonade powder, sugar, and chewing gum.

Late on the afternoon of April 5, the Japanese announced themselves with a barrage of artillery shells, some mortars, and an ineffective air raid. Durant and the other residents set themselves for an attack. "Hardly had we stood-to," he recalled, "when about two hundred yards away over the track, a bugle began a most elaborate solo, presumably the Jap 'advance.' For a moment our people could hardly believe their ears but then they opened up with everything they had, and as the Japs broke cover and reached our wire, they were met by a concentration of fire which broke them completely and within forty-five minutes they had packed it in. The next morning in front of our positions we found any number of Jap packs and rifles, lengths of Bangalore torpedo, and in a hollow, two ponies, but the Japs, as more often happens, had got their dead away."

White City held fast as the enemy probed for soft spots. A pair of light tanks clanked close, but .50-caliber machine guns drove them off. During this period the Chindits dispatched fighting patrols. Durant led one, with Gurkha soldiers equipped with a Vickers machine gun and a three-inch mortar to rescue comrades pinned down in a village four miles from the stronghold.

As those in White City hunkered down under the siege, trooper N. P. Aylen, a member of the 45th Reconnaissance Troop with the 16th Brigade, having hiked from Ledo to Aberdeen, then participated in several battles that centered around villages controlled by the Japanese, had returned to the stronghold. After several days of rest and refitting, on Easter Sunday, April 9, he and his comrades marched out of Aberdeen, now assigned to the 77th Brigade of Mike Calvert to assist in the reduction of the pressure around White City.

Aylen said that when they were within roughly ten miles of the Chindit citadel they could hear the sounds of battle nightly. "Round [White City] the Japs had flung a cordon of four thousand troops. [They] pounded the position with field artillery and invariably followed up with a bayonet attack. The defenders sent up Very lights and mowed down the attackers with machine guns. This went on night after night without respite. We obtained news from the defenders daily by wireless. Once we heard that two hundred Jap bodies had been counted on the barbed-wire defenses after an extra-large-scale attack. The Japs actually succeeded in capturing an airstrip on one occasion, but before they could consolidate this gain, a fierce counterattack was launched by African troops. Many of these threw away their rifles and went in with their favorite weapon, the machete. The Japs hung on grimly and fought to the last, but the airstrip was finally recaptured."

As Aylen and his group advanced toward White City, their patrols skirmished with Japanese until one column, at the village of Seipin, encountered a large force of well-dug-in enemy. Mitchell bombers blasted the village. "It was an exhilarating sight to see our [planes] cooperating with ground troops and we watched the air battle with keen interest. Having unloaded their bombs, the Mitchells made off. Unfortunately, the Jap positions had been just outside the village and devastating as the bomber attack was, the Japs had been so well dug in that the bombs busting a short distance away had not affected them. British and Gurkhas went in with rifle and bayonet but were met with a hail of fire against which they could make no progress."

The day passed, and White City's soldiers remained embattled. Aylen's unit pulled back, learning that those who assaulted Seipin had suffered heavy casualties. Subsequently Aylen reported that in a protected section of jungle, his group was addressed by Calvert. "In quiet tones he gave us a summary of events and explained that the defenders of White City were feeling the strain from night attacks. It was up to us to bring them immediate relief 'at all costs.'"

The strategists organized a new tack to apply their power against the Japanese forces. They came within three miles of White City as Calvert squeezed his troops between the block and the enemy. The withering fire of the attackers cut down much of the hapless mules with Calvert's brigade. He would later write that he was so close to the Japanese that they could hear him speaking as he radioed Cochran asking for tactical air support. He endured some uncomfortable moments as machine guns aimed toward the sound of his voice. Then P-51s roared in, and their strafing silenced the Japanese machine gunners.

"Presently, the battle in our vicinity began in earnest. An enemy patrol had penetrated to the right of where we lay and a hail of fire poured into our positions. I felt a sharp pain in my knuckle and a slight tug at my chest and hugged the earth as close as possible while the storm continued. I looked up, dreading to see our Vickers gunner slumped over his gun, but he was still in the same position, pouring intermittent streams into the enemy, regardless of the storm which was raging round him. The intensity of the fire died down, and presently our column commander and the brigadier came . . . coolly walking round the positions in spite of the fire coming in from all directions. . . . I glanced down to find my shirt soaked in blood from a gash in the chest.

"After the battle had lasted for some time, we received the order 'Prepare to withdraw.' We moved back cautiously and had to lie flat when a hail of bullets came in our direction. Our first and most difficult obstacle was to cross a wide track which had been covered by enemy fire. We dashed across during a lull in the firing, taking wounded men with us on improvised stretchers. As we had moved into the battle we had been followed by Gurkha troops who had taken up positions in our rear. Now, as we moved back along the track, every few yards revealed the body of a Gurkha who had died at his post."

The retreat continued, and during each pause the medics used the time to apply first aid. At one halt, a burial service was held for two of the wounded who had died. The men were cheered after meeting a West African unit that gleefully recounted their ambush of seven truckloads of Japanese troops and supplies. Altogether, an estimated one hundred Japanese had perished, and four wounded men were taken prisoner. Said Aylen, "We began to feel a real affection for our black comrades-in-arms."

A noticeable silence around White City occurred the first night of the withdrawal by Calvert's brigade. The same quiet fell during the second evening, and the Chindits learned that the Japanese had also retreated from their ring surrounding the stronghold. Except for an occasional outburst of bullets when small parties of the enemy surfaced, the column remained stationary for several days before traveling to the Broadway airstrip. Litters carried the most severely injured, but, Aylen said, "I was unable to carry a pack owing to my chest wound and had abandoned everything except rifle, ammunition, water bottle, half a blanket, and a copy of [Francis Turner] Palgrave's *Golden Treasury,* which I had carried throughout the expedition." A seven-day march brought them to their destination. An evacuation plane hauled Aylen from the field of battle.

Norman Durant reported, "At first light on April 17 the Jap made his last big attack on the block [White City] when at dawn he put in a battalion against O. P. [Observation Post] Hill, which was held by only a platoon under a rather precious thirty-five-year-old peacetime decorator [Lieutenant David Scholey]. From our hill we got a grandstand view of the attack and ourselves mowed down a number of Japs attacking from the north. By sheer weight of numbers they broke through the wire onto O. P. Hill, and only a magnificent show by the platoon prevented the hill being overrun. Eventually, David Scholey and sixteen men (all that was left of his platoon) held off the attack until a counterattack force of West Africans arrived and cleared the hill. When the Jap withdrew, one was left, trapped in a trench on the hill and was being grenaded by about twenty men. Instead of surrendering he suddenly leapt out and with rifle and bayonet charged the many people standing around. A W. African dropped his rifle, picked up a wooden box containing twelve grenades, and batted him over the head—end of Suicide Joe. David Scholey got a very deserved Military Cross. Killed on O. P. Hill was a subaltern who had come to us five days before as a reinforcement."

The effort to aid the hard-pressed units within White City also involved Hugh Patterson, the commando platoon leader with the 50th Column from the Royal Engineers. They had been engaged in a successful bridge demolition task, and a small plane plucked him from an airstrip for a quick journey to White City. There Mike Calvert sent him on a mission to meet another unit with information on a forthcoming assault on the village of Kadu. Patterson, weakened by a bout of malaria, never managed to contact the officer in command, but the entire plan was scotched because of the heavy attacks on White City. Patterson rejoined the 50th Column while it was en route to Kadu. Because of the impending but subsequently aborted confrontation near that village, he remembered, the column leader, Lieutenant Colonel Christie, "decided to leave out of battle a group of sick and wounded. Incredibly, he left them unguarded in a small patch of jungle just south of the blown bridge at Mawhun. There they were found by a Jap patrol who massacred the lot, except one man, Fusilier French, who feigned death amongst the bodies of his comrades for a couple of days, until the Japs left. He wandered on his own for several more days until, half-demented, he managed to find his column again. The less said about this deplorable incident the better [but he did include it in his memoirs]. We all accepted that we would have to be left if we were unfit to go on but in as safe a harbor as could be found.

"About the tenth of April, the brigade began a series of attacks on Japanese positions in the Mahpin, Myaunbdantha, and Sapein areas. While these worried the Jap, and took the strain off White City, they cost us a number of casualties. [The] 50th Column had a shaky-do one day when they were caught in the open by several machine guns and an [artillery] gun, which forced us to do a 'dispersal'—return by small fighting groups to a prearranged rendezvous. We lost some men but only one mule. The next fortnight was spent by [the] 50th Column in laying small ambushes in platoon strength and skirmishing with parties of Japs who had withdrawn from White City. I had only one proper 'sapper' job to do—the blocking of the roads and tracks south of White City to prevent movement of motor transport to and from the block."

However, just as they began to place mines on the highway and felled trees across the rail line, they heard the sound of trucks on a road a short distance away. Patterson led a party to investigate. Prudently, he had set some soldiers behind him in a defensive posture as he emerged from the brush with another officer. "Pat Scofield and I nosed our way out to find ourselves in the midst of a crowd of Nips, resting by the roadside and who were as surprised as we were.

We crawled back ten yards, and all lay down. We could hear the Japs without them seeing us. We hoped they would follow us in, but they just chattered excitedly and appeared to do nothing in particular. I couldn't see how many there were but it was enough to give us a good battle and our job was to block the roads. We signaled the Bren gunner to stand by while Pat Scofield and I gave them some grenades. The Nips ran like hell when we stood up to throw but we bagged four with the Bren and the bombs."

Patterson and his crew completed the job and then began a dogged march northeast. "Most of us were very tired, worn down with malaria and feeling the strain—especially the officers. When we started retracing our steps to Broadway there is no doubt that we were all hoping to be flown from there." A short distance from Broadway, the 50th Column halted to await orders from Calvert and Lentaigne. Because of his malaria and a knee injury, a brigade surgeon ordered Patterson to be evacuated. "I left the column with a few other sick and sorry, and hobbled to Broadway. It was only twelve miles but it is not a march I care to remember. I did not like leaving my platoon but I should have been a serious drag on them if I had stayed.

"We were to be flown to Sylhet [Assam]. On the plane was Lentaigne, who had just sent the brigade north to Mogaung, where it would destroy itself pulling Chinese chestnuts out of the fire. There was a severe storm over Sylhet, so [we] landed about midnight at a strip on the Imphal plain. Here we had an insight into our new commander's character. He was met by a major on the strip who told the general he would show him to his *basha* [a hut or house]. Lentaigne turned to the other occupants of the plane, who had no blankets or groundsheets—and it was cold out there—and were all seriously ill and told them to sleep under the wings of the plane. One could not help thinking of the reply Wingate would have given to anyone who suggested that he should fare better than his men. Fortunately the major chap came back later and fixed us up in an old *basha* and gave us tea, biscuits, and fried bacon."

While Calvert believed that White City could have been held indefinitely, his commander, Lentaigne, never wholly convinced of the stronghold concept, decided that it was too exposed and ordered it and Broadway abandoned. Instead, the 111th Brigade would construct a new outpost, Blackpool, sixty miles farther north with the backing of the 77th Brigade. Following a strategy worked out earlier by Slim, Mountbatten, and Stilwell, without objections from Lentaigne, future operations by the Special Forces were to support Stilwell in the drive towards Myitkyina.

According to Louis Allen, Stilwell grudgingly accepted the British forces. Stilwell fretted that they would act independently of his orders, and he regarded the withdrawal from White City as a mistake. On the other hand, he had been pleasantly surprised when his British counterparts did not demand his help in the form of Chinese soldiers to assist in the defense of Imphal and Kohima.

Norman Durant, the leader of a machine-gun platoon with the 77th Brigade that had been at the White City block, recalled the first four or five days as "absolute hell. We had done no marching and carried no packs for seven weeks . . . it was getting near the monsoon and was as hot as it could be. We had to climb some very stiff hills and as the Jap was all round the block, we had to keep moving pretty fast. Many men fell out on the march and I felt nearer exhaustion than at any time before or since, but once we got into the hills life became a picnic."

The only demand upon his unit was for raiding parties to sabotage the road and railway. The pace had been reduced to six miles per day and the bivouacs alongside mountain streams were furnished with abundant water and fresh fish, obtained by throwing in grenades. Air drops dumped luxuries such as oatmeal, canned fruit, canned milk, and rice.

Galahad Regroups and Faces a New Mission

The three battalions of Merrill's Marauders had remained in the vicinity of Nhpum Ga and Hsamshingyang following the desperate battles to relieve the 2d Battalion. The survivors buried their fallen comrades in a small cemetery marked by bamboo crosses; disposed of their dead animals; rested; and received treatment for their minor medical problems, such as ulcerations from leech bites, dermatitis, intestinal tract upset, and the various fevers endemic to the region.

Word spread that the entire outfit would soon engage in another mission. According to James Hopkins, the men of Galahad now regarded Stilwell with considerable hostility. "Some officers who were familiar with the facts pointed out that General Stilwell had been very critical of General Wingate when he lost one-third of his brigade in Burma in 1943. The Marauders had, up until this time, lost almost as many—and, like the Chindits, had many sick and dazed in their ranks. Now, in spite of his [Stilwell's] statements about the British general, we were forced to believe that he was prepared to sacrifice his own troops."

Hopkins was referring to a budding plan to capture the airfield just outside the strategic town of Myitkyina. The fluid nature of the fighting in Burma, where no contiguous front line separated the warring parties, where the steep hills and mountains, swift-flowing streams, and thick jungle handicapped deployment, led to a somewhat disconcerting ebb and flow. The company of Gurkhas and Kachin Levies led by Scott, and with other units, determined to eliminate Sumprabum as a base. Others marched on the village only to find that the Japanese had slipped away, unnoticed.

The departure from Sumprabum of enemy soldiers lessened the threat of an attack on Stilwell's legions. The forces under Lentaigne, however, had been reduced, not only by the attrition of combat and disease, but also the 16th Brigade, led by Fergusson, was considered too shattered from its futile labors against Indaw and the exhausting march that followed. Aircraft bringing in supplies and reinforcements to Aberdeen flew the entire outfit back to India. Still, the Chindits fielded three mobile brigades plus the troops manning the strongholds.

During one of the rare visits to Hsamshingyang by a Stilwell staff officer, Colonel Henry Kinnison, the general's G-3, Hunter learned that Stilwell had been considering a task force aimed at the airstrip near Myitkyina. Hunter said that after Kinnison left, he organized a staff study on the feasibility of such a move. They drew on intelligence from the OSS agents, Kachins, and a missionary priest. When Hunter was told to send a staff officer to Stilwell's headquarters he dispatched Major Louis Williams, his adjutant, with the rough plans for seizure of the airstrip.

To the surprise of Williams, Frank Merrill, seemingly recovered from his cardiac seizure, was present and took Hunter's plans. Undoubtedly Merrill, aware of his superior's desires, had already been investigating the possibilities. A few hours later the Galahad commander presented Stilwell with a script for the capture of the objective. According to Williams, as reported by Hunter, the general growled to his own chief of staff, Haydon Boatner, "With all the time you've had, you haven't got a plan for taking Myitkyina and here Frank comes up with a good plan in a couple of hours." Hunter said Boatner told him Stilwell had never spoken of such an operation. Hunter said "competitive jealousy existed between Merrill and Boatner" and commented, "The record as it becomes more clear indicates that the 'Boss' played one against the other as though each were competing for the starting spot as quarterback."

The actual blueprints for the campaign probably drew from more than the preliminary sketch by Hunter and revisions by Merrill. The

Myitkyina Task Force would deploy not only elements of Galahad but also the 150th Infantry Regiment of the Chinese 50th Division and the 88th Regiment of the Chinese 30th Division. Both would be flown in over the Hump. After delousing and issuance of new uniforms, they would put in their appearance.

A Chinese-speaking officer, Colonel John McCammon, from Stilwell's staff, was named executive officer. That bumped Hunter to third place in the task force command. "I, evidently, had not made the Stilwell team," said Hunter. "The men of Galahad resented this more than I did. They embarrassed me at times by openly offering their sympathy." Hunter's injured pride may have been somewhat assuaged when Merrill assigned him to lead the spearhead of the attack force. Given his choice of unit, he took the 1st Battalion, commanded by Lieutenant Colonel William L. Osborne, a veteran of combat in the South Pacific as well as the first two Galahad campaigns.

16

Myitkyina Morass

At the end of April, Stilwell's army began to slog toward Myitkyina. The 1st Battalion, commanded by Hunter, joined by the Chinese 150th Infantry Regiment, was designated the H Force, while Colonel Henry L. Kinnison Jr. led the 3d Battalion with the Chinese 88th Infantry Regiment in the K Force. A Kachin guerrilla unit, organized by OSS 101, stayed with McGee's 2d Battalion, the M Force, which trailed as a block against a potential Japanese strike from the rear. Heavy rains that dissolved trails into deep mud slowed the columns, and pack animals slipped over the sides of cliffs, consuming time and energy.

A brief battle at Ritpong by the K Force destroyed an enemy company, and on May 13 Kinnison's group engaged in intense combat against a pair of Japanese companies at Tingkrukawng, about halfway to the objective of Myitkyina. The battle there preoccupied the enemy and enabled the H Force to drive almost unimpeded toward the target. Although the M Force met no significant opposition, its route involved extra physical exertion, and the troops, already pummeled severely at Nhpum Ga, showed signs of fatigue.

Hunter's task force of Marauders, Chinese, OSS operatives, and some Kachin guides forged ahead, climbing hills and working its way through the Pidaung forest. Hunter commented, "The silence of a column of four thousand men marching in a cave of darkness through unknown and unfamiliar surroundings is almost deafening in its intensity. The absence of the usual chatter, horseplay, and wisecracks emphasizes the tenseness gripping the men."

When the H Force crossed a railroad with telephone and telegraph lines between Myitkyina and Mogaung, a Nisei Marauder climbed a

263

pole, tapped the lines, and reported hearing nothing to indicate the Japanese were aware of the task force. Hunter ordered the lines not be cut because that might cause the Japanese to send out a repair crew, which would discover the H Force presence. Farther on they came upon a village. Rather than leave anyone who could inform the enemy, Hunter arranged for his OSS people and the Kachins to bring every man, woman, and child along "as our guests for the night." The task force was now in position to attack the Myitkyina airfield.

The combat forces included the Chinese 150th Infantry Regiment, of the Chinese 50th Division, a mixed bag with an estimated one-third veterans of combat in their own nation and the remainder raw recruits. Their "arsenal" consisted of Chinese rifles, Maxim heavy machine guns, antiquated .30-caliber machine guns, and a few 60- and 80-millimeter mortars. Before beginning a sixteen-day march into Burma, the regiment had trained but briefly. Captain Thomas Kepley, the American adviser attached to the 1st Battalion, reported, "The Regimental CO seemed willing enough to push his troops forward but had a terrible fear of getting lost, not knowing the country, nature of the terrain, and his knowledge of map reading was limited." The inadequacies of the Chinese officers in matters of map reading and understanding a compass would prove highly injurious.

For the last stages of the journey toward Myitkyina that was not a problem as the 1st Battalion of Galahad led the procession, with an artillery battery from the 22d Chinese Division trailing them. However, Kepley noted, "The Chinese officers had to be warned on each occasion of an air drop to caution their men about getting off the fields while planes were dropping. With this precaution, there were still a few killed by bags of rice."

On the night of May 16, a three-man patrol led by Sergeant Clarence E. Branscomb, a veteran of the Solomon Islands campaigns, reconnoitered the airfield. Branscomb said that when Hunter gave him his instructions he handed him his last fifth of whiskey, which the scouting party consumed while walking and then creeping toward the objective. They discovered labor gangs who packed up before midnight and left via trucks. "We crawled around in the grass trying to work our way around the airport perimeter. After almost knifing each other a few times, at about 2:30 A.M. I picked up the radio and started walking down the middle of the runway, thinking if those emplacements were occupied, we'd soon find out—besides our time was up. I sat the radio down and called Caifson [Lieutenant Colonel Johnson, the battalion deputy commander]. I could hear him fine, but he couldn't hear me. So we invoked the code 'one is no, two is yes.' He asked me if there were Japanese on the field. I answered, 'one.'

He asked me if there were holes in the runway. I answered 'one.' He asked should he call India and send the gliders in? I said 'two.'" Branscomb and his companions returned safely, but the gliders were temporarily held for arrival after daylight and word that the airfield had been fully secured.

The OSS and Kachins extracted every bit of useful intelligence about the enemy disposition from the local people. Among the valuable tidbits of information: there was no barbed wire surrounding the field; the revetments were not fortified; fifty-five-gallon drums of oil checkerboarded the airstrip to prevent sudden landings; about two thousand Japanese had been in Myitkyina in the past; Pamati, a hamlet southwest of the airfield, housed a unit of Japanese military police; they seemed to have relaxed their controls over villagers; some twenty-five geishas were in residence.

The perimeter organized by Hunter placed the Chinese with a deep, swiftly flowing river immediately behind them. That would prevent them from a pell-mell retreat, particularly since few of the Chinese troops could swim. Hunter drew up a battle plan for the Chinese 150th Infantry Regiment to attack on a broad front and overrun the airport. Osborne, the CO of the 1st Battalion, would lead an assault on Pamati and sweep to the east, capturing the ferry point of the Irrawaddy at Zigyun. At ten in the morning the troops moved out and very quickly seized all of their objectives. Hunter himself walked out onto one of the runways, where Kachins were rolling the fifty-five-gallon drums away. He heard aircraft motors, and a flight of P-40s roared overhead. "We cranked up the radio," said Hunter, "and made contact with the flight leader, who immediately asked, 'Zipper, do you have any targets? We are here to support you.'

"I answered, 'No targets as yet. Look over the city, please.' On their return I asked them to relay a message and stressed its importance. The message was 'Merchant of Venice.'"

Jubilation oozed through the American command in Burma. "About 3:30," wrote Stilwell, "we got 'Merchant of Venice'—i.e., transports can land. WHOOPS! [sic] Enormous relief to get Merrill's report. About 3:30 two transports landed. At 4:00 we saw transports and gliders going over. Thereafter, a stream of planes both ways. Told them to keep going all night. We may have 89th [Chinese Regiment] in by morning.—WILL THIS BURN UP THE LIMEYS [sic]." Indeed, Mountbatten expressed chagrin at not being kept informed of the activities under Stilwell, but it is possible he simply forgot the strategy drafted early in the month. He was undoubtedly discomforted by a demand from Churchill for an explanation of how "the Americans by a brilliant feat of arms have landed us in Myitkyina."

Stilwell and Chindit Operations

On behalf of the campaign in northern Burma, on May 17, the day the Myitkyina airstrip was captured, Slim had placed the Chindits, now commanded by Major General Joe Lentaigne, under Stilwell. Serious disagreements quickly marked the collaboration of the separate forces. Stilwell's plans included seizure by the Chinese 22d and 38th Divisions of Kamaing, a hub for the Japanese south of the Galahad penetrations to Shaduzup and Nhpum Ga. They were to be aided by the Chinese 1st Provisional Tank Battalion, under U.S. colonel Rothwell Brown. The initial drives by the Chinese, while pushing the Japanese back, were extremely costly to the two divisions: 1,450 soldiers killed and another 3,450 wounded. *Spearhead,* by James E. T. Hopkins and John M. Jones, complained, "The Marauders could not understand why General Stilwell's four American-trained and -equipped Chinese infantry regiments could not be depended on to hold the airfield and capture the city. The Chinese had been well cared for and had seen little of the hardship and combat the Marauders had been enduring for four months." In fact, the Chinese units had absorbed considerable punishment both from the environment and the enemy and in many instances were no more physically fit than the Americans.

Kamaing lay at the conflux of the Mogaung River and the Indaw Chaung, and perhaps thirty miles farther south on the river lay another Japanese bastion, the river town of Mogaung. The Chindit Morris Force, which had begun its long-range penetration with eleven hundred men, was east of the Irrawaddy, confronted by a Japanese reinforced company strongly entrenched at Waingmaw, about five miles from Myitkyina. Stilwell ordered an attack on Waingmaw, unaware, perhaps, that the monsoon rains had flooded the neighboring fields chest deep. Repeated thrusts exposed the already weary Chindits to withering scythes of machine guns. Over the following eight weeks the Morris Force shrank to a fraction of the original number of officers and men. Stilwell ultimately acquiesced to requests for the survivors to be flown out.

Stilwell was even more discomfited by the situation at the stronghold of Blackpool. The 11th Brigade, under Major John Masters, its de facto head because its nominal commander was busy elsewhere, started on May 8 to create Blackpool, near the villages of Namkwin and Hopin. It was a difficult feat, since monsoon rains had begun to pelt down and the Japanese began shelling them and launching attacks even as they turned the first shovels of dirt for trenches and leveled the landing strip. Nevertheless, within ten days the brigade established the block, and two other brigades, the 77th and the 14th, would soon arrive to defend the flanks.

Massive, head-on assaults by Japanese soldiers, bolstered by heavy artillery and automatic weapons, rocked Blackpool. Just over two weeks after having planted the Chindit flag at the site, the situation for the residents became untenable. The Japanese were so close to the strip that they menaced the transports with antiaircraft, and precious bundles frequently fell among the enemy. It was impossible for the transport pilots to land and pull out the wounded. They could only drop supplies to the 77th and bombs on the enemy. As the monsoon season stormed in all its fury, the thick rain clouds eliminated air supply and support.

After the 14th Brigade had assisted in the evacuation of White City, it had moved farther north to help establish Blackpool to prevent the enemy from advancing on the embattled Marauders and Chinese around Myitkyina. On several occasions a large clash with the Japanese seemed imminent, but neither column actually came to grips with the enemy. The need to hurry to Blackpool, the thickness of the jungle, and the soaking monsoon rains denied the opportunity to engage. Earlier the troops had been, according to Philip Graves-Morris, "reasonably fresh and capable of giving a first-class account of themselves," but the difficult march up and down slippery slopes and across the treacherous streams—the inroads of malaria and typhus—and a growing shortage of food took their toll. "We were all to see the devastating effect of continuous rain, jungle gloom, mud, and toiling, backbreaking marches was to have on men's minds, as many cheerful normal men became depraved, collapsed, and asked to be left to die or even hastened their end by their own hands."

In a much weakened condition, the two columns slopped toward Hopin. Forming a perimeter to stymie the Japanese, the Chindits now engaged the enemy in numerous small-arms firefights, accompanied by artillery barrages and deadly snipers. "The Japanese," said Graves-Morris, "were showing great initiative in trying to make the British positions . . . untenable and continually infiltrated small parties to ambush the track that led from the supply drop area.

"The conditions of living in the block under constant pressure from the Japanese by day and night, in heavy rainstorms and with no amelioration by hot meals made the relief of 84th Colm advisable. The CO therefore, requested that 65th Colm, who were still working on preparation of the seaplane landing base [at Indawgyi Lake], should relieve 84th Colm."

Masters radioed a message asking permission to pull back. But even before receipt of a response, he realized that an immediate withdrawal was necessary. Accounts of the escape depict terrifying scenes. Stretcher bearers, unable to tote the litters amid heavy shelling, dropped the wounded and fled. Louis Allen wrote, "Some of the wounded who knew they would not survive the march out or who were too terribly mauled by shell fragments, were shot by friends."

Loss of Blackpool, however, opened up an alley for the Japanese to move reinforcements from the Japanese 18th Division into the town of Mogaung and toward Kamaing and Myitkyina. Once having attained relative safety, there was angry talk among the Chindits about the failure of the 14th Brigade to come forward in a timely fashion. Masters heaped blame on Lentaigne for his failure to visit and realize the awful conditions to which he had condemned them. Oblivious of or uncaring about their state, Lentaigne directed the 111th Brigade to advance on Mogaung from the west, while the 77th attacked from the east. The badly battered, depleted, and physically and emotionally exhausted Chindits reacted with incredulity to Lentaigne's new orders.

The British general was carrying out the strategy designed by Stilwell. The American's plan had envisioned a squeeze on the badly battered Japanese 18th Division defending Kamaing. Toward that end he had plotted the capture of Mogaung, a town at the apex of an inverted triangle with Kamaing and Myitkyina. At the end of May the 77th received its orders to attack Mogaung via the hills to the north. Some twelve miles from the objective they began to meet enemy patrols and an occasional sniper. Calvert, in command of the 77th, had signaled Lentaigne that he believed he could take Mogaung by June 5. He had badly miscalculated. Gradually the opposition stiffened, and because of the exceedingly dense vegetation, the Chindits, with their mules, stuck to paths, giving the Japanese the ability to anticipate their movements. Still, the column pressed on until it ascended to a height above Mogaung, three miles in the distance.

Durant, with a segment of the 77th Brigade, was not engaged in the debacle at Blackpool, and after several weeks without serious activity was somewhat restored in body and spirit. However, as the monsoon rains fell on him and his unit, he coped with the discomfort. With Mogaung as the objective, Durant recalled, "We left our packs and all the mules behind [in] the hills and manhandling [machine guns] and mortars we began moving north along the hilltop. Progress was very slow as the ridge consisted of a series of steep hills with passes in between and the job of carrying the guns and mortars up these slopes was a difficult one. We were in our usual formation for a march through thick country, the whole battalion in 'column snake,' single file, with a platoon slightly ahead as advance guard, a Vickers gun with the second platoon, followed by the remaining platoon of that company.

"After we had been moving for about an hour firing broke out ahead and we halted. Ten minutes later a message came for me to bring the first Vickers right forward and reaching the leading platoon I found that they were being fired on from a range of about twenty yards and could see nothing, the jungle there being very thick. Already the very competent company commander, Major Victor Howes, had been killed, sniped through the head, and the leading platoon commander had a burst in the knee and thigh from which he died in hospital a couple of weeks after. There were also some other rank casualties. We mounted a Vickers, laced the area, followed that up with grenades and then a rifle platoon went in just as the Japs left their positions and made off down the hill. They left behind two dead and a great bucket of hot rice and fish! From the positions dug there we learnt that we had been held up all that time by six Japs but this is a very good example of how, in this thick country where it is impossible to deploy, one determined man with a light machine gun, well dug in, can hold up a battalion for hours."

Durant recounted that his unit took up a position after a Gurkha force "put in a magnificent attack through thick creepers and deep mud against well-dug Jap positions." Subsequently, he said, "Shortly after dark a party of eight Japs carrying rations came chattering happily down the road from Mogaung and one of my gunners let them come within twenty yards and made short work of them with a Vickers. Later that night a Jap patrol sent out to find out what the firing was about stumbled into our perimeter and were practically entirely wiped out."

To capture Mogaung, Durant's Staffordshires advanced over open ground with sufficient clumps of bushes and trees to afford some cover. "Archie Wavell's [son of the British general] company with whom I moved was on the left and in contact on his right was the other [company]." Durant's section halted momentarily, awaiting the company on the right to clear its area. "We heard firing break out on the right and after some time a runner came up to say that they had run into a number of Jap snipers whom they couldn't see and from whom they were suffering heavy casualties. A platoon commander who had been flown in as reinforcement the day before had been killed and the company second in charge had been hit in the leg, besides several other O.R. casualties. They could make no headway and to save casualties were withdrawing. That left us in a nasty salient. Archie had one platoon on the right, facing out towards these reported snipers, one platoon four hundred yards away on the left, facing the village which was our objective, and one platoon in the center, facing the river. We knew it was only a question of time before the snipers turned their attention to us. The first we knew was when Archie's 2-in-C (a motherly, married, and family character who should never have been in) was shot through the head and killed instantly as he fussed about getting people under cover. At the same time everything opened up on the left as the Jap tried to push out the platoon facing the village and things got so serious that the center platoon had to be moved over to give support.

"The sniping on the right became heavier and still it was impossible to see where the firing was coming from. I had a Vickers mounted as if for AA and sprayed all the large trees, but it was entirely blind shooting. A platoon came up to reinforce us and was sent round to the right to clear what they could, but they hadn't gone fifteen yards before four men were down and the rest pinned down. The Jap then began, quite successfully, to grenade the wounded and when [we] tried to bring them in, two more men were hit. Archie Wavell, trying a new line, set off with a section but within a few seconds was back holding his left hand, which was hanging by a shred of muscle, having been hit by a sniper at twenty yards' range. He was astonishingly calm, gave out orders, and then walked back unassisted to the RAP [aid station].

"Meanwhile, on the left casualties were equally heavy and as it was getting dusk we were none of us feeling too happy, and even when the order came for us to withdraw we knew that somehow we had to get the wounded in. They seemed to be covered by two snipers so David Wilcox stationed himself where he might be able to get a shot. Someone began rustling the bushes nearby. The Jap moved and David shot him at [the] same time, getting a graze under his chin from a second sniper's bullet. But he saw him as well, and having a beeline was able to fire quickly enough to get him. It was a very courageous action, well deserving of a decoration."

The remainder crept and crawled away to join the others of the battalion, consoling themselves that while they had taken considerable losses, they had also gleaned much information about the disposition of the enemy. "The next day," said Durant, "we dug in like beavers and were shelled regularly and once again my phenomenal good luck held, for one shell burst within five yards of me, wounding my batman, killing the man next to him, and leaving me unscathed. It was very wet and all the trenches filled in with water as soon as they were dug, but the men seemed quite happy and cursed Joe Stilwell's

Chinese for not appearing, even making up a little song which they sang throughout the days with the greatest satisfaction:

I'm coming, I'm coming
Though my pace is very slow,
I hear the Chindit voices saying,
'*Jalo Joe.*' [Hindi for "Hurry up" and pronounced *jill-ho.*]"

While Norman Durant with the South Stafford Chindits had entertained themselves with their bitter ditty, Calvert's brigade lost as many as 130 killed or wounded in the battle. The delay in moving into Mogaung allowed the Japanese to bring in more troops until as many as four battalions defended against any further advance. The Chinese troops still had not appeared by June 13, more than a week later than in Calvert's timetable for subduing the town.

The Siege of Myitkyina Begins

There was precious little time to savor the conquest of the airstrip outside Myitkyina. Almost immediately, Hunter became irritated if not downright irate as flight after flight of cargo planes and transports touched down carrying everything but what he said he needed most, food and ammunition. To his consternation, the arrivals included an antiaircraft unit, a company of aviation engineers, and another regiment of Chinese soldiers. On his own, Major General George Stratemeyer, head of the Eastern Air Command in India, and a deputy to Stilwell, had substituted these elements for the scheduled shipments of food and ammunition. Stratemeyer's explanation was that he feared for the security of the airstrip. For the Marauders and the two Chinese regiments that had seized the objective, the alteration, which left Hunter's forces short of food and ammunition, was a critical error.

To complicate matters further, for inexplicable reasons, Hunter said neither Merrill nor Stilwell had informed him of the battle plan after the capture of the airfield. What occurred immediately following the seizure of the Myitkyina base is somewhat in dispute. Tuchman's book asserted that with expectations of a quick conquest of the town of Myitkyina, "Stilwell decided the honor should go to the Chinese; two battalions of the 150th Regiment advanced on the town on the afternoon of May 17, but coming under Japanese sniper fire at dusk, dissolved into confusion, fired on each other in error and continued shooting and killing each other in uncontrollable response until they were pulled out." Discredit for this tragedy of errors went uncertified as the official army history does not specify who directed the attack, and Hunter said he had busied himself trying to sort out the chaos enveloping the now functioning airstrip.

Thomas Kepley, the American liaison officer with the 150th, observed, "The regiment was given a mission to attack and capture the railroad station and yards in the town. Again, no knowledge of terrain and ability to read a map caused the Regt. CO to select [sic] going to the railroad instead of along the road. After dark that night, the Regt. started toward the railroad but stopped before reaching there because of the extreme darkness. During the late evening and night, the 89th Regiment [30th Division] were flown in by plane. At daylight the next day, fighting began with this regiment because neither knew the other's exact location. It [subsided] only when ordered by headquarters [on the airstrip] to stop."

Hunter summoned the 2d and 3d Battalions of Marauders to the Myitkyina airstrip. They arrived in a state hardly fit for battle, fatigued, plagued with sores and skin diseases as well as an epidemic of dysentery that caused some men to cut away the seats of their fatigues rather than take the time and effort to drop their pants during intestinal distress. Along with all of the battle injuries a new and deadly infection, *tsutsugamushi* fever, a form of typhus brought to Burma by the invading Japanese Imperial Army, began to ravage the Americans and the Chinese.

At a headquarters established at Shaduzup, Merrill had met with Stilwell to discuss the immediate moves. The Galahad chief, said Hunter, told Stilwell that there were about two and a half Japanese battalions in the town, with more rushing up from the south. Colonel Joseph W. Stilwell Jr., the general's son and his intelligence officer, rejected this information and put the number of defenders at a modest three hundred. During the next few weeks the head count for the enemy continued to depend on which intelligence officer one questioned. Postwar history concluded that Stilwell's headquarters, by a wide margin, consistently underestimated the strength of the Japanese. The same day on which he conferred with Stilwell, Merrill was struck with another cardiac breakdown. Merrill was evacuated and no longer played a role in the Burma campaign.

Hunter made still another attempt to seize Myitkyina. "I had intended to send the 150th Regiment against the city as soon as food and ammunition arrived. It came three days late, on the twentieth. The 150th was ready to go. Unfortunately, I gave them an azimuth as an axis of advance. Reading his compass wrong, Colonel Huang [the Chinese regimental commander] got off in the wrong direction and had to come back and start all over. This time we lined them all up in a column of battalions, a simple attack formulation not easily fouled up."

When Hunter took off in a jeep to inspect the progress of the Chinese he suddenly encountered a Japanese machine-gun nest. A bullet caught his driver, Private First Class Barlow Coon, in the chest. Hunter pulled him from the wheel and quickly steered back to the airstrip. Coon received plasma and was loaded aboard a C-47. Just as it took off, a flock of Japanese Zeros swooped down, strafing the transport. Coon was killed and a nurse wounded. Major Bill Laffin, a Marauder intelligence specialist who had just taken off in an L-5 for a look at the Japanese defenses in Myitkyina, was shot down and killed along with his pilot.

Hunter said that the U.S. fighter patrol responsible for air cover had radioed in the clear that they were low on gas and returning to base. The Japanese, lurking in the clouds, heard the message and seized the opportunity to hammer the field unmolested. Hunter's wounds required medical attention. "My face looked like I was in the last stages of syphilis. I was pockmarked all over my head, shoulders, and forearms."

Initially, Colonel Huang's soldiers drove deep into Myitkyina. Stilwell sounded a triumphant note: "One hundred fiftieth has command post in railroad station. Japs backed into bazaar section. Resistance now localized and we are reasonably sure of the place. Japs apparently all in confusion and trying to pull out, Chinese casualties heavy."

Kepley described the action beginning on May 19 as the 150th again advanced at night until it attained positions a few hundred yards south of the railroad yards: "The Japs let the two battalions through them and a few minutes afterward attacked the Regt. CP. The two battalions got to the railroad yards and were then hit from front and rear. They fell back in confusion to Regt. who had to withdraw several hundreds of yards to the rear. The 3d Bn CO was killed in this action and also the 2d Bn liaison officer, Major [Frank] Hodges."

Unfortunately, their triumph in advancing to the railroad station was short-lived because of still another friendly-fire engagement. Japanese gunners, firing at the battalion occupying the buildings around the terminal, dropped some of their shells among the battalion moving up behind. They retaliated, and their bullets and bombs ripped into their comrades ahead. Soon the two Chinese outfits mistakenly began shooting at one another. The advance battalion, punished fore and aft, broke and fled, and the entire regiment melted away from the gains in Myitkyina. Hunter attributed some of the confusion to British-supplied uniforms that were identical in color to those of the enemy. Only the helmets differed. When the shooting died out, the remnants of the 150th, which had suffered 671 casualties, were assigned to guard the strip and replaced as an attack force by the Chinese 89th Regiment.

The same entry by Stilwell that announced the temporary success of the 150th also included an ominous note: "[T]hey [the Marauders] are to finish the job [Myitkyina]." His decision to throw the remnants of Galahad into the battle would seal the animosity or downright hatred for him by the Marauders. They had been led to believe from the beginning of their long-range penetration that they would be pulled out after three months, following the model formulated by Wingate. Their time was now up. Furthermore, they understood that once the airport and its immediate environs had been seized, they would be removed from combat. James Hopkins said Merrill had promised that upon capture of the airfield, "Galahad personnel would be relieved and flown to an already selected site where a rest and recreational area would be constructed. General Merrill even told Colonel Hunter that money had been put aside for this purpose. None thought that General Merrill would fail to keep his promise." Hunter insisted that at no time did the members of Galahad expect to be rotated to the States except in accord with the standard War Department policies, which in fact did not specify any limits to a combat tour by foot soldiers.

Without capture of Myitkyina, the entire venture of Galahad and the Chinese legions would have been deemed a failure in Stilwell's eyes and reinforced the generalissimo's commitment to keeping his troops at home. But the exigencies of the Burma war aside, the wretched condition of the Marauders augured poorly for a battle led by them. During the period following the seizure of the airport, the two botched attacks and a lull followed. The Japanese began to flood the town with troops, building up a garrison that may have numbered as many as five thousand. Stilwell's intelligence, as noted, continued to badly underestimate the defenders. Some Marauders have suggested that G-2 officers deliberately set the numbers low in order not to discourage the Chinese commanders, who were notoriously reluctant when they believed they faced formidable resistance.

With Merrill out of the picture, Hunter, as of May 22, again took charge of the Marauders, but under the reorganization decreed by Stilwell, Hunter was subordinate to Colonel John McCammon (appointed unofficially a brigadier general by Stilwell). Battalion surgeon Hopkins said, "General Stilwell's plan to let the Marauders finish the job at Myitkyina can only lead me to believe that he had no knowledge of what they had been through, how few men remained, and how— almost without exception—the men required hospital care for diagnosis, treatment, and rehabilitation before returning to combat. His attitude must therefore have been due to lack of knowledge, total indifference to the health and survival of his troops, or early senility."

The Marauder 3d Battalion had executed a successful drive that brought it as far as Radahpur, a scant three miles from the town and a small auxiliary airstrip, but soon began to feel the pressure of the Japanese sliding around and through Charpate, four miles from the airstrip. The Americans retreated to Charpate, a better terrain for defensive purposes.

The disposition of the American and Chinese forces placed the 3d Battalion, under Lieutenant Colonel Charles Beach, on a line from the Irrawaddy to Charpate, with the task of blocking any passage from the north and northwest into Myitkyina. Battalions from the Chinese 88th and 89th Regiments formed a line from Charpate south. The 1st Battalion from the Marauders held the airport and the village of Pamati on the Irrawaddy along with the 150th Chinese Regiment and elements from the 89th. This force was more or less due west of Myitkyina. Lieutenant Colonel George McGee's 2d Battalion of Galahad, with portions of several Chinese units, shut off Japanese reinforcements and supplies coming up from the south. In theory, the deployment prevented the insertion of additional enemy forces, but in fact, the perimeters were highly porous, too few men to adequately protect the frontage. The Marauders and some of the Chinese were in no condition to keep a tight grip on the real estate. Under these circumstances, the Japanese bypassed villages and filtered into Myitkyina. The 3d Battalion, at Charpate, started to take incoming fire and probing attacks by groups of Japanese. Colonel Henry Kinnison, who had initially commanded a force that included the 3d Battalion of Galahad and a regiment of Chinese, died of the virulent new typhus. Altogether 149 men contracted the disease, and many would succumb.

Stilwell called May 22 "Black Monday." He noted, "Bad news from Mitch [the GI name for the town]. Now they saw 800 Japs go into Charpate last night. And 200 crossed the river from the east. McCammon says 'situation is critical.' Not a thing I can do. It has rained heavily all morning. We can't get troops in, also the field is in bad shape at Mitch. Radioed McCammon to take out Charpate if information was true. Later message said Japanese both in front of and behind 3d Battalion of Galahad. General air of discouragement down there, and of course corresponding worry here. Q: Get Pick's engineers [as reinforcements]? Yes. At least alert them and use as replacements for Galahad. Meanwhile push 42d [Regiment] in and follow with 41st [both Chinese] if necessary." He apparently had rejected the possibility of borrowing a British division from Slim.

The situation at Charpate was worse than Stilwell suspected. There were too few men in the 3d Battalion to plug the gaps for a secure perimeter. There were a number of skirmishes or brief outbursts of fire as the troops fought enemy interlopers, or mistakenly shot at their own people or Chinese. On the night of May 23 a substantial group of Japanese slipped beyond an outpost, and by the time someone realized what was happening, the foe was in their midst. In the dark, rainy night bullets and grenades were exchanged and bayonets wielded. Seven Marauders died during the struggle for Charpate and eight more were wounded seriously enough to be flown out. The survivors counted fifteen enemy bodies and estimated that they had wounded another thirty-five. The 3d Battalion was ordered to move two miles south and tie in with the Chinese 88th Regiment.

The 2d Battalion of Galahad occupied Namkwin, four miles from the airport and between the 3d and 1st Battalions. On a humid, hot May 20, Major Bernard Rogoff, the battalion surgeon, personally escorted twenty-five desperately ill men on a trek to the airport to arrange their evacuation. A day later a similarly sized contingent also departed. During this period, mortar and artillery fire accompanied skirmishes with the enemy, adding to the casualty list. Galahad was beginning to lose seventy-five to a hundred men a day. Nor were the Chinese forces any more robust. The shattered 150th Regiment had been reduced to a mere six hundred men, less than the complement of a single battalion. The regiment's 3d Battalion was ordered now to advance.

At one point Galahad's 2d Battalion passed seventy-two hours without anything to eat other than what they could scavenge from their surroundings. In their weakened condition, the ravages of disease intensified. Hunter said, "Stilwell's staff was issuing orders which were impossible to comply with by battalions at less than half strength and with few remaining pack animals." Hunter perceived a lack of concern and absence of coherent direction. He drafted a letter to Stilwell detailing the deficiencies, which in his mind indicated an orientation that favored the Chinese units rather than the American one. After showing the missive to McCammon, who suggested some deletions, Hunter personally delivered it to Stilwell. The general read it in Hunter's presence, pronounced it "a strong letter," and then did nothing to correct the problems.

Nearly a week after Hunter delivered his letter, Stilwell relieved McCammon and replaced him with his own chief of staff, General Haydon Boatner. That could hardly have assuaged Hunter, who felt he should have been in charge, and Boatner was one of those he suspected of discriminating against the Marauders.

Stilwell decided to bring replacements from the engineers building the road. From May 25 to 29, the 209th and 236th Engineer Combat Battalions left their bulldozers, trucks, shovels, picks, and axes on the Ledo Road and flew to Myitkyina to become part of the assault forces aimed at the entrenched Japanese. Most of these soldiers possessed little of the infantryman's skills or knowledge.

Lieutenant John F. Eichelberger Jr., with the 236th Combat Engineers, in CBI from about the same time as the Marauders, said, "Without any warning or preliminary notice, we got an alert at 1500 [3:00 P.M.] that we were going into combat the next day, 27 May. We were told to be at the airstrip at 0600 [6:00 A.M.] at Ledo and that we would be fighting Japanese."

On arrival at the airstrip he remembered, "It looked like a no-man's-land. There were more bomb craters on that place than Carter's got pills. The plane came down in a zigzag fashion and he still had to zigzag after he got his wheels down. When we got off the plane there was another plane trying to steer right ahead of us. One of our lieutenants started lining his platoon up. He said, 'Fall in.' I hollered, 'No, don't do that.' One of the Marauders said, 'You know you will get yourself killed.' The Japanese opened up with artillery and they scattered." The engineers spent their first few nights living in muddy foxholes, while the Marauders from the 1st Battalion exploited any period of relative quiet to teach their new colleagues use of M-1 rifles, carbines, machine guns, grenades, and mortars.

There were other, more dubious efforts to beef up the Myitkyina forces. Well before deployment of Galahad, the U.S. Army understood that rather than ship individual replacements for the Marauders, whose combat tour was accepted as three months and faced a casualty rate as high as 85 percent, entire new and trained units would be sent to CBI. But the plan for a deliberate continuity never left the conference room. In April 1944 the War Department circulated a call for volunteers to serve in the Far East through its army camps, and twenty-six hundred men were recruited. John Evanoff was with the 97th Infantry Division at Fort Leonard Wood, Missouri. "The Orient had always fascinated me, so I volunteered. At first they rejected me because I was a company clerk. But my MOS [military occupational specialty] was 653, mortarman, and they accepted me."

Within days Evanoff joined a contingent that sailed for India, reaching Bombay on May 25. By the first week of June, the nucleus of what would become known as "New Galahad" landed at the Myitkyina airfield. (There were actually tens of thousands of other American soldiers already in India and Burma who might have been deployed. These were the African Americans engaged in quartermaster duties

278 The Jungle War

and in building the road from Ledo. Most of them had passed through
basic training, learning to handle small arms, before assignment to their
service and engineering companies. However, the segregated army of
World War II, except for a few units, denied black soldiers active combat duty.) The first nine hundred soldiers who had volunteered for
duty with what was called New Galahad marched from the airstrip to
the headquarters Hunter had established at Radahpur, a village north
of Myitkyina. When he hiked out to meet them, he discovered a column of men drinking water from contaminated shell holes and a rice
paddy. No one seemed to be in charge, and Lieutenants Russell Shave
and Gordon W. Campbell would later explain that contrary to what
had been said, these reinforcements were not cohesive, functioning
units. "Men and officers were practically strangers. Companies were
organized hastily and without regard to qualifications of the men involved. Countless men were having their first initiation in the mechanical functioning of the M-1 rifle. Infantry tactics were, to a great
number of men, something entirely alien from the training they had
received in the States. Men were physically weak from the long ride on
the troopship to this theater and no time was given them to become
acclimated." They were even less prepared for what faced them than
the engineers. Hunter immediately installed a rigorous training program for the first to arrive and those who followed. He notified Boatner of the newcomers' physical condition and their ignorance of the
necessities to function as combat troops. "His protests," said James
Hopkins, "were answered by sarcasm and he was ordered to get into
Myitkyina."

Eichelberger reported, "The Galahad fellows were giving us instructions in BARs, Bren guns, the 60-millimeter mortars, and 80-
millimeter mortars. All the officers that went to OCS had taken an
advanced officers course in mortars, but it seemed to me that I was
the only one who knew how to set a mortar up. So I was made the
mortar officer."

When the enemy attempted to carve out a new airfield near their
holdings in Myitkyina, Eichelberger was directed to "set up our machine
guns, so we could hose down the strip." A liaison plane watched from
overhead and reported success in driving the workers away. Subsequently his unit set up a 37-millimeter cannon and fired blindly into
a jungle area. The explosions blew away the foliage and revealed camouflaged buildings that housed the enemy.

The Japanese responded with their own artillery. Eichelberger
remembered moments when his company was settling into a new area.
Suddenly artillery, using their standard support piece, struck. "I called
it a whiz bang. It went wham, whiz, burp. That's about the way it

sounded. You heard the shell go off and then the wake of the shell and finally the gun.

"My platoon sergeant got hit and was on a litter to be evacuated when they opened up again. I remember a boy by the name of Hoot Gibson. Anybody with the last name of Gibson, of course, was Hoot [the name came from a popular film cowboy]. He was pretty well shook up. I reached and got hold of his jacket on the left side and started pulling him into the hole with me and a shell hit his right hip and his right arm went down the hill. I looked down and Lindsey [the platoon sergeant] had been hit on the litter. It just opened him up. I hollered down the hill, 'Now Lindsey is dead, bring that litter up here and get Hoot out!'" The stretcher bearer dumped the dead man off and then rushed up with others to haul away the wounded man. "People who watched said machine-gun bullets chased them all the way. They missed."

Mortar-shell bursts in the limbs of nearby trees threatened the men in their foxholes. Eichelberger said, "I decided to do the only engineer job there was. I started cutting down trees to stop the tree bursts. I gathered up all kinds of dud shells and managed to get a couple of cases of old waterlogged TNT and some blasting caps and used the walkie-talkie to set the charges off. I would tie a block of TNT to a tree and add a 75-millimeter shell and maybe a 4.5 bazooka shell, anything that had explosive in it. The biggest one . . . had a ten- or twelve-foot diameter." One of those toppled into a place where Eichelberger had been reluctant to patrol because it was packed with booby traps. When the tree crashed down, the trunk and limbs triggered numerous explosive devices.

Sergeant George Davey of A Company in the 236th had been a bulldozer operator and said that shortly after reaching the area, he and others bivouacked in a deserted village. On the way to the river for water, they passed a dead enemy soldier. "One of the fellows came over and said, 'I see a Jap.' We thought he was talking about the one on the pile of brush. Just as he said that, a Japanese machine gun opened up and we all took cover. I got behind a big tree. The Japanese were firing the machine gun and it was taking the bark off the tree. It was a huge tree. As I looked behind, all the other fellows were on the ground, including our lieutenant. They wasn't doing anything, just laying there. The machine gun had wounded quite a few guys. I fired my rifle a few times but it didn't do any good. I wouldn't pinpoint where the Japanese machine gun was. I ran back to the lieutenant and asked him if I could go get a bazooka.

"He told me to go ahead, so I ran up the trail to the village and saw Sergeant White coming up the trail. Someone had already told them what had taken place. So he came along with an armful of rockets and the bazooka. I grabbed the armful of rockets he was carrying and down we went to where all the Japanese had all those fellows pinned down. We got up behind the big tree that I had been standing behind and knocked out the machine-gun nest. We picked up all the wounded and made makeshift stretchers. The Japanese had killed—I forget how many it was. It was certainly two or three dead and a lot of wounded."

Aware of the weakness that had hampered Galahad during its previous forays, the command had arranged for batteries of artillery to be flown in. Unfortunately, they were not set up to deliver the kind of mass barrage fire that could wilt defenses. On June 10, Boatner directed a coordinated attack by all the units surrounding Myitkyina against the Japanese. The defenders stoutly resisted and even initiated a counterattack, driving one company from New Galahad backward. Individual acts of valor by original Galahad members included Private Howard T. Smith, who took over after his platoon leader was killed and by himself destroyed a pillbox; Private First Class Willard Lilly knocked out a machine gun; and Lieutenant Melvin D. Blair rescued a wounded soldier and erased an enemy machine gun. Among the many casualties was Lieutenant Colonel Combs, the former American liaison chief for the 150th Regiment, named to command the two combat engineer battalions. Badly wounded, Combs cautioned soldiers that it was too risky to try to reach him. When they finally did it was too late, and he died of his injuries. The Japanese cut off two companies of the 209th Engineers for sixty hours before they could escape, with twenty dead and twenty-five wounded.

Hunter apprised Boatner of the misadventures of the recent additions to the American forces and the latter answered, "General Stilwell had been informed of the unreliability of the troops and many other handicaps that you are encountering. . . . These troops were known to be unseasoned and untrained when they were sent in. I know that you are suffering unusually heavy casualties as a result. For this, I accept full responsibilities as commanding general.

"There can be no withdrawal or slackening of our efforts. The enemy situation must be much worse than ours. They are and have been completely cut off from their base." Boatner was correct in that the Japanese garrison suffered from many of the same afflictions as the Allied troops—disease, even worse medical care, and shortages of food and water.

Boatner radioed Stilwell on June 23 that from May 18 through June 21, 2,478 Chinese were evacuated and noted they had suffered "one killed per wounded," which adds up to a staggering loss of almost 5,000 soldiers in that one-month period. During the same time, 447 Americans had been taken out. In his final paragraph, the task force general brought up an unpleasant matter. "Unless we have some special shortcut, I am afraid our self-inflicted 'wounderers' might get away and beat trial. To send them back—then have an investigation with papers to go to Delhi and return will mean witnesses will disappear, forget, etc. Have two sets of charges now for men of New Galahad manning the perimeter."

The men of Old Galahad undoubtedly welcomed anyone in uniform who might take their places. Not only were those still on their feet kept on the line, but also Stilwell and Boatner summarily decreed that those who had been evacuated and were able to tote a rifle, regardless of the medical diagnosis, would immediately be returned to the Myitkyina task force. Boatner, in a letter to Stilwell, would claim, "From Galahad's rear in Dinjan, I hear that 250 of Old Galahad are being equipped and will be flown back today. They will be of tremendous help. Rumor has it that they were roving around the countryside and many AWOLs. Colonel Osborne just saw me and spoke most earnestly about how he felt those men are malingering and wants to go back to get a few more officers and many men back here."

Hunter himself wrote that he felt the evacuation rate of Galahad people was becoming excessive, and none were returning from their hospital stays. He admitted that almost every member of the organization was suffering from malaria, dysentery, diarrhea, exhaustion, or fever but was obliged to slow the removal of those pronounced ill. After a conference with the Galahad physicians, he set a policy for evacuation for sickness. Those individuals seen by a doctor for three days and with a fever of 102 or higher would then go before a board of three battle surgeons, who would conduct an examination before the soldier qualified for evacuation.

Hunter constantly applied pressure to Major Melvin Schudmak, serving as the Myitkyina task force surgeon, to slow the pace of evacuations. To ensure that only those truly deserving of hospitalization were brought out, Schudmak sent an officer to the 20th General Hospital to confer with the medical authorities there. They advised Schudmak's representative that only 5 percent of the evacuees could be considered fit for duty in the forward area.

Howard G. Garrison, a company commander at Myitkyina, in a letter to Scott McMichael, author of an article on Galahad in *Parameters*, a publication of the U.S. Army War College, said, "[Y]ou say that medical evac tags were alleged to have been removed from wounded and sick personnel and they were returned to duty during the fight for Myitkyina. I can personally attest that this happened . . . and I received some of my medical evacs back from the airstrip."

James Hopkins, 3d Battalion surgeon, and Captain A. Lewis Kolodny, the doctor from the 2d Battalion, had both been shipped to the hospital because of severe dysentery and were at a convalescent center when they heard that several hundred sick and recovering Marauders were being trucked to the Dinjan airfield for transport to Myitkyina. They intercepted the convoy and forced the return of the men to the convalescent area.

Desperate conditions breed desperate efforts to escape. A company clerk with one of the combat engineer battalions said, "During our stay in Burma from May 28 until August 9, at least six or seven men shot themselves to get out. It seemed that the only way out was feet first, and they didn't want to go that way. They were going to court-martial them but it seems they never got around to this. If they would court-martial them, they would dig into the facts and ask the question 'Why did they do it?' The first fellow that shot himself I was told to put him down in the sick book as being hurt—not in the line of duty—he wasn't to get pay for it. But this didn't last long. I was told to change it and put him down in the sick book as a regular entry.

Stilwell remained unhappy about the infinitely slow progress toward "Mitch." His diary entries reported, "Just bellyaches from Boatner. He's pushing—but—etc., etc." "Gloomy report from Boatner. Everybody running away and hell to pay generally, and Japs about to take the offensive." "Terrible letter from Boatner, bad news from Myitkyina. U.S. troops are shaky. Hard to believe. Either our officers are all rotten, or else Boatner is getting hysterical. I'll have to go down." When he did fly to the Myitkyina airfield, he hiked six miles in mud and rain. He noted, "Saw Hunter and talked it over, not so bad as painted, the men looked good." Obviously he saw troops from the New Galahad rather than the bedraggled veterans.

Judging from the consensus of statements by Galahad veterans and the published comments of Hunter, Hopkins, and others, Stilwell was despised as an uncaring commander out of touch with the troops and willing to sacrifice them to enhance his own achievements. In a study project for the U.S. Army War College, Lieutenant Colonel Henry L. Kinnison IV, grandson of the Galahad commander in the first days of the siege of Myikyina who died of scrub typhus, quotes Lieutenant Colonel George A. McGhee Jr., the 2d Battalion leader and a defender of Stilwell. McGhee, in his account, argued that Hunter actually provided very little direction to the Marauders in the quest for Myitkyina. He said Hunter never met with the battalion commanders as a group. "Hunter," wrote Kinnison, "remained at the airstrip and never constituted a staff or communications capability to support his responsibilities."

McGhee detailed a meeting with Stilwell at the edge of the airfield runway. "After I reported to him, he asked me in a calm, informal manner about the situation in the Namkwin area . . . what we had run into, what was my estimate of the number of Japs there, and other questions pertaining to the tactical situation. I told him substantially the same information that we had been reporting to [task force] headquarters, to include that we had not identified any Jap force of more than company size. Contrary to Hunter's experience, I found him interested and easy to talk with; he displayed no irritability, no impatience, and no outward indication of the serious problems [with] which he was most surely concerned at the time. I have a high regard for General Stilwell as a professional soldier and as a considerate individual. From my point of view, he has been unjustly treated in many accounts as far as his relations with the Marauders were concerned."

Much of the controversy about Stilwell's actions involves the question of whether he should have obtained trained, tested units from Slim rather than try to use combat-raw Americans. Louis Allen reported that the British 36th Infantry Division was available for an airlift from its India base, but Slim in his autobiography described the 36th as undergoing "refitting" at the time. It had been heavily engaged in the Arakan. Allen was one of the sharpest critics of the American, writing, "The universal verdict on Stilwell is not kind . . . the Chinese detested him, the British—with the possible exception of Slim—loathed him, his own men hated and feared him."

17

Finales for Marauders and Chindits

Outside of Mogaung, the Chinese troops still had not appeared by June 13, already more than a week later than in Calvert's timetable for subduing the town. One small addition to Calvert's forces came from a twelve-man detachment wielding flamethrowers. Its commander was Arthur Binnie, who had taken over the Bladet group after its original leader had been injured in the glider landing at Chowringhee. Binnie, who had been evacuated with severe malaria, but returned, had been trained to head the flamethrowers. The unit then parachuted into position.

On June 18, in response to a summons from Calvert, P-51 Mustangs raided the foremost Japanese positions, and then a dawn crescendo of mortars and machine guns struck a village near Mogaung. The Lancashire Fusiliers, the King's Liverpool, and the erstwhile band from Bladet all advanced, pouring bullets and literally fire on the defenders.

Binnie commented, "Although the tactics [for the flamethrowers] were discredited, their use was such a shock to the Japs that the village fell into Calvert's hands with minimal casualties to our attacking force." The same could not be said for his own squad. "In this action, I lost the sight of my right eye from a Jap grenade, one soldier was killed, and the remaining ten soldiers were all wounded to some degree." The Chindits counted a hundred dead Japanese.

That evening, the long-awaited Chinese began to arrive. Their arrival boosted morale. Hunter said, "This was good news for it meant that the area to the north of us was practically clear of Japanese. Perhaps now we could stop looking over our shoulders."

284

The newcomers exhibited an unwarlike reticence. They showed a lack of enthusiasm for attack, particularly a frontal assault, and were in no hurry to evict the enemy from its positions at Mogaung. Nevertheless, among their units was artillery, a critical component sorely lacking in the Special Forces. Major Wayne Cook was an American adviser who had helped train a number of Chinese artillery units at the Ramgarh camp in India. After several other assignments, Cook joined the 6th Battery, 2d Battalion of the 38th Division Artillery. "The 6th Battery," said Cook, "was considered the best of the Chinese army in India. I would rate it as excellent. The cooperation of the battery commanders with me was superior. The biggest problem was in obtaining enough hay, grain, and ammunition for the unit. At one time, during the Battle of Kamaing, the Jap lines were only about three hundred yards in front of the battery position, and in spite of the heavy Jap fire, the battery kept on shooting. One Jap entered the gun position, firing at everyone and hitting no one. A Chinese soldier emptied a tommy gun on him but also missed. When the Jap ran out of ammunition the Chinese took him prisoner."

Cook reported that the battery reached its area near Mogaung on June 19. "We went into position immediately and sent out a forward OP. We saw some Japs on the opposite side of the river and put some surprise fire on them. We were the first artillery to fire on Mogaung, June 20. At that time we were supporting the [Chinese] 114th and 113th Regiments and the British 77th Brigade. On June 21 the 113th surrounded a company of Japs at a point five miles north of Mogaung. We put a concentration down on [them] that was effective from the first round and killed fifty-seven Japs and wounded many more. The infantry moved in and killed the rest."

With the appearance of additional Chinese bringing in more artillery, Calvert directed a drive on the town on June 24. His 77th Brigade infantrymen numbered little more than five hundred, but he had two battalions of the Chinese at his disposal plus more air support and some flamethrowers. The Japanese vigorously defended themselves after a mortar barrage with heavy counterfire. Captain Michael Almand, hobbled by trenchfoot, which was endemic, upon seeing his Gurkhas stymied by a machine gun, charged forward through the muck throwing grenades until he silenced the weapon. He was killed in the action and received a posthumous Victoria Cross.

In the face of the stubborn resistance, Norman Durant had set up his machine guns. "The flamethrowers were now summoned from the rear and as they moved past where I was lying, a shell burst, and puncturing one of the weapons, set it on fire. The wretched man who was carrying it was a mass of flame but managed to get it off and all we could do was to roll him into some water in a nearby ditch. The others went forward but it was a long time before the Japs there [holed up beneath the ruins of a brick house] were finished off. Only one broke out, all his clothes on fire, and was shot down. The remainder preferred to stay where they were and get burnt to death. We found that the officer had committed suicide by shooting himself through the head with his revolver."

The combined forces of Chindits and Chinese advanced slowly against continued stiff defenses. But a day later, patrols sifted into the town and discovered that the remainder of the Japanese had departed. Durant remarked, "Every man had fought magnificently under very unpleasant conditions, and although our casualties had been heavy we had achieved our objective and killed a lot of Japs on the way. The Chinese were full of admiration but thought we were quite mad, for with Oriental patience, they would have taken a week to do the same attack and probably suffered 5 percent of our casualties."

On June 27 Stilwell noted, "Good news from Mogaung. We have it." The news broadcast by the British Broadcasting Corporation from Stilwell's headquarters announced that the Chinese had seized the town. Calvert and his staff were outraged at the snub of the Chindits. The Chinese commander from the 114th Regiment apologized to the furious Calvert. "If anyone has taken Mogaung, it is your brigade and we all admire the bravery of your soldiers." Calvert sublimated some of his fury with a message to Lentaigne at headquarters, "Chinese reported taking Mogaung. My brigade now taking umbrage." (One British officer claimed that some of the command staff spent considerable time trying to locate the town of Umbrage on a map.)

Stilwell wanted the ravaged brigade to head down the railway toward the abandoned Blackpool and roust the Japanese who had settled into positions in a pair of villages on the Namyin River. Calvert balked at his orders and traveled to the Myitkyina base to have it out with Stilwell. In his memoir *Prisoners of Hope,* Calvert described the scene with Stilwell, who greeted him, "Well, Calvert, I have been wanting to meet you for some time."

"I have been wanting to meet you, too, sir."

"You send some very strong signals, Calvert."

"You should see the ones my brigade major won't let me send."

That broke the ice, as Stilwell began laughing. "I have just the same trouble with my own staff officers when I draft signals to Washington." Calvert then replayed the ferocious fight for Mogaung. Stilwell interrupted several times with a plaintive, "Why wasn't I told?" Louis Allen ascribed that professed ignorance to "his sycophantic staff

[that] played down the British role and that the true nature of the battle had been kept from him. He was not even aware that 77th Brigade was the same body of men who had been flown in four months before."

One person unable to celebrate the subjugation of Mogaung was Haydon Boatner. On June 26 Stilwell confided to his diary, "Chased Boatner to the showers. He cried and protested, told him no argument." Ostensibly Boatner was relieved because of his malaria, but actually Stilwell was unhappy with his subordinate's gloomy assessment of the situation. To replace him he brought in Brigadier General Theodore F. Wessels from the Southeast Asia Command. At the same time, Stilwell put Hunter in charge of all of the U.S. troops around Myitkyina.

Long-Range Penetration Peters Out

The two columns from the 14th Brigade also had been earmarked for the battle for Mogaung. After backtracking from the environs of Indaw, the brigade started on the long, difficult trip. The physical and emotional conditions of the men had continued to deteriorate under the assaults of disease, the enervating climate, the inadequate nutrition of K rations, and the incessant floundering beside their mules in the mud and swamps. Some humans straggled behind; the animals that could not continue were put out of their misery with a bullet. Their route carried them over a thirty-five-hundred-foot high ridgeline, and attrition reduced the battle group for both columns to a mere two hundred men. The "soft skins"—noncombat or unfit-for-duty troops—numbered three hundred, and they were detailed to try to evacuate the sick and dying. In any event, they could not get into position to actually participate in the final assault on Mogaung before it was seized.

Like the others involved with Wingate's Special Forces, Phil Cochran's air force showed signs of burnout. "We were showing signs of wear and tear. My fighter pilots were getting sick with extreme fatigue. Some were losing their desire to fight and fly. It was the same with the bomber pilots. The transport and light-plane fliers were growing ill. They had some of the heaviest evacuation jobs. We had harder work than ever in winding up the job and wore ourselves out, wore ourselves ill."

Cochran himself fell ill enough to warrant hospitalization. He chose one in Delhi, a place well removed from his headquarters because, he said, "I didn't want my men to see I was sick." His cocommander,

John Alison, had left the scene about a week after Wingate's death. Hap Arnold had recalled him to the States to create three new air commando units, each twice as large as the original version.

Calvert and his badly depleted Chindit brigade had left Mogaung to the Chinese. With the grudging approval of Stilwell, they began a two-week trek to Shadwzup through deep mud, crossing deep fast-flowing streams enriched by monsoon rains and coping with omni-present leeches. But they finally reached the airstrip and Durant, along with the others, flew to India.

At least equally beat up was the portion of the 111th Brigade com-manded by John Masters. With the Morris Force split off for an ad-vance on Myitkyina from east of the Irrawaddy, Masters figured his able-bodied soldiers at 119, down from an original complement of 2,200. Stilwell insisted that they be retained, and it required the inter-cession of Mountbatten. He reached an agreement with the American for the medically qualified Chindits to be evacuated and the remain-der taken out as soon as the British 36th Division took the field. On August 1 the remaining troops departed with Masters.

Other Burma Forces

The northern Burma front also involved a British-led non-Wingate force, the Gurkha 4th Battalion, formed from the remnants of the Burma Frontier Force (BFF) and the Burma Military Police. They were supplemented by Kachin Levies and had begun a long march from Fort Hertz toward Myitkyina through Sumprabum, now held by British forces. They encountered stiff Japanese resistance at several points, which eroded under constant pressure over a period of weeks. I. O. G. Scott, who in the prewar years had enjoyed his duty with the BFF and been wounded earlier, had rejoined the 4th Battalion.

"That crusty old brute Stilwell," said Scott, "did not appreciate that all this had to be done and he assumed that we were sitting on our backsides and resting and he sent us a series of frantic messages ordering us to get a move on. He had been hammering away at Myit-kyina with two divisions of Chinese and the remains of a brigade of Americans for many months but had been unable to capture the place. If he had been unable to capture the place with that considerable force I really did not understand what difference it would make to have the remains of a battalion, because that's all we now amounted to. After a conference it was decided to send all the Levies (less one company) and two companies of the battalion down to Myitkyina by jungle tracks." Scott was chosen to command this "jungle force," known as Scocol. The remainder of the battalion would follow another route.

Scott received only fifteen mules to bear one day of rations and other paraphernalia for his roughly three hundred men. Air drops were to supply Scocol during the expected eight-to-ten-day march. It was another miserable hike, through torrential downpours with the attendant leeches. "Every quarter of a mile or so we had to stop to remove these horrible pests, which penetrated all parts of the body. Even if removed by using a cigarette or salt there is always considerable bleeding."

Equally difficult were the river crossings, as the monsoon deluge widened ordinarily easily fordable rivers, demanding pioneer squads to build rickety bridges or manufacture flimsy bamboo rafts. They pushed on, through the thick bush. As they approached within 15 miles of Myitkyina, Scott dispatched patrols that reported signs of the Japanese presence, mainly in the form of half-starved or sick soldiers who offered "scant resistance."

Scott then led a group in search of the main body of the battalion. On this venture, Scott said he suddenly heard heavy firing no more than four hundred yards off. "There was no mistaking the crack of a Jap rifle and it was pretty clear that the battalion was indeed in the vicinity but so were the Japs and we were roughly in the middle of the battle! It was a nasty moment and as we tried to get away from the battle we found the jungle got thicker and thicker. It was a solid mass of creepers and thorns and the only way to move at all was to hack a way with kukries." On the following day they contacted the battalion. "We then became a part of the siege of Myitkyina."

Across the Sino-Burma border, farther east of the route taken by Scott and his compatriots, the Chinese Y Force also had headed for Burma, through the Salween gorge, where in 1942 the Japanese army underwent a fearful pounding during the final days of the AVG. The American strategists had long been urging such an advance as the final step in opening up the road from Ledo. When first proposed, the invasion could count on nearly five months of good weather, but the postponements due to Chiang Kai-shek's unwillingness to commit his forces until he saw tangible signs of the British and American presence in northern Burma meant that by the time the Chinese started out, only a month or so remained before the monsoons. Brigadier General Frank Dorn, one of Stilwell's staff who had accompanied him during the 1942 walk out of Burma, was chief of staff for the U.S. advisers with the Y Force.

On paper the Y Force consisted of five armies, but in fact each of these amounted to roughly the size of an American infantry division of fifteen thousand. The Chinese forces were reasonably well armed, although a comparable U.S. unit packed considerably more firepower. Their avenues into Burma required passage through mountains that rose as high as nine thousand feet, and fording the omnipresent fast-flowing, deep streams. The bridges across the Salween River, the major watery impediment, had been destroyed in 1942 and never replaced. The Y Force crossed by footbridges constructed by engineers; rubber boats; and a ferry made out of oil drums.

The situation for the first Japanese defenders was precarious. Their supply lines were tenuous at best. The U.S. advisers reported that Chinese soldiers at one area discovered that the starving enemy resorted to cannibalism, eating those killed in battle when they ran out of rations. Against stiffening resistance the invaders drove toward the border, with Chennault's Fourteenth Air Force adding tactical air power to the offensive. The effectiveness of the American liaison was limited by the refusal of their hosts to accept suggestions. The commanders balked at advice to infiltrate around enemy strongpoints and insisted on wasteful frontal assaults. It was difficult for the Westerners to understand how a company commander could on his own execute a soldier but it required a group army order to shoot a horse or a mule. The offensive stagnated, and the Y Force halted fifty to seventy-five miles short of Burma.

The Myitkyina Siege Continues

Task Force commander General Wessels, under instructions from Stilwell, on June 29 directed a battalion of Chinese from the 42d Regiment to strike at the Japanese positions on a line that would cut off the enemy north of the town. Ordinarily the Chinese unit consisted of 400 soldiers, but its numbers had been reduced to about 250, some of whom were noncombat cooks and orderlies. Hunter agreed to provide an I and R platoon to assist. The group penetrated through the defensive positions at Sitapur, adjacent to the town proper. Then the Japanese reacted with infantry, mortars, and artillery. The attacking force immediately dug in, creating a small but strongly designed perimeter. They held a patch of ground so tiny that parachuted supplies of ammunition drifted off into the Japanese lines.

Hunter, according to *Spearhead*, dispatched F Company from New Galahad to enlarge the perimeter, starting out at night. They entered a large flooded rice paddy, and when heavy fire fell on the troops, they moved back to await daybreak. Just before dawn, the column worked its way through a bamboo grove and broke out into a large, open area. (The Japanese had planned to construct a second airstrip there until interrupted by the Allied forces.) The acting company commander (his predecessor had been killed), First Lieutenant Lewis Broadbrooks, in the lead, saw a group of Asians whom he believed were part of the Chinese unit. There were some friendly greetings between the groups, but when one of the strangers suggested they stack their arms, Broadbrooks realized his mistake and sounded the alarm. He was bayoneted to death while others from F Company took cover and opened fire.

The hapless unit from New Galahad had lost its way and blundered into the midst of the Japanese, who brought to bear their rifles and machine guns. They cut down a great many of the Americans. For eight hours the survivors of F Company fought to survive and escape. Of the 160 soldiers whom Broadbrooks started with, only 32 made their way to safety.

With their saviors routed, the battalion from the Chinese 42d Regiment was in dire circumstances, and Wessels sounded the order for a withdrawal. The task force leader arranged for another attack, on July 12. On his own initiative Major General Howard C. Davidson of the Tenth Air Force dispatched thirty-nine B-25s to bomb the enemy positions. Hunter said he had immediately suggested that men from the Marauders and New Galahad serve as ground controllers or observers. For some inexplicable reason, the offer of help was rejected. The New Galahad soldiers, many of them from the engineer battalions, had occupied emplacements as few as fifty yards away from enemy troops but withdrew two thousand yards to allow the B-25s ample room.

Hunter watched from his headquarters at Radahpur. "When the first string of bombs appeared the silence was shaken by gasps of horror, followed by curses, as each of us realized that the bombs were going to fall short, so short in fact that they would land on or very near to the troops awaiting to jump off when the word was given that the last bomb had been released. All this was apparent to the Galahad staff even though we were three miles away.

"There was a mad scramble for the phones in an attempt to put a stop to this fiasco. Task Force Headquarters could do nothing. . . . I recall that the bulk of a platoon was killed, only six or seven very shaken men survived. The platoon was pulled out and moved to a quiet guard post on the road to the north. I went to talk to the survivors. There wasn't much I could say and I refrained from any display of histrionics."

Within ten days more Chinese reinforcements arrived, and the weeks of siege obviously attrited the Myitkyina defenders. Estimates placed the Japanese dead at almost 800, with another 1,180 wounded. The noose around the town had tightened sufficiently so that no more reinforcements could slip through holes to help their beleaguered countrymen. The final push began on July 25 with a concentration of artillery by Chinese guns guided by Colonel George Sliney, a veteran and expert artilleryman.

Behind a barrage of high explosives and under the cover of smoke, the New Galahads punched through the enemy defenses and took control of the northern section of Myitkyina. Hunter, as their commander, held them there, advising task force headquarters that the rest of the mission should be completed by the Chinese. He reasoned, most properly, that as the ring about the city tightened, the possibilities for the attackers to be firing at one another increased greatly. Within Myitkyina, the defenders recognized they were doomed. The garrison commander committed suicide on August 1 after giving permission for others to escape if they could.

American adviser Thomas Kepley, with the 150th Regiment, said the Chinese commander was determined not to pull back again. "His whole regiment was brought up and given a section of advance from the Irrawaddy west. Their methods were sometimes a little crude. Each day, a little advance was made by digging trenches forward into the enemy emplacements." The trenches mentioned by Kepley would be connected laterally.

Major Fred Huffine, serving as assistant G-3 (operations section) for the 150th Regiment, reported the almost yard-by-yard advance. "Progress was slow. Eventually the 149th Regiment came in from Mogaung and replaced the 42d Regiment on the left." According to Huffine, the Japanese exploited the heights within Myitkyina and only after seizure of a particular crossroads did the Chinese eliminate the enemy automatic weapons able to "look down their throats. The regiment advanced daily and never yielded an inch of ground to numerous Jap counterattacks.

"The division commander, General Pon, became tired of house-to-house, street-to-street fighting. He evolved a plan to infiltrate and take the town. This plan used 100 volunteers from both regiments and division headquarters units. It was well organized to the last detail. Groups of 15 men, each with 8 hand grenades, 2 days' rations, their individual arms with, in the case of rifle, 200 rounds of ammunition, Thompson Sub MG, 800 rounds, L MG, 2,000 rounds, would go to prearranged crossroads and high ground some 900 yards deep in the north section of the town. This infiltration took place on the night 2–3 August, and although coincident with the Jap order to leave the town, it was highly successful in killing many Japs and taking Myitkyina."

When the last of the Japanese had been killed, captured, or escaped at Myitkyina, the casualty toll on the Allied forces listed 272 Marauders killed and 955 wounded; the Chinese lost 972 dead and 3,184 wounded. Figures on those who succumbed to disease or were evacuated for noncombat purposes were listed as 980 Americans and 188 Chinese. The capture of the town also marked the finale for Merrill's Marauders, most of whom had already been removed from Burma.

In fact, Old Galahad and New Galahad, according to Hunter, were dissolved by Stilwell. At a meeting in the general's private quarters, Hunter said he was surprised to find a third man present, Brigadier General Thomas Arms, a training officer for the Chinese troops. Hunter recounted, "Stilwell opened the conversation by stating, 'Hunter, I am going to organize a brigade out of what is left of Old and New Galahad. We will organize the 475th Infantry Regiment. On the way and due in Bombay shortly is the 124th Cavalry. I would like you to command the 475th. You can go back and get some teeth put in [Hunter had dental problems], take two months' leave in the States, and get back in time to move south with the 475th. How does that strike you? General Arms will be your brigade commander.'"

Nonplussed that Wessels, who was about to bag Myitkyina, apparently "hadn't made the team either," Hunter concluded he would not accept. He had lost whatever faith he had in Stilwell and in good conscience could not follow or support him. Hunter felt himself long abused by Stilwell, passed over on several occasions when he believed he should have been elevated to command slots and denied a promotion to general. The life of Merrill's Marauders thus passed on a final sour note.

The final element of the Chindits to depart Burma were the 65th and 84th columns of the 14th Brigade. In a rest camp they established in the hills overlooking the Mogaung valley, the men shaved off their beards, cut their hair for the first time since March, and gorged themselves on unlimited food from drops. "The incautious," said Graves-Morris, "soon found that shrunken, sickened stomachs could not manage the increase in food. A final march in scorching heat brought them behind the newly arrived 36th Division positions on their way to Mogaung. A train carried them to Myitkyina, where the last of them flew to northern Assam."

In the face of the morass developing around Myitkyina, Stilwell had drawn grim satisfaction from the news about China. His July 2 diary note reports, "Message from George Marshall: 'How about going to China and fixing things up!'" As Stilwell had predicted, the Chinese armies were unable to contain the Japanese forces who drove toward Chennault's air bases. In a letter to his wife he explained, "Over in China things look very black. It would be a pleasure to go to Washington and scream, 'I told you so.' But I think they get the point. This was my thesis in May last year, but I was all alone and the air boys were so sure they could run the Japs out of China with planes that I was put in the garbage pail." Nowhere on the record does Chennault claim he could defeat the Japanese in China via his air force.

18

Matterhorn

The operations in northern Burma of Merrill's Marauders and Chinese units were all part of the Quadrant strategy agreed on in Quebec in 1943. At that time the Combined Chiefs of Staff recommended the use of B-29s, the newest long-range heavy bomber, to hit targets in Japan from bases in China. The effort would require a massive engineering project, construction of airfields capable of serving the B-29 not only in China but also India. In fact Matterhorn, the B-29 project, required five fields for the big bombers linked to the oil tanker depots by pipelines. One concession from the original script eliminated the requirement that Air Transport Command carry the supplies for B-29s over the Hump. Instead, the big bombers would bring in the materials themselves.

The engineer battalion with Captain Richard Johnston, who supervised black troops engaged in building the road from Ledo, had been maintaining a stretch of their handiwork when the entire outfit was ordered to Kharagpur, India, to construct the 20th Bomber Command headquarters. With no equipment suitable for laying an airfield, the road builders used a battery of their small cement mixers to pour the ten-inch-thick base.

Johnston said, "We worked around the clock in two twelve-hour shifts because we were way behind schedule when we started." In the midst of these operations Johnston was detailed to aid an Indian steel company erect a plant to supply rolling stock for railroads. Having finished this stint for a private manufacturer, Johnston returned to work on the Ledo Road. While he was at this task, Stilwell arrived just before they built a bridge over the Irrawaddy. It was necessary to use one of the pontoon boats with an outboard motor to ferry him across the water. Stilwell was in his usual uniform, a Chinese enlisted man's cap and a well-worn GI raincoat. "Joe Cunningham was one of our black troops and he was not too diplomatic. He looked at him and Stilwell was huddled in the corner, shaking with malaria. Cunningham stared at him and said, 'Man, them draft boards are sure getting hard up for men when they bring an old "mother" like you over here!' Stilwell laughed hard and said, 'I agree with you 100 percent.' Cunningham had no idea who he was, and he didn't much care either."

More or less simultaneously with the airfield construction in India, sites for B-29s in China also were built. Austin Betts, the army engineer who had been involved in drafting the plans for the B-29 project, followed through on the actualization at Cheng-tu in western China. Betts found that the job entailed more than moving rocks and dirt or pouring concrete. "Within the Nationalist forces there were warlords whose loyalty to the generalissimo was suspect at best . . . we had to deal with individual governors, more or less independently, with any help we could get from the central government. We know that the governor of Yunnan Province had a lot of trucks he had either begged, borrowed, or stolen, and had hidden . . . that would have helped our transportation situation. To get those committed to the effort was an exercise of some considerable magnitude . . . as I remember it, we paid pretty heavily to get some of that capability . . . he was just an out-and-out crook with no more willingness to support the operation than he felt was in his own best interest and not that of China.

"I dealt almost totally with Chinese engineers who had been organized to support our construction activities. Most . . . had been trained in the United States. Virtually all of them spoke English. The way we built our airfields was to request that [Chinese engineer] organization to go into an area and build an airfield to our specifications. We would furnish them the overall plan for the airfield, general location of buildings, size of each building, physical layout of runways and facilities that we would want as part of the airfield. The Chinese engineers would go to the site, preempt the land under the authority of Chiang Kai-shek, usually having to work with the local governor. Then they would recruit the labor force, by conscription largely.

"They did some of their construction, things that required some skill by contracting with local Chinese contractors, but the major airfield work was done by hand. Just thousands and thousands of people, men, women, and children who had been conscripted by the political forces from villages all around the area . . . far because they had to walk to the job. They would live primitively right there on the job. When they did it they were released back to their village.

"We did have to deal with the generalissimo himself in getting approval of each airfield because in most cases it meant preempting the rights of the farmer by taking his land. With very bad inflation that they had in China, it was impossible for the government to pay them what the land was really worth, regardless of how many yen were paid. There was a real question about whether a man got what the land was worth. He couldn't go two miles away and buy a comparable piece of property. Unquestionably, the little farmers suffered by this transaction."

The hardship on the peasants, the machinations of the powerful, and the corruption notwithstanding, four Cheng-tu B-29 fields and three supporting fighter strips were ready by May 1, 1944. Two of the bases in India went operational in March, with others completed several months later. On paper, the 58th Bomb Wing's four groups each had four squadrons that operated seven B-29s—a total of 112. In addition, a 50 percent reserve boosted the bomber availability to 168. To man the aircraft, the air corps assigned double crews. In an effort to reduce the size of the ground force, each member of the flight crew was trained in one nonflight speciality. That system was not wholly successful and adjustments were required, including the deactivation of the 58th Bomb Wing. The 20th Bomber Command actually would consist of four very heavy bomb groups totaling 150 B-29s and 20 C-87 cargo planes.

Although Matterhorn would not depend on the Air Transport Command, the B-29s required a substantial support element, about twenty thousand men working at aircraft maintenance, ordnance, communications, radar, and various other tasks, including the usual complement of cooks, bakers, and clerks. The first projections of supply tonnage fell well short of the mark. The big planes required many more engine replacements than had been anticipated. In practice, the B-29s could not handle the theoretical amounts of cargo set down by planners. Brigadier General Kenneth Wolfe, the commanding officer of the 20th Bomber Command, ordered several B-29s stripped of all combat equipment except for tail guns and minimal radar, enabling them to tote seven tons of aviation gasoline per trip instead of three. According to one B-29 pilot, each sortie against the farthest targets, the Japanese home islands, required five trips over the Hump by a bomber to build up enough gasoline. The priorities of Matterhorn shifted some of the tonnage destined for Chennault's Fourteenth Air Force to the 20th Bomber Command, much to his displeasure.

The historian for the 20th Bomber Command reported a preemptive strike in the internecine war, writing, "Faced with the necessity of executing a combat mission on the directed date, despite its reduced transport capacity, the command had only one alternative: to reduce the delivery of equipment, supplies, and personnel to all units in the forward area [Cheng-tu] to the bare essential required to sustain life and permit the airplanes to take off for the target. These instructions were so stringent that all surface transportation to the forward area ceased with the exception of one vehicle per base. No supplementary rations were supplied to the garrisons in the area. All supplies of PX rations were eliminated. There was no shipment of clothing, less than 25 percent of the mail. No hospital rations and no additional personal or organizational equipment were supplied."

While Betts, his American subordinates, and tens of thousands of coolies carved airfields in China, the B-29 crews who would use them had trained in the United States. From inception of the B-29 in 1939 to its operational status only four years elapsed. In fact, the air corps ordered quantity production even before the first model left the ground. The massive dimensions of the Superfortress, its performance requirements, and its innovations reflected bold imagination. Its size dwarfed the standard four-engine B-17 and B-24 heavy bombers, giving the B-29 the designation of very heavy bomber. Top ceiling was rated at 38,000 feet, and at the optimum height of 33,000 feet, it could sprint 361 miles per hour. With a four-ton load of bombs, the range was 3,500 miles. The massive engines and the aerodynamics made it a "hot" airplane to fly, and some of its first pilots, accustomed to its more forgiving predecessors, viewed it as difficult to handle. With a pressurized cabin and remote-control, power-driven gun turrets—12.50-caliber machine guns—and a 20-millimeter cannon as a tail stinger, the B-29 packed a formidable arsenal.

One Superfortress pilot, Richard Carmichael, from a poor Texas family, obtained an appointment to West Point through service in the National Guard. When he graduated in 1936 he, like a quarter of his class, elected flight school. On December 7, 1941, at about 8:00 A.M., he was at the controls of one of eleven B-17s en route to the Philippines, with a stop at Hickam Field, Hawaii. The machine guns for the Flying Fortresses were neatly packed in crates stowed in the fuselages.

Carmichael remembered, "Somebody tapped me on the shoulder and said, 'Look at all those white puffs up there in the air ahead.' I looked up and said, 'Well, the navy must be practicing.' We got close enough to hear the control tower was under fire. By this time we could see airplanes. We alerted and I called in and asked for landing instructions. We had to fly around the ships and as we started into this pattern on the downwind leg, the navy started shooting at us. At the same time, somebody said, 'We have a pursuit airplane, a Japanese plane on our tail.' Things had gone to hell in a handbasket. Everything was happening. All the battleships, all the smoke there—they had already been hit and were on fire." Carmichael found refuge for his B-17 on a strip used by fighters and that was under attack even as he landed.

Carmichael eventually reached Australia with the 19th Bomb Group, flew missions against Japanese targets in the Dutch East Indies, ferried General Douglas MacArthur on one leg of his trip after he fled the Philippines, and had returned to Kansas to learn how to fly B-29s. Assigned as commander of the 462d Bomb Group, part of the 58th Bomb Wing, Carmichael said, "We all liked it. It was an easy, honest airplane to fly. It didn't spin out, or do anything you didn't expect. It was just like the old B-17. Both airplanes would get you home under really bad conditions." However, in their first inception, B-29 engines had a tendency to overheat and catch fire. Carmichael noted, "The engine problem got progressively worse after we got to India because of the heat, humidity, and the dust. On-the-ground cockpit temperatures could hit 140 degrees. When we got to China we had different conditions and we had to fly over the Hump. To get over the Hump was touchy; only one out of five airplanes had radar." Carmichael observed that beyond matters of strategy and morale, Matterhorn was an opportunity to test the B-29 under combat conditions. Typically, the missions flown by the B-29s began at airfields in India and then staged forward from Chinese airfields.

The first operation struck not at Japan but at Bangkok. Because of delays in the training program dating back to problems that surfaced in Kansas, General Wolfe decided to reduce the risks by making it a night attack and with the aircraft bombing individually rather than in a tight formation. However, that ran counter to the philosophy of the air corps, daylight precision bombing and Hap Arnold insisted on sticking to the book. Wolfe postponed the mission for a week while crews underwent intensive practice in formation tactics.

On June 5, 1944, the big birds took off for Bangkok, a two-thousand-mile round trip. Intelligence indicated that enemy defenses would provide a test but not a severe one. There were 112 aircraft scheduled for the operation. One crashed immediately, killing all aboard, and 14 aborted. Others never found the target. Cloud cover and haze cut visibility. Some aircraft joined the wrong elements, while others wandered from their formations and headed for Bangkok by themselves.

"The way I remember it," said Carmichael, "is that I was scared as hell. What I was scared of was a B-29 running into me because we got down there, and there were planes all over the target. We were in and out. We had no good plan of separation. Everybody was given the same altitude to bomb from. Some people would keep in formation through the clouds. Some of them couldn't. I remember seeing the river in Bangkok, but my attention mostly was looking out to see who we were going to run into. Every time we would come out of a cloud, there would be a B-29 over here and one over there."

The official history of the 20th Bomber Command reported that of the seventy-seven B-29s that bombed Bankok, forty-eight of them did so by radar, a technique in which crews had received limited instruction. Some dropped their ordnance from more than twenty-seven thousand feet, while others made their runs at only seventeen thousand feet. The Japanese fighters offered only halfhearted passes at the attackers, doing little damage, but weather and mechanical troubles downed five of the Superfortresses. Two ditched in the Bay of Bengal. Air-Sea Rescue plucked all but two of the crew of one from the water, while in the second watery landing, the ten airmen washed ashore and with the aid of Thais were recovered. Navigational errors, clouds, and engine malfunctions forced twelve to land at B-29 fields other than their home bases, and another thirty set down at airfields outside the 20th's command. The crashes killed fifteen.

One day later, while still gathering in the widely dispersed B-29s, Wolfe received an order from Hap Arnold demanding an attack on Japan proper as a way to discourage the current Nipponese campaign against the more forward airfields of the Fourteenth Air Force. Initially Wolfe could only promise fifty-five B-29s for the date of June 15, but Arnold insisted on a minimum of seventy. Frantic efforts equipped the Superfortresses with extra tanks required for the thirty-two-hundred-mile round trip, and the 312th Fighter Wing yielded much of its precious stock of gasoline to fuel the bombers. Wolfe marshaled a force of eighty-three aircraft, but several were scratched.

The target was Yawata, on the southern island of Kyushu, home to vital coke plants for the manufacture of steel. Washington forbade Wolfe from going along, but Brigadier General LaVerne "Blondie" Saunders, who had piloted the first B-29 to China, led the mission. Eight reporters and three photographers went along to provide publicity for this land-based attack on Japan.

Takeoffs began shortly after four in the afternoon. A total of seventy-five B-29s were listed, but only sixty-eight lifted off. One crashed immediately, and four more returned to base because of mechanical failures. It was shortly before midnight when the first B-29 signaled bombs away at Yawata, and it was followed by forty-six more raiders. Because of malfunctions, half a dozen jettisoned their loads before approaching the target, and several more hit alternate targets.

Carmichael remarked, "I took my classmate [Dwight] Monteith with me. Blondie was a great guy for getting his staff [Monteith was the commanding officer for the 20th's forward echelon] to get out and ride on these missions with the troops. He liked to get them down and get their hands dirty, get them shot at, too. We usually flew the four-airplane box [formation] on that type of mission, but not at night. At night was in trail; we had altitude and time-departure separation. I gave Monteith a good ride over Yawata, at nine thousand or ten thousand feet. We could afford to go in low at night. They didn't have any night fighter resistance that I remember. There was a gap [in antiaircraft] between seven thousand and twelve thousand feet."

Again, the 20th Bomber Command lost nothing to enemy air defenses or fighters, but seven went down for mechanical or weather-related reasons or pilot error, with fifty-five casualties. Photo reconnaissance indicated minimal bomb damage at Yawata. The coke plants were untouched.

These first two efforts exhausted the Matterhorn fuel stocks and other necessities. Not until three weeks after the run at Yawata was the 20th Bomber Command ready to strike again. At that, it was considered a "harassing" raid of eighteen B-29s against several targets in Japan. Only one plane aborted, and after striking again at sites on Kyushu, the remainder returned without a loss.

A more serious venture dawned on July 29 as seventy-two of the B-29s aimed toward a complex of industrial plants at Anshan in Manchuria. The nagging problems with B-29 mechanical systems reduced the number of actual raiders to sixty. On this daylight mission the Superfortresses flew the four-plane diamond-shaped formation and bombed from twenty-five thousand feet. At speeds of 182 to 212 miles per hour over the target, the planes made it difficult for enemy fighters to bore in, and the American gunners claimed three probables and four damaged. One B-29, hit by flak and with a malfunctioning engine, was jumped by five enemy fighters. Among them was a P-40 still wearing its Chinese-American Composite Wing insignia, obviously captured at some point by the Japanese. It promptly shot out another engine, and eight men parachuted into occupied China. Chinese guerrillas brought them out. For the first time, the intelligence experts reported significant damage inflicted to the objectives.

Matterhorn's Behind-the-Lines Helpers

The B-29s attacking deep into occupied territory in China and even all the way to Japan required knowledge of meteorological conditions over the target. The solution lay in small weather stations established near the coast and within Japanese-controlled areas. Specialists from the navy and marines were assigned the task, and among them was Robert M. Sinks.

Born in 1923 and raised in West Frankfort, Illinois, Sinks graduated from high school in 1940 and began attending Southern Illinois University, where he joined the naval reserve. By March 1942 he had been called up and sent to boot camp at Corpus Christi, Texas. "They said I'd make a good pilot but I got lost the minute I got in the air. I had trouble seeing colors and I am dyslexic. They decided to make me a meteorologist and trained me in Corpus Christi."

By early 1943, Sinks qualified as an aerographer, and when the call for volunteers to serve in China came, he signed up. Assigned to Washington, D.C., Sinks underwent not only further instruction in aerology but also in code, cryptography, and enough Chinese for him to be able to communicate once he reached China. "We were told at the time, 'When you go to China you'll be doing other functions besides meteorology. You will be training people.'" He and the eight others in the group were brought into a room with Admiral H. E. Yarnell and a number of other high-ranking officers. "They told us that the job we were about to set out to do was extremely important and that six of us would not make it. All nine of us survived," Sinks recalled, "and I think it was because of the training we received." At the marine camp in Quantico, Virginia, Sinks became an expert with a submachine gun, learned to use a rifle, pistol, and hand grenades, and learned parachute jumping. During survival training he discovered that he could eat cattail plants.

Flown over the Hump, Sinks spent several months at a special camp outside of Chungking as part of the Sino-American Cooperative Organization [SACO], a joint effort between the U.S. Navy Group China and Chiang Kai-shek's secret police. SACO's mission was to train Chinese guerrillas, gather intelligence, and conduct insurgency operations behind the Japanese lines.

When he went operational, Sinks flew to the air base at Kan-chou, from where he traveled with his equipment by sampan and on foot, a slow, thirty-day trip. He did not wear a uniform but the clothes of a Chinese peasant, although he was still obviously recognizable as an alien. Coolies toted the gear, which included his submachine gun and carbine, while he packed .45- and .38-caliber pistols. They were at Huaan, China, about sixty to eighty miles from the coast. "That's where we were to set up a camp for training guerrillas and I also set up a meteorological station to send up radiosonde balloons." The devices transmitted weather data relevant to attacks on Japan or on

Formosa (now Taiwan). "This was all Japanese-held territory. Huaan
was right in the middle of nowhere. There were no roads leading to it.
The only way you could get to it was by coolie or by river transportation. The Japanese had never been there for the entire war. When we
started working with the guerrillas, we promised never to take a guerrilla more than twenty-five miles from his home. Most of these people
had never been ten miles from their homes in their entire lifetime. He
was going to be paid, fed, and trained. The biggest thing was the
guarantee that his family would be taken care of if something happened to him. If you promised to pay money, the Japanese would
probably outbid you.

"I was ordered to go to the coast to set up weather stations right
across from the Japanese naval base at Amoy [on the China coast]. I
was to set up places along the coast." These installations were staffed
with an American radioman and Chinese trained by Sinks. "We had
coast watching stations all the way, almost from Shanghai to Hong
Kong. I was in charge of those across Fukien [a province in southeastern China]. We covered several hundred miles.

"We had portable anemometers for wind, things for pressure,
mercurial barometers. I was in charge of the balloons. We figured the
maximum amount of time we had was probably an hour [before the
activity was discovered and the Japanese reacted]. I got the [big] balloons up at night. Instruments were in the balloon and they sent radio
signals [the radiosonde system]. I had a receiver and was able to plot
the temperatures, pressures, and different things. An amazing part of
it was that fishermen off the coast of Taiwan brought in two of the
boxes from the radiosonde one time. They knew we Americans were
there and we gave them a little something for doing that, which pleased
them. It showed us that those things were getting all the way over to
Taiwan.

"In the daytime I would send up pie ball balloons. You merely
watched [them] and you had a theodolite [surveying instrument that
measures horizontal and vertical angles]; mathematically you could
figure the wind direction." The pie balloons, while small, could be
seen with instruments at altitudes of twenty thousand feet. While visible, once they left Sinks's area, a pie ball balloon was difficult if not
impossible to shoot down because it was so small.

"I made my own hydrogen for the big balloons," said Sinks. "I
didn't use helium. I made hydrogen by taking iron filings along with
caustic soda and water. I had a tube, like a cylinder for selling gas. I'd
put the filings and water in and the last thing put in was the caustic
soda. I had a Chinese fellow standing there with the cylinder and he'd
twist [the valve]. By the time that was fully tightened, it would build

up to fifteen hundred pounds of pressure. It was dangerous to fool with, but that's how we made our hydrogen. Later, I ran out of iron filings. I found some American and Japanese planes that were shot down. I had the Chinese file the metal into powder, and that made it faster. It worked wonderfully because aluminum [used on the aircraft] had more of a reaction to caustic soda.

"I ran out of caustic soda and there was no way they could parachute that in. It had to come another way. I got 120 pounds of caustic soda from the Japanese naval base. The Chinese were trading with the Japanese all the time. There was some crooked guy [a guard] down there. We figured out that it probably cost the American taxpayer about $8,000 to get that caustic soda.

"As the war progressed and the Philippines were taken, we were able to get penicillin dropped to us. We had a lot of guerrillas who were killed and we had some who were wounded. They sent us penicillin but we had no way of keeping it, no refrigeration. We found that Standard Oil had a boat in Amoy, and we bought that boat. A Chinese trader bought it from the Japanese and brought it up the river. We took the refrigerator off; it worked on our auxiliary generator really well. Then they took the boat back and sold it back to the Japanese without the refrigerator."

Although a bitter war raged, in this backwater of China moments of truce occasionally occurred. Recalled Sinks, "China is a great citrus fruit grower and they produce some of the best *satsumas,* which are like tangerines. We were buying them one time and the Japanese were not more than fifty yards away, buying some, too. Everybody ignored each other!"

The meteorology stations provided more than weather information and guerrillas. Sinks noted, "The submarines were progressing against Japanese shipping. We took the Philippines, and the Japanese ships were moving closer to the coast. They were trying to bring their troops from down in South China and the Dutch East Indies back to the Japanese homeland. They always had to come into the harbors because they would not be out at night. The continental shelf out there is such that because of tides, the water level was too low for submarines [to operate submerged].

"A group of ships one night was spotted by marine sergeant William Stewart. He saw them moving along the coast and immediately radioed back to us. He said they were probably going for the harbor at a certain place. His radio message was in code and I had to rework the message and put it into code. It was then relayed to Chungking by our radio because we had much stronger transmitters. [Chungking] in turn sent it out to the fleet.

"It was picked up by the submarine *Barb,* whose skipper was Eugene B. Fluckey. He moved his submarine in but had to fire his torpedoes on the surface. He immediately sank a ship; in fact, he sank three ships and damaged three others, but he only got credit for one. He then had to get away and at night he was being chased by a Japanese destroyer. He submerged and that destroyer ran itself onto a reef. The skipper of the *Barb* [Fluckey] got the Medal of Honor."

The blows against their ships had aroused the Japanese, who began to make life for the coast watchers difficult. "It took maybe three or four weeks," said Sinks, "to get Stewart back. I remember a radio message saying, 'If you hear from me, let my dad know I'm still alive.' We got him back and it was decided Stewart had done a *fantastic* job because we were able to find literally thousands of bodies that washed ashore from those ships [sunk by the *Barb*]. He had been out, doing this for about a year. They decided he would be sent back to Chungking. We thought he should have been awarded the Silver Star or something, but because of certain circumstances [most likely the association with Chiang's secret police] SACO was not allowed to give medals."

Sinks himself nearly fell victim to a Japanese patrol. He and a companion named Davis fled. Sinks said, "The Japanese were shooting at us. I was in front of Davis, and he was trying to get around me. We were in a rice paddy, so you couldn't go any way but straight. Thank God, the Japanese were poor shots. I always told everybody I broke the four-minute mile and did it carrying a submachine gun, six full clips of ammunition, with someone trying to [pass] me."

Further Intelligence

While Matterhorn debuted, the Fourteenth Air Force of Chennault struck at closer Japanese installations. A critical component of its efforts, as well as those of the B-29s, lay in the photographic displays of targets and evidence of the success or failure of missions. Frederick H. Kline, whose ancestors had settled in Pennsylvania in the early 1700s, was a specialist in this aspect of intelligence.

Born in 1918, Kline, when he finished high school, earned a scholarship to Grove City College and in 1940 held a degree in chemistry and premed. "Realizing I couldn't go to school, do odd jobs, and play basketball in graduate school if I went into medicine," said Kline, "I took a job with United States Steel."

"Having read Herman Raushing's book *[The Revolution of Nihilism]* which is a life history of Hitler, I was pretty well up-to-date on what was going on in the world. I decided the country was pretty good to me, and in spite of my cream-colored Packard and a few other things, I became a volunteer selectee [the draft had been instituted in November 1940]."

After six months of learning how to be an infantryman, Kline obtained an honorable discharge and then applied for a four-year stint in the army air corps. At the urging of a superior, Kline applied for officer candidate school as an aviation cadet in photography, his hobby. "The school was a two-year course, boiled down to three months. Everything was accelerated, we operated eighteen hours a day. We got six hours of sleep, four meals, and no time off on weekends." The dozen students in the class used a Speed Graphic camera, the standard tool of newspaper photographers, flew in P-38s photographing areas around Denver with aerial cameras, and converted the pictures to maps. He learned to work with a trimetrogan camera that shot a vertical and two oblique angle views to produce from an altitude of ten thousand feet the same horizontal width of a ground photograph. On conclusion of his studies, he received a commission as a second lieutenant in the permanent reserves. Subsequently he attended an air corps intelligence school. When Kline finished the program he was given his choice of theaters. Having read about the Flying Tigers in China, he succumbed to the romance of that adventure and applied for duty there, although the AVG had long been dissolved.

Shortly after Kline landed at Kunming, he was ushered into Chennault's office to explain the bomb damage assessment photographs at Formosa. "The Japanese were shipping out bauxite," said Kline, "used to make aluminum for their airplanes. We knew they were probably doing this at night, so we couldn't find them because we weren't too well equipped for night stuff. We went down to the big harbor of Takao at the northern end of Formosa and had a diversionary attack on the docks there. It was late in the evening, and we dropped mines right across the harbor—a lot of mines. Then the next morning at dawn, we sent a reconnaissance plane down there, and he took pictures of probably the biggest tonnage of sunken shipping that was ever accomplished in that part of the world. These ships came out—all kinds, cargo ships, escort ships—and some of them they pulled back and beached. We analyzed them and estimated the potential tonnage.

"Chennault had standing orders that if anything of consequence came up, any hour of the day or night, he wanted to know about it. As soon as we got all of that stuff together, it was pretty late at night [when] somebody got hold of Chennault and he [said] he'd like to see some of this stuff in his office. I went up beside him to lay these pictures out on the desk for him to look at, to actually see what these tonnage figures meant.

"He said, 'Soldier! Get on the other side of the desk! I have only one ear that I can hear out of.' That was my introduction to General Chennault. He needed that [intelligence] desperately, because that's the information he sent back to get what little supplies he could get from the rest of the military. By doing this we were paying our way, so to speak. His door was open to anybody in his command. He had a small command at the time, so he could do this. If you had any problem, you could feel free to take them right to the top."

Subsequently Kline became the photographic officer and the photo intelligence officer for the 341st Medium Bomb Group at Yankai, about 170 miles north of Kunming. "We were given the objective of interdicting the supplies that the Japs were trying to take [from] what was then French Indochina. They would try to get the supplies over to the coast on boats or on a railway along the coast. We went down there on a bridge-busting job, which continued essentially the rest of the time we were there." The B-25s also struck at coastal shipping, frequently strafing with a 75-millimeter cannon, driving vessels out to sea where submarines might torpedo them.

Although unauthorized, Kline flew a number of missions. "We had a 75-millimeter cannon mounted between the pilot and copilot in the nose of the B-25J. The shell could penetrate metal and we could hit locomotives and moving trains. It was a sure kill." Kline created a set-up in front of the cannon that enhanced judgment of distance, speed, and angle. "I got so that I could probably get about one out of three shells on target, which was very good. When Chennault found out about it, he grounded me." He preferred that Kline work on ways to improve targeting accuracy rather than risk being shot down.

Hump Flights Continued

The demands from Washington for large-scale B-29 operations, while preserving the means for Chennault to function, strained the supply system, with much of the burden falling on the Air Transport Command and pilots such as Tom Peays. Raised on a ranch in Coke County, Texas, upon graduation from high school in 1936, he applied for the navy, but the recruiting officer told him to attend college. Peays enrolled at Texas Tech in Lubbock, majoring in animal husbandry.

He entered the Civilian Pilot Training Program and qualified for a commercial license. A private training center hired him to teach air corps aviation cadets the rudiments of flight. Sometime after Pearl Harbor, the military created its own flight training centers and Peays, still a civilian, began to work for the Air Ferry Command, moving aircraft around the United States. Because of fears that on overseas assignments he and other civilians could be classified as spies if shot down, Peays was inducted into the army as a flight officer service pilot.

In late 1943 Peays, as a pilot on a C-54, traveled to Calcutta from Miami. He began an assignment ferrying fifty-five-gallon drums of high-octane aviation fuel over the Hump. "I preferred the C-54," said Peays, "because it was such a comfortable and safe airplane, but I flew the C-109 [a B-24 with belly tanks] most of the time. We had electric flying suits. You plugged them in, and that's what kept us warm. There was no heavy clothing except for our boots.

His usual destination was Kunming. "Most of the time my flights were from six to eight hours, one way. Thunderstorms were sudden. Maybe we could see them build up, but especially at night we couldn't tell. They were killers. They did things to airplanes that airplanes were not built to withstand. There was hail and wind and up-and-down drafts. The storms would take that airplane up so many feet per second and then drop it just as fast. Your engine would be running away or it could be in a stall situation.

"We had to be concerned about the mountains and rocks because our instruments would home in on the magnetic fields in those rocks on the mountains. On one particular night we found that when there would be lightning, our instruments would go dead [as far as being useful]. Our magnetic compass would home in on something over to the side. We knew that was not right. The only thing we could do was fly needle and ball and stay on a beam. The people who used it [the beam] lived. The people who didn't flew into the mountains because there was no way they could keep from turning that airplane to where it pointed. I stayed with that beam. Your hands would get sweaty, but I would listen to that beam and I'd wear those earphones and my ears roared all of the time. Tintinnitus, they called it. In my opinion it was from wearing those earphones and listening to the beam for hours and hours at a time.

"We had superchargers in the B-24s and could get pretty close to thirty thousand feet. We didn't have passengers unless we were coming back. When we did, we would take a lower route." For the most part, personnel traveling over the Hump, explained Peays, were carried by army pilots not engaged on bombing missions. "They were flying the low route," said Peays, "and we lost a lot of them." The "low route" was at an altitude of ten thousand to twelve thousand feet and also was known as the "aluminum trail" because of the shiny streaks of metal scattered over the mountains. Only once, near Myitkyina, did Peays ever see enemy aircraft. He ducked into some thick clouds, and the fighters, lacking the instrumentation for blind flight, did not follow.

Matterhorn Closes Down

Chennault, increasingly anxious over the progress of the enemy ground forces toward his bastions, urged that the B-29s be directed against the Japanese-occupied ports in China, through which supplies for the oncoming troops passed. That proposal did not mesh with the long-range objectives for B-29s. Instead, Saunders, having replaced Wolfe, scheduled a return visit to Yawata during the daylight hours with a smaller force attacking that site during the night.

A crew member for Van Horne's *Jukebox* reported, "Takeoff was after midnight so as to arrive over the target around 9:00 A.M. We flew alone during the dark hours and were to rendezvous for formation along the Japanese coastline. Two hours out we were flying through turbulent weather with fuel splashing into the forward bomb bay from the two tanks there, and St. Elmo's fire lighting up the propeller tips like an airborne fire rocket on the Fourth of July. All unneeded switches were turned off and the bomb door was opened manually to rid the bay of fuel and fumes. Once clear of these, the doors were closed with electrical power.

"We knew this mission was going to be different because the chaplain had given us Catholic boys the provisional last rites of the church. Now we are crossing the China Sea and as we approach Japan, several miles off to our right, we see several of their naval ships sitting in the water. (We will report this to the U.S. Naval Command.) Then a few miles nearer, some very brave American men were in a submarine sending us a message: 'We will be there to pick you up, if needed.'" The navy had instituted a "lifeguard" system, which stationed subs underneath waters near targets for its carrier-based planes and extended it to include saving air corps crews who ditched.

In his narrative, the anonymous crewman for Van Horne continued, "At the coast we join in on [Lieutenant] Colonel [William F.] Savoie's left wing, and [First Lieutenant Ernest] Picket was on the right wing. No. 4 had an engine malfunction and was forced to land in China. We pick up our course for the bomb run. Each plane will be flown straight and level for a good bomb drop.

"On our course ahead the enemy has put up flak in a box pattern for us to fly through. Two formations ahead get through, but now the fighters attack. One bomber is rammed in the wing section. For the first time we see our buddies go down in flames. As we started through I saw an explosion in Picket's plane, evidently near the front, as it looked as if the men were blown forward from the cockpit area. The planes go down, but we are happy to note parachutes opening. Some will be saved.

"Colonel Savoie's and our plane do get through, but we are then attacked by the fighters. We make our drop, but Savoie's plane now seemingly is hit. They are losing altitude. We have very little damage and turn for home. Our gunners receive credit for three fighters. We will never know what claims Savoie's gunners had. We later heard they bailed out near the China coast. Later reports indicate over half of Savoie's crew had been picked up and are well and in the hands of friendly Chinese. They will be brought safely out of Japanese-held territory." Indeed, Savoie and four others made their way back.

The 794th Bomb Squadron was hard hit over Yawata. The history of the Billy Mitchell Group read, "[Lieutenant] Colonel [Robert] Clinkscale's crew in *Gertrude C* released their bombs and with bomb doors closing, found a twin-engine Jap fighter closing very fast in a head-on course. According to Major [Don] Humphrey in 279 *[Postville Express]* in No. 3 position, the fighter laid over on its side and rammed its right wing into the right wing of No. 334 just outboard of the No. 1 engine. The fighter catapulted in flames over the top of Humphrey's right wing, leaving his right wing embedded in the wing of No. 334, which burst into flames and began to disintegrate.

"Captain [Ornell] Stauffer in No. 368 *[Calamity Sue]*, flying in the No. 4 position, flew into No. 334's debris and went down over the target. Captain Cristie's crew in No. 217, flying in No. 2 position, reported No. 334 finally pulled up on its tail and then spiraled down out of sight. Witnesses in another formation claimed the vertical stabilizer had also sheared off. Pieces of the wreckage also damaged No. 217. The entire crew on *Gertrude C* was listed as KIA while several from *Calamity Sue* survived after a year as prisoners of war."

During this mission to Yawata one of the B-29s from the 462d Bomb Group aborted, and Richard Carmichael led the three-plane formation over the target. "We were hit on the run in from the IP [initial point] to the target by antiaircraft fire which wounded my central fire control officer, Chester Tims. It may have started a little fire or something in the back end. There was a little confusion in the cockpit, trying to find out or help do something about what had happened. Instead of turning left, as I should have, out from Yawata over the sea, it looked like there was more flak and more fighters that way. I elected to turn right and I kicked my butt all the way through prison camp for making that decision. I was picked up immediately by a Betty, a Japanese twin-engine bomber, above me about one thousand or two thousand feet.

"We were under attack by fighters all the way this time, as well as antiaircraft. The excitement in the cockpit, something wrong back below, wounded man, maybe a fire—there was a lot of distraction. Nobody saw this plane up above us. We didn't expect to be attacked by bombs. Finally Ed Perry, the navigator, hit me on the leg and pointed up there. When I looked, the bombs were falling from the Betty. All I could do was try to make a steep turn. I always said I missed them all but one. That got us in midship and started a fire in the bomb bay. Ed Perry grabbed a fire extinguisher, squeezed himself around the four-gun upper turret that extended vertically all the way down through the fuselage, only to find the device empty."

Carmichael flew out to sea toward Iki Island while his radio operation tried to contact a submarine supposedly stationed offshore for rescue in an emergency. "We were getting lower and lower and faster and faster and hotter and hotter and burning more and more. We started bailing the crew out a little before we got to the island because the first three people out of the rear end hit in the water. We lost Chester Tims because he was wounded and he hit in the water; we figured he must have drowned. The copilot hit in the water. He was lost, not because he drowned, but because Japanese fighters came around and shot him. They attacked everybody they could in a parachute. The radio operator also was lost. Just as I jumped out, the airplane broke apart and hit the island in two pieces. I hit in a field. The first person I saw was a little Japanese soldier coming toward me. I had a pistol and he had a rifle. Behind him I saw a whole bunch of angry farmers coming with long sticks. I knew I wasn't going to put up any resistance. I let that little soldier, who couldn't have been over sixteen or seventeen—but he had a rifle—come up and gave him my pistol." Several farmers managed to rap Carmichael with staves, but the soldier drove them off; and along with the seven other survivors of his B-29, Carmichael became a POW.

The India-China-based B-29 campaign went on, but the results continued to disappoint Hap Arnold. On August 29 Major General Curtis LeMay replaced Blondie Saunders as head of the 20th Bomber Command. Previously with the Eighth Air Force in England, LeMay had built a reputation by developing effective formation tactics and more effective bomb runs.

Before LeMay relieved him, Saunders had scheduled another attack on Anshan. Chennault's apprehensions of a Japanese thrust at the Cheng-tu bases and weather forced postponements. Reacting to complaints from Washington about the numbers of B-29s going after targets, Saunders instituted maintenance and personnel policies that pushed the available B-29s at the forward staging areas to 115, and 108 of these actually lifted off the runways. Of these, 95 found their way to the factories at Anshan. LeMay flew in one ship as an observer. For once, clear skies unveiled the targets, and the Japanese ground and air defenses were negligible compared to the uproar that greeted the raiders over Yawata. The postraid photographs showed significant damage, causing a drop of 30 percent in production at the Showa Steel Works. Just four planes were lost.

Under LeMay, the pace of B-29 missions increased. Repeated visits to Anshan, Yawata, Palembang, and raids on Formosa sites—the Okayama aircraft assembly plant, Heito airfield, and Takao harbor—were dictated not only by their strategic import but also by the limitations of operating from the western China bases. The Formosa expeditions at least tied in with the U.S. Navy's carrier raids on that island and with the beginnings of the campaign to oust the Japanese from the Philippines. The strikes at Okayama and Heito produced excellent results. However, the steady advance of the Japanese troops in China menaced the Cheng-tu fields. Chennault's pleas for B-29s to help fend off the enemy went unanswered. American strategists had decided that rather than confront Japan's army in China, the war would be won by seizure of the Philippines and Okinawa as springboards for an invasion of Japan itself.

Matterhorn had been conceived under the premise of early sustained bombing of Japan, but the attacks were neither early nor sustained. Furthermore, the capture of the Mariana Islands by U.S. forces in the summer of 1944 opened up a much better avenue for attacks on the Japanese home islands, eliminating the requirement to stage forward from India, placing all of Japan, not just Kyushu, within range and lopping off as much as a thousand miles from round trips.

LeMay flew to the Marianas on January 18, 1945, to assume command of the 21st Bomber Command, taking with him key personnel from the B-29 program. His shift signaled the end of Matterhorn and the new theater for Superfortress operations, although missions from China continued into February.

19

The Prisoners of War

Americans taken prisoner by the Japanese were spread out from the Philippines through Japan, Korea, Burma, and China. O. R. Sparkman, captured in China immediately after the declarations of war, had been crowded into an old barracks at the former Chinese post of Fort Woosung, Shanghai. Along with the marines, the camp held survivors from Wake Island as well as some of the first British taken in Burma. "We still had our own officers with us," said Sparkman, "and they were still demanding our rights." Sparkman and his companions believed they would be repatriated and were bitterly disappointed when they learned differently.

Sparkman described the routine and the dearth of food. "You had to get up every morning and count off. They would check to see if everybody was there. And it was cold. Then you went over to the cookhouse and got the rice—they called it a soup. I think there were about six pounds of meat for fifteen hundred men. Sometimes you'd see a chunk of meat once a week. You'd get a teacup full of rice. It was pretty gritty.

"One morning they were serving rice and [a fellow prisoner] dipped in and he come up with half of a rat in a cup of rice. The rat had been trying to eat at night and fell in and drowned. This old boy says, 'I don't want it.' I says, 'Heck, give me that rat and the rest of it too.' I suppose I throwed the rat out. There was an old kitten in the camp and I was going to cook that, but one of the Chinese of the *USS Harrison* beat me to it because I saw the skin laying there to dry out." During his 3½ years as a POW, Sparkman's weight would fall from 140 to 110 pounds.

At first the Japanese employed the prisoners to build a "park." Later they learned it was a rifle range. "It was about three miles out

313

there and we'd march out every morning. We would draw our picks and shovel. We had a narrow-gauge track like in an old mine. The box on the wheels would hold about a yard of dirt. We were supposed to start out with four men, fill the box, and push it around on the track. The soil was dumped into water holes, five or six feet deep. They got us down to three men and then two. Two men digging thirty-five yards of dirt a day, that's a lot of dirt." For six days a week, from sunup to sundown, they labored under the baleful eye of a guard who lashed out with a lead-loaded riding crop. On Sunday, a chaplain held church services; a Japanese Christian preached.

One day, more than two years into his captivity, while leaning on his shovel he heard the sound of an airplane and looked up. "That was the prettiest airplane I ever saw. A real sharp nose, streamlined. It was a P-51. And there was a little old plane trying to get up from the airfield, a trainer. That P-51 hit the trainer and then there was a big old bomber trying to get down. He made a wide sweep and he knocked that thing down. Everybody felt a lot better after that."

Sparkman and his compatriots had begun digging shelters for the Japanese, and visits to the vicinity by American aircraft began to increase. As the air war rained down on Shanghai, Sparkman, along with the other inmates, rode boxcars to Pusan, Korea, where they worked on the wharfs. After a short period of time they boarded ships to Japan and embarked on an extended trip that carried the men to Tokyo. Food consisted of minuscule portions of items such as a small box with rice and dried grasshoppers. Changing trains in Tokyo, Sparkman saw the results of U.S. air raids. "There were bodies still laying in the streets. There were fires everywhere. It was burning; the whole town was burning." Some of his companions reported that women had thrown rocks at them to vent their fury over the attacks.

Sparkman's journey ended at Japan's northernmost island, Hokkaido. He was put to work in a coal mine previously deemed too dangerous for local citizens. He wore a coat, issued by the Red Cross, when in the mine, where water lay ankle deep. He shoveled coal while enduring humiliations from aged guards who slapped the prisoners if they failed to bow. The diet amounted to rice with seaweed and occasionally horsemeat with maggots clinging to it.

Henry B. Stowers, a marine from the 1920s, recalled that a double ring of electrified barbed wire surrounded the encampment. Said Stowers, "You knew that if you touched it you were dead. Later a number of young fellows actually committed suicide by going out on rainy dark nights . . . they decided the war would last six or eight months and they couldn't hold out that long. They would grab the fence. Sparkman [and others] were recruits and we had to keep their morale up.

'Look, fellows, this thing will be over very soon.' But we never said three months or six months. The old pros knew it would take three or four years.

For Stowers the worst of the ordeal lay in the hard work and poor food. "We would go out in the morning and work twelve hours— hot—in July and August, working ditches and building roads. We'd have no water with us and no lunches. We'd have a bowl of rice in the morning. You'd come back and you'd have another bowl of rice and maybe some cabbage soup for dinner. Our cooks would have a pot of boiled water to drink."

As an old China hand he was aware of dangers, such as cholera and dysentery, disregarded by many of the younger men. "Their lips would get parched and their tongues would swell up. They couldn't talk because of that hot sun. They'd see a Chinese out in a canal, dipping up water with his hands and drinking it. We would tell them 'Don't do it.' You tell an eighteen-year-old boy that and then you see the fellow out drinking nice cold water and splashing it on his face and suddenly he'd just break ranks and go out there and start drinking it. Three or four days later you'd have to bury him."

Not until the late summer or autumn of 1942 did the first trickle of Red Cross packages arrive, although Stowers saw the Japanese take many of the materials for themselves. The meager supplements to the diet included small cans of butter, powdered milk, cream cheese, vitamin pills, and cigarettes. He noted that his guards avoided the vitamin pills, fearing they were poison. The prisoners traded the smokes to the Japanese for items such as lard or salt. In his first three months at Woosun, Stowers's weight fell rapidly, from 210 pounds before it stabilized at 112.

For the most part, the older Japanese soldiers, veterans of Guadalcanal and other areas of combat, behaved more professionally toward the prisoners. Young reservists and Koreans drafted for duty as guards were much more likely to mistreat their charges. Stowers said he and the others talked about escape, but as Caucasians they would be quickly noticed. "We knew that the coolies for five pounds of rice would turn you in." Morale perked up after two years, he said, when the first B-29s bombed Shanghai and the surrounding area. The increased frequency of raids by P-40s and P-51s caused the Japanese to abandon the "Mount Fuji" [an earthen backstop for a rifle range] construction project. "After each bombing, they [the guards] would raise hell, cut your rations, maybe not even feed you that night. All privileges as you had would be cut off."

Like almost all Allied prisoners of war of Japan from World War II, Stowers reported that the inmates were consumed by images of food.

"You would dream of it at night, and you'd wake up and your whole face would be wet, salivating where you had dreamed of eating some greasy beef stew or steak or pork chops. You'd wake up in the morning and just wipe saliva from all over your face. You didn't dream of girls! You never heard, like you normally would in the barracks, about all the girlfriends they had. They talked about recipes and keeping warm and getting out alive."

In May 1945 the northern China marines embarked on a long, slow train ride that eventually rattled into the port of Pusan, Korea. During this journey, five of the captives escaped. Chinese guerrillas aided three of them to reach safety. Two were found and killed. The Japanese showed one body to the remaining prisoners. Stowers had been invited to join the group. "I told them thanks, but no thanks. I didn't believe we could make it."

Although the war was grinding toward an end, the Japanese made no attempt to alleviate the pain of the prisoners. In Pusan they endured extended hours of hard labor loading salt aboard ships. Subsequently, Stowers boarded a transport bound for Japan. American aircraft dive-bombed the vessels, sinking two, but the one with Stowers, although hit, managed to reach Honshu, a lower island. Taken to Yokohama and then Tokyo, Stowers reported, "We got attacked by hundreds of civilians. There were about fifty of us in the group. I took my shirt off and told everybody around me to form a little group, the Indians and the cowboys. We took our shirts off and our shorts, put rocks in them, and used them to fight these civilians off. The Japanese guards, soldiers, finally came in and rescued us and got us out of there."

Like Sparkman, he eventually reached the coal mines on Hokkaido, a cold, miserable, primitive place. There were two shifts, each twelve hours in duration. The clothes worn in 1941 had long ago disintegrated, and the prisoners wore a Japanese soldier's uniform, but despite the frigid clime of Hokkaido, they were barefoot.

One might believe that the experiences of the northern China marines in captivity were the nadir for prisoners of war, but those incarcerated in Burma underwent a worse ordeal. Otto Schwarz, born in 1923 in Newark, New Jersey, grew bored with high school and dropped out after two years. He enrolled in the Civilian Conservation Corps before enlisting in the navy. After service on smaller ships, the seventeen-year-old Schwarz received a transfer to the cruiser *Houston*, armed with eight-inch guns. Assigned to turret No. 1, his battle station in the forward powder magazine placed him far below the waterline.

Already on a high alert with guns manned at all times, the *Houston,* in the Philippine Sea, sounded "general quarters" with news of the bombing of Pearl Harbor. "It seemed to me," said Schwarz, "that we were almost jubilant about the war starting. Of course, that soon changed after we got our noses bloodied and we found out what life was really all about. We were all rather young and we were ready to go. We wanted to get at them."

He admitted that he had the common stereotype of the enemy and caricatured them. "A typical Japanese was about four foot tall and wore round glasses and was not too intelligent and ate women and little children for breakfast. When they captured people, they broke their ankles so they couldn't run away." Schwarz and his shipmates believed the war would not last more than five or six months after the United States got involved. "Even when we got captured, I remember someone saying, 'Well, they'll be here in a few days or a week to get us back.'"

After the Battle of the Java Sea, the *Houston* was one of the very few large Allied warships still afloat. On February 28, 1942, the cruiser and a few other vessels sought to fight off a far superior Japanese invasion force at the island of Java. "Very rapidly," remembered Schwarz, "it became obvious we were in trouble and the ship started to lose speed. Then next thing, we were given orders to abandon ship." In total darkness, amid fires and choking smoke, he led a party up to the deck where he donned a life jacket. Shells continued to explode about him, hurling chunks of teakwood deck through the air. He leaped into the sea and began to swim away from the sinking ship. In the night he heard an occasional scream as he paddled toward Java. Just after dawn, a Japanese landing boat neared him and he and another refugee from the *Houston* were pulled into the barge.

After being knocked around by interrogators, Schwarz joined hundreds of other prisoners, many of them British, at a place known as Bicycle Camp on Batavia. Living conditions were fairly benign, with no hard labor and an adequate diet. But in the fall of 1942, Schwarz embarked on a series of unpleasant voyages, taking him first to Singapore, then Rangoon, and finally Moulmein. At sea, the prisoners were jammed belowdecks, locked in without ventilation or sanitary facilities. Hunger became omnipresent.

He and his companions arrived at Thanbyuzayat, a base camp. "That's where we met our new boss, [Lieutenant Colonel Y.] Nagatomo. He lined us up and read us a speech in which he told us that we were the rabble of a lost army, that the Japanese were going to build this railroad over our dead bodies. We found out that he meant every word of it. From Thanbyuzayat we marched [fourteen kilometers] up into our first jungle camps."

Schwarz estimated the contingent at some six hundred Americans and twelve hundred Australians. The 14 Kilo Camp was little more than a clearing in the jungle, with no fences other than some strands of barbed wire. "They didn't need anything because there was nowhere you could go. You couldn't escape anywhere. Nobody in their right mind could possibly entertain the notion that there was any way you could travel through thousands of miles of uninhabitable jungle with no food, no clothing, no weapons, nothing [actually the distance to British lines along the border would have been just under a thousand miles]. And being a white man in a black man's world, there was no way you could get anywhere. I helped bury a couple of people who tried, a couple of Aussies. They brought them back and they were sentenced to death and shot."

At 14 Kilo Camp the incarcerated slept in long bamboo huts with barely any more room than the width of a man's shoulders. Possessions, such as they were, hung from the bamboo ceiling. "We started by cutting the roadbed for the railroad. We had very crude instruments, and we carried the dirt in either a native-woven basket or we had burlap rice sacks. We were assigned in the beginning one meter a day to dig per man." The Japanese used plans captured from the British. The former colonial power had contemplated construction of such a railroad but abandoned the project because of no means to bring modern construction machines into the jungle, and the cost in money and lives would be intolerable. Although thousands of captured soldiers worked on this railway of death, many more natives, conscripted by the new rulers, died laboring on the project. This railway was the basis for the epic 1957 film *The Bridge on the River Kwai*. According to Schwarz, "The entire male populations of villages were just wiped out." The regimen at 14 Kilo at first was fairly easy compared to what lay ahead. Gradually, the quota for dirt dug rose until it vanished totally and the men worked without limits.

At the first base camp some vegetables and even meat from a herd of cattle sustained the prisoners. But as the crews cleared a roadbed farther and farther into the jungle, the supplies of food dwindled to a trickle. Said Schwarz, "We were going out at five o'clock in the morning and staying out until eleven or twelve o'clock that night, maybe getting one meal in that period of time, nothing but dry rice and maybe a little watery soup. Our standard breakfast was a handful of rice with one teaspoonful of sugar water." Schwarz, like most of the others, developed diseases such as malaria, dysentery, and beriberi.

Conditions worsened rapidly as the prisoners moved deeper into the Burma bush. Koreans, conscripted as noncombatants, replaced Japanese soldiers as guards. "They were treated pretty badly by the

Japanese," observed Schwarz. "They were beaten on many occasions and were considered quite a bit lower as people by the Japanese. They had to have somebody to dump it all on, and that became us. Sometimes the Japanese would treat you very nicely in the morning and then they would get drunk during lunch and beat you up after lunch. We could learn which Japs hated us to the point where they would practice their brutality on us and then avoid them. I don't remember meeting a Korean that did not beat up the prisoners. You expected to get beaten up, but they would actually kill people.

"I [saw] them shave guys' heads and kneel them down on a gravel path out in the sun, put a bamboo stick behind their knees, and make them kneel down on that bamboo stick. I've seen them take a foxhole and fill it with water and put a guy in it up to his neck in water for days and days and days. I saw one Englishman who tried to escape. [They made] him swallow dry rice and then drink gallons of warm water and then they jumped on his stomach with hobnailed boots. They even tortured animals, dogs, and chickens and anything. You were always getting bashed and beaten and hit."

The schedule for building the railroad fell behind because of an absence of adequate equipment, the debilitated workforce, and the monsoons. In May 1943 the Japanese engineers organized what the captives called the "Speedo" program. "All you ever heard from a Jap or a Korean," said Schwarz, "was 'Speedo! Speedo! Speedo!' Nobody ever worked fast enough, long enough, or hard enough, and it became a nightmare. It was a constant atmosphere of urgency, constant bashing by rifle butt and bamboo poles. We started carrying extremely heavy cross-ties made out of teakwood. We used to carry them with two men, one on each end. Then it got down to one man and we were getting weaker all the time and yet doing heavier work. It meant getting all the sick men out on sick call and some Jap private deciding who was sick and not sick, despite our own doctors. The sick calls were becoming bigger and the bigger the sick calls the less food they gave us because they cut the rations for the sick."

Monsoon deluges brought the greatest discomfort. "The footing was bad, everything was a torrent of water. In the middle of the huts it'd be like a swimming pool, a stream running down your hut. You never were dry; nothing you owned could ever be dry, and this went on for months. You actually didn't need clothes because they weren't any good to you. If you had clothes on, they'd be soaking wet all the time. We started to get a lot of pulmonary problems, bronchitis and all from the constant cool wetness. Tropical ulcers were all over the place. As soon as you cut yourself, you became infected and ended up with an ulcer."

The victors offered no treatment, but instead when they determined individuals unfit for work, they trundled them off to an area
at the 55 Kilo Camp and, said Schwarz, told them, "Build yourself a
hospital." That is exactly what several doctors and medical orderlies
did, saving some lives that otherwise might be lost. Nevertheless, death
was commonplace. "When we first went in the jungles, every time a
guy died, we'd blow *Taps* or play *Last Call*. Everybody'd stop whatever
they were doing and stand at attention. After a while we just forgot
about it because they were blowing all the time. Four or five men died
every day."

Schwarz himself was sent to the 55 Kilo hospital by his captors,
who expected him to succumb there. "The only thing that saved me
was I got in with a bunch of Australians who took me under their
wing. These guys were going out at night and trading with the natives
[from a nearby village]. They were giving me meat and eggs and things
they snuck into camp."

After six months there, Schwarz returned to the railroad project,
now at 100 Kilo Camp, where the line started to emerge from the
jungle. Living conditions for him improved. The Japanese transported
his contingent to Thailand. They cut bamboo but did no heavy work.
The first Allied bombers appeared, lifting morale. Taken to Bangkok,
Schwarz, locked in a boxcar at the railroad yards, endured some anxious nights while bombs pounded the area. Following such raids, the
Japanese vented their anger with extra beatings. The captors became
infuriated at the Americans, who maintained a cheerful attitude, laughing or joking.

Subsequently, the prisoners were shifted to Saigon and housed at
a former French military base. Said Schwarz, "It had very good huts.
With a lot of working parties, we had a lot of opportunities to steal
[food, shoes, soap, and even pieces of cloth useful for barter with
natives], to put on a little bit of weight, and gain a lot more strength."
The captives performed the tasks of stevedores on the docks, repaired
an airfield, and did odd jobs at oil refineries. At the latter, the men
indulged in sabotage, opening caps on gasoline drums just enough for
a slow trickle to ooze out.

Kelly Bramlett, a Texan born in 1922, began his military service
as a member of the 2d Battalion of the 131st Field Artillery. Assigned
to Headquarters Company, Bramlett trained as a telephone lineman
for the communications and fire direction section. Destined for service in the Philippines, his battalion was at sea after leaving Honolulu
when the Japanese struck at Pearl Harbor. The ship changed course
and steered first for Australia, but on January 11, 1942, Bramlett came
ashore in Java.

"After the Japanese landed, we thought we might be evacuated. We didn't know at this time that the cruiser *Houston* and the Australian cruiser *[Perth]* had been sunk during the landing." On February 5 Bramlett got his first but long-distance view of the enemy when Japanese bombers high overhead flashed in the sky. However, the raid inflicted very little damage. Lacking any antiaircraft guns, the defenders tried to ward off attackers the next time using their artillery, ancient French 75s. They also removed .50-caliber machine guns from wrecked B-17s and scattered them around the base. The assaults on Malang reduced the available aircraft until the handful still flyable fled for Australia, leaving behind the disheartened artillerymen to help defend the island.

Bramlett was with a portion of the battalion sent to assist some Australian troops near a tiny town, Butizenzorg. The guns supported the Aussies until the Japanese slipped behind the defenders, who in vain tried to retreat to Bandung. Within four or five days, on March 9, the Allied forces surrendered to the Japanese. Bramlett and others tried to flee over the mountains in search of a boat but soon gave themselves up. "Everyone thought, it won't be but just a matter of a few months until they'll release us. Our troops will be in and get us out."

He was not impressed by the first Japanese troops. "They just looked small. They didn't look like soldiers. Most of them had the little sneaker tennis shoes, the wrapped leggings, and the little baggy pants and little caps. They weren't neat. Their uniforms were all sloppy, even their officers."

Whatever their appearance, the conquerors soon established their supremacy with more and more "bashing." Bramlett and his comrades toiled at the Dunlop Rubber Warehouse, shipping out tires and other items to Japan. That work was not strenuous, but at Bicycle Camp (allegedly so named because soldiers mounted on bicycles previously occupied the installation) the prisoners bore 100-kilo (220-pound) bags of rice on their shoulders. The two thousand or so Australians, English, Dutch, and Americans lived in separate barracks but could freely mingle with one another in the streets behind barbed wire. Bramlett recalled the facilities, with showers and latrines, as the best in his years of captivity. The Allied medical personnel doctored the ill with the remains of their stock of drugs. At this point, still in possession of their last pay, the men could, through their officers, buy food from the local people. Some officers took advantage of the situation to live better than the enlisted men. While at Bicycle Camp, Bramlett saw the survivors of the sunken cruiser *Houston* arrive.

The basic amenities disappeared during transport to the mainland via Singapore on a rust bucket of a ship. The prisoners were so crowded in that one couldn't lie down. Oven-temperature heat baked them and the air turned most foul. But at Singapore's Camp Changi, the captives again ate reasonably well and lived in clean, open barracks, once the domain of British soldiers. That idyll ended in January 1943 with a voyage to Burma. An air attack by the Allies sank some of the convoy, and Bramlett helped pull Dutch and Japanese out of the water and onto his boat.

Like Schwarz, Bramlett testified to the constant brutality of the Koreans, who assumed responsibility for guarding the prisoners. "They liked to slap a man in the face. They seemed to get a big bang out of that for some reason, especially a big guy. I remember one instance where they tried to slap this fellow and he was too tall. They couldn't reach him to hit him in the face. They got on some steps. They used the bamboo poles to 'whup' you."

Like Schwarz, Bramlett recalled a near-starvation diet that knocked his weight down from 160 pounds to about 90. He endured the misery of the monsoon rains that rotted clothing until everyone wore only what amounted to a pair of shorts, and some garbed themselves with a resemblance to a G-string. Lice became constant companions, but rats became scarce because the prisoners trapped and ate them.

Bramlett treated his ulcer by packing it with salt until it healed. He helped hold down patients when a medic employed the "spoon" technique for scraping out the dead flesh. He observed, "A Dutch doctor used live maggots. Put them in there and put a bandage over it and left them there until they'd eat all this rotten flesh out. It seemed about as good a thing as you could do and less painful."

Amid the constant presence of death and excruciating pain, Bramlett said, "Most guys in a way became more aware of Christianity. A lot of them were young guys and hadn't thought about it. But at that point they became more aware. You'd see guys sitting around reading their little testaments [sic], which most everyone had." He characterized 100 Kilo Camp as "the worst place of all. I helped bury eighteen people there one morning. It wasn't anything to bury eight, ten, or twelve a day."

When the rail line was completed in November 1943, Bramlett boarded a train. "We went over the bridges to Kanchanburi [Thailand] over the Bridge on the River Kwai. The English built that bridge," he noted. He reported that Japanese held a ceremony upon completion of the infamous structure, an incident replicated in the film, although without the sabotage.

The B-29 pilot, Richard Carmichael, endured physical abuse by his interrogators. "They would hit me in the face with fists, books, and bookends. They would make you kneel and put these bamboo poles across your calves. Somebody would get on either end and start working on those calf muscles. They would put pencils between your fingers and start working on them."

The Japanese, as with the Doolittle fliers, organized a court-martial, charging Carmichael and three others with indiscriminate bombing that killed civilians. "There were three judges. We had to prove ourselves *innocent.* We were guilty until proven innocent. They had these big maps of Yawata and all the plots of the bomb bursts that didn't hit the target. [They alleged] [w]e didn't have any bombs on the target. We had them all out killing civilians. [We were not] as in Germany deliberately bombing the cities. [Actually, the policy in Europe was strategic bombing, manufacturing plants and transportation hubs, but many bombs fell on civilians.] It was a military target, a recognized one. It was just our overage, shorts, rights, and lefts. They were real serious about this. We were using high explosives. What got us off the hook was the fire raid. When LeMay brought those B-29s down to five thousand to nine thousand feet, that mass attack with firebombs made us look pretty good by comparison. So they decided not to shoot us."

Carmichael and three from his crew entered a regular prison camp on a small island. It housed several hundred people: a mixed bag of others from downed B-29s; soldiers taken in the Philippines; the former Flying Tiger and marine fighter pilot Greg (Pappy) Boyington; Dick O'Kane, the commander of the submarine *Tang;* and even some stray Britons.

It was less onerous than many prison camps. The inmates worked in gardens raising cucumbers, radishes, and carrots, collecting human excreta from local outhouses to fertilize the crops. As the war dragged into its final months, Carmichael became uneasy. "It looked like they were going to fight to the bitter end, not necessarily the populace, but the military. They put us to work digging tunnels, caves, inside of hills not far from where our gardens were. We presumed this was part of their last-ditch-defense system. The caves dug back in there pretty deep. You have to assume that this was going on all over Japan.

"The Japanese saw to discipline. They inspected us daily, twice a day. Morale varied. One young boy in Boyington's group just completely gave up and died. He finally got to the point where he wouldn't eat. All of us were skin and bones, hungry all the time. Most of us had a resigned attitude. It was common, among all pilots, anybody that is foolish enough to fly an airplane to accept kind of a fatalistic attitude. You figure, hell, it is going to happen sometime, why not now?

"We didn't have anything to read. We just either slept or we talked. Everybody would tell their life's story. The most popular sport was talking about what they were going to eat after they got out. Food was uppermost in our minds all the time because the single most deleterious effect of the whole year in prison camp was hunger."

20

The Tide Turns

By mid-1944, the flow of battle in India and Burma definitely favored the Allies. Slim's plan, which amounted to sticking in place and letting the enemy punch away until physically and emotionally exhausted, ended the threat to India. The fierce campaign to seize the Imphal plain by the three divisions of invaders had begun to ebb, and the costs to both sides verged on exorbitant. At the siege of Kohima in April, the two sides shot, shelled, and slashed one another over a confined terrain of steep terraces and thick woods. The opposing forces dug in so close to one another that a Japanese soldier digging his foxhole actually threw dirt into a British trench. The defending garrison could not evacuate their wounded and received only meager amounts of supplies. But the Japanese were worse off: they had no airlift to drop matériel and their overextended supply line broke down completely. When a British relief force broke through, the status of the combatants reversed, with the Japanese now on the defensive.

As commander of the Fourteenth Army, Slim, with the approval of General Sir George Giffard, head of the Eastern Army, could now mount his own offensive aimed at nothing less than the eviction of the Nipponese from all of Burma. The first phase involved a push to the Chindwin, fifty miles or so from the deepest inroads of the Japanese invasion of India. The task rested with the man who directed the defense of the Imphal plain, Lieutenant General Sir Geoffrey Scoones. Slim described him as "an informed, thoughtful soldier with a clear mind of analytical type. My staff sometimes complained that he produced lengthy appreciations in which all factors and courses of action were conscientiously considered."

When Slim himself visited the 23d Division, a trip that required him to travel part of the distance on foot, he said, "Whole sections of the road had vanished in landslides; the troops soaked and filthy, were struggling forward across steep slopes through mud with the consistency of porridge half-way up to their knees. . . . The litter of the Japanese rout was everywhere; their corpses shapeless lumps in the mud." He remarked on the mood of the Indian soldiers. "Their sufferings from wet, cold and jolting during these interminable journeys were grim but those I spoke to all assured me in their various languages that they were all right, when quite obviously several of them were, alas, far from it. It stuck me then, as so often that I had very brave soldiers. So had the enemy. A Japanese officer with a horribly shattered leg was brought back roughly bandaged in a jeep ambulance. A British officer was shocked to see the wounded man's hands were bound. He stopped the jeep and ordered the Indian guards to untie him. They explained that the prisoner had several times torn the bandages from his leg. Even now, with his hands tied, he had attempted to rip them off with his teeth. The Japanese soldier, even in disaster, retained his one supreme quality—he chose death rather than surrender."

In this endeavor, the 5th Indian Division, brought out of the Arakan, pressed the heavily attrited Japanese 15th Division. The 7th Indian Division, also switched from its positions in the Arakan, hammered at the very center of the Japanese lines. Slim credited the 23d LRP Brigade, which he had siphoned off from Wingate's forces, as a key instrument for the advance. "Through the jungle and over the hills, by tracks, passable only on foot or at best by pack animals, the columns of the brigade, air supplied, thrust round the enemy flank and struck at his communications from the Chindwin. Apart from the enemy resistance, the mere physical exertion of slipping and sliding, heavily loaded, up and down these soaking tracks was a test that only tough, well-trained and determined troops could have passed."

Rather than cut their losses, however, most Japanese elements refused to flee across the border, even as monsoon rains drenched the battlefields. Pushed ever backward toward the rampaging Chindwin, the Nipponese discovered that rather than offer the protection of a natural buffer, it drowned many in its flooding path. By July, the casualty toll for the Japanese drive on the Imphal-Kohima front had reached an appalling sixty thousand, while the British and Indian forces counted seventeen thousand, a number that did not include those who fell victim to various diseases and afflictions due to terrain or climate.

Although the momentum of battle had gone over to the Allied side, the Japanese, while leaving India, showed no signs of abandoning Burma; they continued to reinforce their army in that country. At the same time, it became apparent to Slim and his staff that any hopes of a seaborne invasion to capture Rangoon had been eliminated by the massive deployment of the Allied navies for the Normandy invasion. Unlike Germany, the Japanese still possessed enough sea power in the Indian Ocean to have been a major hazard had any landings been tried.

The Stilwell-Chiang War Approaches Its Climax

On the Sino-American side, the ultimate confrontation between Chiang and Stilwell accelerated toward the inevitable. Even before the final conquest of Myitkyina, Stilwell had smugly commented on the inability of Chiang Kai-shek to mobilize his forces enough to halt the Japanese offensive aimed at the airfields that supported the B-29s and the Fourteenth Air Force operations directed by Claire Chennault. Faced with this threat, the generalissimo, instead of utilizing the armies on hand, insisted that the Y Force dispatched to northern Burma and embroiled in a stalemate there after crossing the Salween River return to China to face the enemy at home. Furthering the internecine struggle, Chennault requested ten thousand tons a month in supplies and that he be allowed to draw on Matterhorn stocks at Cheng-tu. His demand was tantamount to a monopoly over what the Air Transport Command flew over the Hump with additional materials the cargo B-29s brought to China. Chiang supported him with messages delivered to President Roosevelt.

When Stilwell traveled from his headquarters in Burma to Chungking, he carried with him a gloomy forecast from Frank Dorn, his representative with the Y Force in the northern sector of the country. Dorn advised Stilwell that Chennault's staff was confiding to newspapermen that items destined for the Fourteenth Air Force were being diverted to other organizations, making it sound as if Stilwell was sabotaging the airmen. Furthermore, Dorn noted that huge stocks of arms and other equipment given to the Chinese as much as a year earlier remained in warehouses instead of being issued to the troops.

In Chungking, Stilwell bargained with the generalissimo until they reached an agreement to boost the Fourteenth Air Force's allotment to roughly ten thousand tons. Stilwell expected to skim fifteen hundred tons of the total from Matterhorn. In his diary, Stilwell penned a sarcastic note: "Date with Peanut at 3:00. As expected, chiseling gasoline for the Fourteenth Air Force. All he wants is the world and nothing in return."

When Stilwell met with Chennault, the latter pressed him for a commitment to send the B-29s against the Japanese military center at

Hankow. Stilwell seemed willing enough as Chennault argued. "He [Chennault] felt confident that with the help of the VLR [very-long-range B-29s against Hankow] he could stop the drive, but emphasized the necessity for immediate action." Stilwell's diary reported, "[S]aw Chennault and his staff and told them what would be done."

If Stilwell indeed promised the goods from Matterhorn and heavyweight missions to smash Hankow, he either deliberately misled Chiang and Chennault or else unknowingly overstepped his bounds. The War Department flatly rejected the arrangements. There would be no matériel taken from Matterhorn for Chennault's purposes, and the B-29s would only attack Japanese industry, rather than detour for missions to support the campaign within China. The decision seemed not to dismay Stilwell at all. He replied, "Instructions understood and exactly what I had hoped for. As you know, I have few illusions about the power of air against ground troops. Pressure from [the generalissimo] forced the communication."

While still bogged down in front of Myitkyina on July 2, Stilwell had poured generous dollops of spleen over Mountbatten and then the generalissimo. Of the former Stilwell wrote in a letter to his wife, "I have been thinking of Mountbatten as a sophomore but I have demoted him to freshman." He then preened with self-satisfaction: "Over in China things look very black. It would be a pleasure to go to Washington and scream 'I told you so,' but I think they get the point. This was my thesis in May last year, but I was all alone and the air boys were so sure they could run the Japs out of China with planes that I was put in the garbage pail. They have had their way and now the beans are spilled but what can anyone do about it? It's just one of those sad might-have-beens. The people who are principally to blame will duck all criticism and responsibility. If this crisis were just sufficient to get rid of the Peanut without entirely wrecking the ship, it would be worth it. But that's too much to hope." His remarks were based on the Japanese capture of eastern air bases at Kweilin, Liuchow, Hengyang, and Nanning and also threats to several other strips.

As Stilwell's letter to his wife indicated, Washington had lost faith in the Chinese army if not in the generalissimo. The U.S. Joint Chiefs of Staff memorandum to Roosevelt submitted July 4, 1944, declared, "The Chinese ground forces in China, in their present state of discipline, training, and equipment, and under their present leadership, are impotent. The Japanese forces can, in effect, move virtually unopposed except by geographical logistic difficulties."

The U.S. military leaders reiterated their belief that only improved combat efficiency of the ground forces could provide security for the air bases. They commented, "Chennault's air [power] alone can do

little more than slightly delay the Japanese advances." The memorandum scorned the demands of Chiang for added tonnage over the
Hump to Chennault. It recommended that the president urge the generalissimo to place Stilwell in charge of all Chinese armed forces.

On July 6, while the Japanese still occupied Myitkyina, Roosevelt,
who had promoted Stilwell to four-star general (the rank then held
only by Marshall, Arnold, Eisenhower, and MacArthur), acted on the
advice of the Joint Chiefs of Staff and radioed Chiang. In as tactful a
manner as possible Roosevelt spoke of "the critical situation" and the
need for a single individual to command "all the Allied military
resources in China, including the Communist forces." The president
noted, "I think I am fully aware of your feelings regarding General
Stilwell, nevertheless I think he has clearly demonstrated his farsighted judgment, his skill in organization and training and above all
in fighting [with] your Chinese forces. I know of no other man who
has the ability, the force and the determination to offset the disaster
which now threatens China and our over-all plans for the conquest of
Japan."

FDR pointed out, "It has been clearly demonstrated in Italy, in
France, and in the Pacific that air power alone cannot stop a determined enemy." Chennault had lost currency in the White House. The
president concluded that if Chiang agreed to the assignment for Stilwell, he, Roosevelt, would recommend Lieutenant General Dan Sultan
to take over responsibilities for the Sino-American forces in Burma,
although overall Stilwell would retain command.

What followed was diplomatic terpsichore that time and again
frustrated the Western generals and diplomats. The Chinese leader
responded that he fully agreed in principle but explained that because
"Chinese troops and their internal political conditions are not as simple as those in other countries" he thought there needed to be a
"preparatory period." Roosevelt accepted the delay. The "preparatory
period" allowed the generalissimo to muster a full-bore campaign to
destroy Stilwell's standing. Among those mobilized was the irrepress-
ible financier and finagler T. V. Soong; the highly influential former
chief adviser to the president Harry Hopkins, a close friend to Soong;
and the not so lowly Captain Joseph Alsop, a member of Chennault's
staff and consultant to Soong but, more importantly, a former foreign
correspondent with strong ties to diplomats, government officials, and
the media of the day.

Major General Patrick J. Hurley, nominally a civilian lawyer, a
onetime secretary of war who held his rank in the reserves, had been
appointed as a special representative to mediate between the American
general and the generalissimo. Hurley apparently had the confidence

of both men. Chiang's public reasons for rejecting the power urged for Stilwell centered on his people's distrust of any foreigner in such a post. Their reaction could weaken the generalissimo's power. He insisted he needed to control Lend-Lease. There also was the nettlesome issue of the Chinese Communist armies. What role were they to play in fighting the common foe? What materials from Lend-Lease should they receive?

The New Offensive

Although the occupation of Myitkyina occurred on August 3, 1944, not until two months later did the Allied forces resume the campaign in northern Burma. The strategists labeled the plan to secure the region Operation Capital. Simultaneously, Operation Romulus targeted the Arakan, and Operation Talon specifically aimed at Akyab. For this trinity of objectives the Allies had amassed considerable manpower. The British could field 660,000 combat troops from the empire; 58,000 Chinese and 7,000 Americans were available. Another 275,000 Allied communications and supply soldiers boosted the total to 1 million. The Japanese had 220,000 men in Burma and another 190,000 stationed in the neighboring countries of Thailand, Indochina, Malaya, and Sumatra. Exclusive of Chennault's Fourteenth Air Force and the B-29 command, the USAF and the RAF possessed nearly 900 planes in September and would have another 600 by December. Enemy aircraft were far fewer.

The Y Force China-based armies that had bogged down after crossing the Salween River remained beyond Stilwell's control since the still standing agreement with Chiang denied him command powers over any Chinese troops inside their country. However, the invading armies resumed their offensive. Russell B. Simpson, a first lieutenant and communications specialist attached to the Chinese Fifty-Third Army, said, "On our front, the soldiers were fighting in mountains ten thousand feet high. I think the lowest valley was about five thousand feet. The Japanese controlled the trails leading up the steep mountains, and also had the advantage of truck supply behind each range, while our forces relied almost entirely on air drop for supplies."

A critical battle developed around the walled city of Teng-chung, site of a major Japanese strongpoint. "In the drive toward Teng-chung," said Simpson, "Chinese casualties were very high. The Japanese sat on the high ground looking down the trails and mowed them down until by sheer numbers the Chinese were able to outflank the Japanese, who would retreat to the next crest. One of the major threats was the local hill tribes. They hated the Chinese, who had stolen all their food and animals during their retreat through the area two years before. From time to time Chinese cooks who had been washing rice at a stream were found hacked to pieces with the long knives the tribesmen carried. They did not bother us, but when I passed them, I would have my carbine and .45 ready.

"To each Chinese division in combat was assigned an American surgical team, consisting of five doctors and about thirty technicians. They doctors were fantastic but faced an impossible task. The wounded were turned over to the Chinese for evacuation, which usually meant death, since evacuation was by stretcher over mountain trails, involving several days with no medical care en route and inadequate food.

"We sat outside Teng-chung for two or three months watching Chinese artillery pound the city. Finally, we had the largest air strike of the campaign [by the Fourteenth Air Force], thirty B-25s skip-bombed the wall and created a sizable gap, which assisted the Chinese to break into the city. Fighting was fierce, but the Chinese army group commander would order the troops to advance to a certain point by the next day, or all commanders below the rank of battalion commander would be shot. Needless to say, there was soon a shortage of captains and lieutenants. It reached a point where any soldier who could read and write was commissioned.

"Our role during the siege basically was to coordinate supplies and air support by P-40s of the Fourteenth Air Force. General Dorn and our colonel tried to give the Chinese commanders an incentive to be more aggressive by walking into the city, which the Chinese commanders had been reluctant to do. The city finally fell, and our army advanced to a point near Wanting. We watched from the village while the Japanese pulled out at night along the Burma Road with their headlights on, knowing the Chinese would not attack at night."

Another savage fight enveloped the Japanese positions at Sung Shan, southeast of Teng-chung and athwart the Burma Road as it traveled from Myitkyina to China. The struggle here witnessed desperate back-and-forth exchanges of territory that became copiously smeared with blood. The pivotal moment arrived on August 20 after Chinese engineers dug tunnels underneath the Japanese positions and then exploded huge mines that buried the defenders. Soldiers armed with flamethrowers followed up to incinerate survivors. Sung Chan fell at an estimated cost of more than seventy-six hundred Chinese. Of the twelve hundred Japanese, a mere nine were captured, and ten are believed to have escaped.

Unfortunately for the Allies, the Y Force had absorbed so much punishment that it was in no condition to maintain a drive into Burma.

Moreover, Chiang, in the never-ending negotiations with Washington, tossed in a joker that proposed Stilwell bring the Y Force back to China, and augmented with a few other divisions, he could command the defenses against the Japanese. His responsibilities would not include soldiers in training or in reserve.

While engaged in his marathon political struggle, Stilwell had begun to reorganize his forces for Capital. He now had at his disposal the British 36th Division and the five Chinese divisions from the First and Sixth Armies. Galahad no longer existed, but a new outfit, dubbed the Mars Task Force, emerged. In its ranks were a few veterans of the Marauders, some American replacements formed into the 475th Infantry Regiment, troopers from the 124th Cavalry (dismounted), the 612th and 613th Field Artillery Battalions (pack), a Chinese regiment, a Chinese tank brigade, and a force of Kachins.

Activated on July 26, a week before the capture of Myikyina, the Mars Task Force originally was known as the 5332d Brigade, Provisional, much like its predecessor. For the relatively short period of little more than three months, the brigade trained in the ways of long-range penetration. Unlike the Chindits or the Marauders, Mars would have its own artillery. On November 17 the brigade, broken into two combat teams, based on the 124th Cavalry and 475th Infantry, headed south from their base at Camp Landis (named in honor of the first Marauder casualty) in the vicinity of Myitkyina to wrest control of the territory through which the road from Ledo would follow until its entry into China. The combat teams traveled roughly parallel paths, providing one another with some protection from flank attacks.

The American officer Gerald Widdoff, who had studied Japanese to become an intelligence officer and served in Delhi at SEAC headquarters, had received orders to join the Marauders after Captain William Laffin was killed while flying a reconnaissance mission. "We arrived shortly before the taking of the village of Myitkyina," said Widdoff. "A headquarters was set up in Myitkyina. My Bible-reading roommate from Delhi was brought out with his team to man that post and I and my guys continued with the combat units.

"The G-2 at that new HQ was Colonel Joseph Stilwell Jr. He embodied the best and worst of the professional soldier. Hard on everyone, including himself. At 4:00 P.M. each day, whoever was in his office, working or visiting, had to join in a rough game of touch-tackle football. Every NCO got a shot at pushing the colonel around, and a lot of steam was let off.

"While the unit was being reorganized at Myitkyina [for Mars], my immediate superior suggested I should take the Nisei out and give them a refresher course in basic training. I had to shamefacedly con-

fess that I had never gone through basic training myself [when he enlisted he had been immediately enrolled in a language course] and he
said I should get in with the men and he would assign an infantry
officer. That week was all the basic training I and most of the men
ever got."

Stilwell, on the Cusp of Victory, Falls into the Jaws of Defeat

The Mars Task Force was still being schooled for its mission when the
conflict between Stilwell and Chiang climaxed. Roosevelt's emissary
Patrick Hurley, in uniform, had flown to Chungking along with Don-
ald Nelson, an American industrialist and government official, detailed
to help with China's economic problems. Rounds of talks produced
position papers by the principals, and negotiations dragged on. Fearful that the Japanese forces at Lung-ling would mount a counterattack
and eventually overrun the Chinese and cross the Salween River, the
generalissimo added to the issues a request that the Chinese soldiers
who fought at Myitkyina be redeployed to the Lung-ling front. Chiang
could not order but only ask for these troops because once they entered
Burma they were part of Mountbatten's Southeast Asia Command.
Stilwell argued that there were sufficient replacements available inside
China to reinforce the Salween campaign. Removal of the Chinese at
Myitkyina would weaken, if not destroy, the entire northern Burma
effort.

The issue of the disposition of the Chinese troops and the control
of them was complicated by new possibilities for the Allies. The successes of the British against the Japanese along the Indo-Burmese
border and the drive that captured Myitkyina had inspired the British
and the Americans to look anew at an amphibious and airborne assault
on Rangoon. Operation Dracula, as it was called, offered a chance to
open the prewar pathway from the port city north toward China and
cut down on the grueling and costly jungle campaigns. It also supported the British determination to restore, eventually, the empire
jewel of Singapore. Chiang's machinations, which threatened to abandon the gains at Myitkyina and to retreat from the Salween front,
jeopardized the plans developed by the Western Allies.

President Roosevelt, having weighed the various papers and reports
from the negotiators and the opinions of his military leaders, particularly army chief of staff George Marshall, sent a radio message to the
generalissimo on September 19. In it he stated that unless Chiang supported the northern Burma campaign and maintained the Chinese

forces across the Salween, "you must yourself be prepared to accept the consequences and assume personal responsibility . . . the only thing you can now do in an attempt to prevent the Jap from achieving his objectives in China is to reinforce your Salween armies immediately and press their offensive, while at once placing General Stilwell in unrestricted command of all your forces."

The American president appeared to have made Stilwell's case in the strongest language possible. In his diary the general exulted, "Mark this day in red on the calendar of life. At long, at very long last, FDR has finally spoken plain words and plenty of them, with a firecracker in every sentence. 'Get busy or else.' I handed this bundle of paprika to the Peanut and then sank back with a sigh. The harpoon hit the little bugger right in the solar plexus, and went right through him. It was a clean hit, but beyond turning green and losing the power of speech, he did not bat an eye. He just said to me, 'I understand.' And sat in silence, jiggling one foot. . . . Two long years lost, but at least FDR's eyes have been opened and he has thrown a good, hefty punch."

Neither Stilwell nor Roosevelt, however, seem to have appreciated Chiang's resolve nor his ability to pick himself off the floor and counterpunch. In typical fashion, although seething with anger, Chiang dallied without committing himself. He talked with Hurley but resolved nothing, and the special envoy as well as Stilwell soon perceived that they were not making any progress. At the end of a week, the generalissimo informed Hurley that he could no longer accept Stilwell. In a message to Roosevelt, after commenting that "it was manifest to me that General Stilwell had no intention of cooperating with me, but believed that he was in fact being appointed to command me," he wrote, "In view of the many fine and soldierly qualities which General Stilwell has shown in the past, it is with deep regret that I come to this decision." He then hurled his own harpoons: "[M]y recent experiences with him merely reinforce the experiences of the past two and one-half years, which have firmly convinced me that General Stilwell is unfitted for the vast, complex, and delicate duties which the new command will entail. Almost from the moment of his arrival in China, he showed his disregard for that mutual confidence and respect which are essential to the successful collaboration of allied forces. . . . Far from leading to an intensified effort against the common enemy, the appointment of General Stilwell as field commander would immediately cause grave dissensions in the new command and do irreparable injury to the vital Chinese-American military cooperation."

The missive closed with a pledge to support a qualified American sent to his country as field commander. Not until October 19th did Stilwell openly acknowledge his defeat. His diary entry read, "THE

During the final months of the war, British soldiers picked their way through the wreckage surrounding Burma's famous Bahe Pagoda. (Photograph from Imperial War Museum)

AX FALLS [sic]. Radio from George Marshall, I am 'recalled.' Sultan in temporary command. Wedemeyer to command U.S. troops in China. CBI to split. So FDR has quit. Everybody is horrified about Washington."

Lieutenant General Albert C. Wedemeyer, who had served as Mountbatten's American deputy chief of staff and who was an affable, diplomatic officer, became the generalissimo's chief of staff as well as commander of U.S. forces in the China Theater. That placed Chennault and his air force under Wedemeyer, but he held no more sway over the Chinese armies than his predecessor. Lieutenant General Dan Sultan assumed command of the Chinese and American forces fighting in Burma.

In this war of wills, Chiang had won the final battle. More than likely, however, he owed his triumph to the U.S. perception that mainland China no longer figured as highly in the strategy of the war. At one earlier point, General Marshall had even considered shipping two full infantry divisions to CBI. Quite likely, if Stilwell did take charge, he might soon clamor for American ground troops to inspire and perhaps lead the Chinese. That was not acceptable any longer. The Pacific campaigns of Douglas MacArthur and of the navy under Admiral Chester Nimitz put the Japanese home islands within easy range of the B-29s and carrier-based aircraft. Either the Ryukyu Islands or Formosa could provide bases for an invasion rather than one via Chinese ports. The strategy would eventually settle on Okinawa in the Ryukyus.

Slim, in his autobiography, said, "I think throughout the British forces our sympathies were with Stilwell—unlike the American Fourteenth Air Force, who demonstratively rejoiced at his downfall. To my mind he had the strange ideas of loyalty to his superiors, whether they were American, British, or Chinese, and he fought too many people who were not enemies; but I liked him. There was no one whom I would rather have had commanding the Chinese army that was to advance with mine. Under Stilwell it *would* [sic] advance. We saw him go with regret and he took with him our admiration as a fighting soldier."

Like so many upper-echelon officers, Slim was out of touch with the feelings of the lesser ranks who were well aware of the departing American's attitudes. I. C. G. Scott, a British officer who began the war with the Burma Frontier Force, was enjoying a period of rest in Kashmir, India. "While we were at the Srinagar Club one day, the news was coming about the American fleet sinking the Jap fleet and nobody was listening until there was a 'special announcement' concerning General Stilwell. The reaction to this news was fantastic! American and British all started to stand each other drinks and there was a great celebration, the like of which I had never seen before. He must have been one of the most hated generals of all time and I am not surprised though I did not realize just how much he was hated by his own men!"

Condemnation of Stilwell was not universal. The men of OSS 101 esteemed him highly, and his staff mourned his relief. George Marshall continued to believe in Stilwell, naming him head of the army ground forces, responsible for training and equipping combat troops.

Mars Begins Its Mission

Far removed from the struggle for hegemony, Widdoff and the others of Mars had trudged off in search of the Japanese. "The most difficult part of the early weeks for me," said Widdoff, "was to fend off total exhaustion and keep up with the unit. Everyone from the general [Brigadier General John Willey] on down walked. There was no transport. We had mules but they were only to be used as pack animals. There were no roads. The Burma [Ledo] Road was being built behind us. We would walk up a trail to a mountaintop and then go down the trail on the other side. For the first few weeks I thought I would not make it, that I would reach a point where I could no longer place one foot in front of the other. I thought I would fall by the side of the trail and either die or survive somehow and become a Kachin tribesman. I frequently started the day at the head of the column and ended it with a group of stragglers at the tail.

"Some of the guys who were having the same difficulty would tie their hands to the harness of one of the mules and the poor beast, in addition to carrying a heavy load of artillery shells, would also be dragging a GI. I thought that was too humiliating to even contemplate and struggled on. By the end of the first week I was only halfway back in the column and by the end of the second I was in perfect condition, enjoying the hike each day.

"Mainly what I learned from that walk across Burma, which would come back to help me at many times in life, was that there are extraordinary reserves of strength in each of us which we are rarely if ever called upon to use. When you have reached what you are sure is your very last step, your mind can, if properly focused, lift you to another plateau from which you can seemingly miraculously continue. There also appear to be enormous reserves of strength that can be called upon in psychological exhaustion as well as physical exhaustion.

"The army oversupplied us," remarked Widdoff, "and everyone threw away whatever they could. In Myitkyina they issued a 'jungle hammock,' a lunatic contraption that could only have been invented by someone who had never been in a jungle or slept in a hammock. All of them were abandoned in the underbrush near the camp. The army issued two blankets. Throwing one away lightened the pack considerably. They supplied a poncho. Since it rarely rained [this was the dry season], the poncho was a deadweight. When it did rain, it was so heavy that you were soaked through the poncho. So the poncho got tossed. The mess kit had an upper and lower part and contained a knife, fork, and spoon. Since C or K rations had nothing that needed a knife and since you had a combat knife on your belt, the knife went. Then the fork seemed useless as well as the top cover of the mess kit."

The march that preoccupied Widdoff stretched out to nearly a hundred miles, and by December 9 the men from Mars had secured Shwegu and then faced off against the Japanese at Tonkwa. When the guns of the 612th opened fire, they became the first organic American artillery battery to shell the enemy in Burma. For two weeks the brigade, backed by its pack 75s, sought to dislodge the Japanese, who finally retreated southward. The positions taken by the Americans around Tonkwa were handed over to units of the Chinese 50th Division. Along with the village, the brigade seized the airfield at Nansin.

21

Death Throes
of an Army

By late September 1944, the Japanese military readily saw that with the exception of mainland China, the war was going very badly for them. The Imperial Navy was in shambles, no longer able to prevent American aircraft carriers from approaching close enough to launch waves of bombers and fighters. Marines and army troops waded ashore on island after island, a stepping-stone advance across waters that once protected Japan. In Burma, Japanese forces grudgingly yielded territory to a British drive from India into the center of the country, and the Stilwell-sponsored offensive promised to finally open the Ledo Road gateway for supplies to reinforce the Chinese armies. The Japanese air force no longer seriously threatened Hump flights. The Japanese High Command ordered the resident units in Burma to maintain the stability and security of southern Burma, while in the north, they would cut the India–Burma–China route only "as far as possible." Even more ominous, the troops in Burma, as in other locales, were advised that they now operated *jikatsu jisen*, which meant that they would have to subsist and fight on their own. There would be no aid from Japan.

The British 36th Division, briefly at the beck and call of Stilwell during the latter days of the Myitkyina siege, had been incorporated into the Northern Combat Area Command (NCAC) under U.S. major general Dan Sultan. The 36th Division continued to march southeast of the Chindwin, a track that would eventually parallel the Chinese 50th Division on that division's left flank. Captain G. S. Elliott, a twenty-five-year-old communications specialist with B Company, recalled starting out on October 19 for what, he said, "was to be the

338

most difficult phase of the whole campaign, bringing pain, fatigue, misery and fear, and no small degree of heroism in unlikely places."

A collection of bullock-pulled carts with Indian drivers assembled to bear all of the outfit's kit, from ammunition to rations. In an "inky-black" night, Elliott and his companions engaged in a great struggle to persuade the animals to plow through thick patches of ooze. "We had to push and pull at the bullocks, tweak their tails and shout as loudly as we dared; then we quite literally had to put our shoulders to the wheels and force these primitive, wooden-wheeled carts through the mud, our feet sticking every step. We heartily cursed these wretched animals, even though some had dragged their heavy loads through the mud on their knees."

On October 29 the outfit slowed its advance, as the enemy was known to be in the area. Elliott, still in charge of the pack animals, was slightly behind as the battalion began to comb a wood for fox-holes and bunkers. "Suddenly there was the sound of sustained and concentrated fire from rifle and machine gun, which sounded danger-ously close at hand. Hurriedly placing mules and muleteers safely behind a clump of trees, I approached nearer to the sound of firing, just in time to meet B Company appearing in great disorder and looking thoroughly shaken as indeed they were. It appeared that C Company had attempted to attack a Jap bunker but had been held down by the heavy stream of fire I had heard. B Company were given orders to attack the position by moving along the dry chaung, the right flank of the enemy, and so with D Company make a dual attack on the bunker. But when B Company advanced along the chaung they met with a withering hail of fire, chaos broke out, and discipline, on the only occasion I remember, was ignored in the mad rush for cover. We were very fortunate to have only one killed, though two were wounded and several treated for shock. The CO's annoyance at B Company's behavior was quite understandable."

The battalion dug positions in the woods on the chance of a counterattack during the night. But when daylight filtered through the trees, the British discovered that the Japanese had slipped away under cover of night. During the following day, sporadic contact gen-erated brief skirmishes, creating casualties for both sides. One British patrol, while pausing on a hill, was astonished to see a full company of Japanese soldiers headed by an officer flourishing his sword. The patrol unlimbered their weapons, which included Bren guns, and doused the column with fire. But a day or so later, the B Company commander led his own reconnaissance mission. They stumbled on a roadblock that left the second in command and one other soldier dead.

When found later, both bodies had been stripped of all clothing, arms, and ammunition. Elliott remarked on a soldier who "caught the trigger of his loaded rifle and shot off one of his fingers—a difficult operation and how he accomplished it *accidently* [sic] was a matter for conjecture."

The pace of the advance slowed markedly as the division entered jungle. Snipers heckled them. Occasionally rifle fire ripped through the vegetation and mortar bombs exploded around the unit, startling the mules into a panicky trot to the rear. The snipers in particular bedeviled the oncoming troops. "One could never be sure from which direction they were firing. They might be in the branches of a tree immediately above one's head or they might be a hundred yards to the left or right, before or behind. They might even be in a foxhole at one's foot."

The battalion passed into a clearing with a stand of elephant grass and more jungle ahead, an ideal situation for an ambush. With a Royal Artillery unit now only a mile behind, the infantry called for a shower of shells to blast the turf ahead of them. "A barrage was very effectively laid not more than fifty yards in front of us and on the jungle beyond. It must have been impossible for anything or anybody to remain alive in that area. I tried to count the shells as they burst," said Elliott, "but found it impossible. At the end of the barrage we advanced through the elephant grass and penetrated a short distance into the jungle ahead. Nothing happened. One dead Jap was discovered and an unconscious Jap officer was picked up with a chest wound. [He] later confessed to the unhappy plight of their forces in the area, so many men had been killed or wounded there were only about six or seven men to each officer."

In place of Lieutenant General Sir George Giffard, Lieutenant General Sir Oliver Leese, who had commanded the British Eighth Army in Italy, assumed command of the Eastern Army, under which Slim's Fourteenth functioned. Elliott's outfit relieved the 10th Glosters before the village of Pinwe. With their ranks severely depleted by casualties in action and sickness, B Company, short on officers in particular, was absorbed into C Company. After several more isolated contacts with the enemy, the division enjoyed a period of tranquillity that lasted to the New Year. The troops bivouacked at a spot close to the Irrawaddy where they could wash their clothes and swim while awaiting their holiday festivities. On Christmas Day religious services were held, mail arrived, and Elliott relished a pack of cigarettes and tobacco. "A carol service was held, followed by a sing-song around a huge camp fire." A mobile cinema entertained the soldiers, and on December 28 the actual celebration of Christmas. "The traditional Officers vs. Sergeants football match took place, for here were good fields and little jungle. In the afternoon, after a meal of pork, a plum pudding with rum sauce and a drink of beer, I, along with one or two others, went by jeep to the [field hospital] and entertained the patients there with music and homemade comedy, during which the C.O. of the hospital lavishly treated us with his whisky and cigarettes."

The Chinese 150th Regiment, part of the 50th Division, which had participated in the siege of Myitkyina, had moved southwest on pathway toward objectives along a rail line before veering to the east and across the Irrawaddy. Major Thomas Kepley, the American liaison officer attached to the 1st Battalion, reported that in the first weeks after Myitkyina, the outfit underwent retraining in jungle combat; map reading; use of the compass; and the role of supporting weapons and maneuvers by sections, platoons, and companies. "The Chinese soldiers took an interest in the training which proved valuable in the next campaign."

In mid-December the 150th headed into a rugged mountain range. "A small attachment of American engineers," said Kepley, "ferried the regiment across the Irrawaddy without accident. From December 31, 1944, to January 1, 1945, the regiment relieved the American 475th Regiment [Mars] at Tonkwa. While there British patrols from the 36th Division contacted us." Between them, the 36th Division and the Chinese Sixth Army had carved out a thousand square miles of territory.

Continuing their advance into thick vegetation and mountainous terrain, the Chinese encountered a considerable enemy force, according to Kepley. "We had attached to us an air support team of two officers and three enlisted men. With close cooperation with the air corps and aggressive actions of the Chinese troops, the heights were taken. The Japs pulled back and the river [an Irrawaddy tributary] was bridged by the 50th Division engineers, and the troops crossed against slight opposition. Here our first real problem of air drops began. The tendency for the Chinese commanders to want more ammunition than needed, often not taking into consideration what the enemy might do and running off and leaving it, was noticed. As the Chinese officers in this regiment were very cooperative, this was soon worked out."

The British Fourteenth Army Advances

Quite apart from the achievements of the Chinese Sixth Army, Slim, with Leese's blessing, had geared up for an offensive into the solar plexus of Burma. The forces under Slim held at least one considerable advantage: the Japanese air arm in Burma had been reduced to a puny sixty-four planes, while between the RAF and USAF, the Allies possessed twelve hundred. The Myitkyina airfield plus other strips provided bases within easy range of targets. Slim could expect that he would have no trouble protecting his ground forces from harassment from the air, and he could count on significant onslaughts against the enemy. Slim eventually could also expect additional men and matériel as the Allied armies in Europe had begun to approach the German border, while his adversaries could not expect such aid. However, in December 1944 the Japanese still retained a formidable five divisions plus affiliated units to oppose Slim's central Burma campaign. There also were seven battalions formed from the Burma National Army (BNA), a force of Burmese who rebelled against British rule. Their value was questionable because the Japanese had not treated them well, and unlike the Kachin Rangers, who supported the Allies, the BNA was rapidly losing allegiance to its new masters.

According to historian Louis Allen, the British now switched from ambitions to occupy key towns and instead focused more heavily on destroying the enemy forces. An offensive with that purpose started on December 3, 1944, with elements of Slim's Fourteenth Army crossing the Chindwin River on an eastern track toward Mandalay. The Chindwin could have served as a strong natural defense line because its heavily jungled and steeply hilled eastern bank offered excellent terrain for a defense. However, the Japanese chose not to contest the crossings.

Ahead of the British lay the Irrawaddy, a thousand yards wide but dotted with many islands in midstream. At Sagaing, across from Mandalay, the Irrawaddy hooked a sharp right before it flowed south. With the Chindwin to the west, the configuration produced a triangle known as the Shwebo plain. It was relatively flat land, dry and dusty in December. Slim expected that the Japanese would confront him there, and with strong tank support, a decisive battle could be fought, but he had not reckoned with the sagacity of Lieutenant General Heitaro Kimura. Sacked in 1943 for defeat on Guadalcanal, Kimura had been restored to prominence as commanding general of the Burma Area Army. He disdained to risk his assets on the Shwebo plain.

Slim said, "It looked as if this battle, like so many of mine, was not going to start as I intended. It was time for me to use a little of that flexibility of mind that I had so often urged on my subordinates." Kimura's strategy was to withdraw behind the Irrawaddy. Slim divined, "He hoped, not without reason, to cripple us as we struggled to cross the river, and then, with the help of the monsoon, to destroy us as we limped back to the Chindwin."

The Fourteenth Army commander declined to advance into such a possible snare and instead sought a way to outflank the concentration around Mandalay. He reasoned that if he struck at the area of Meiktila and Thazi, he would menace a network of supply dumps crucial for the Japanese presence as far off as Rangoon. Kimura at Mandalay would be forced to commit his resources, but success depended on the British troops reaching Meiktila before Kimura moved on the hub. The key lay in fording the Irrawaddy at Pakokku without the Japanese becoming aware of the deployment.

A sufficient portion of Slim's soldiers would secure the Shwebo plain, making it appear that this was in preparation for a direct blow at Mandalay. To avoid notice of the true objective, the main body of IV Corps of the Fourteenth Army would secretly travel down a valley along the Myittha River. However, the British general wanted to spearhead the attack on Meiktila with armor, but the existing trail would not support tanks and heavy vehicles. The British engineer corps, however, working with "bithess," a special composite material that resembles asphalt, put down a hundred miles of serviceable roadway in roughly six weeks.

Another segment of the operation involved a massive effort to haul supplies along the rivers. Major General William Hasted, Slim's chief engineer, using troops and workers from construction companies in India and local Burmese labor, chopped down teak trees to manufacture crude rafts or barges capable of carrying as much as a Sherman tank. Outboard motors powered the craft. Tank transporters, borrowed from the armored units, drove a hazardous track from Dimapur to Kalewa on the Chindwin, bringing motor launches. The British even salvaged a variety of Japanese landing craft, tugs and small steamers, from the bottom of the river. Slim's pride and joy were a pair of "warships" built by his engineers. Made of wood with a light coat of armor around the bridge, they mounted guns ordinarily used for antiaircraft use. He christened one *HMS Pamela* in honor of Mountbatten's youngest daughter and the other *HMS Una*, for his own child. He noted a "dignified rebuke from Their Lordships of the Admiralty who pointed out, more in sorrow than in anger, that only Their Lordships themselves were authorized to suggest names for His Majesty's ships."

Slim's grand design almost faltered when three squadrons of C-46 Dakotas suddenly stopped hauling his matériel and flew off to China. Operation Ichi-Go, an offensive by Japanese ground forces that captured some airfields and menaced others in China, required Wedemeyer to remove the 14th and 22d Divisions of Chinese soldiers from Burma to reinforce the troops falling back under Japanese pressure. Beyond his engineers and the prodigious efforts at boat and barge building, Slim depended heavily on the air transport system to provide initially 750 tons a day and then 1,200 by March. The prospectus for-warded by Slim through Mountbatten had impressed Hap Arnold in Washington sufficiently for him to authorize 400 more cargo planes for CBI. Although many were quickly shifted to supply the Chinese and the Fourteenth Air Force, some serviced the British offensive in Burma.

Air Supply for the Burma Offensive

Nicholas Sanchez, a Texan, was among the latest to crew aircraft fly-ing the Hump. A seventh-generation direct descendant of the founder of Laredo, Nick Sanchez graduated from high school in 1941 and immediately began to work part-time as an announcer at a local radio station. "I was on duty that morning that the Japanese bombed Pearl Harbor. I was just [finishing up] when all of a sudden, a 'bing, bing, bing, bing' came on the bulletin. The end result was that I didn't go home for four days."

Some weeks later, after his employer failed to raise his salary, San-chez volunteered for service. When asked his preference, he chose radio school and trained in Sioux Falls, South Dakota. Subsequently he be-came a member of the 4th Combat Cargo Group, composed of four squadrons, each of which had twenty-five aircraft. The unit began with C-47s and then C-46s. His outfit, the 15th Squadron, flew to Sylhet, India, arriving in November 1944. "We got there about four or five o'clock in the afternoon. The next night we got our first shock because somebody had Tokyo Rose [Iva Ikuo Toguri d'Aquino, who broadcast from Japan] on the air and she officially welcomed the 4th Combat Cargo Group and named the commanding officer."

At first the group supplied the British Fourteenth Army in Burma. "We flew everything from food and ammunition to toilet paper. We would land at just about any place that a plane could land. By no stretch of the imagination could these be considered airfields a lot of times. One time we were landing at night and we only went by com-munications with the tower. The tower was a man with a radio in a jeep. We saw some flashes of light and we said, 'Hey, tower! What are those flashes of light?' The tower responded. 'You damned fool! Don't you know there is a war on? The Japs are shelling us! Get out of here!' We got out real fast.

"We were supplying everybody. We would fly in the morning. The Indians and the Burmese would load our airplanes and we would fly [to a location]. Some other crews would unload them. We would take off again and come back with a second load, sometimes with a third load because we had a crew, pilot, copilot, crew chief, and radio operator, and we flew that one plane every day that plane was in commission. No other crew could take it over. Sometimes we flew ten, fifteen, twenty days straight, but we would fly it everywhere."

The Road to Mandalay

One spearhead for Slim's campaign was the 19th Indian Division, an unblooded organization but one with a high proportion of prewar regulars, commanded by Major General Peter Rees and attached to the Indian army's IV Corps. It progressed rapidly until it met Elliott's 36th Division the second week of December to provide a connected front stretching from the Indian Ocean to China, albeit the impassable Himalayas loomed as the most northerly border.

Although evidence on corpses and from the few prisoners indicated that the Japanese were often fielding large numbers of inexperienced newcomers, the Nipponese fought as fiercely as ever. Near Ngazun on the Irrawaddy, the Japanese commander ordered his thirty-five-man unit to fight to their last breath. When the troops of the Durham Light Infantry had secured one area, all thirty-five were dead in their foxholes. A Japanese officer suddenly leaped from concealment onto the top of a British tank, where its commander stood with the turret open. With a savage sweep of his sword, the officer decapitated the tanker, shoved the body aside, and plunged inside the tank. He stabbed a gunner to death and grabbed for the dead man's pistol. The driver manager to shoot him. In another encounter, a weaponless soldier tried to bite a British officer in the throat.

As part of Slim's plot to keep the enemy preoccupied while he brought the main body of IV Corps down to a siege of Meiktila, the 19th Division shifted east from Shwebo to the Irrawaddy and prepared to cross it at points forty and fifty-five miles north of Mandalay. The enemy accepted the bait and threw both the 15th and 53d Divisions against the expected bridgeheads. Although the two Japanese units had drawn some replacements, both organizations were well below their normal complements, adding up to perhaps eighty-five hundred soldiers between them.

Despite the stubborn resistance, the British forces, abetted by tanks, steadily advanced. Slim marveled at their progress under difficult conditions and with little roadmaking equipment. "Most of the division went on foot but guns and lorries had often to be winched and man-hauled up steep slopes, and in one place the only way to get the track round a cliff was to cantilever it out on timber supports.

It was vastly exhilarating to fly over the division in a light aeroplane. Through gaps in the treetops . . . I could see on every rough track files of men marching hard with a purposefulness that could be recognized from five hundred feet. Behind them gangs, stripped to the waist, were felling trees and hauling them to make rough bridges across the numberless streams and gullies while guns waited to move on."

General Rees instructed his commanders, "If the Japanese are obviously pulling out fast, act boldly and go fast while the going is good and take risks." But he cautioned, " I do not intend to incur unnecessary casualties in any ill-prepared rushes at organized defenses."

Actually, the 2d and 20th Divisions also had arrived from the south in time to assist in the encirclement of Mandalay before heading for Meiktila. The former had seized Shwebo and the plain about it when the Japanese refused to bring the bulk of their forces into Slim's hoped-for trap. The organization had been slowed by the difficulty of getting over the Irrawaddy at a sector fifteen hundred yards wide and easily defended even by a thin line of Japanese. The 20th Division's approach involved an even deeper swing, rousting small clumps of enemy soldiers in its path. Farther west, the 7th Division, striking in the direction of Pakokku, chose to get over the Irrawaddy at Nyaungu and Pagan, notable for its twelve hundred red and white pagodas, from the tops of which British forces could be readily observed.

The 7th Division commander, Major General G. C. Evans, picked the 2d Battalion of the South Lancashire Regiment for a critical crossing. Because of tricky, unmarked shoals, Evans ruled out a night operation. To maintain surprise, however, the first wave, embarking at dawn, would not start their outboard motors until well out in the river. Unfortunately, some refused to turn over, and several of the assault craft, never robust, sprang leaks. Frantic to keep the attack from breaking down, the officer in charge ordered the landing craft to proceed whether or not they were in proper sequence. The current pushed the leading boats downstream, and those behind, thinking this was the intended course, followed. Instead, they traveled right into the mouths of the enemy guns, manned not by Japanese but by various factions of rebels against British rule. Within a few minutes two company commanders were dead and several boats sunk. Only the intercession of P-51s, P-47s, and B-25s with some RAF Spitfires that lay down covering fire kept the machine gunners from sighting on the floundering amphibious force and allowed rescue of survivors. Some were lifted off sandbanks by Americans in L-5s.

One isolated South Lancashire company managed to sneak ashore, and on the following day the remainder of the brigade forced its way over the river. Six miles farther south, a Sikh battalion had the good luck to face off against a dispirited band from the rebel Indian National Army. They ran up a white flag, and their representatives explained that the Japanese troops had withdrawn, enabling the Sikhs to occupy Pagan without resistance.

The New Stilwell Road

The Allied offensive in Burma in late 1944 and early 1945 operated on a wide but noncontiguous front. In northern Burma, Major General Dan Sultan directed the Mars Task Force, which, working beside the Chinese 30th and 38th Divisions, had headed due south from Myitkyina. While the two Chinese units seized Bhamo, the Mars men, forty miles south, turned east toward a key Burma road site at Namhpakka. They depended entirely on air drops for supplies. Wounded and sick soldiers were evacuated by use of small, single-engine, liaison-type planes.

The Americans tramped through a rugged terrain marked by a series of isolated hills and extended ridges. The Japanese, as usual, had taken advantage of what nature provided, entrenching themselves in these elevations. It was necessary to eliminate the Japanese from every range to prevent fire on the territory achieved. The most difficult site faced was the Loi Kang ridge, with two villages, Loi Kang and Man Sak.

On the morning of February 2, troopers from the 124th Cavalry left their line of departure following a softening up by field artillery and mortars from Mars's own guns as well as those of Chinese batteries. F Troop started out in a jungle valley and began a fifteen-hundred-yard approach toward the four-hundred-foot-high escarpment held by the enemy. Leading one platoon was First Lieutenant Jack Knight, one of seven brothers in uniform. His brother Curtis was the first sergeant, and the two had entered the army when the Texas National Guard 124th Cavalry was federalized.

As the troopers forced their way up, Jack Knight was accompanied by Sergeant Wayne Doyle, ordinarily the company cook but who had volunteered to serve as Knight's runner. They encountered a pair of enemy soldiers, and Knight gunned them both down. When he had gained the crest he summoned the rest of the unit, which quickly began digging in under heavy mortar explosions and shells from the Japanese 77-millimeter high-velocity gun known as a "whizbang." Small arms also peppered their positions.

An account of the scene by the CBI Veterans Association said Knight reconnoitered the area and on the southwestern slope discovered a pillbox and foxholes. "He threw a grenade in that pillbox, saw another, and went for it. He called back, 'There's a whole nest of 'em down here.' He kept going and found himself in the center of a horse-shoe formation of well-built dugouts.

"Fear was no part of Jack's makeup. He preferred doing a danger-ous job himself to calling on his men. By this time they were coming over the side of the hill to see what was going on. They later described him as looking and acting as if he had to get all of those emplacements by himself. He was fighting like a madman. A grenade sailed toward him from one of the pillboxes. Men yelled at him. Instead of dropping to the ground, he backed up. Shrapnel hit him in the face. He was out of ammunition. He dropped back a few feet to Lieutenant Leo C. Tynan Jr., an artillery observer who had stayed with him from the start of the attack.

"Tynan shared his carbine ammunition and Knight turned back to the hornets' nest. His only comment was, 'I can't see.' One eye was closed and blood was running down his face. The men, now fight-ing around him, were dropping like flies. He hesitated long enough to organize them by arm motions, shouting, 'Come on, we've got 'em now!'

"He was out front again. He grenaded another rat hole. Another Jap grenade wounded him again, and he went down. Curtis [his brother] called out, 'Jack's hit!' and ran toward him. He fell, seriously wounded. Jack pulled himself up on his elbow and cried, 'Curtis, are you hurt?' Someone else answered, 'Yes!' Jack pleaded, 'Go on back! Somebody get Curtis back!' Propped on one elbow, he then urged his men forward, beckoning to them with his free arm. He tried to reach another, his sixth pillbox, when a Jap bullet hit him and he lurched forward, dead.

"When the tumult of the battle was over and the excitement of making evacuations, digging in, avoiding sniper fire, and exchanging stories died down, the most oft-repeated words were 'The bastards got Jack Knight.'" Knight was posthumously awarded a Medal of Honor, the only one bestowed in CBI. The citation read, "Preceding his men by at least ten feet, he immediately led an attack. Single-handedly he knocked out two enemy pillboxes and killed the occu-pants of several foxholes. While attempting to knock out a third pill-box, he was struck and blinded by an enemy grenade. Although unable to see, he rallied his platoon and continued forward in the assault on the remaining pillboxes. Before the task was completed, he fell mortally wounded." Mountbatten ordered the site be designated "Knight's Hill."

The successful venture by Mars and the Chinese First Army had secured the final piece of real estate to open the road from Ledo to

Chungking, 350 hard but negotiable miles away. On February 4 Brigadier General Lewis A. Pick, the chief engineer for the project, led the
first truck convoy from Ledo into Chungking, where fireworks greeted
the American drivers, who brought 75- and 105-millimeter guns plus
supplies. Beside, the highway engineers worked to extend a pipeline
carrying vital oil from Burma to China.

Named the Stilwell Road in honor of the now departed general, it
was by no means a smooth-surfaced turnpike. Robert B. Toulouse, an
air force supply and maintenance captain, led a group of vehicles on a
twenty-one-day journey from start to finish in late February and
described the condition of the road as "packed dirt and rock."

A schoolteacher in south-central Missouri when drafted in June
1941, Toulouse said, "Hitler frightened me. I felt that he had made so
many military advances that it would inevitably involve the United
States. We really kind of ignored the Japanese." In 1942 he chose to
attend an officer training program in chemical warfare and after graduation was assigned to the air corps and eventually the 301st Air
Depot Group. After thirty days at sea, his unit arrived in Bombay. At
a base called Kanchrapara, a short distance from Calcutta, the 301st
assembled its equipment, which would be devoted to repair and supply for aircraft in China. From a base in Assam the GIs then drove
their vehicles off flatcars to begin their journey to Chungking.

Toulouse recalled, "I was the lead person that had to go and make
arrangements with the next camp. I drove most of the Burma Road
[that label was frequently interchanged with Ledo and Stilwell] by myself because I had to arrive, make arrangements for food, a place to
stay, and if there were any facilities for gassing up our vehicles. These
camps were established for what would appear to be about a day's
distance apart. It took twenty-one days to drive the Burma Road.
That wasn't constant driving. Most of the time we'd get in in the late
afternoon, but sometimes it would be earlier.

"There were no protective barriers on the outside lane of the road.
You could look down for hundreds of feet, sometimes even a thousand, to various fields that were down there. A lot of people had not
driven trucks. I had never driven a truck in my life. They asked us at
the start if anybody who was then driving a jeep would be willing to
try to drive a truck. The truck was a two-and-a half-ton truck with a
three-quarter-ton trailer, everything loaded. I wasn't in the lead vehicle just out of Assam, but the very first one going up a steep climb
stalled out after it started up. None of us knew how to get down into
double-low gear on a four-wheel-drive. I remember a sergeant running by each truck, telling us how to shift down." Toulouse remarked
that there was little danger of attack by Japanese aircraft. However, he

saw some bombed-out vehicles, both U.S. and Japanese, pushed off the right-of-way. According to Toulouse, the organization of more than two thousand soldiers engaged in driving vehicles included two all-black truck companies. "The gossip was that Madame Chiang Kai-shek said, 'No black people coming into China.' So these two truck companies didn't get to go."

IV Corps Envelops the Enemy

Slim's IV Corps soon slipped a noose around Meiktila at roughly the same moment as the 19th Division poised to assault Mandalay. Neither Japanese garrison could hope for relief, and the attackers had no need to fear interference at their backs. For his part, General Kimura divined that although the situation was desperate, the one chance for survival of his armies in Burma lay in a defeat of Slim's Fourteenth Army in central Burma. On that basis he gathered in as many troops as he could, taking many from the northern front facing Dan Sultan, with his three Chinese divisions and the Mars Task Force. Kimura pulled out pieces from the Arakan and even reversed the passage of a regiment bound for Thailand to add more reinforcements. With the Allies in full control of the air, Kimura executed this remarkable deployment through adroit movement of his people at night, by boat, train, truck, and on foot.

Slim countered with the addition of another division, the 5th Indian. All of his strategy teetered toward collapse on February 23 when Chiang Kai-shek abruptly demanded that his three divisions and the Mars Task Force engaged as the Northern Combat Area Command all immediately fly to China. Not only would that allow Kimura to draw in a considerable number of otherwise engaged soldiers and require Slim to protect the Stilwell Road, but also the generalissimo, fearful that the Japanese were about to overrun his country, insisted on using American transport planes, some of which Slim depended on for his air drops.

Slim and Leese protested vehemently, and Mountbatten even flew to Chungking to remonstrate with Chiang. The Chinese leader remained adamant. Mountbatten then turned to the British and American Chiefs of Staff, who agreed that their aircraft would continue to service Burma until either June 1 or the fall of Rangoon. That gave Slim sufficient time to maneuver, even though by March 11, orders had been cut for the removal of the Chinese divisions and the Mars Task Force.

22

Final Bloody Days

Although their situation was nearly hopeless, the Japanese in Mandalay and Meiktila readied themselves to make the armies at their gates pay dearly. The three British divisions destined for the Meiktila siege—the 7th, 17th, and 20th—had all gotten over the Irrawaddy by February 20 and broken out of their bridgeheads to march or in some cases clank toward the city. For the tanks of the 17th Division, that was an eighty-mile crawl through dry ravine beds, plowing through the thick dust of the still-dry season. In villages along the way, groups of Japanese resisted the foot soldiers with conventional fire. To halt the Shermans and Stuarts, ground versions of the aerial kamikazes strapped explosives to their chests, hurled themselves on the engine louvers or between the tracks, and detonated the charges. What stuck in the minds of the British was the tenacity of the enemy; they would fight to the death.

The center of Meiktila straddled the land where two lakes on a north-to-south axis pinched together. Despite that watery confluence, from March through May the area resembled a desert rather than the usual jungle. The garrison holding the town numbered some thirty-two hundred men, abundantly supplied with arms and ammunition. They dug in under buildings, on the banks of the lakes, and constructed concrete and earthen redoubts.

On February 28 the Indian 255th Tank Brigade, accompanied by two infantry battalions and a self-propelled twenty-five-pound battery, swept around the northernmost tip of the South Lake to strike from the east. The well-entrenched Japanese threw artillery and anti-tank shells at the armor, while machine guns with interlocking fire and well-concealed snipers hit the infantrymen hard. Nevertheless, the attack penetrated deep into Meiktila, with corpses from both sides strewn around the streets. As night fell, the tanks were withdrawn rather than exposing them to destruction under cover of darkness. That allowed Japanese soldiers to infiltrate back to positions they had earlier abandoned.

Slim had been at the Mandalay front on this first day. As reports of the action at Meiktila reached him, he resolved to visit the scene. "I was very angry when the RAF informed me, with the utmost politeness but equal firmness, that they would not fly me to Meiktila—it was too dangerous. The airstrips had not yet been properly repaired, they were frequently under fire, and Japanese fighters were reported. It was no use pointing out that a whole brigade had been landed on these same airstrips, that they were being used every hour of daylight by unarmed RAF and USAF transports. . . . I was told that the RAF would be delighted to fly any of my staff anywhere at any time, but not me, not to Meiktila, not now."

By pure happenstance, however, a visiting American general arrived at the Monywa headquarters with his own B-25. "I asked him if he would like to come with me and see something of the Meiktila battle. As I hoped, with characteristic American generosity, he suggested we make the trip in his aircraft." Slim immediately accepted, and on the morning of March 1 they took off, "I feeling rather like a schoolboy who had dodged his masters and was playing truant for the day." The B-25 picked up IV Corps commander Lieutenant General Sir Frank Messervy and brought them to the Thabutkon base. "It was quite peaceful, though there was a little popping not far away and a few dead Japanese on the edge of the field."

After their arrival, said Slim, "He [Major General D. T. 'Punch' Cowan, commander of the 17th Division] soon put Messervy, me, and our American friend in the picture of the fight, which, judging by the noise, smoke, and constant zooming of aircraft diving on their targets, was no skirmish. Indeed, this day . . . saw the bitterest fighting of the battle." Cowan directed his men while suffering intense grief. His son, wounded at Mandalay, died during the campaign.

Slim and his party then ventured to the northern side of the town, where Gurkhas from the 48th Brigade edged forward in short dashes with the support of a single Sherman tank and mortars. The touring group itself was only five hundred yards away from some enemy machine guns in bunkers. The tank maneuvered for a position behind the emplacements. Several rounds whizzed beyond the targets, heading straight toward the brass-hat observers. "One army commander," said Slim, "one corps commander, an American general, and several less distinguished individuals adopted the prone position with remarkable unanimity. The only casualty was an unfortunate American airman of our crew, who had hitchhiked with us to see the fun. As the metal whistled over his head he flung himself for cover into the cactus hedge. He was already stripped to the waist and he emerged a blood-stained pincushion." Under the gaze of Slim, the Gurkhas now closed on the bunkers, poking their tommy guns through embrasures and driving the still-living inhabitants to exit, to be shot down. It was a day of gory hand-to-hand struggles.

While night shrouded them, the defenders schemed to thwart an expected onslaught the following day by tanks. Along the ground over which the armor would probably trundle, the Japanese dug holes and inserted a man with a five-hundred-pound aerial bomb, nose up. The soldier held a brick in his hand, and as the tank closed on his position, he would slam the brick on the percussion cap, exploding the bomb, the tank, and himself. "The area," said Louis Allen, "had become a human antitank field."

Lieutenant Colonel Alan Wakefield, an intelligence officer with the brigade, having been over that same ground the previous day, noticed the pockmarked turf. He instructed the tankers to halt and cover him while he went forward. At each hole, he shot the soldier in the head, and not a single one of the human mines exploded. The Japanese had been ordered to blow themselves up when a tank neared. They thus ignored the approach of a single British officer. Wakefield went untouched either by his victims or by enemy soldiers overlooking the site. Because Wakefield initiated the action on his own, no one recommended him for a medal for his worthy feat.

On March 3, the siege of Meiktila turned into a slaughter, punctuated by a futile *banzai* charge of the remnants of one regiment, while others in groups fled toward Thazi. Organized resistance from the cobbled-together defenses collapsed, and it became a matter of hunting down small parties and individuals. More than two thousand bodies were counted, but the total probably was considerably higher, with a number of corpses submerged in the lakes and others buried in the subterranean bunkers.

Seventy miles to the north, the fight for Mandalay had raged on. Rees, with his 19th Division, having traveled four hundred air-supplied miles in fewer than five weeks, detoured his 62nd Brigade to seize Maymyo, a hillside town some thirty miles to the east. A mobile column dubbed Stiletto led the march, with Rees hectoring them to keep up the pace. When a chaung blocked the tanks, Rees ordered his sappers to shove three trucks on their sides to provide a bridge for the armor. The general scolded the engineer officer at the site for not having come up with this solution, ignoring the junior officer's reasonable fear of reaction to such a prodigal use of vehicles. Another column reported its troops exhausted and its vehicles breaking down. The commander suggested that they start again the next morning. Rees rebuked him, insisting he keep up the pressure and not to pause during the night.

Maymyo was a diversion from Rees's main objective, Mandalay, with its thousand-foot-high pile of rock, Mandalay Hill, which was festooned with pagodas and the British Empire's Victorian-age redoubt Fort Dufferin. It contained a palace built of teak, Government House, a jail, a club, and even a polo ground. A seventy-five-yard-wide moat surrounded the brick walls, in themselves 30 feet thick at the base and rising to a height of twenty-three feet. With the Japanese garrison under orders to hold to the last man, Louis Allen remarked that jungle war would revert to a medieval siege. Mandalay Hill, a citadel of devotion to coexistence and nonviolence, would play host to the ultimate violence man could inflict on man.

In an on-site BBC broadcast on March 9, 1945 (on file at the Imperial War Museum in London), Rees himself delivered an almost bullet-by-bullet report. "I'm now in the northern suburbs of Mandalay. The fighting is going on. Mandalay Hill is just to the southeast of me. Our troops have got onto the top. On the way up they've killed a fair number of Japanese, captured matériel. So far the number of corpses reported [is] twenty to thirty Japs. . . . The Gurkhas are the people who got up there first. They, in some extraordinary way, managed to get round last night in spite of a very fatiguing day marching through the dust. They worked their way round and got a small detachment up first, then more and now they're busy clearing the top of the hill. We're sending up a company of the Royal Berkshire Regiment to assist. . . .

"Meanwhile, right at the bottom of the mountain at the north end there's still stubborn fighting going on, Japanese in machine-gun nests and antitank defenses there, and at the moment Gurkhas and Baluchis, supported by British tanks, are dealing with that. The rest of the Royal Berkshires are just behind me, and their last company is just slogging in from the north, very dusty, in very good spirits. We had to send them back yesterday evening in the dust to clear a village near which I had my headquarters last night, when they kindly cleared it for me. They had British tanks and Bombay grenadiers to help them and at least fifty corpses were seen before they finished the Japanese. At first the Japanese resisted, very like hornets, but when they saw that the game was really up, then they scattered and ran like rabbits. . . .

"Now in Mandalay itself, the southwest, the Frontier Force Regiment are busy cleaning the place. There are Japs about there still, a certain amount of shooting, but it isn't clear yet whether they're going to offer stubborn house-to-house resistance. We've had some 105 shells at us this morning. Not many, and we haven't had any for some time now. Now here it's a very sunny, hot morning, it's very dusty, the troops are very dusty, and they're pouring with sweat. For some days now they've been going all out, they've been going more than all out. They've had a negligible amount of sleep, but their spirit and élan is tremendous."

While the Gurkhas possessed the crown of Mandalay Hill, the defenders, as they did throughout the war, had previously gouged subterranean chambers in the sides of the hill from where they sniped and machine-gunned anyone within sight. The Gurkhas responded with satchel charges that exploded in dugouts, ignited gasoline poured into crevices, smashed through steel doors using antitank shells, and followed up by rolling in drums of flammable fluids that were touched off with grenades. The tactics slowly eliminated the Japanese presence, and the 19th Division focused on its next objective, Fort Dufferin.

The sturdy walls of the nearly two-square-mile bastion yielded to 5.5-inch howitzers, but the earthen breastworks built behind them easily foiled artillery shells. British tanks stalled when met by resolute antitank gunners. Exercise Duffy, a night excursion, brought two companies with scaling ladders and flamethrowers across the moat in small boats. The enemy discovered them, and the automatic fire became so heavy that Rees called off the attack.

Unwilling to expend his people in head-to-head battering, Rees summoned bombers, but although they poked many more holes in the ramparts, the Nipponese held firm. On March 20, after another airstrike, four Anglo-Burmese, civilian prisoners, emerged from one of the Fort Dufferin gates bearing a white flag and the Union Jack. The Japanese Fifteenth Army commander had taken mercy on his beleaguered soldiers and given them permission to fall back. They slipped out through a sewer drain on the southern side, leaving Mandalay to the British.

As Slim had previously theorized, the attacks on Mandalay and Meiktila forced his opponents to confront the Fourteenth Army before it conquered all of central Burma. Rather than await the Japanese counterattack, the 17th Division rolled south and southeast, leaving behind a considerable force to protect Meiktila, its airfields, and the neighboring supply dumps. Pitched battles ensued, with the British tanks beset by the enemy artillery. The Japanese strategy was hampered by disorganization as units arrived on the scene piecemeal. Furthermore, some of their resources included pieces of the Indian National Army, never a puissant force and now one dispirited by the obvious momentum of the British forces. Still, skillful deployment enabled the Japanese to seriously interfere with air operations east of Meiktila. Aircraft ran a gauntlet of enemy guns as they landed and took off. At least two transports were destroyed, some fuel storage tanks blasted, and a number of casualties inflicted on the arriving soldiers. Still, the relentless pressure on the Japanese whittled away at their ability to remain in the field.

At the same time, the transfer of units from the northern front had weakened the Japanese there sufficiently for the British 36th Division, under Major General Frank Festing, to achieve rapid advances. Similarly, the Chinese Sixth Army, retained for the moment in the Northern Combat Area Command (NCAC), and the Mars Task Force also had gained large chunks of ground, including the old Burma Road town of Lashio. Once the 36th Division contacted the Mars Brigade on March 30, under a previous agreement, Festing's troops transferred to the Fourteenth Army and headed to Mandalay to relieve the 19th Division. To prevent the enemy from repossessing the territory taken by the NCAC and to protect the Stilwell Road, OSS 101 was tasked to raised a sufficient force of Kachin Rangers to maintain a Nipponese-free zone. Bill Peers recruited a thousand of them.

An African Soldier's Tale Completed

Isaac Fadoyebo, the teenage native of Nigeria and medical orderly assigned to the 29th Casualty Clearing Station with the 81st West African Division in early March 1944, had barely survived an ambush of his unit during the failed second offensive in the Arakan. Fadoyebo had then evaded capture by crawling into the bush. With his friend David Kagbo he had found refuge in the village of Nyron, inhabited, said Fadoyebo, by Bengalis. Although Japanese soldiers were in the vicinity, no one betrayed the precise location of the pair.

Their main patron in Nyron was a man named Shuyiman, who furnished them with food and ersatz cigarettes, *pata,* made of woven rice straw. They occupied a hut some distance from the village. "We were in a world of our own," said Fadoyebo, "and so cut off from the rest of the universe that we had no idea of dates or days of the week. Our Bengali was not good enough to extract from our visitors any information regarding dates, not even the current month of the year. We could not also say whether it was Monday or Tuesday morning. A day was just a day. We were also blank about the progress or otherwise of our troops.

"We knew for sure that they had retreated and that they were all outside Burma [a misperception], but our hearts were set on obtaining information about the progress of subsequent invasion by the Allied forces if any. 'For how long are we going to continue to live in fear and on the charity of poor people?' we started asking ourselves. Shuyiman and other friends kept on telling us that our troops were progressing satisfactorily. We did not know the source of their story. We had to accept the situation as it was; slept at night, woke up in the morning, ate if we were able to lay hands on food, and offered prayers to God for further protection."

Religion increasingly absorbed Fadoyebo. "It got to the stage at which I felt I was directly communing with God, my Maker. He seemed to have assured us that our lives were no more in danger and that we would eventually survive the ordeal. A few days after my imaginary communion with God, David Kagbo woke me up one afternoon and informed me that he saw two Japanese soldiers with rifles at alert position filing past the back of our hut and suggested that we should vacate the hut. I told him I was not going anywhere. He looked worried and visibly shaken. His eyeballs turned red as death stared us in the face once more. I felt sure he was not sure of what he thought he saw. I did not see the Japanese soldiers myself. I [would] have trembled also if I had seen them. I kept cool and completely unruffled as I began to feel the presence of the Good Lord."

Kagbo left the hut and hid. Fadoyebo waited silently four hours. "I knew he was still alive since I did not hear gunshot or any other sound and in the evening as I was busy fighting off the mosquitoes he reappeared. He did not like the firm attitude I maintained. I did not like his either. Later, we ironed out our disagreement and the inevitable union continued.

"Shuyiman did not look disturbed when he heard the story. We had been so long in the vicinity that the news of our presence must have been widely circulated. The Japanese troops were no doubt aware of it, perhaps through the machinations of the hostile Burmese inhabitants hence they kept trying to fish us out. If they had known that we were a set of dying or harmless people they might not have worried themselves so much. Having live enemy soldiers in one's territory might constitute a security risk; the possibility of radio communication with their own troops disclosing the Japanese strength or military position could not be ruled out."

Fadoyebo insisted that the deity protected them. "Every attempt by the enemy to have us liquidated had always been aborted through the inscrutable design of Providence. It seemed as if God Himself had ordered us to maintain silence each time they [the Japanese] came searching for us. We could not have been silent all the time. There were times we talked loud and even joked but it had pleased God that each time they came quite close to us, we would not be in the mood to either talk or move any part of our bodies. If they had come at the time of our prayers or at any of our *pata* smoking sessions or at a time we engaged in loud conversation with our visitors or at a time we had to set [a] fire, which usually produced a lot of smoke, we would have been easily betrayed."

The faithful Shuyiman, who risked his own well-being by his hospitality, came one night with two others to bring the African soldiers to his own home, close to the Kaladan River. "David Kagbo was quite fit for the journey. I was not. I could do it with a pair of crutches if available but they were not. Instead they [brought] a walking stick, which was not even strong enough to bear my feather weight. When it broke, they looked around the bush and fetched another that was a lot stronger." Kagbo, Shuyiman, and one of the villagers acted as an "advance party'" while Fadoyebo and another man trailed them.

"We had to pass through a rice field with ponds. Apart from my physical disability [the residue of his leg wounds], I was yet to regain my strength in full. I was so weak and feeble that I fell down three times before we got to our destination. By my estimation, the distance we did was less than half a kilometer, and it took us approximately one and a half hours, whereas David Kagbo and the others made it in no time." Climbing the rickety steps to Shuyiman's raised bungalow exhausted Fadoyebo. He had so little energy he could barely pluck the persistent leeches from his body.

The two refugees noticed an intensification of Allied bombing and strafing, with one explosion close enough to shake their hideout. Soon, Fadoyebo said, he could hear the noise as the Japanese troops began retreating after dark down the Kaladan River. In fact, from Shuyiman's house, a hut with a thatch wall not plastered with mud, he said, "We could see clearly during the day anybody passing along the footpath on the bank of the river. At night bright moonlight facilitated our glimpse of the retreating Japanese soldiers."

The sound of gunfire became more frequent, and one morning, Fadoyebo said, "I actually saw what could be described as the remnants of the Japanese forces passing through the village in broad daylight with their rifles on their shoulders and some quantity of ammunition strung round their waists. They were moving away sluggishly, probably to join their colleagues who had retreated earlier. They were about a dozen in number.

"The following day the whole village was agog all of a sudden. Behold, our suffering had come to an end. The members of the Gurkha Regiment of India had entered Nyron in triumph. Actually, they were on patrol and were few in number. They must have been informed of our presence as soon as they entered the village and as a result came straight to Shuyiman's door and ordered we be brought out.

"For the first time after months in hiding, David Kagbo and I came out in the open. We whooped with joy, shook hands, and hugged each other. It was like a dream. Almost immediately, we were surrounded by a huge crowd. I was so wildly excited that I was no longer in control of myself, in gentle hallelujah chanting songs of praise. Of course I was carried in an improvised stretcher by two 'coolies' and David Kagbo 'marched' along with the patrol team."

From his rescuers, who were "not particularly literate in English," Fadoyebo learned that Christmas 1944 was a few weeks off, although by his own crude calendar it was only August. Brought to the main encampment, the pair received new outfits of green battle dress and canvas shoes. After several days with the Gurkhas, they were flown out, and Fadoyebo then endured surgery, a sustained period of recuperation, and return to his native land. His physical disability was eventually assessed as 60 percent.

Recovery of the Arakan and Rangoon

Japanese had begun a withdrawal from the Arakan once the British offensive began in December 1944. The Indian 25th Division, backed by commandos, tanks, and artillery, along with many aircraft from the RAF, poised for an assault on Akyab Island. But on January 3, 1945, an artillery observer flew over Akyab and saw no signs of the enemy. He landed, and the local residents informed him that the Japanese had slipped away. They left behind them airfields from which the British could now blast the former Flying Tiger base at Toungoo and even Rangoon.

On all fronts, the British forces in Burma advanced with wholesale surrenders by the members of the Indian National Army despite the unpleasant conduct of their Japanese masters, whose swords slashed arms of those caught deserting. By one route, Rangoon lay almost 340 miles from Meiktila, and a second, more circuitous pathway stretched 100 miles farther. Slim sent his XXXIII Corps from the Fourteenth Army the longer way, and IV Corps followed the shorter one. He reasoned that the Japanese could not possibly find the manpower to block both at once. Speed was primary, since the monsoons were nigh, and he would have to hand over some of his air support to China by June 11.

Mountbatten, dubious that the ground forces could get to Rangoon by the deadline, had planned an airborne and amphibious assault on the city under the code name Dracula. In addition, as Churchill eyed the gems of the prewar empire, the British Chiefs of Staff expected to mount seaborne attacks on Malaya and then Singapore. The slowdown of the Allied advance in Europe, marked particularly by the fiasco of the airborne Market Garden in the Low Countries, had lessened the availability of resources for Dracula. However, the military strategists directed by Mountbatten, realizing that Rangoon's importance took precedence over other objectives, agreed to allocate one division and a parachute battalion to Dracula. Neither Slim nor his immediate superior, Oliver Leese, favored the proposed landings if the scheme drained resources from the Fourteenth Army.

Because of the approaching monsoon season, Slim plotted his twin axes of attack to be led by motorized forces that could trundle forward more swiftly. At the same time, the farther south the offense went, the worse the roads. A wild card finally fell the way of the Allied soldiers when the Burmese National Army, an insurgent force that had aided the Japanese against their imperial masters, but now grievously disappointed by their treatment, rose against its ally.

The Japanese attempted to halt the IV Corps thrust about twenty-five miles beyond Meiktila, at Pyawbwe. Punch Cowan dispatched three brigades in a pincer maneuver along with an armored column that could complete a circle around Pyawbwe. Although there were anxious moments when a high embankment and a ditch halted the tanks, leaving the accompanying foot soldiers exposed, the opposition eventually was overcome. The armored force, known as Claudcol in honor of its leader, Brigadier General Claude Pert, rumbled on, destroying the remnants of a division, killing 230 men at Yanaung and another 200 at Ywadan as the defenders, bereft of antitank guns, could not withstand the British firepower.

In the second prong of the drive for Rangoon, XXXIII Corps traveled at a much slower pace than IV Corps. The latter ripped through the Japanese at Toungoo and Pegu in fewer than three weeks, covering more than three hundred miles to be within twenty miles of Rangoon in spite of monsoon torrents that arrived two weeks ahead of schedule. The former, having to deal not only with the enemy units in central Burma but also with those streaming into the area from the Arakan, encountered stiff resistance as they traveled a course centering around the Irrawaddy. They had gone perhaps a hundred miles in the same period as their colleagues to the east.

On May 1, in an overture to Operation Dracula, bombers from the RAF and the USAF smashed targets at Rangoon. The bombardment was a prelude to the drop of the Indian 50th Parachute Brigade at Elephant Point, a spit of land at the mouth of the Rangoon River as it enters the Gulf of Martaban. Because the delta waters were extremely shallow, warships could not come within range to add their firepower. When the first Gurkha troopers landed, the only resistance came from about thirty Japanese soldiers inexplicably left behind. One survived.

On the next day, the amphibious force, staging out of Akyab and Ramree Islands and shielded by more than two hundred fighters, a pair of battleships, and escort carriers, cruisers, and destroyers, landed on both banks of the Rangoon River. They met no opposition. The Japanese had abandoned the city and the Mingaladon airfield eight miles out of town.

While there was no doubt that the Japanese in Burma had been routed, intelligence sources reported as many as seventy thousand soldiers still in the country, along with large numbers in Thailand and Indochina. Among these was the Rangoon Defense Force, a body of some four thousand composed of Japanese civilian workers in Rangoon hastily mobilized to be soldiers, and about twelve hundred drawn from a naval guard.

After their quick-step march south toward Rangoon, Slim's forces paused for replenishment of men and supplies. The heavy downpours of the monsoons slowed the traffic, and the remaining Nipponese concentrated on withdrawing across the Sittang River to their still-secure holdings in Thailand. The naval guard element of the Rangoon Defense Force slogged through the soggy terrain with their enemy at their heels. As the surviving four hundred of the original twelve hundred neared the Sittang, the Indian and Gurkha soldiers, backed by artillery, closed in on them. When the shelling, shooting, and bayonet thrusts ended, only three had escaped. Other units lost smaller percentages but were hit hard.

By the end of July, the Japanese, hectored by artillery and the advancing British, and weakened by outbreaks of cholera, beriberi, and dysentery, had pulled back to the Sittang. The atomic bombs fell on August 6 on Hiroshima and on August 9 on Nagasaki. These signal events passed without immediate effect on those fighting in Burma. Because of the daily deluges, the once-placid Sittang had morphed into a raging torrent and become as threatening to the retreating troops as British guns and planes. Discipline and order collapsed. Hundreds if not thousands of men, seeking to make their way across on flimsy bamboo rafts, slipped into the merciless currents to be swept downstream, screaming, to their watery deaths.

Even as some scrambled ashore on the eastern banks, the war had already been over for days.

Aircraft flew overhead, but instead of bombs, they dropped leaf-
lets reading, "Japanese soldiers! The war has come to an end!" They
were instructed to lay down their arms and yield to the Allied units.
Some of the troops believed this a propaganda trick. However, local
Japanese commanders had begun to get the word, and arrangements
were made for cease-fires. The entire business was complicated by the
British and American Combined Chiefs of Staff investing General
Douglas MacArthur with overall responsibility for the surrender.
MacArthur decreed that only after formal ceremonies in his own the-
ater could others do the honors in Southeast Asia. MacArthur's stric-
tures ignored mandates given Mountbatten, supreme commander for
Southeast Asia, who had already begun to mount the campaign for
Malaya and Singapore. Worse than having to mark time—ships of the
invasion fleets were already at sea—the delay risked the welfare of
Allied prisoners. Allied representatives in the theater having already
begun negotiations with various enemy commanders in occupied terri-
tories managed to parachute teams of medics into the prisoner camps
to bring emergency relief. On September 2, MacArthur had his day
aboard the battleship *Missouri*. (In the backwaters of Burma, however,
that news did not reach some of the Japanese stragglers for weeks.)
Starting the next day after the ritual surrender, liberation and succor
came to the wretched captives lodged in Southeast Asia.

Liberation

William (Ray) Peers recalled his last days in the war. "We had quite a
few guerrillas down around Canton, on the Vietnamese border, and
some farther out to the coast. I was in that area looking at some of
these organizations when the bombs were dropped and the armistice
called.

"I got back to Kunming as rapidly as I could. I finally got a bite
to eat, also a quick snort. I hadn't had any sleep for about forty-eight
hours. I just barely got to bed and I was awakened by the commander
of the OSS forces [in China]. 'We just got a message from General
Wedemeyer who said, put in the rescue teams to the Japanese POW
camps.' I said, 'Well, go ahead and put them in.' He said, 'We don't
have any teams.' I said, 'Well, goddamn, here you've known this for
over a month and you don't have these teams in being right now?'
No, he didn't have a goddamn thing, to put it bluntly.

"I got together some people I had brought up from Burma that I
knew, knew what to do. We organized five five-man teams. We had a

commander, a doctor, a radio operator, and an interpreter, and one other individual. We worked all night and at seven o'clock the following morning we had them ready to go. The air force was very cooperative. They gave us all the latest aerial photos of all the areas that we had to go into, which included Mukden, Peiping, Weishien, and a camp outside of Chungking. Another team went to Seoul, Korea. In all cases they were parachuted in. A lot of them were held under gunpoint but they were finally able to get their mission accomplished."

Former marine guard O. R. Sparkman, working the coal mines in Japan, recalled that the first hint that the war had ended came when one marine reported he had not bowed and the sentry did not knock him around. The prisoners learned of the atomic bombs and the guards were changed, a move taken to avoid retaliation against those who had been punishing the inmates. Then the Japanese brought food and even beer. The former prisoners could hike to a nearby village without interference. U.S. Navy planes flew overhead, dropping coffee and other items packed inside mattresses. A B-29 dumped a pair of fifty-five-gallon drums welded together. One struck a shack and killed two girls inside. But the prisoners recovered cigarettes from it, and Sparkman lit up one that still had blood on it. Other packages contained chocolate; canned fruit; and DDT, the insecticide to rid the men of severe flea infestations.

The morning came when prisoner Henry Stowers, having completed his night shift, headed back toward the camp, expecting to meet the day workers, only to find them still inside the barbed-wire fence, "all standing around in little clumps talking. The Japanese had one radio and they were all huddled around it. We were too excited to sleep." The senior noncom, a sergeant major named Dietz, declared, "Either the Japanese have won it or we've won it. Each one of you go back and tell everybody to get any weapon he has." Stowers said, "They told us, if they lost the war, they would kill us all and commit harikari. They were so fanatic that we weren't sure.

"Dietz went down—I was with him—and this arsenal of knives and clubs and everything suddenly appeared." Dietz then approached the fence behind which stood the camp commandant, a young lieutenant who spoke some English. "Dietz said, 'Lieutenant, the Americans won the war, and we want the surrender of this garrison. I'll take your sword, and we'll treat you as honorable prisoners of war.' He stood there a long time and finally he unbuckled his belt and handed his sword to Dietz and then wheeled and saluted and walked off. The guards still stayed in the camp, and an hour later the lieutenant marched them off. We weren't sure whether they had turned the electricity [on the fence] off, so we threw some wires on it and checked it. They had turned it off. We took over the camp but the Japs all got away."

Given their freedom, some of the prisoners sought revenge against one particularly brutal guard. They caught the culprit and brought him back to the camp with a rope around his neck. "They were going to hang him. Some of the older hands talked them out of it." Three days later a plane flew over and a medical evacuation team parachuted into the midst of the encampment. Other aircraft dropped food. Subsequently, aircraft began ferrying the freed men to Yokohama, and the long voyage back to the States began.

When word of the first atomic bomb detonation occurred, prisoner Otto Schwarz said, "They went crazy. They all got drunk and started burning all the records." He was in Saigon when he heard that the war had ended but that the prisoners would remain in Japanese custody. "We were told by our NCOs who, I supposed, were told by the Japanese. They expected a lot of trouble because the natives in Saigon were beginning their uprising against the French. The Japs did not want to take the chance of us busting out and getting involved."

Schwarz attempted to join a group about to be shipped to Japan and narrowly missed execution when the guards discovered him. He was saved only after he pleaded that it was because of his great interest in Japan, which he understood was very beautiful. Subsequently, he fled his camp to seek refuge with the French residents of Saigon. A band of local anti-French rebels captured him along with two friends and lodged them in a civilian jail. A priest interceded on his behalf, and the sailor from the *Houston* returned to the prison camp. Final release came with the arrival of Americans who parachuted into the camp. Not until September 5, more than three weeks after Emperor Hirohito agreed to a surrender, did Schwarz board a C-47 for the flight to Calcutta and eventual repatriation.

Bomber pilot Richard Carmichael, who detected an improvement in the attitude of the guards after the great incendiary raids on Tokyo in February 1945, recalled, "One morning in August, everybody, regular prisoners and special prisoners, were all turned out in formation in the big assembly area. There was a Japanese officer, a lieutenant colonel, I think, up on a wooden platform in front of us who relayed to us the emperor's speech of surrender." A few days elapsed and then Carmichael was repatriated.

23

After-Action Report

W orld War II was officially over, and CBI, a concept of strategical convenience, disappeared into history. At least as much as in Eastern Europe, the conflict had ripped apart the fragile political fabric of the region. In China, after the final Japanese advance that swallowed strategic territory, including sites of the Fourteenth Air Force, the Chinese armies, both those of Chiang Kai-shek and the Communists, had begun to regain ground from the now depleted and unsupported Japanese forces. American officials tried to broker an agreement between the two Chinese factions, but neither party believed they could work together. The stage was set for the civil war that ended with Chiang's defeat. In 1949 he formed a government for the Republic of China based on Taiwan, formerly Formosa.

World War II destroyed the old colonial framework. Any possibility that the British could retain India, its "jewel in the crown" as a loyal member of the empire, disappeared with World War II. Although a sizable Indian faction had favored the Japanese as a potential liberation force, too many Indians had loyally and valiantly served for the people to accept anything less than independence. Nor could the exhausted British government and its military hope to retain Burma. Although the Burmese, unlike the Kachins, Karens, and other ethnic communities, did not oppose the Japanese, they, too, eventually successfully pursued nationhood, as did Malaya and Singapore. So, too, did the former French colonies gain their independence over the next decade. Siam, which had become Thailand in 1939, stayed independent. Indochina broke into South and North Vietnam, Laos, and Cambodia. The Dutch East Indies became independent Indonesia.

To the media and those removed from CBI, it had seemed like a sideshow marked by a few headliners—the Flying Tigers, the Chindits, and Merrill's Marauders. But for those largely anonymous soldiers and airmen who fought there, it was the ultimate struggle. The totals for Burma and the Imphal/Kohima campaign indicate 106,144 Japanese casualties, of whom more than 40,000 were killed in action. The British forces, including Wingate's two expeditions, suffered 71,244 casualties. The 3,000 men from Galahad or Merrill's Marauders for the entire campaign that culminated at Myitkyina counted 272 dead, 955 wounded, and 980 rendered unfit for duty because of illness. There are no reliable statistics on casualties for the armies that fought in China. Nor is there any accounting of the tens of thousands of civilians in the CBI campaigns.

General J. Lawton Collins, one of the better World War II American commanders with experience in the South Pacific before he headed the U.S. First Army's VII Corps in Europe, once told an audience that the first three things to consider before a battle were "terrain, terrain, terrain." In CBI the lay of the land, the waters that coursed through it, and the environment dictated strategy and tactics while exacting the stiffest of prices from the warring armies. No other theater of war witnessed as high rates of debilitating diseases, saw hungrier troops, or more physically exhausted troops. Given their choices, military commanders from both sides would have preferred to fight elsewhere, but geopolitical strategy forced them to meet on these most violently hostile grounds.

Some historians credited the early successes of the Japanese in Burma to experience in jungle warfare, but that is not true. The Imperial Army, however, was experienced in war, having fought in China for four years before a single one of its soldiers set foot on Burmese soil. Lessons about use of natural terrain, maneuvers of large and small bodies of men, supply, weaponry, and the exigencies of combat—albeit against a weak foe—provided a sound base for future operations. The Nipponese soldiers who invaded Burma learned how to survive in the jungle on the job. Under the circumstances, they adapted extremely well and for the most part fought bravely and under skilled leadership.

In a different sense, terrain also frustrated the Japanese in China. In this case it was a matter of the size of the country. At the end of the war, they still held a vast amount of territory. The Nipponese Army punched its way deep into China but at the prohibitive costs of hugely extended supply and communications lines. As long as Chiang's troops could retreat west and the Chinese Red Armies remained in the northwest, Japan could not remove its soldiers.

The Allied forces started out poorly equipped for war. Many of their weapons, from aircraft to artillery, were antiquated. The tools for bridging or crossing streams were lacking. Considering that so many of the men pulled in from disparate countries in the British Empire lacked the homogenous loyalty of the enemy, they rallied to their cause surprisingly well. Slim commented that the British erred by taking a static defensive stance early in the war. "Merely to hold ground, unless relief and reinforcement are at hand, is fatal." He admitted that during the first stages, the Allied forces were weaker than their opponents, who seized the initiative. He credited the Japanese with skill and determination but thought their downfall lay in their lack of flexibility.

Certainly there were times when the Japanese upper echelons clung to plans at moments when they were obviously doomed, as had the Colonel Blimps, both British and American, who refused to consider the Japanese worthy warriors. In territory where the fronts often stretched many hundreds of miles with huge gaps in the line and communications uncertain, a premium was based on the ability to improvise and act without orders.

But the eventual defeat of the invaders in CBI was due to more than military philosophy. Logistical superiority played a key role in the eventual victory. The output of war matériel, particularly by the United States, dwarfed that of its enemies. In one sense that could be a curse; emphasis on supply detracts from mobility, particularly in an area where the road and rail networks are as primitive as they were in most of CBI. Faced by this problem, Slim noted a solution that grew out of necessity. Whereas in more developed countries 400 tons a day was considered necessary to keep a division fighting, in Burma and India they found that they could maintain a comparable unit in action with only 120 tons a day. Some of that disparity can be chalked up to the difference between what those from a British or an American culture require compared to the expectations of Indian and African recruits accustomed to less.

While the Japanese were both ruthless and resourceful at living off the land, the Allies more than compensated for any shortfall in that respect through control of the air. That enabled the air transport commands to air-drop supplies in enormous amounts and to ferry troops who fueled the many campaigns. By 1944, Japanese fighters and bombers were more of a nuisance than a genuine threat to operations in Burma. The once-superior Zero and its descendants could not match the P-47s, P-51s, and Spitfires, particularly as the Allied troops seized airfields closer to the sites of battles.

CBI was graced or marred by the presences of several of its more notorious actors. It provided the arena for "special forces," the Chindits, and the Marauders. The achievements of Wingate's legions are matters of continuing debate among military historians. John Bierman and Colin Smith, in their biography of Wingate, trace the scorn for him to a pervasive feeling in army circles that he was a divisive influence. Slim in his autobiography dismissed the achievements of the Chindits: "I came firmly to the conclusion that such formations, trained, equipped and mentally adjusted for one kind of operation only, were wasteful. They did not give, militarily, a worthwhile return for the resources in men, material and time that they absorbed."

A contrary view came from Sir Robert Thompson, an RAF liaison officer with both of the Chindit expeditions, and a recognized authority on guerrilla and insurgency movements. He considered Operation Thursday a significant factor in weakening the enemy offensive toward Imphal and Kohima. Lieutenant General Mutaguchi, the Fifteenth Army commander who led that drive, said after the war, "General Wingate's airborne tactics put a great obstacle in the way of our Imphal plan and were an important reason for its failure."

Even in death, Wingate created controversy. In 1947, an Anglo-American group disinterred the remains of those killed in the crash of the B-25 carrying the Chindit leader. Three years later, the U.S. government, citing an agreement with the British, argued that since the majority of those who died were Americans and since the remains could not be separated for identification, they should be buried in a single grave at Arlington National Cemetery, just outside of Washington, D.C. No one notified Wingate's widow or son of the decision. When the news reached his family, survivors of an aide, and the two British correspondents aboard the ill-fated plane, furious letters, Parliamentary debate, and press comment challenged the interment. In 1974 Wingate's family received some solace as the cemetery dedicated a headstone to him.

As Wingate had predicted, the other major special force, Galahad, did not follow his prescription for long-range penetration but became a spearhead for the Chinese troops under Stilwell. Neither Merrill nor Hunter had the ego or the panache of Wingate, and they owe their reputations to their organization rather than the other way around, as with the Chindit leader. If they do not have the celebrity, at least there has been little criticism of either Merrill or Hunter for their direction. Most of the survivors speak of them with admiration and affection, recognizing their concern for their people as well as their leadership in combat.

Claire Chennault seems to have been an individual tailored for a unique situation. Only someone with his abiding faith in his unorthodox theories could have created the AVG and honed it into an effective operation. He knew how to both teach and lead. Even a fellow as habitually undisciplined as Greg Boyington accepted Chennault as a leader. The Flying Tigers did real damage to the Japanese when no one else could, and their function as a morale booster can hardly be discounted. Only a maverick such as Chennault, an airman who understood his craft—but not the overall aspects of modern warfare—could have led that organization. Quite likely, its actions and those of its successor, the Fourteenth Air Force, had as much to do with Chiang staying the course as did the entreaties, promises, and warnings from Washington and London.

The major American figure of CBI, Joseph Stilwell, while celebrated in books by Barbara Tuchman and Theodore White, is a less heroic figure among his contemporaries. He was obviously not a "people person." As noted earlier, he was detested by the Marauders, and most of the British with the exceptions of Slim and possibly Mountbatten. Stilwell clashed often with subordinates such as Chennault, and even some originally close to him, such as Haydon Boatner, lost their affection. Almost from the start, Chiang Kai-shek desperately wanted to get rid of him.

No one can discount Vinegar Joe's dedication to duty. He was often ill; he would die from stomach and liver cancer little more than a year after the war ended. But he seemed indefatigable in his travels to his far-flung responsibilities—Chungking, Delhi, Myitkyina. He put on no airs, demanded none of the rituals due rank, stood in chow lines and ate C rations from a mess kit, and would literally get down in the dirt with the common soldier to get across his points. His immediate staff, which grew to include a son and two sons-in-law, were loyal to the utmost, and the OSS chief Ray Peers considered Stilwell an excellent officer and boss.

While the Marauders would dispute it, Stilwell sometimes appeared to show concern for the enlisted man. "He paid special attention to people at the bottom," said a Chinese officer quoted by Barbara Tuchman. Stilwell insisted on mess officers making an extra effort. The armed forces magazine *Yank* called him "the GIs' favorite" after he canceled rules that forbade soldiers to have pets and barred "officers only" signs from restaurants and bars. When he learned that the 20th General Hospital in Ledo had no fans, he ordered Dan Sultan, then his deputy in Delhi, to procure the devices, which were removed from the Imperial Hotel, which housed the U.S. staff. Colonel Isidor Ravdin, the surgeon who commanded the 20th General Hospital in Ledo, had been among those who objected when Stilwell ordered some of those Galahad men evacuated from Myitkyina brought back. Nevertheless, Ravdin rated him as one "who thought more of his men than any commanding general I have known."

In an undated diary passage at about the times of the battles for Myitkyina, Stilwell offered some thoughts on the psychology of command. He listed "high character," which he did not define, as the most important attribute and placed second "the power of decision." For all of his certainty about objectives, Stilwell was curiously vague when it came to issuing battle orders. For example, his instructions to Merrill consisted of "You know what I want, Frank."

In his introspection, Stilwell continued, "He must reward promptly and punish justly." There is little evidence that Stilwell carried out the first requirement. "He must be accessible, human, humble, patient, forbearing." Such qualities were in short supply when he dealt with the British, the Chinese government, and Washington, D.C.

"Unless a commander is human," wrote Stilwell, "he cannot understand the reactions of his men. If he is human, the pressure on him intensifies tremendously. The callous man has no mental struggle over jeopardizing the lives of ten thousand men; the human commander cannot avoid this struggle. It is constant and wearing and yet necessary, for the men can sense the commander's difficulty. There are many ways in which he can show his interest in them and they respond. . . . Then you get mutual confidence, the basis of real discipline."

Stilwell apparently won the confidence of the Chinese commanders whom he brought to Burma, but he obviously never managed to convey to the men of Galahad his "interest in them." He paid tribute to the men on the line, going so far as to denigrate generals who "cover themselves with medals, won at the expense of the lives of their men, who are thrown in regardless, to compensate for faulty or poorly thought-out plans." That was the charge brought against him by the Marauders in their final days.

He claimed that most generals, including himself, envied the buck private because the lowly individual "carries the woes of one man; the general carries the woes of all." He concluded that he was probably not a good commander because "I doubt myself."

For all of his ruminations suggesting considerations for the lesser ranks, Stilwell exhibited a cold, peremptory side. He publicly called for the execution of Chinese officers whom he believed shirked their duty. In the heat of the Myitkyina siege he expressed no concern for the ordeal of the Galahad contingent. For their part, they felt he misled them both on the length of time they would be in combat and on the nature of their mission. He seemed to have had no sense of the contribution a commanding officer can make to morale when the troops are on the line. His disdain for the showier trappings of a soldier fitted his own persona, but the attitude cost him not just the affection of the troops but also their regard for him as a leader.

Of all of the headline figures, William Slim emerged with little revisionist detraction. Slim was tough enough to tolerate an insubordinate like Wingate while allowing him sufficient resources to pull off his long-range penetrations. He stood up to Stilwell while appreciating what the American was attempting to do. He accepted suggestions from subordinates. Self-deprecating in his autobiography, Slim refreshingly acknowledged a number of errors on his part, but there's no gainsaying that he directed the major operations that finally defeated the Japanese. In contrast to too many generals, Slim showed up at the front, appearances that not only won affection from the troops but also gave him a firsthand look at what they had to contend with and their condition. When the war ended, in keeping with the public notion of CBI as a marginal matter compared to Europe, he received none of the fanfare of his contemporaries Bernard Montgomery or Harold Alexander, and Churchill gave most of the credit for the theater's success to Mountbatten. But after a brief period in retirement, and over the objections of his predecessor Montgomery, Slim was named chief of the Imperial General Staff. His memoir of CBI, *Defeat into Victory,* became a best seller in his home country.

Looking at these leaders, one aspect of their personality leaps out. War is a poor stage for anyone with more than a minimum of self-doubt. Stilwell, Chiang, Mountbatten, Wingate, Slim, and Chennault, to name some of the major players, manifested diamond-hard determination. But that asset can chisel in two ways. While promoting decisive action, the mind-set also may exclude other possibilities, an ability to evaluate all the possible consequences.

The war in CBI was fought by tens of thousands of largely anonymous men, recruited or drafted from their far-off homelands. Whatever the qualities of those whose names made the historical accounts, the final word of what they did lies in a passage from Slim's autobiography: "The war in Burma was a *soldier*'s [his italics] war. There comes a moment in every battle against a stubborn enemy when the result hangs in the balance. Then the general, however skilful and farsighted . . . must hand over to his soldiers, to the men in the ranks, and to their regimental officers, and leave them to complete what he has begun. The issue then rests with them, on their courage, their hardihood, their refusal to be beaten either by the cruel hazards of nature or by the fierce strength of their enemy. That moment came early and often in the fighting in Burma [India and China as well].

Sometimes it came when tired, sick men felt alone, when it would have been so easy for them to give up, when only will, discipline, and faith could steel them to carry on. To the soldiers of many races who . . . *did* go on, and to the airmen who flew with them and fought over them belongs the true glory of achievement."

Bibliography

Published Works

Allen, Louis. *Burma: The Longest War, 1941–1945*. New York: St. Martin's Press, 1985.

Bidwell, Shelford. *The Chindit War*. London: Hodder & Stoughton, 1979.

Bierman, John, and Colin Smith. *Fire in the Night*. New York: Random House, 1999.

Brett-Jones, Anthony. *Ball of Fire*. London: Gale & Polden, 1951.

Calvert, Michael. *Fighting Mad*. London: Airlife Publishing, 1996.

————. *Prisoners of Hope*. London: Leo Cooper, 1971.

Chennault, Claire L. *Way of a Fighter*. New York: Putnam, 1949.

Collis, Maurice. *Last & First in Burma*. New York: Macmillan, 1956.

Craven, W. F., and J. L. Cate. *The Army Air Forces in World War II*. Vol. 5. Chicago: University of Chicago Press, 1953.

Dunlop, Richard. *Behind Japanese Lines*. Chicago: Rand McNally, 1979.

Evans, Lieutenant General Sir Geoffrey, and Antony B. James. *Imphal*. London: Macmillan, 1962.

Fergusson, Bernard. *Beyond the Chindwin*. London: Collins, 1945.

Herries, Meiron and Susie. *Soldiers of the Sun*. New York: Random House, 1991.

Hopkins, James E. T., and John M. Jones. *Spearhead*. Baltimore: Galahad, 1999.

Hotz, Robert B. *With General Chennault*. New York: Coward-McCann, 1943.

Hunter, Charles N. *Galahad*. San Antonio, Tex.: Naylor, 1963.

Jones, John M. *The War Diary of the 5307th Composite Unit (Provisional)*. Palo Alto, Calif.: Merrill's Marauders Association, 1991.

Kinnison, Henry L. IV. *The Deeds of Valiant Men* [Study Project]. Carlisle Barracks, Pa.: U.S. Army War College, 1993.

Ogburn, Charlton. *The Marauders*. New York: Harper, 1959.

Peers, William R., and Dean Brelis. *Behind the Burma Road*. Boston: Little, Brown, 1963.

Romanus, Charles F., and Riley Sunderland. *Stilwell's Mission to China*. Washington, D.C.: U.S. Army, Center of Military History, 1953.

————. *Stilwell's Command Problems.* Washington, D.C.: U.S. Army, Center of Military History, 1956.

Rosbert, C. Joseph. *Flying Tiger Joe's Adventure Story Cookbook.* Franklin, N.C.: Giant Poplar Press, 1985.

Samson, Jack. *Chennault.* Garden City, N.Y.: Doubleday, 1987.

Scholtz, Duane. *The Maverick War.* New York: St. Martin's Press, 1987.

Slim, Field Marshal Viscount William. *Defeat into Victory.* New York: Cooper Square Press, 2000.

Stibbé, Philip. *Return via Ransoon.* Barnsley [England]: Les Cooper, 1995.

Thomas, Lowell. *Back to Mandalay.* New York: Greystone Press, 1951.

Tuchman, Barbara. *Stilwell and the American Experience in China, 1911–1945.* New York: Macmillan, 1970.

Weston, Logan. *The Fightin' Preacher.* Alexander, N.C.: Mountain Press, 2001.

White, Theodore, ed. *The Stilwell Papers.* New York: William Sloane Associates, 1948.

Ziegler, Philip. *Mountbatten.* New York: Alfred A. Knopf, 1985.

Unpublished Memoirs and Oral Histories

Acker, John A. Letter to Ray Lyons. Carlisle, Pa.: U.S. Army Military History Institute, n.d.

Alison, John. Oral history. Maxwell AFB, Ala.: U.S. Air Force Historical Research Center, 1979.

American advisers with Chinese armies. Reports. Carlisle, Pa.: U.S. Army Military History Institute, 1942–1945.

Atkins, Henry. Memoir. London: Imperial War Museum, n.d.

Aylen, N. P. Memoir. London: Imperial War Museum, n.d.

Baird, Ralph. *Mars Task Force.* Internet history. http://www.cbiinfo.com/jack.html.

Betts, Austin W. Oral history. Carlisle, Pa.: U.S. Army Military History Institute, 1971.

Binnie, Arthur S. Memoir. London: Imperial War Museum, 1977.

Boatner, Haydon. Papers. Carlisle, Pa.: U.S. Military History Institute, n.d.

Bowerman, John. Papers. Carlisle, Pa.: U.S. Military History Institute, 1942.

Breitweiser, Robert. Oral history. Maxwell AFB, Ala.: U.S. Air Force Historical Research Center, 1975.

Carmichael, Richard. Oral history. Maxwell AFB, Ala.: U.S. Air Force Historical Research Center, 1980.

CBI Veterans Association. *They've killed Jack Knight.* World Wide Web.

Cochran, Philip. Oral history. Maxwell AFB, Ala.: U.S. Air Force Historical Research Center, 1975.

Donovan, William. Papers. Carlisle, Pa.: U.S. Military History Institute, n.d.

Durant, Norman. Memoir. London: Imperial War Museum, n.d.

Elliott, G. S. Memoir. London: Imperial War Museum, n.d.

Fadeyebo, Isaac. Memoir. London: Imperial War Museum, 1988.

Firth, A. D. Memoir. London: Imperial War Museum, n.d.

Fisken, Geoffrey B. Oral history. Denton: University of North Texas, 1993.

468th Bomb Group. Internet history. http://cbiinfo.com/468th_bomb _group.htm.

Garne, R. O. Memoir. London: Imperial War Museum, 1986.

Graves-Morris, P. H. Memoir. London: Imperial War Museum, n.d.

Hill, David Lee. Oral history. Maxwell AFB, Ala.: U.S. Air Force Historical Research Center, 1977.

Holloway, Bruce. Oral history. Maxwell AFB, Ala.: U.S. Air Force Historical Research Center, 1978.

Jeffreys, Peter. Memoirs. London: Imperial War Museum, 1946, 1992.

Johnston, Richard L. Oral history. Denton: University of North Texas, 1999.

Kinloch, Bruce. Memoirs. London: Imperial War Museum, n.d.

Kline, Frederick H. Oral history. Denton: University of North Texas, 1998.

Leber, John R. Oral history. Denton: University of North Texas, 1999.

MacMorland, Edward. Diary. Carlisle, Pa.: U.S. Army Military History Institute, 1941–1942.

Martin, W. Papers. London: Imperial War Museum, 1944–1945.

McKnight, John. Memoir. London: Imperial War Museum, n.d.

Merrill's Marauders, Internet accounts.

Neale, Robert. Oral history. Maxwell AFB, Ala.: U.S. Air Force Historical Research Center, 1962.

O'Brien, T. P. Diaries and records. London: Imperial War Museum, n.d.

Older, Charles. Oral history. Maxwell AFB, Ala.: U.S. Air Force Historical Research Center, 1962.

Patterson, Hugh. Memoir. London: Imperial War Museum, n.d.

Peays, Tom. Oral history. Denton: University of North Texas, 1999.

Peers, William R. Oral history. Carlisle, Pa.: U.S. Army Military History Institute, 1977.

Quaid, David. *Merrill's Marauders: War in Burma*. Videotape, n.d.

Rissik, David. Memoirs. London: Imperial War Museum, 1944–1945, 1980s.

Sanchez, Nicholas. Oral history. Denton: University of North Texas, 1999.

Schwarz, Otto. Oral history. Denton: University of North Texas, 1979.

Selee, Richardson. Diary. Carlisle, Pa.: U.S. Army Military History Institute, 1943–1944.

Sinks, Robert M. Oral history. Denton: University of North Texas, 1999.

Sparkman, O. R. Oral history. Denton: University of North Texas, 1999.

Stafford, Allen E. Oral history. Denton: University of North Texas, 1999.

Stowers, Henry B. Oral history. Denton: University of North Texas, 1973.

Tatchell, Rodney. Memoir. London: Imperial War Museum, n.d.

Thompson, Henrietta. "Walk a Little Faster." Unpublished accounts of members of 1942 Stilwell exodus from Burma. Carlisle, Pa.: U.S. Army Military History Institute, 1980.

Toulouse, Robert B. Oral history. Denton: University of North Texas, 2000.

Tricoli, Tony. Interview by author, 2003.

Tutt, L. E. Memoir. London: Imperial War Museum, n.d.

Twentieth Air Force. Internet history. http://www.20thaaf.com/.

Widdoff, Gerald. Interview by author, 1999.

Index